*Spirituals and the Birth of a
Black Entertainment Industry*

SPIRITUALS

and the Birth of a Black Entertainment Industry

SANDRA JEAN GRAHAM

UNIVERSITY OF ILLINOIS PRESS
Urbana, Chicago, and Springfield

Publication of this book is supported by the
AMS 75 PAYS Endowment of the American
Musicological Society, funded in part by
the National Endowment for the Humanities
and the Andrew W. Mellon Foundation;
by the Babson Faculty Research Fund;
and by a grant from the H. Earle Johnson Fund
of the Society for American Music.

Supplemental materials for this book are available at
http://www.press.uillinois.edu/books/graham/spirituals/

Library of Congress Cataloging-in-Publication Data
Names: Graham, Sandra J. (Sandra Jean) author.
Title: Spirituals and the birth of a black entertainment
industry / Sandra Jean Graham.
Description: Urbana : University of Illinois Press, [2018] |
Series: Music in American life | Includes bibliographical
references and index.
Identifiers: LCCN 2017057358| ISBN 9780252041631 (hardcover :
alk. paper) | ISBN 9780252083273 (pbk. : alk. paper)
Subjects: lcsh: African Americans—Music—History and
criticism. | Jubilee Singers. | Spirituals (Songs)—United
States—19th century—History and criticism. | Minstrel
shows—United States—History—19th century.
Classification: LCC ml3556 .g77 2018 | DDC 782.25/30973—dc23
LC record available at https://lccn.loc.gov/2017057358

Contents

PART ONE

The Rise of a Jubilee Industry

PART TWO

Spirituals for the Masses

Acknowledgments

People often ask how I became acquainted with spirituals and why I study them. Spirituals have been a part of my life for as long as I can remember—in Sunday school, church choir, summer camps, family sings at home. Minstrel songs were also a big part of my musical upbringing, although I didn't know where they came from at the time. It wasn't until I studied ethnomusicology in graduate school that I became aware of the multifaceted and extremely complex history of these genres.

After graduate school I moved to California, where I discovered Friends of the Negro Spirituals, founded by Sam Edwards and Lyvonne Chrisman. Sam explained to me how the organization came about: "Lyvonne and I were listening to some music of Moses Hogan, and somehow, through him, there was some kind of visitation of the spirit that told us that we had to go forth and set an organization of this kind. Since that time, in 1998, we have been working really, really hard to make sure that the Negro Spirituals are understood and appreciated by the public and indeed by many cultures in the community. So our mission has been to educate the public, to make sure that we get the word out that there are some songs that were created by the enslaved ancestors and that we want them to be understood and to be appreciated as well. We are not against singing; we love singing, but at the same time, we believe that the public would better appreciate and work harder to preserve spirituals if the people better understood what they are all about."

When I joined Friends of the Negro Spirituals I was asked to come to the front of the hall with a few other new members. Sam had us raise our right hand and repeat after him, "I do commit to the promise of working hard to preserve the heritage of Negro Spirituals through educating the public." Like Sam, I'm not against singing. But I would prefer singing with a consciousness of the rich cultural work that performers, composers, and arrangers of spirituals have accomplished since these songs first came into being. I hope this book honors the pledge I made that day.

• • •

The research for this book was partially supported by a 2005 National Endowment for the Humanities Summer Stipend and a 2005 Faculty Development Grant from University of California, Davis; in addition, generous grants from the Babson Faculty Research Fund in 2013 and 2015 supported the final stage of writing, and a 2017 mini-grant helped support production expenses. I am thankful for research assistance from archivists at Fisk University, Hampton University, Harvard Library Theatre Collection, and the Library of Congress. Several individuals generously shared their research with me: Rob Bird, John Graziano, Donna Hamilton, Alan Lewis, David Newman (a descendant of J. B. T. Marsh, chronicler of the Fisk Jubilee Singers), and the students in Paul LaRue's Research History Classes 2000–2003, Washington Senior High School, Washington Court House, who shared with me their collection *Ohio's African American Civil War Heritage*, of which Ben Nichols's essay, "Samuel Lucas—Actor, Composer, Member of Fifth Regiment United States Volunteer Colored Infantry," was particularly helpful.

In the "above and beyond" category I thank the following individuals, who made time in impossibly busy schedules to comment on drafts and listen to me reason out loud: Tamar Barzel, Gwynne Kuhner Brown, Kathryn Craft, Jon and Mickey Elkus, Nancy Graham, Beth Levy, Bill Mahar, Jean Snyder, Henry Spiller, and Joe Weed. Anonymous reviewers commented on my work in generous and rigorous detail, and I can't thank them enough. The errors that remain are mine alone to claim. Luciano Chessa and Chris Simmons provided research assistance so long ago I doubt they even remember it. Jackson Williams prepared the musical examples. I honor the late Judy McCulloh of University of Illinois Press, friend and mentor, who started this book on its journey to publication; Victor Yellin, whose rigorous intellect made my life difficult but my work always better; and Larry Gushee, who got me thinking in new ways about Sam Lucas. Although I never had the opportunity to meet Eileen Southern, her work has influenced mine profoundly.

This book has been over a decade in the making, and a large cast of people buoyed me along the way. Special thanks to Joanna Bosse, Donna Buchanan, Judy Gilbert, Felicia Miyakawa, Brian Moon, Gillian Rodger, and Josephine Wright. A collective thank-you to my brilliant and caring colleagues in the Society for American Music and the Society for Ethnomusicology, who nurtured my soul and my scholarship.

Last, thanks to Laurie Matheson, the editor who finished the journey that Judy McCulloh started, for her patience, wise counsel, and moral support. I hope it was worth the wait.

Introduction

Black men and women took to the popular stage in unprecedented numbers after the Civil War. By the late 1870s hundreds of black entertainers were performing in concerts, minstrel shows, musical plays, circuses, and variety shows. Whether in big cities or rural backwaters, they drew large numbers of blacks to their performances, changing the faces of nineteenth-century audiences. Collectively, they constituted the first black entertainment industry in the United States, and until about 1890, these diverse genres were connected by one common ingredient: black sacred song, known as the spiritual.

Black entertainment had emerged in fits and starts over the previous hundred years. Katrina D. Thompson, in her persuasive book *Ring Shout, Wheel About: The Racial Politics of Music and Dance in North American Slavery*, posits that the first entertainment venue in America was slave society, and that white perceptions of slave entertainers were shaped by misrepresentations of black culture in a series of widely read publications.[1] For example, the journals and travel narratives of white explorers, missionaries, and adventurers traveling in West Africa in the late 1600s and 1700s almost always commented on the ubiquity of music and dance, which accompanied both ceremonial and everyday activities. Their accounts portrayed Africans as innately musical but also in desperate need of Christianization to curb behavior that their white observers deemed superstitious, barbarous, childlike, and lascivious. Such dehumanizing rhetoric became a template for white reactions to black music making in the New World.

Barbarous as it purportedly was, black musical behavior fascinated whites, some of whom took every opportunity to exploit it for personal pleasure and profit. Beginning with the Middle Passage, ship captains coerced slaves to sing and dance on deck—often while bound in chains—for their entertainment. Likewise, plantation owners would sometimes order their slaves to dance and sing even after an exhausting day of work in the fields. Some masters had a platform stage built for these performances, and they would pit their slave dancers against those of a neighboring plantation. Slavers discovered that slaves who could play an instrument, execute an impressive jig, or sing a powerful song brought higher prices; consequently music, song, and dance became a staple of the coffle, the slave pen, and the auction. Such coerced entertainments helped fabricate one of the enduring mythical characters of the southern plantation: the carefree, submissive, dancing slave. Writes Thompson, "Music and dance . . . became tied to the violence of slavery, turning a form of amusement into one of terror."[2]

In addition to slave musicians who played for dances and other social occasions attended by whites, there were free blacks who composed popular songs, played in bands and led them, and even performed in stage entertainments. There was a strong culture of music making in black middle-class homes and communities, with the same type of piano, vocal, and chamber music found in white parlors. Black musicians were everywhere but were especially numerous in urban centers. Most of these musicians never attained recognition beyond their locality, however, and those who did were seldom able to sustain enduring careers.[3]

There were notable exceptions. In 1818, for example, the bugle player, violinist, composer, and bandleader Francis "Frank" Johnson (1792–1844) became the first African American to have his compositions published as sheet music, which eventually numbered over two hundred. He went on to train a large circle of black musicians, tour nationally with his band, and appear in integrated concerts with white musicians. In 1837 he and four bandsmen were the first Americans of any race to perform abroad, in England.[4] His band played not only classical compositions but also marches and dance music for balls. Elizabeth Taylor Greenfield (ca. 1819–1876), the first black concert singer in America and the best-known black concert artist of her time, toured for just a few years in the early 1850s to great critical acclaim before she turned to teaching and directing an opera troupe.[5] Anointed the "Black Swan" by her admirers after her contemporary, the immensely popular white singer Jenny Lind, she performed works by Handel, Bellini, and Donizetti, as well as popular ballads, accompanied variously by piano, harp, guitar, and orchestra. Thomas J. Bowers (ca. 1826–1885), a tenor known as "the colored Mario" after the Italian opera star Giovanni Mario, toured with Greenfield in 1854, and thereafter performed sporadically. Justin Holland (ca. 1819–1887) was an Oberlin College–educated guitar virtuoso. He settled in Cleveland, Ohio, where he performed, taught, and arranged over three hundred classical compositions and popular songs for guitar, many of them commissioned by the leading music publishers of the day.[6]

All of these exceptional musicians had in common a devotion to European and American art music, which they mixed with popular parlor songs (e.g., Stephen Foster's "Old Folks at Home") in concert, according to the conventions of the day. They participated in and made their own contributions to systems of education and entertainment that had been defined and continued to be controlled by white Europeans and Americans.

If few black musicians were able to sustain lengthy performing careers in the early 1800s, theatrical livelihoods for blacks were even more precarious, as demonstrated by the short-lived historic African Grove in New York, which opened as a permanent theater in 1821. Serving as a training ground for black actors and musicians, it featured musical productions, abridged versions of Shakespeare plays, historical dramas, pantomimes, and farces, most of which catered to its black audiences with themes of revolt and triumphant struggle, on occasion addressing slave life directly.[7] On the one hand, the theater was a success and even became a tourist destination for whites visiting New York. Beleaguered by white troublemakers who disrupted performances, however, the African Grove was shut down several times by the police. The worst attack took place on 10 August 1822, when a gang of some twenty vandals, likely hired by the manager of the neighboring Park Theatre, entered the African Grove with tickets and proceeded to extinguish the lights, strip the actors and shred their costumes, and destroy the furniture and scenery. As an item in the *New York American* noted, blacks had been virtually excluded from white theaters, and yet when they started their own enterprises they were "hunted with a malice as mean as it seems to be unmitigable."[8] The African Grove closed its doors after only three seasons, unable to recover financially from the effects of repeated assaults.

The alternative to the legitimate stage for those who wanted a theatrical career was blackface minstrelsy, although very few black performers entered this profession before the war. The virtuosic dancer William Henry Lane, known as Master Juba, made history as the first black member of a white troupe when he joined the Georgia Champion Minstrels in 1845, and Thomas Dilward, known as Japanese Tommy, performed with various white troupes in the 1850s and 1860s, although he was valued more for his short stature—he barely reached three feet—than for his talents as a violinist, singer, and dancer.

The fortunes of black minstrel entertainers, and black entertainers generally, improved during Reconstruction, although every success came with a cost, and there were innumerable failures. It is with these new opportunities that this book begins.

Scope of the Book

Spirituals originated as folk songs, and their soundings were embedded in black daily life before the war (chap. 1). During the 1860s a number of white Union officers in charge of black regiments, impressed with the singing of spirituals and other black folk songs in army camps, described them in articles that were published in northern newspapers and magazines. The culmination of this burgeoning interest in black folk song was the first anthology of spirituals with musical scores, *Slave Songs of the United States* (1867), edited by William Francis Allen, Charles Pickard Ware, and Lucy McKim Garrison. Despite the value of these detailed written descriptions, they failed to convey the essence of spirituals, which was located in sound. One antidote to this problem arrived a few years later.

In 1871 the Jubilee Singers, a troupe of black students from Fisk University in Nashville, Tennessee, began touring to raise money for their school (chap. 2). Singing hymns and popular songs of the day by white composers, they struggled financially until they began singing arrangements of their spirituals. From then on their fortune was made, in the United States and well beyond. In 1873 they began a tour of England under the patronage of the Earl of Shaftesbury and other dignitaries, even giving a private performance for Queen Victoria. They toured Scotland and Ireland, sang in Switzerland and Holland, and toured Germany. Numerous anthologies of their spirituals were published in the United States and England and were translated into Dutch and German. The Jubilee Singers introduced spirituals in concert halls, white and black churches, and charitable institutions. Such was their fame that they became synonymous with the songs they sang, so that spirituals became known as jubilee songs. It's hard to exaggerate their influence. The Jubilee Singers reached audiences in the millions—through their performances, publications, and the countless newspaper reviews and articles they inspired over the course of their six-and-a-half-year career.

Their influence lives on today at Fisk University: Jubilee Hall, dedicated in 1876 and funded by the Jubilee Singers' tours, still stands; the campus celebrates Jubilee Day every 6 October to commemorate the start of the singers' first tour in 1871; and the Jubilee Singers still sing and travel. In 1980 the university even registered the name "Jubilee Singers" as a trademark. The twenty-first-century singers honor their lineage: "We stand on the shoulders of the original Jubilee Singers, continuing their legacy, as we sing Negro spirituals."[9]

Originally spirituals had been a communal folk music. George White, the troupe's white director, translated this folk music into a musical style that he believed would appeal to the discerning ears of concertgoers. In so doing he created a new genre: the arranged, or concert, spiritual (chap. 3). The public gave its repeated approbation to the tune of $20,000 after only six months of concertizing in the northern states; ultimately the singers raised $150,000 for their school before disbanding in 1878.

When the first competitors emerged in 1873–74, the Fisk singers became the standard to which their rivals aspired (chap. 4). Some of these rival jubilee troupes were imitators, and others were innovators who put their own stamp on the style and performance of the concert spiritual. The importance of these troupes has been underappreciated. While the Fisk students were touring abroad, for example, it was the Hampton Institute Singers, the Tennesseans, the Hyers sisters, and many others like them that kept the sound of jubilee song ringing in the ears of American patrons.

Although jubilee groups were household names by the late 1870s, they had no impact on mass entertainment until minstrel performers began to parody them (chap. 5). White minstrels in blackface had long lampooned certain religious practices, but the reports on black religious behavior from Civil War correspondents provided them with new fodder. Minstrels began to feature camp meeting songs (a relation of the spiritual) and depictions of slave life more generally in their shows, feeding a growing postwar nostalgia for the Old South among whites. Once jubilee singers became a cultural phenomenon, it was hardly surprising that minstrels began to parody jubilee troupes and the spirituals they sang. "Carry the News," "Rock'a My Soul," and "Contraband Children" are early examples of white compositions modeled to varying degrees on spirituals. Examining the relation of these songs to black culture, how they evolved, and how they traveled among different minstrel performers—both white and black—highlights the complicated relationship between folk and popular song, cross-fertilization between black and white performers, and issues of authenticity. With the increased visibility of black performers, whether jubilee singer or minstrel, audiences began to shift their loyalty from white minstrels' portrayal of slave life to "the real thing"—even though performances by blacks enacting slave stereotypes created by whites were scarcely less counterfeit.

With the Fisk Jubilee Singers and their arranged spirituals, George White unwittingly furnished the model for a popular song genre that would permeate minstrel, variety, vaudeville, plays, and spectacles for a good fifteen years: the commercial spiritual, a newly composed song based on the slave spiritual but written for entertainment and profit (chap. 6). It's worth devoting serious attention to this song genre that was anything but serious, despite its propagation of racist stereotypes. Not all commercial spirituals were created equal, and they performed complicated cultural work, especially when the composers, performers, and audiences happened to be black.

Both traditional and commercial spirituals found their way into the legitimate theater in the late 1870s (chap. 7), when productions of *Uncle Tom's Cabin*—the most well known and frequently performed story on the American stage—began incorporating jubilee troupes. There was a glut of productions into the new century, most of which strayed far from Harriet Beecher Stowe's original conception for her novel (which, for the record, contained no jubilee singers). At the same time a fledgling black musical theater movement pioneered by the Hyers sisters, Elizabeth Hopkins, Sam Lucas, and a cohort of other performers was taking shape, providing another venue for spirituals and commercial spirituals. Not to be left behind, other plays and melodramas followed suit, inserting their own jubilee singers even when they weren't germane to the plot. All of these shows, plus the retrogressive plantation shows of the 1890s like *Black America*, which aspired to re-create plantation culture with slave cabins and a multitude of field hands singing spirituals in open-air cotton fields, provided work for hundreds of African Americans.

By the late 1870s and into the 1880s jubilee singers had become so commercialized that the boundaries between "traditional" and "commercial" spirituals were often blurred in the jubilee marketplace (chap. 8). Fisk-like troupes that sang to support a school or religious institution were outnumbered by independent enterprises performing for their own profit. Some independent jubilee troupes competed for audiences by including plantation sketches, creating comic portraits of slave life using costumes, sets, and music. These carried the influence of minstrelsy and stage productions of *Uncle Tom's Cabin*. Consequently, despite the established association of "jubilee troupe" with the singing of spirituals, or "jubilee" songs, by the 1880s the so-called jubilee troupes found in Tom shows, variety shows, minstrel shows, and circuses mostly sang popular songs, with nary a spiritual to be heard. With the proliferation of jubilee performers, then, the term "jubilee" became an empty signifier.

A companion website to the book provides additional information on select troupe personnel, excerpts of recordings, and profiles of some eighty-five jubilee groups who formed and concertized in the last quarter of the nineteenth century. References to specific web materials occur in the text; the website may be found at http://www.press.uillinois.edu/books/graham/spirituals/.

. . .

By singing arranged spirituals in public, the Fisk Jubilee Singers ignited a chain reaction that rippled throughout multiple levels of popular culture for the rest of the century. Those cultural ripples cumulatively transformed spirituals from a genre of limited recognition into a national music, and the performance medium of jubilee singing into the basis of an entertainment industry.

That industry gave employment to thousands of singers, dancers, instrumentalists, songwriters, impresarios, and specialty artists of all kinds. The most successful black entertainers won the respect of black and white audiences alike and were able to sustain careers of ten or even twenty years and more. But every entertainer, no matter the degree of success, faced the same risks both on and off the stage: financial instability, racial degradation, physical danger, and the psychic toll of performing slave stereotypes day after day, year after year—for to abandon them would have been career suicide. For example in 1890—long after the Fisk Jubilee Singers had become world renowned— Frederick Loudin was denied lodging at a hotel in Cleveland while touring with a group of Fisk singers that he directed. Black minstrels frequently found themselves in a similar situation, and resorted to sleeping in an unheated hall where they had just performed or in a train station. Minstrel Billy Kersands made a career out of utilizing his unusually large mouth to great comic effect, only to wrestle with, as Mel Watkins imagines, "the conflict between satirizing social images of blacks and contributing to whites' negative stereotypes of blacks."[10] In short, white fantasies about slave culture delimited America's first black entertainment, just as they had delimited perceptions of Africans a century earlier. The happy, dancing slave of the coffle was transported to the theatrical stage. For this reason, some might argue that calling this the first "black" entertainment industry is a misnomer. Certainly whites participated in and even controlled virtually every type of entertainment, whether as owner, director, impresario, theater manager, performer, composer, playwright, audience member, publicist, or reviewer. Nevertheless, it was an industry built on black culture, black ingenuity, and black bodies, and it was embraced by black audiences who valued seeing their own community members onstage and knew how to look beyond the endlessly recycled stereotypes for subversive and affirming messages. Furthermore, over time blacks gradually took control over their own enterprises, even if caste prejudice ultimately constrained the material they could perform. A coterie of black composers of popular music emerged, black newspapers became more numerous and trumpeted the feats of black entertainers, and black directors and impresarios became important creative forces. The debates over cultural appropriation, exploitation, and stereotypes that arise from an examination of nineteenth-century performance are still relevant to much black entertainment today.

That spirituals influenced such a wide variety of popular amusements in the last quarter of the nineteenth century illustrates the symbolic distance these songs had traveled since the Civil War. That such a large number of entertainers coalesced around the performance of spirituals demonstrates the centrality of these songs and their offspring to a black entertainment industry. That the popularity of talented black songwriters relied initially on songs styled on spirituals likewise spoke to the spiritual's centrality in black entertainment. The groups and individuals that appropriated spirituals during these decades had wide-ranging and often conflicting agendas, from the educational to the commercially exploitative. This book examines how those agendas affected the musical style of spirituals and shaped black entertainment philosophies and business practices. For the patrons of these black entertainments were buying not only diversion but also conceptions of racial identity, in heaping doses.

Spirituals and the Birth of a
Black Entertainment Industry

CHAPTER 1

The Folk Spiritual

Spirituals are religious folk songs created by African Americans in the early nineteenth century. Favorite textual references include Old Testament heroes battling stronger foes (David, Moses, Daniel, Jonah) and the Israelites' bondage in Egypt under Pharaoh—obvious parallels to the condition of African Americans. In *The Souls of Black Folk* W. E. B. Du Bois famously christened them "sorrow songs," but the term fails to capture their multiple dimensions. In lyrics that demonstrate a selective approach to Christianity, spirituals reflect a variety of attitudes and themes, among them righteousness on Judgment Day ("Just as you live, just so you die . . . Judgment will find you so"), the jubilation of crossing over into heaven ("Oh, my little soul's going to shine, shine . . . all around the heaven"), the pathos of earthly suffering ("We'll die in the field"), faith ("Children, we all shall be free"), and patience ("Keep a inching along . . . Jesus will come by and by"). Some spirituals had a ritual function ("Good-by, brothers," sung as worshippers took leave of one another at the end of a religious meeting). Their poetry is a forceful mix of first-person declaration and metaphor that communicates in images rather than through cohesive narrative—an aesthetic that links them to the Yoruba praise poetry known as oriki, as Shane White and Graham White have observed.[1] Rhyme schemes are erratic, a consequence of a compositional practice rooted in improvisation. A capsule summary can do little justice to the scope, imagination, and power of these songs.[2]

Folk spirituals were transmitted orally. In the absence of a permanent written or aural record they lived only in performance, and each performance was unique. With a variable text and a loosely defined melody a folk spiritual was, as White and White have written, "a frame to be filled as the moment dictated."[3] Folk spirituals were communal music in which everyone participated, regardless of musical aptitude. The typically responsorial structure consists of solo calls and communal responses that often overlap, creating a dense, continuous flow of sound. Textual and melodic repetition encourage participation by making the songs easy to remember. The most common song structures are chorus plus verses of four lines each; verses only; and two-line verses with refrain. When present, choruses rather than verses launch the song. Verses often have an "internal refrain," as in "Swing Low, Sweet Chariot":

> I looked over Jordan, and what did I see,
> *Coming for to carry me home,*
> A band of angels coming after me.
> *Coming for to carry me home.*

The melodies typically have fewer pitches than those of the familiar seven-tone major scale. When only five of the seven pitches are used, for example, a gapped scale results:

do re mi fa **sol la** ti **(do)**

The gaps between *mi* and *sol*, and *la* and *do*, define the interval of a third—an interval that characterizes the melodic contour of many spirituals. The chorus to "Swing Low, Sweet Chariot," for example, begins with two such (descending) gaps of a third:

Mi	**do**	**mi**	**do-**	**do-**	**la-sol**
Swing	low,	sweet	char–	i–	ot

Gapped-scale melodies don't have a key in the conventional sense. For example, if we assigned the key of F major (where F is *do*) to the unharmonized melody of "Swing Low," we would place B♭ (*fa*) in the key signature. But there is no *fa* in the melody, so there's no need for a B♭. Furthermore, the absence of *ti* prevents the strong pull to *do* that is characteristic of melodies in major keys.

An even greater challenge in talking about the melody of folk spirituals has been articulated by John W. Work III, among countless others: "All Negro folk-singers regard the melody of their song with a free attitude," as evidenced by the fact that "in the course of a song repetitions of the refrain or verses are most always varied."[4] In addition to melodic variations, singers might produce pitches slightly higher or lower than the pitches of major and minor scales. They might slide into a pitch, or slide off one. They ornament tones with shakes of the voice or lots of additional quick notes (melismas). They intersperse moans, groans, cries, and shouts. They tend to sing spirituals without instrumental accompaniment in a heterophonic texture—a kind of "thick" unison in which the voices follow the same general melodic outline but lack synchronicity.

Spirituals can be rhythmically free or governed by a beat, and tempo matches the mood and occasion. Rhythmic spirituals usually have a duple meter (counted in two or four), which facilitates body movement during physical labor or holy dancing. Spirituals in other meters exist but are rare. In folk performance spirituals might be rhythmically layered, accompanied by foot stomping and clapping in cross rhythms, and rendered with a rhythmic freedom or swing that can't be represented easily in printed music—to say nothing of notes that are lengthened, shortened, or omitted, as Work notes.

Folklorist/anthropologist Zora Neale Hurston's characterization of spirituals as unceasing variations around a theme explains why spirituals are best described by their manner of performance, which depended on context.[5] Whereas a spiritual to accompany work might require a quick tempo with a regular beat, which would make a highly melismatic singing style impractical, a spiritual growing out of a prayer might be slow and rhythmically free, leaving plenty of time for ornamentation.

Considered in aggregate, spirituals were songs of survival; they created a temporary escape for the spirit that was denied to captive bodies. The same song could have vastly different meanings according to the occasion, the geographic region, and the way it was performed (e.g., tempo, number of singers, ornamentation, accompaniment). Spirituals were not only sacred songs (for worship, baptism, funerals) but "secular" songs as well (for cotton picking, rowing, loading riverboats, singing children to sleep, plucking on banjos to relax at the end of a day). They could serve as a coded signal for a secret nocturnal religious meeting (e.g., "Steal Away") or for escape to the North on the Underground Railroad ("Run to Jesus").[6]

The multipurpose nature of spirituals can be accounted for by a typically West African worldview in which all elements of the divine are incorporated within the everyday world, as Lawrence Levine has argued.[7] But this didn't preclude a distinction between "sacred" and "secular" song and dance. Whereas on some plantations slaves who were religious filled their free time with praying, singing, and shouting, the "nonbelievers" patted (making percussive sounds on their body), sang, fiddled, and danced.[8] This incipient schism between sacred and secular became even more pronounced after emancipation, mirroring the increasing social, economic, and geographic diversification of the African American population.

Origins

It's impossible to pinpoint the origin—or origins—of the spiritual, as is true of any long-standing oral tradition. The spiritual seems to have several related ancestors: the slave shouts, ring dances, and chants of African origin; Anglo-American hymnody; and camp meeting songs.

Eileen Southern found the seeds of what became known as the spiritual in an 1801 hymnal by Richard Allen, who in 1786 organized the first congregation of the African Methodist Episcopal (AME) Church, in Philadelphia. *A Collection of Spiritual Songs and Hymns Selected from Various Authors by Richard Allen, African Minister* contained the texts of fifty-four hymns from Methodist and Baptist sources, with some possibly written by Allen himself. (Southern has identified most of the writers, who are not credited in the hymnal.) No other autonomous black congregation at the time seems to have produced a hymnal, making Allen's the earliest surviving anthology of hymns favored by blacks for congregational singing.[9]

The hymns in Allen's anthology are linked to the spiritual in their use of "wandering refrains"—short, easy-to-learn choruses that singers could attach to any hymn they wished. Wandering refrains allowed everyone in the congregation to participate in the singing without knowing the verses. Contemporaneous accounts of hymn singing in northern churches suggest that these refrains were sung repeatedly (e.g., "a thousand times," for "half an hour"), serving as an opportunity for group improvisation and ecstatic worship.[10] Refrains in spirituals could have functioned similarly.

Another precedent of the spiritual was the camp meeting hymn. Camp meetings were an offspring of the evangelical movement in America known as the Second Great Awakening (ca. 1790–mid-1800s); the first meeting was held in July 1800, in Kentucky. Spanning several days, these open-air revivals attracted whites and blacks in the hundreds and even thousands. In the first two decades attendees camped out in tents, warmed themselves by large fires, socialized, prayed, listened to preachers, and sang. The proclivity of some worshippers for emotional gyrations (jerking, falling, rocking, crying, grunting, groaning) eventually sparked dissent among the various Protestant denominations involved in the revivals. Some succumbed to critics who urged more sedate worship, whereas others retained the so-called sensory excesses. As revivalism spread to the East and throughout New England, the worship style became less emotional. Camp meetings in the Northeast were associated mainly with middle-class Congregationalists and Presbyterians, whereas camp meetings in the West and South were largely the domain of Methodists and Baptists. By the 1830s revivals were part of mainstream American culture.[11]

Camp meeting hymns, like spirituals, usually had a verse and refrain; in this they bore some resemblance to the hymns with wandering refrains in Richard Allen's hymnal. The simplicity of their repetitive music and lyrics was essential to facilitate group participation, especially in the earliest years of the revival movement when most of the participants were illiterate.

As Eileen Southern has noted, "The camp meeting was primarily an inter-racial institution," in which black worshippers sometimes outnumbered white.[12] Camp meetings ran the gamut from integrated to strictly segregated worship spaces for whites and blacks. Whites who described camp meetings in letters, diaries, and journalism almost always mentioned the singing—particularly that of the blacks, which they characterized as loud, overpowering, tumultuous, and full of exultation.[13] The white Methodist preacher John F. Watson, who overheard blacks worshipping in their quarters during an after-hours session at an 1819 camp meeting, reported hearing "short scraps of disjointed affir-mations, pledges, or prayers, lengthened out with long repetition *choruses.* These are all sung in the merry chorus-manner of the southern harvest field, or husking-frolic method, of the slave blacks." Watson was distressed because "the example has already visibly affected the religious manners of some whites." In some camps as many as sixty people crowded into a tent after the official worship had concluded, where they continued "the whole night, singing tune after tune . . . scarce one of which were in our hymn books."[14] Those ecstatic hymns became known as "shouts," and shouting became a style of hymnody especially prevalent among southern rural blacks and whites.

Given that African Americans and some whites shared similarly emotional styles of worship, Watson's revelation that the two groups' worship styles influ-enced each other isn't surprising. Like the black attendees, many of the whites attracted to camp meetings were on the social and economic margins, so it's logical that the two groups had qualitatively similar psychic and emotional needs.[15] The following recollection by ex-slave Cordelia Thomas, describing the emotional worship style of whites and blacks, suggests that both groups sang spirituals at camp meetings:

Missy, you jus' don't know nothin' 'bout 'citement if you ain't never been to one of dem old-time camp-meetin's. When folkses would git 'ligion dey would holler and shout a-testifyin' for de Lord. After de meetin' dey dammed up de crick and let it git deep enough for de baptizin'. Dey dipped de white folkses fust, and den de Niggers. You could hear 'em singin' a mile away dem old songs lak: *On Jordan's Stormy Banks I Stand,—Roll, Jordan Roll,—All God's Chilluns is a-goin' Home,* and—*Whar de Livin' Waters Flow.*[16]

It was in the after-hours sessions of camp meetings that African styles of performance emerged most strongly: multiple layers of voices creating dense musical textures; strong chest voices; interjections of moans, screams, shouts. One distinctly African practice was the ring shout, in which participants per-formed a shuffle step counterclockwise in a circle to the accompaniment of singing. (A related ring dance was modified for the praise house on plantations and was held after the regular worship service.)[17] The goal of this holy dance was religious ecstasy (often called "getting happy"), in which the Holy Spirit entered and inhabited the body. A shout could last for hours.

Although some masters prohibited (or showed no interest in) religious instruction among their slaves in the early nineteenth century, most succumbed to the persuasion of evangelists who argued that all blacks should be converted to Christianity.[18] It's hard to generalize further, for individual circumstances dictated when and in what manner slaves worshipped (see figure 1.1). As narratives from ex-slaves make clear, however, masters closely controlled formal religious instruction, to prevent insurrections:

> We went to de same church as de white folks did; only thing was we had to go in de evenin' atter de white folks. De white folks would go along an' read de Bible for de preacher, an' to keep dem from talkin of things dat might help dem to git free. Dey would sing songs like "Steal Away," "Been Toilin' at the Hill So Long," an' "Old-Time Religion." [Interview with William Henry Towns]

> Didn't have no colored churches. De drivers and de overseers, de house-servants, de bricklayers and folk like dat'd go to de white folk's church. But not de field hands. Why dey couldn't have all got in de church. My marsa had three hundred slaves, himself. . . . They had colored preachers to preach to de field hands down in de [slave] quarters. Dey'd preach in de street. Meet next day to de marsa's and turn in de report. [Interview with Rebecca Jane Grant][19]

Former slaves Frank Roberson and Charlie Van Dyke recalled that the sermons of white preachers repeatedly commanded obedience to the master and condemned lying and stealing.[20] Black preachers, fearful of white reprisal, parroted such messages. Slaves who wished to worship unencumbered by white presence resorted to the "invisible church" of the woods, where under the cover of darkness and at a far remove from master and overseer they prayed, sang, danced, and exhorted communally. Although the exception rather than the rule, there were plantations where blacks and whites worshipped together. Uncle Shang Harris recalled, "Thanksgiving we give thanks in de church on our knees. Warn't no slave gallery. White and colored all together and shouted together."[21]

Spirituals, then, had antecedents in formal hymns with wandering refrains, camp meeting hymns, and various African musical practices. They also had secular analogues in the songs and dances used for corn huskings, work, and festivities. Compositional methods varied. One method, common in oral cultures around the world, involved improvising on previously composed materials: "singing an old song anew," in the words of George Pullen Jackson, by combining

FIGURE 1.1. This wood engraving by illustrator Frank Vizetelly, titled "Family Worship in a Plantation in South Carolina," was originally published in *Illustrated London News* 43 (5 Dec. 1863). About twenty slaves are in attendance, under the watchful gaze of the white owners. Plantations often relied on itinerant preachers, who might make it to their stopping places only once every few weeks, depending on circumstances. Courtesy of the New York Public Library.

parts of Euro-American hymns and snatches of African melodies.[22] Alternatively spirituals might be improvised, either individually or collectively—leaping "almost wholly from the heart," as John Wesley Work II put it in 1901, or evolving gradually over successive performances.[23] A preacher might extemporize a spiritual in the course of a sermon; a spiritual might develop from a prayer; or responses from worshippers during a sermon might grow into a refrain. Whether fashioned on preexisting ideas or consisting of new material, each was an original, anonymous creation.[24]

For the greater part of the twentieth century, inquiry into the origins of spirituals was shaped by a wider debate among artists and intellectuals over the relative European versus African heritage of African American culture. For example during the black nationalist arts movement of the 1920s and 1930s known as the Harlem Renaissance, writer-scholars Alain Locke and Zora Neale Hurston celebrated the "African-ness" of folk spirituals; although they appreciated the highly rehearsed concert arrangements of these songs, they felt that adherence to formal rules rendered the arrangements "European" and unworthy of the name "spiritual"—indeed, Hurston called them "neo-spirituals."[25] Two prominent scholars who came to represent opposing views in academia were the black sociologist E. Franklin Frazier (1894–1962) and the white anthropologist Melville Herskovits (1895–1963). Frazier argued that slavery in the United States had dismantled African social structure and thereby erased African cultural practices. Herskovits, who studied with anthropologist Franz Boas at Columbia University and spent a decade doing fieldwork in Haiti and Africa, argued in *Myth of the Negro Past* (1941) that even if Africans in the United States didn't retain their material culture, they retained their cultural memory.[26]

George Pullen Jackson's determination to find the musical roots of black spirituals in British folksong melodies placed his theories at the center of a vigorous origins controversy in the 1980s among the scholars Dena Epstein, William Tallmadge, and John Garst.[27] Jackson was a white professor of German at Vanderbilt University and an amateur musician. His writings in the 1930s and 1940s sought to explain why some black spirituals resembled Anglo-American hymns in words and melody, as well as why certain spirituals (e.g., "Swing Low, Sweet Chariot") were present in both black *and* white traditions. Because he relied solely on hymnals and tune books as evidence, his argument merely demonstrated which songs were printed first—hardly a valid methodology for dating and attributing songs created in oral tradition. Only when Jackson was unable to trace white ancestry for 630 of the black spirituals in his pool of 892 was he was forced to credit them as black creations.[28]

Debates over origins tended to focus on what remained of African culture after Africans were brought to the United States—often termed "African retentions," "African survivals," or simply "Africanisms." But the *what* was less important than the *how*—the processes, interactions, and attitudes that *created* African American culture. The *how* has been the focus of scholarship since the 1970s. Spirituals reflected African worldviews as applied to distinctly American experiences, in music that fused African modes of performance with Euro-American musical styles. Spirituals were not only without doubt African American compositions, but they were uniquely American.

The term "spiritual" is one of three species of song—with psalms and hymns—designated in the Bible (e.g., Colossians 3:16; Ephesians 5:19). The earliest known use of the term "Negro spiritual" occurs in a diary entry of 3 December 1862 by Colonel Thomas Wentworth Higginson, a white officer who commanded the first black regiment (the First South Carolina Volunteers) to serve in the Civil War.[29] But "Negro" was not a consistent qualifier until the twentieth century, when debates about white versus black origins began to intensify. Today the term "Negro spiritual" is sometimes replaced with "African American spiritual," but it is increasingly common to dispense with qualifiers altogether. An artificial history of white-to-black influence, necessitating differentiation between white and black spirituals, has been propagated for too long. In the same way that blues, jazz, and ragtime have no racial qualifier, so it should be with spirituals. All of these genres were African American creations, rooted in African American lived experience. As Lawrence Levine has written of the spirituals, "It is not necessary for a people to originate or invent all or even most of the elements of their culture. It is necessary only that these components become their own, embedded in their traditions, expressive of their world view and life style."[30]

Spirituals during the War Years

The Civil War provided white northerners with their first extended exposure to plantation slave culture. Army officers, missionaries, educators, and war correspondents wrote descriptions of singing, shouting, and dancing among plantation slaves, giving their northern readers a taste of what many southerners had already experienced. The earliest commercial publications of slave songs were the products of these wartime contacts.

"Go Down, Moses" was the first spiritual published as sheet music. In 1861 the Young Men's Christian Association (YMCA) sent the Reverend Lewis Lockwood to Fortress Monroe in Hampton, Virginia, to help address the desolate living conditions among the "contrabands" there. (General Benjamin Butler, the Union commander at Fortress Monroe, had designated the runaway slaves who came under Union protection "contrabands of war.") During his stay Lockwood heard them singing "Go Down, Moses," which he described in detail for the *National Anti-Slavery Standard* (12 Oct. 1861). Later he sent a copy of the spiritual to YMCA secretary Harwood Vernon, and Vernon expanded on Lockwood's account in a letter to the *New York Tribune* (21 Dec. 1861). Within weeks the spiritual was published in a sheet music edition under the title "The Song of the Contrabands: O! Let My People Go" by Horace Waters, New York—with credit given to Lockwood as collector and to Thomas Baker as vocal/piano arranger.[31] From today's vantage point the first commercial publication of a spiritual seems a momentous event, but in 1861 few took notice. It's unlikely the published song resembled its model, given that it was translated first from vocal performance to musical notation, and then again from transcription to arrangement for voice and piano—the latter by someone who didn't witness the original performance.

Some of the most comprehensive descriptions of slave song during the war years came from the Sea Islands, a chain of some one hundred islands off the Atlantic coastline of South Carolina, Georgia, and northern Florida. The islands were home to a host of plantations—and approximately ten thousand contrabands—abandoned by their Confederate owners during the war.[32] On 7 November 1861 Union forces occupied one of those islands: Port Royal, off South Carolina. In a federally organized effort that became known as the Port Royal Experiment, the ex-slaves operated the plantations with oversight by white northerners, while military personnel, missionaries, and abolitionists initiated various philanthropic ventures among the freedmen, foremost among them education.

The northerners who participated in this early experiment in Reconstruction pronounced the slaves' language and song primitive, colorful, foreign, and exotic. Although they might well have used those descriptors for any slave culture they encountered, Sea Island culture was distinctive. The slaves in South Carolina generally, and in the Sea Islands particularly, were a mix of West and Central African peoples in which Bantu ethnicities predominated (52 percent of the slaves imported to South Carolina in 1804–1807 came from Angola). American planters chose them for their knowledge of rice cultivation—South Carolina's main crop—and physique. Bantu peoples shared a relatively homogeneous linguistic and cultural background that tended to predominate over West African presence in the islands, giving rise to a Creole culture known as Gullah. Gullah culture was marked by a high degree of African retentions in language, foodways, religion, folklore, crafts, work traditions, and music. Gullah culture remained relatively immune to acculturation for two reasons. First, the islands were geographically isolated from the mainland, and the plantations usually had large slave populations with only one or two white overseers. Second, illegal shipments of Africans to the Sea Islands continued through the 1800s, the last one recorded being 420 Africans to Jekyll Island, Georgia, in 1858.[33] This meant that Gullah culture was regularly refreshed with African languages and cultures.

In June 1862 nineteen-year-old Lucy McKim accompanied her father, James Miller McKim, on an inspection of the Sea Islands for the Philadelphia Port Royal Relief Committee.[34] Struck by the unusual music of the slaves, this accomplished musician transcribed the words and music to several songs.[35] Although her descriptive reports found an eager audience, the same cannot be said for the two spirituals that she collected, arranged, and published in sheet music editions: "Poor Rosy, Poor Gal" and "Roll, Jordan, Roll" (1862).

McKim's experiences were paralleled by those of Unitarian minister Henry George Spaulding, who wrote an article on plantation life in the Sea Islands called "Under the Palmetto," published in the *Continental Monthly* of August 1863. A capable musician, Spaulding wrote detailed descriptions of "Negro 'Shouts' and Shout Songs" and transcribed the words and melody of five of them. In preparing his sheet music edition of the spiritual "Times Hab Badly Change' Old Massa Now; Song of the Freedmen" (Boston: Oliver Ditson, 1866), Spaulding transcribed the melody from the singing of a slave but composed new words, because he couldn't understand the original lyrics. Spaulding's publication followed McKim's into oblivion.

It wasn't Lockwood's or McKim's or Spaulding's fault that their representations of slave spirituals failed to attract a sizable audience. Spirituals were songs that lived in performance, not on paper. They lived in vibrant voices, local dialects, interactive communal singing, variable tunes and rhythms, and expressive body movement—none of which could be conveyed in a musical score. Even more important, the general public had no aural model for interpreting these unfamiliar songs. In the 1860s people bought sheet music because the songs were already familiar to them from popular entertainments.

The culmination of this nascent interest in black song was the landmark publication in 1867 of *Slave Songs of the United States*, edited by William Francis Allen, Charles Pickard Ware, and Lucy McKim Garrison.[36] Most of the songs were collected by Allen, Ware, and Thomas Wentworth Higginson.[37] Fearing that emancipation would lead to increasing acculturation of blacks and therefore the extinction of their folk songs, the editors sought to preserve the music while it was still possible. Although they aimed for a geographically diverse collection, most of the 136 songs in the anthology came from South Carolina.

There's no need to reproduce here the well-documented publication history of *Slave Songs* and the biographies of its compilers,[38] but it's worth noting a few well-known features of the anthology that relate to the later stylistic evolution of spirituals. The editors produced a remarkable document of folklore two decades before folklore studies became a professional discipline in the United States. They attempted a scientific approach, notating variant tunes and texts, inserting notes about performance, and describing in detail the difficulties of notating what was to them a completely unfamiliar sound. Coaxing the Gullah to sing their old songs, even without the prospect of transcription, was "no easy matter," as Allen wrote in his introduction—"such is the dignity that has come with freedom" (x). Although the transcribers strove for accuracy, "the best we can do . . . with paper and types, or even with voices, will convey but a faint shadow of the original" (iv). The editors published the melody only, taken "from the lips of the colored people themselves," and made no attempt to arrange the music (iii). Although Allen theorizes that the slave songs were composed partly "under the influence of association with the whites, partly actually imitated from their [i.e., African] music," he writes that "in the main it appears to be original in the best sense of the word, and the more we examine the subject, the more genuine it appears to us to be" (vi). He rejected as spurious the spirituals "Give Me Jesus," "Climb Jacob's Ladder," and "I'll Take the Wings of the Morning" because "we find [them] in Methodist hymn-books" (vi, n.). In other words, the editors were interested in "genuine black creations" that were tinged only marginally, if at all, with white influence, exposing a prejudice in favor of (mythical) racial and cultural purity.

Finally, the editors' notes on performance context (when and how a song was performed) reveal that individual performances of songs differed, and that repertories varied by region. It's remarkable that the editors thought to make such distinctions at a time when blacks were stereotyped as primitive savages.

The songs in Allen, Ware, and Garrison's compilation are almost exclusively *sperichils*—as the Gullah called them—with a handful of secular songs sent in by other contributors. Although Allen suggests that secular songs have a much higher degree of the "barbaric element" than religious songs (vii), he claims that he encountered no secular music or instruments in Port Royal. But secular music was probably as common in Port Royal as it was elsewhere in the South; rather, Allen likely ignored it in favor of religious song, since his work with the Freedmen's Commission involved "the serious and earnest side of the negro character" (x). Allen also admits that his collection only skims the surface of a narrow segment of black song, which further suggests the existence of greater diversity (x).

Slave Songs engendered widespread interest upon publication and sold out its print run within a few weeks. Nevertheless its impact was limited by the merger of its publisher with two other companies. A second edition finally appeared four years later, but it wasn't until the Harlem Renaissance that the book was rediscovered, thanks to a 1929 facsimile edition.[39] Since then it has become a well-known fixture of American musical history.

In his discerning book *Culture on the Margins: The Black Spiritual and the Rise of American Cultural Interpretation*, Jon Cruz situates nineteenth-century chronicles of spirituals within a confluence of romantic-humanistic and social-scientific paths that began to radically alter perceptions of black life. He argues that uncomprehending whites in America heard spirituals initially as "noise" and only eventually as music that had meaning and beauty. He summarizes the public perception of the black spiritual as a transformation from testimony—in the writings of Frederick Douglass, Spaulding, and Higginson—to cultural artifact in *Slave Songs*. The testimonial mode of hearing championed by Douglass "sought out the inner world that was presumably reflected in the expression of slaves. Their songs were to be grasped as testimonies to their lives, as indices of their sense of social fate."[40] This mode of hearing required that listeners perceive the singer of slave spirituals not as chattel but as a human being with a soul. "Every pathos-oriented listener who understood that the spirituals were slavery-induced cries of anguish to God could be a full-fledged cultural interpreter, a reader of what had hitherto been the slave's secrets," writes Cruz.[41]

With the publication of *Slave Songs*, spirituals became cultural artifacts, to be collected, captured, and preserved. The act of collecting was characterized by what Cruz calls "disengaged cultural engagement."[42] Although *Slave Songs* expanded knowledge of black culture, the editors' selective approach to what they documented—primarily religious song—resulted in a limited recognition of black expressivity. This "mode of social and political enclosure" resulted in what Cruz calls "a new *cultural-interpretive reservation*." Not only did the romantic perspective of the collectors prevent them from complete dedication to the transformation of the freedman's social status—reservation as a form of hesitation—but their limited recognition confined black expressivity on a kind of cultural reservation.[43] The expansion driven by these new collectors was a step forward, but it also created new boundaries that would have to be broken.

The repositioning of cultural boundaries is conceived in another way by cultural studies scholar Ronald Radano. He argues that spirituals were especially suitable for analysis by the editors of *Slave Songs* because they contained both European and African qualities. Therefore Allen, Ware, and Garrison could celebrate the slaves' civility ("merely an extension of their own whiteness") while fetishizing their qualities of difference (i.e., "the qualities of blackness incommensurable with white experience").[44]

Black music-makers were *literary* representations in the writings of Higginson, Allen, and other observers of the Civil War era. The sounding of black voices and the physicality of black bodies were absent. Even Frederick Douglass was "heard" more widely through print than through his oratory at that time. This situation changed radically in the 1870s.

The Rise of a Jubilee Industry

CHAPTER 2

The Jubilee Singers of Fisk University

With the gradual dismantling of slavery, from President Abraham Lincoln's Emancipation Proclamation on 1 January 1863 to the states' ratification of the Thirteenth Amendment on 6 December 1865, education became a critical step toward self-reliance for the approximately four million freed women and men. Until legislatures in the southern states agreed to fund public education for all citizens, the creation of schools for African Americans was shouldered largely by various northern philanthropic organizations. Fisk University president George Gates recalled the "romantic beginnings" of several early black colleges:

> Hampton had its heroic early days, gathering round the personality of General Samuel Chapman Armstrong. Tuskegee's romance rests largely on the ever inspiring story of the rise from a little slave boy into the strong American citizen of world honor, Dr. Booker T. Washington. The romance of Fisk's early beginning will always be associated in the popular mind with the Jubilee Singers and Jubilee songs.[1]

Fisk (1866), Hampton (1868), and Tuskegee (1881) may have owed their inception to the single-minded determination of their founders, but they owed their survival to the courage of small bands of students—jubilee singers—who sang school buildings into existence with the profits of their concert tours. What began as a desperate attempt to raise money for the struggling Fisk School ended up establishing a new style of performance that quickly became a tradition. It was a process of musical transformation that its progenitors could never have anticipated. This "early beginning" was hardly a "romance," however, but rather a struggle involving privation, anxiety, racism, and financial disaster—as well as faith and ultimately triumph.

■ ■ ■

One of the most active philanthropies in early black education was the American Missionary Association (AMA), which started hundreds of schools during and after the war. Formed by Lewis Tappan in 1846 in Albany, New York, the AMA distinguished itself from other abolitionist societies by refusing to accept money from slaveholders and by appointing four African Americans to its founding board of twelve men.[2] By 1865 the AMA officially allied itself with the Congregational Church, although it welcomed anyone of appropriately evangelical sentiments and moral behavior.[3]

In 1865 the AMA decided to start a school for blacks in Nashville, which had been the first southern capital to fall to the Union Army during the war. Why Nashville? There was need: the city had no public school for blacks but a large base of 10,744 potential students, 3,580 of whom were under the age of fifteen.[4] It was accessible from the border states as well as the Deep South. Furthermore Tennessee had a hearty strain of liberalism—it was the sole southern state that had not criminalized the education of slaves before the war, and its governor from 1865 to 1869, East Tennessean William Gannaway Brownlow, hailed from a part of the state that had been loyal to the Union.

But Nashville was conservative, and the hunt for sites was frustrating. The search team consisted of two newly hired AMA employees: field secretary Erastus Milo Cravath (1833–1900), district secretary of the Middle West Department Edward Parmelee Smith (1827–1876), and John Ogden (1824–1910), who was superintendent of education of the Freedmen's Bureau in Tennessee. One prospect after another evaporated as soon as sellers learned of the intention to build a school for blacks. The team finally found a potential candidate in the "Negro district"[5]—the former Union Army hospital—but the government's asking price of $16,000 for the land was far beyond the AMA's means. Unwilling to let this property slip through their fingers, Cravath, Ogden, and Smith pledged $4,000 of their own money. The AMA reimbursed its three agents, paying three-quarters of the purchase price, and the Freedmen's Bureau contributed the remaining $4,000.[6]

But there was still a stumbling block: $16,000 purchased the land but not the buildings. The deal was completed only through the financial benevolence of Union General Clinton B. Fisk, who at the time was assistant commissioner of the Freedmen's Bureau for Tennessee and Kentucky. Thanks to him the Fisk School opened its doors on 9 January 1866, with John Ogden as its principal.

By now the story of Fisk University and the accomplishments of the Jubilee Singers has been told, and told well, from many perspectives. The Jubilee Singers have rightly been recognized as role models whose concert tours evolved into a dignified campaign for civil rights. But what did their spirituals *sound* like? And why did they sound that way? What was the manner of performance, and how did it differ from the way folk spirituals were performed? How did audiences *hear* the Jubilee Singers? Because these questions are crucial to understanding the broader impact of spirituals, the chapters in part 1 of this book explore the new "sounding" of postwar performances and the strategies that created this new sound. The foundations of those strategies lie in the backgrounds of those who first administered the Fisk School.

Fisk's Educational Philosophy

E. M. Cravath, who was thirty-two when the Fisk School convened its first classes, had a long and lasting influence on the direction of education there. His childhood home near Homer, New York, had been a station on the Underground Railroad, and this early exposure to abolitionism shaped the course of his entire life. As AMA field secretary in New York City he oversaw the association's educational work in the South, and from 1875 until his death in 1900 he served as president of Fisk University.

Largely owing to Cravath's and Ogden's influence, Fisk was distinguished by its devotion to the liberal arts. Course offerings included arithmetic, reading, writing, spelling, geography, and music, buttressed later on by Latin, science, and theology—all of them firmly rooted, by AMA mandate, in Christian ideals. (Principal Ogden's monthly reports to the AMA recorded not only academic progress but the number of religious conversions.) The majority of white southerners, who barely tolerated vocational schools for freedmen, were even more hostile to this intellectual curriculum. Governor Brownlow acknowledged their antagonism in his remarks at the dedication of the Fisk School on 9 January 1866—nine months to the day after Lee surrendered to Grant. He pragmatically advised the students to be "mild and temperate" in their "habits and spirit" and "conduct towards white people," and teachers to be "exceedingly prudent and cautious, and do nothing offensive to the predominant party here."[7]

The idealistic mission of the Fisk School came under immediate and continuous assault. Not only were students harassed and accosted on their way to and from school, but the teachers—all of them white northerners of various evangelical religious backgrounds—were dubbed "white niggers" by Nashville's white society. The social challenges were exacerbated by a chronic shortage of funds. The school buildings, dilapidated from day one, needed constant care and expansion. Even so, Fisk fared better than other "colored" schools in Nashville, where buildings were burned, teachers brutalized, and students murdered.[8]

The student body at Fisk, which numbered five hundred by February 1866, was a motley group of male and female, young and old, Christian and non-

Christian, freed and born free. Most of them, regardless of age, required the most basic primary education. Although the majority were day students, there was a small group of some thirty to forty boarding students, which the Fisk faculty referred to as the "family." Each student had daily responsibilities in the "home," or dormitory. Students led a highly regulated existence, as was customary in all boarding schools of the day:

> [Boarders] rose promptly at the ringing of the first bell and studied from 5:30 to 7:00 in the morning; lights were put out at 10:00 P.M. Each student on campus was expected to attend chapel every morning and Wednesday afternoon, and regular services on Sunday. Visits to rooms of other students were prohibited during study hours (5:30 to 7:00 A.M., 8:30 to 12:00 noon, 1:00 to 4:00 P.M., and 6:30 to 9:00 P.M.). Males and females were not allowed to visit each other or friends in their private rooms under any circumstances. All interviews had to be public and in the presence of a teacher. Tobacco in any form, ardent spirits, and games of chance were strictly forbidden at all times and places while the student was connected with Fisk. To teach economy and prevent needless expenditure, pupils were required to deposit all their money with the treasurer upon entrance.[9]

Although the classrooms, faculty rooms, and family sitting rooms were heated, boarders' rooms—again, as was customary—were not. This made for uncomfortable winters, since Nashville residents were well acquainted with temperatures below freezing. Food was meager and barely edible. Not surprisingly, illness was a frequent visitor among students and faculty.

A year and a half after its founding, the Fisk School was incorporated in Tennessee as Fisk University. Since the students were still at a primary school level, this was more an act of faith than a reflection of present realities. By 1869 Fisk consisted of a normal school (organized in 1867, for teacher education), high school, model school (in which students practiced teaching), theology department, practical commercial department, and the college.[10] Fisk was poised to produce craft workers, clergy, professionals, and teachers.

The Prehistory of the Jubilee Singers

The Music Man: George L. White

Music played a central role at Fisk almost from its inception because of an unlikely music teacher named George Leonard White (1838–1895). Natural ability and enthusiasm appear to have been his main qualifications for the job, for he never studied music formally and left school at the age of fourteen.

He apparently inherited his musical aptitude from his father, a blacksmith by trade who played occasionally in a local band. At some point White taught himself to read music and to play the violin and the fife. A self-effacing man before the public, it was as a teacher and director, not as a performer, that White found fulfillment.[11]

White was born in 1838 in Cadiz, Cattaraugus County, in southwestern New York State. Missionary activity in this sparsely populated Indian territory had begun in 1798 with the Quakers, the first whites to settle in the county and establish a school on the Seneca reservation. In 1826 a Presbyterian mission was organized, and around 1850—when White was a boy of twelve—the Methodists and Baptists arrived.[12] Perhaps their ethos of "elevating" the Indian race through religion and education impressed the youthful White, for he ended up devoting his life to similar labor. A deeply religious man, White worked as a teacher in Ohio during his early twenties, where he directed the choirs of school and Sunday school groups consisting mostly of African Americans.

White's wartime experiences led him to Fisk. A member of the Seventy-Third Ohio Regiment, he survived the battles at Chancellorsville, Virginia, and Gettysburg, Pennsylvania, before accompanying General Joseph Hooker to Chattanooga, Tennessee, in November 1863. Consumptive and gravely weakened from the war campaigns, White was confined to the hospital for some months. He was then made first sergeant in the army's regimental band, and subsequently clerk to General Hooker's headquarters.[13] But even these positions proved too stressful for his health, which remained delicate for the rest of his life. Accordingly, the army gave him a medical discharge in 1864, and he went home to Ohio to recuperate. White returned to Tennessee in 1865 to serve in the quartermaster's department in Nashville. Shortly thereafter he was appointed to the Freedmen's Bureau as an assistant to John Ogden, who having helped the AMA buy its land was about to become the Fisk School's first principal.

When the Fisk School opened White began volunteering there, teaching penmanship, music, and, during his daily lunch break, half-hour singing classes. Before long he was a full-time fixture at the school: in 1867 he married Cravath's younger sister, Laura, the first female teacher at Fisk, and by the end of that year he had been appointed treasurer by his new brother-in-law.

When he arrived at Fisk at the age of twenty-eight, White's six-foot frame, full beard, and blue Freedmen's Bureau uniform made for an imposing physical presence. His opinionated and headstrong nature was balanced by generosity and tireless pursuit of his ideals. The father-child relationship he cultivated with his choristers accorded with both the concept of family promoted by the school and the characteristically paternalistic attitude of sympathetic whites

FIGURE 2.1. George White in his thirties. From Marsh, *The Story of the Jubilee Singers* [1880], rev. ed., facing p. 12.

toward blacks at the time. "He loved us very, very near," said one of the singers, according to Mary Spence, the daughter of the man who in 1870 would become Fisk's next principal, Adam Spence. Some fifteen years after White's death she recalled that White never thought of his students "as of one race and himself as of another. They were simply his children."[14]

Entering into his musical work at Fisk with his customary spirit, White built on his noontime singing classes by organizing a full-length student entertainment at Nashville's Masonic Hall in May 1867 (see figure 2.2). Educational achievement was on display in choral and instrumental music, speeches and colloquies, and gymnastics. Such school events were typical of the time, and this one had nothing out of the ordinary—except for its African American participants. Among them were at least seven future Jubilee Singers: Georgia Gordon, Jennie Jackson, Josephine Moore, Maggie Porter, America Robinson, Thomas Rutling, and Eliza Walker.

The concert's success—it raised four hundred dollars—was an implicit endorsement of black education. The program of songs, assembled from music

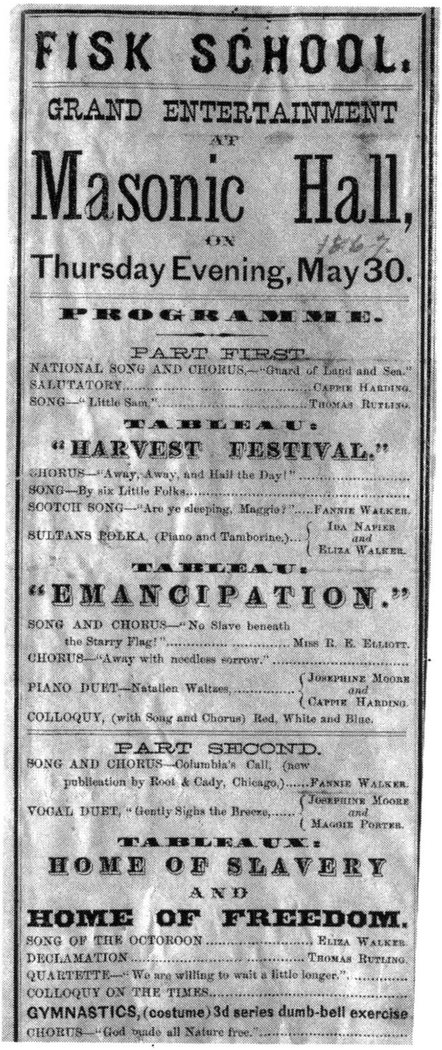

FISK SCHOOL.

GRAND ENTERTAINMENT

AT

Masonic Hall,

ON

1867.

Thursday Evening, May 30.

PROGRAMME.

PART FIRST.

NATIONAL SONG AND CHORUS,—"Guard of Land and Sea."

SALUTATORY.......................................CAPPIE HARDING.

SONG—"Little Sam,".......................................THOMAS RUTLING.

TABLEAU:

"HARVEST FESTIVAL."

CHORUS—"Away, Away, and Hail the Day!".......................................

SONG—By six Little Folks.......................................

SCOTCH SONG—"Are ye sleeping, Maggie?".....FANNIE WALKER.

SULTANS POLKA, (Piano and Tamborine,)... IDA NAPIER *and* ELIZA WALKER.

TABLEAU:

"EMANCIPATION."

SONG AND CHORUS—"No Slave beneath the Starry Flag!".......................................MISS R. E. ELLIOTT.

CHORUS—"Away with needless sorrow.".......................................

PIANO DUET—Natalien Waltzes,.............. JOSEPHINE MOORE *and* CAPPIE HARDING.

COLLOQUY, (with Song and Chorus) Red, White and Blue.

PART SECOND.

SONG AND CHORUS—Columbia's Call, (new publication by Root & Cady, Chicago,)......FANNIE WALKER.

VOCAL DUET, "Gently Sighs the Breeze,...... JOSEPHINE MOORE *and* MAGGIE PORTER.

TABLEAUX:

HOME OF SLAVERY

AND

HOME OF FREEDOM.

SONG OF THE OCTOROON.......................................ELIZA WALKER.

DECLAMATION.......................................THOMAS RUTLING.

QUARTETTE—"We are willing to wait a little longer.".......................................

COLLOQUY ON THE TIMES.......................................

GYMNASTICS, (costume) 3d series dumb-bell exercise

CHORUS—"God made all Nature free.".......................................

FIGURE 2.2. Program of the Fisk School's First Grand Entertainment. Courtesy of Fisk University, John Hope and Aurelia E. Franklin Library, Special Collections, Julius Rosenwald Archive.

primers, religious songbooks, and sheet music of the day, became the prototype for the repertory, format, and aesthetics of future jubilee concerts.

The Early Repertory: People's Song

The Fisk School Grand Entertainment featured mostly religious, sentimental, and patriotic songs by northern white American and British composers. New

England music educator and church musician Lowell Mason (1792–1872) was represented by "Away, Away, and Hail the Day!," "Away with Needless Sorrow," and "Tramp, Tramping On!" All three are found in *The Song-Garden*, Mason's compendium of psalms, hymns, and secular songs designed to imbue America's youth with upstanding values while teaching them the elements of music.

The duet "Gently Sighs the Breeze," an ode to the end of the day by English songwriter Stephen Glover (1813–1870) and lyricist J. E. Carpenter, represented the sentimental tradition. The song had become wildly popular through the performances of the beloved soprano Jenny Lind (1820–1887) and the Italian contralto Marietta Alboni (1823–1894). Future Jubilee Singers Maggie Porter (soprano) and Josephine Moore (alto) sang it for the Fisk entertainment, in a display of individual talent that would become a permanent feature of the Jubilee Singers' concerts.

In the patriotic vein were "Columbia's Call" (1867) by George Frederick Root (1820–1895), an entreaty for the country to reunite now that the war was over, and "No Slave Beneath the Starry Flag," an abolitionist song composed by Susan McFarland Parkhurst (1836–1918; known as Mrs. E. A. Parkhurst), with words by the Reverend George Lansing Taylor. Parkhurst's song could have served as an official anthem for the AMA. Published in 1864, it was dedicated to the Honorable Henry Wilson, U.S. Senator from Massachusetts, who urged that the conscription bill be amended so that immediately upon serving in the military a slave would be freed. It's hard to imagine from today's perspective the courage it took to sing this song publicly in a city rife with racial and political antagonisms, let alone mount such an entertainment in the first place. It's also hard to fully appreciate George White's resourcefulness in producing two nights of an exhibition involving scenery and props, costumes, a piano, and some twenty-five vocal and instrumental songs, in addition to overseeing rehearsals, theater rental, tickets, and publicity—all while teaching music part-time at a school where resources were scarce to nonexistent. The success of the first entertainment encouraged White to stage another one the following year, this time featuring popular numbers from opera, sung in English.[15]

White drew from white song traditions not only for the Fisk entertainments but in conducting musical evangelism in the black Sabbath schools of Nashville and its environs.[16] In 1868 he sold nearly fifty copies of the American Tract Society hymnbook *Happy Voices* (1865) to various Sunday schools, applying the profits to Fisk's general expenses.[17] Although *Happy Voices* served its purpose, for his own students White preferred something more current, such as *Fresh Laurels for the Sabbath School*, compiled in 1867 by William Bradbury (1816–1868), another New England composer in the Mason-Root circle.[18] "We intend to have our Ch[urch] service in good shape, and need the same books & helps that *white* folks have," explained White. In order of priority he wished to purchase *Bradbury's Anthem Book* (1860), some Sunday school music, a hymnal, and a "good Choir Book" such as "the *Jubilee* or *Key note*, or *Sacred Lute*, or *Temple Choir* or *Triumph*. The anthems & S. S. music are first, because we had *special work* to do with them and *have nothing of the kind*."[19]

By "*white* folks" White meant the educated, Protestant evangelical northerners typified by AMA missionaries. His desire for a book of anthems—more musically complex compositions to be sung in parts by trained voices instead of the congregation—illustrates his goal of advancing his singers' musical skills while bringing souls to Jesus. The choir books he lists in his letter are all by composers in the Lowell Mason school of composition. In fact, *The Temple Choir* (1867) was compiled by Theodore F. Seward, who in 1872 transcribed the Jubilee Singers' spirituals for their first publication and in 1874 began assisting White in directing the Jubilee Singers. This is the earliest evidence that White knew Seward, at least by reputation if not personally. The emphasis on white religious song is somewhat ironic in that White eventually led the Jubilee Singers to fame through black religious song—the spirituals.

■ ■ ■

The spectrum of music in late nineteenth-century America encompassed three broad, often overlapping categories—traditional, popular, and art music—whose fluidity arose from style, content, and especially performance context. Each had attendant associations of class, race/ethnicity, region, nationality, religion, and gender. Folk spirituals were traditional music. The songs on the first Fisk School Grand Entertainment were popular music that collectively asserted middle-class values: religious songs (Sunday school songs, gospel hymns); parlor songs (ballads, dramatic narratives, sentimental songs); solo piano music for amateurs; and message songs (patriotic, abolitionist). One song in particular illustrates the fluidity of categories: "Little Sam" by Will S. Hays—which was "sung by all the best minstrel troupes."[20] What was a minstrel song doing on a program sponsored by a missionary organization? Although minstrelsy had traveled far on the path toward respectable family entertainment by the late 1860s, it was hardly a diversion that the AMA would endorse.[21] As sung by future Jubilee Singer Thomas Rutling, however, Little Sam's story of a black youth devoted to his brother and mother could have impressed white listeners as Rutling's autobiography. In a program dedicated to the effects of education, with piano accompaniment rather than minstrel instruments, and surrounded by virtuous message songs, the latest popular "minstrel" song became a "parlor" song.

Much of what would be called "art" music today was actually popular music in the nineteenth century. On the one hand opera was art music, the province of the upper classes and the object of erudite comment in newspapers and music journals. And yet the lower and middle classes could also be found in opera audiences, and a troupe of blackface minstrels could transform an opera into a lower-class popular music entertainment in the time it took to perform one hilarious spoof.[22] Between these two extremes were the types of opera choruses, duets, and arias comprising the second Fisk entertainment. They were mainstays of the cultivated popular tradition, accessible not only in sheet music and song anthologies but ubiquitous on the concert stage as well, in performances by touring families like the Hutchinson Singers or by celebrated singers of art song, whose repertory intermingled opera numbers with parlor songs like Henry Bishop's "Home, Sweet Home" (which itself comes from an opera, *Clari, the Maid of Milan*, 1823).

Most of the native composers featured on the first Fisk entertainment were self-taught musicians and advocates for reaching the widest audience possible. Public schools began incorporating music into their curriculums only in the 1830s—thanks to Lowell Mason—and the United States lacked the infrastructure of conservatories and music academies present in Europe. Native composers of popular song were pragmatic. George Frederick Root, a student and an eventual colleague of Mason, recognized his own limitations in the face of the abundance of imported music that Americans had at their disposal. "I saw at once that mine must be the 'people's song,'" he wrote in his autobiography. "I am simply one, who, from such resources as he finds within himself, makes music for the people, having always a particular need in view." Regarding technique, he wrote, "It is easy to write *correctly* a simple song, but so to use the material of which such a song must be made that it will be received and live in the hearts of the people is quite another matter."[23] From a Western music–theoretical point of view, people's songs were anything but "correct," filled as they were with part-writing "errors" (e.g., parallel octaves and fifths) and unimaginative accompaniments that academically trained composers were taught to avoid. But such considerations were irrelevant to the masses; the best songs of Root and his compatriots set soul-stirring lyrics to melodies that did indeed live in the hearts of "the people." Spirituals would soon join their ranks.

Ella Sheppard: The Invisible Director

Ella Sheppard (1851–1914) made seminal contributions to the enduring success of the Jubilee Singers and their sound. After enrolling as a student at Fisk in fall 1868

FIGURE 2.3. Ella Sheppard as a student at Fisk. From Pike, *The Jubilee Singers*, 49. Courtesy of the New York Public Library, Schomburg Center for Research in Black Culture, Jean Blackwell Hutson Research and Reference Division.

she became George White's right hand, singing soprano with the choir, assisting with the rehearsal and direction of the singers, and supplying piano, organ, and occasionally guitar accompaniment as required. Later as a Jubilee Singer she led the group onstage, signaling when to begin a song, deciding whether to give an encore, and guiding recovery from inevitable mishaps. She even transcribed and arranged some spirituals. It was Ella Sheppard who sustained the troupe's success through management upheavals and internal strife, even though her multiple talents and modest temperament were frequently overshadowed by more overtly charismatic soloists. (Over the years these included Maggie Porter, Jennie Jackson, Thomas Rutling, and Frederick Loudin.) After the original Jubilee Singers disbanded she performed sporadically and in 1882 married Fisk graduate George W. Moore, a clergyman. The couple spent most of the next decade in Washington, DC, where Ella Sheppard began a new career crusading for various social and religious causes that brought her into a circle of prominent black leaders, among them Frederick Douglass. In 1892 the middle-aged Ella Sheppard returned with her husband to Nashville, where she coached a new generation of Jubilee Singers that included the folklorist Thomas W. Talley and the music and history scholar John Wesley Work II. Although she was a director of the Jubilee Singers in practice if not in title, her contributions were routinely overlooked until Andrew Ward's comprehensive history of the Fisk Jubilee Singers, *Dark Midnight*. Her talent, skills, and diplomacy were essential to the Jubilee Singers' success.

It is worth rehearsing parts of Ella Sheppard's biography, both as a reminder of the severe obstacles most students had to overcome to get an education as well as an introduction to her musical background. Ella Sheppard was born into slavery on 4 February 1851 in Nashville. She was of mixed African, American Indian, and white heritage. Her parents, Simon and Sarah Hannah Sheppard, belonged to Benjamin Harper Sheppard and his wife, Phereby (née Donelson, Andrew Jackson's grandniece), of Nashville and later Okolona, Mississippi.[24] Sarah served Phereby as head nurse and housekeeper, and Simon was, for a while, the coachman.[25] Benjamin had allowed Simon and Sarah to marry, although as slaves their marriage wasn't recognized legally. Ella (referred to here by her first name for clarity) was their second child, born six years after their first child died. Her parents "feared for seven years that they would be eventually separated by the mistress," wrote Ella. "My father, who had previously hired his time, had bought himself from his young master, who was his half-brother, for $1800.00. He had been repeatedly promised by the mistress, to whom mother belonged, that when he should accumulate $1300.00 more he could have my mother."[26]

Phereby kept tabs on Sarah by training Ella to spy on her mother. Upon receiving the unsuspecting Ella's first report, the mistress exaggerated it and threatened Sarah. Fearing that Ella would grow up learning to lie and deceive, Sarah contemplated murder-suicide. "In agony of soul and despair," wrote Ella, "she caught me in her arms, and while rushing to the river to end it all, was overtaken" by an elderly slave, who convinced her to reconsider. "Hugging her helpless baby to her breast," continued Ella, Sarah "walked back into slavery to await God's own time."[27]

In another telling of this story the elderly slave says, "Don't do it, honey; wait, let de chariot of de Lord swing low and let me take one of de Lord's scrolls and read it to you." The old woman then mimes the unrolling of a scroll and reads its prophecy: God "had important work for that baby" and directed "that its life should not be taken."[28] Jubilee Singers director Theodore Seward eventually worked this latter version of events into the program notes for the spiritual "Swing Low, Sweet Chariot."

In 1854 the owners prepared to move to Mississippi, which would have separated Simon from his wife and child. When Benjamin reminded his wife of her promise to let Simon buy Sarah, the three-year-old Ella overheard Phereby cry out in anger: "Sarah shall *never* belong to Simon; she is *mine* and shall *die* mine.

Let Simon get another wife." Ella found herself in a situation all too common in plantation culture, for "when a master separated man and wife it was as final as the grave." Ella's mother made a bargain with her mistress, agreeing to remain her slave if she would sell Ella to her father immediately. Sarah hardly expected her to agree, but the next day Ella was sold to her father for $350. "I remained with my father in Nashville," wrote Ella, "and my mother was taken to Mississippi, the most dreaded of all the slave states."[29]

Simon started a livery stable. He tried again to buy Sarah, with no success. He later purchased a slave woman and married her, but complications ensued. Creditors threatened to seize Ella and his new wife because of business debts and because Simon hadn't yet obtained his wife's free papers. So the family made a sudden move to Ohio, the nearest free state, where they set up house in Cincinnati just before the war. Ella attended a "colored school" there for about two years, from the ages of ten to twelve, until poor health required her to take a two-year leave.

Even though her father had to start over and acquire furniture and household items one by one, and Ella's stepmother had to take in washing and ironing as well as occasional boarders, Ella's parents managed to purchase her a piano. At the age of thirteen she began piano lessons with a German woman, which continued for a year and a half. But the death of her father in the summer of 1866 threw the family into a tailspin once again: Ella and her stepmother had to sell all of their possessions, including the piano, to satisfy debts. The benevolence of James Presley Ball, a free black photographer in Cincinnati who took an interest in Ella, allowed her to continue her music education a while longer.[30] "He offered to give me a thorough musical education," remembered Ella, "with the understanding that I was to repay him at some future day. I took twelve lessons in vocal music of Madame Rivi," who taught in the music department of the exclusive Glendale Female College.[31] The circumstances were humiliating: Ella, who was Rivi's only black student, was forbidden to reveal her teacher's identity and received her lessons late at night (9:00–9:45 p.m.) in an upstairs room that she had to access through a rear entrance.[32] In the middle of the first quarter, however, Ball lost the means to support Ella's study, and her lessons ended.

Ella tried to support herself as a teacher, as did many African Americans at the time who were literate or semiliterate. She taught for five months in Gallatin, Tennessee, but her pupils were so poor that she couldn't make a living. With the six dollars she managed to save she went to Nashville in September 1868 and enrolled as a student at Fisk, where she paid her way by taking in sewing and giving music lessons. By this time she had had piano lessons for a year and a half and voice lessons for perhaps three months (assuming the lessons were weekly)—which added up to more formal training than George White had. At the end of her first year at Fisk she was offered the position of music teacher effective fall semester 1870, and she remained the only black staff member at the school until 1875.

Unveiling Spirituals at Fisk

"There was a strong sentiment among the colored people to get as far away as possible from all those customs which reminded them of slavery," recalled Fisk Dean H. H. Wright in 1911; the students "would sing only 'white' songs."[33] George White, for one, reinforced this attitude in the name of education, at least initially. But during the 1870–1871 academic year he and a few white administrators began to have a change of heart.

As Ella Sheppard took up her appointment as music teacher that fall, Fisk welcomed a new principal to replace Ogden: Adam K. Spence (1831–1900), a professor of Greek and French who was expected to help guide the development of Fisk as a liberal arts college. A native of Scotland, Spence was "of a deeply spiritual nature, being conscientious in the extreme."[34] Spence's early life was characterized by poverty and sacrifice, and when his family immigrated to America in 1833, his father became active in abolitionist and prohibitionist causes.[35] Spence met and befriended E. M. Cravath while they were both students at Oberlin. Although Spence's sobriety was off-putting to some, others found in him a kindred spirit based in his ardent love of music. During his twenty-five-year career at Fisk he championed spirituals for use in worship; initiated the Mozart Society, which eventually became the University Choir; and tirelessly promoted artistry in music performance. He remained on the faculty even after Cravath became president in 1875.

Exactly how and when Spence, White, and other teachers at Fisk first heard students sing spirituals remains unknown. Certainly spirituals were in the air, heard "in all of the religious meetings of the Negroes," as Fisk Singer Georgia Gordon recalled,[36] their sound flowing onto the Fisk campus from nearby churches. One African Methodist Episcopal church was so close to the school that a Fiskite could "stand on our chapel steps & hear the minister preach, the people pray & the choir sing."[37] White may have also encountered spirituals during his musical evangelism in Nashville, or even during his Sunday school days in Ohio. But the Fisk students didn't sing spirituals openly on campus.

One day in the summer of 1871, Spence recalls, George White, "with an air of mystery," invited a teacher or two into Spence's parlor, along with three or four students. After drawing the curtains and locking the doors, the students "sang in a doubtful and ashamed manner some of those Spirituals now known as Jubilee Songs, the real value of which was then unrecognized."[38] These two or three students must have been future Jubilee Singers, for they had to be students who knew White well and who were inclined to trust (or obey) him.

Ella Sheppard's account corroborates Spence's version and explains the reason for the students' shame. "The slave songs were never used by us then in public. They were associated with slavery and the dark past, and represented the things to be forgotten. Then, too, they were sacred to our parents, who used them in their religious worship and shouted over them."[39] William Allen encountered a similar attitude when collecting spirituals for *Slave Songs of the United States*: "It is often, indeed, no easy matter to persuade them to sing their old songs, even as a curiosity, such is the sense of dignity that has come with freedom."[40] The students weren't ashamed of the songs, but rather of the circumstances that gave rise to them. It took some time for their uneasiness to lessen, according to Sheppard:

> We finally grew willing to sing them privately, usually in Professor Spence's sitting-room, and sitting upon the floor (there were but few chairs) we practiced softly, learning from each other the songs of our fathers. We did not dream of ever using [the slave songs] in public. Had Mr. White or Professor Spence suggested such a thing, we certainly had rebelled. It was only after many months that gradually our hearts were opened to the influence of these friends and we began to appreciate the wonderful beauty and power of our songs; but we continued to sing in public the usual choruses, duets, solos, etc., learned at school.[41]

Sheppard, who was devoted to White until the day he died, describes the experience in generous terms—"gradually our hearts were opened to the influence of these friends." Dean H. H. Wright put it more bluntly: "Professor Spence and others . . . were often obliged to agree with and sometimes scold and drive, or perhaps plead with the young people" to sing their songs from slavery.[42]

Georgia Gordon, a member of White's singing class who joined the Jubilee Singers' 1873–1874 concert tour, recalls that White "had no intention at first of using these songs in public." Instead his music class rehearsed and rendered "a drama arranged by Mr. White called 'Nicodemus the Slave,' and . . . the cantata 'Queen Esther' [William Bradbury's 1856 *Esther; the Beautiful Queen*, given by the Fisk students in March 1871]. The wonderful success of these productions opened Mr. White's eyes to the larger possibilities and led to his insisting upon our practicing the slave songs, and later led to his conception of organizing a company to travel for the benefit of the school."[43]

If White had his students rehearsing slave songs in the spring of 1871, the students could have been practicing them for up to six months before the troupe departed on its first concert tour on 6 October, which confirms Sheppard's recollection that it was "only after many months" that the students became comfortable in sharing their songs in public.

As director of the Jubilee Singers, White is often credited with bringing spirituals to the popular realm. But John Wesley Work II—a professor of Latin and history at Fisk University who directed a touring troupe of Fisk Jubilee Singers from 1899 to 1903 and who knew Ella Sheppard, Spence, and Cravath—asserts that Spence was "largely responsible for the salvation of the Negro music."[44] This is because once the Fisk Jubilee Singers began touring it was Spence who maintained spirituals as a living tradition at the university, insisting that they be sung at chapel services. Initially this involved considerable fortitude. When Spence would rise and "'start' one of these songs," wrote Work, "requesting the students to 'join in,' they would 'join in' with a chorus of cold silence":

> They knew enough to comprehend slavery dialect and bad grammar, and they would have none of either. Elijah, Messiah, and Creation were different and meant better things than the times and conditions represented by these songs. But Professor Spence would analyze and explain individual songs and show their beauty. This he did day in and day out, illustrating with his own sweet voice and sweeter soul the virtues expressed by the music, until he finally led them to an understanding.[45]

Ironically, Spence's efforts required him to battle some of the very attitudes fostered by the liberal arts curriculum he had been hired to oversee.

Forming a Troupe

By spring of 1871 the Jubilee Singers existed in conception if not in name. White had cultivated a select group of singers and had begun to talk among the faculty of forming a troupe to tour and raise money for Fisk.

It wouldn't be surprising if White's inspiration to form a traveling troupe lay in the singing family phenomenon, especially popular from the 1840s through the 1860s. Audiences flocked to hear groups like the Rainer Family from Austria and the homegrown Alleghanians and Orpheans. One of the most famous, and infamous, of the singing families was the Hutchinson troupe from New

Hampshire, who promoted native American music and pioneered the use of popular songs as agents of social change, championing abolition, temperance, and women's suffrage. In 1859 the Hutchinson Family Singers toured with the Luca family, an African American troupe from Connecticut that had formed in 1850.[46]

The parallels between the Hutchinson family's career and the inception of the Jubilee Singers could hardly be mere coincidence. Although the Hutchinsons initially toured as a quartet featuring siblings Asa, John, Judson, and Abby, they disbanded in 1849 when Abby married and retired. From then on the family performed in various incarnations.

In the winter of 1870 Abby Hutchinson Patton (1829–1892) wintered in Magnolia, Florida, on the St. Johns River—a popular destination for visitors in the nineteenth century because of its warm mineral springs. Her brothers John and Henry, who were at the time performing as a trio with Samuel B. Spinning, paid her a visit. John wrote in his autobiography, "Abby had become very much interested in the colored people and took us to their meetings, where we found much to delight us in their songs. Some of them we learned and brought back with us and they so pleased our audiences that we published them."[47] Abby arranged three spirituals, printed in a sheet music edition under the collective title *Camp Meeting Songs of the Florida Freedmen* (1870): "Don't Stay Away," "Wait a Little While," and "Turn Back Pharaoh's Army." Of "Room Enough" (an alternate title to "Don't Stay Away") John wrote: "This song set to one of the simple and pathetic melodies of the freedmen, became very popular, was taken up after being heard in our concerts and is still often sung in gospel meetings and similar services in the North."[48] John's brother Asa (1823–1884) particularly embraced this set of spirituals, performing them as well as "Pray, Nicodemus, Show Me the Way"; in fact, he sometimes sang as many as eight spirituals in one concert.[49] The Hutchinsons were unique at the time as white entertainers singing parlor arrangements of black folk song.

Their Florida sojourn at an end, the Hutchinson trio of John, Henry, and Samuel Spinning made their way back north in 1870, giving concerts along the way. Southerners treated the well-known abolitionists with contempt and refused to patronize them. "When we reached Nashville," John wrote, "we found the Southern prejudice still against us. We advertised a concert, but the audience was so meagre that we postponed it."[50] Fisk University, however, gave them a warm welcome:

Professor White . . . invited us to go to the school and sing to his colored pupils. We gave them some of our best pieces. At the conclusion he said, "I wish you to hear some of my singers." We said we would be most happy, and resigned the platform to them. I was delighted by their wonderful harmony. The whole world has heard it since. I suggested to the professor that he bring a choir of his freedmen to the North, for I was sure it would prove a great financial as well as musical success. The result of the suggestion was a tour of the Fisk University Jubilee Singers, which so soon followed.[51]

If only we knew what songs these two groups sang for each other! Certainly the Hutchinsons showed off their newly learned spirituals. The Fisk students, who hadn't yet introduced their spirituals to the Fisk teachers, would have selected songs from recent local concerts, all of which consisted of white repertory. If the encounter happened this way, it would be fascinating to know what the students thought of these white strangers singing spirituals for them.

It may be that John Hutchinson (figure 2.4) took a bit of undue credit in claiming he inspired White to take his singers on the road, but it's possible that Hutchinson's visit validated White's intention to tour, inspiring him to move forward with a concrete plan.

If the Hutchinsons seemed a ready-made model for the future Jubilee Singers, in other ways they served as a cautionary tale. Whereas enthusiasts embraced the songs' social message and extolled their simplicity, denigrators complained that the concert hall should offer a vacation from politics, and some deemed their simple songs unworthy of cultivated listeners.[52] Causing further turmoil were the free blacks who attended Hutchinson concerts and sat in sections normally reserved for whites only.[53] This same musical caste warfare would plague the Fisk Jubilee Singers when they began their public career.

The parallels between the Hutchinson Family Singers and the Jubilee Singers are inescapable. Organized on the concept of family, they both began their careers with "cultivated" repertory that was gradually given over to "native" songs that better represented their respective identities. Their songs were identified with social causes, even if the texts themselves weren't always didactic. As champions of progressive causes they both found a warmer welcome in the North than in the South. In addition, it seems that White consciously programmed several songs from the Hutchinsons' repertory: "Good-Bye, Brothers," "Great Is the Lord, and Greatly to Be Praised," "Holy Lord God of Sabaoth," "Home, Sweet Home," "If I Were a Voice" (a signature Hutchinson song), "Stars of the Summer Night," and "What Are the Wild Waves Saying?"[54] Even more significantly, the spirituals sung by the Hutchinsons—"Don't Stay Away" (under the title "Room Enough"), "Turn Back Pharaoh's Army," and "Wait a Little While"—were among the earliest spirituals in the Jubilee Singers' concert repertory.[55]

FIGURE 2.4. John Hutchinson, mid-1860s. From Hutchinson Family Scrapbook, photograph courtesy of the Lynn Museum, Lynn, MA.

The Decision to Tour

For the impulsive White, the decision to tour was relatively easy. Cravath had recently been discouraging White from mounting such elaborate musical productions as *Esther*, urging him to focus instead on his role as treasurer and keep Fisk from falling into financial collapse. But White stubbornly believed he could do both at the same time and ignored his brother-in-law's directives. The measured Spence, on the other hand, was troubled by the many complexities of a decision to tour, which he enumerated in a ten-page letter to Cravath, who was serving as AMA district secretary in New York at the time. Spence's letter began with a vivid description of life at Fisk—where an odor of disease still lingered about the hospital barracks serving as living quarters—and ended by debating the merits of establishing a traveling band of singers to fund an endowment. Spence first addressed the propriety of sending out students to do this work:

I find there is a general feeling of opposition to the scheme although have had no faculty meeting on the subject. A good many think it beneath the dignity of our institution to be represented by a strolling band of singers, or negro minstrels as they term it. Some fear the success of the thing as a musical performance, some financially and others that it would not even get us the interest nor wish. Then again it is viewed from the stand point of its effect on the institution directly, tending to dignify musical talent too much, and the singers themselves, turning them temporarily and perhaps permanently from their studies, dissipating their minds and lowering their piety, as many of them are Christians.

I think these are the varying arguments brought against the plan with perhaps this in addition that we are seeking to build up a school in which the religious element should especially enter in to all that is done, and that our hope is especially in that class of people who sympathize in such a school.[56]

Spence identified five main concerns. First, a band of traveling singers—regardless of whether they were perceived as blackface minstrels—would be an undignified representative of Fisk University, especially given that Victorians regarded entertainers as disreputable. The moral character of the Fisk students' songs (as exemplified by their school-sponsored local entertainments) couldn't compete with the spectacle of a "pioneer band of genuine Ethiopian minstrels without the aid of burnt cork," in the words of Fisk trustee Judge John Lawrence.[57] Second, financial and artistic success remained a gamble—and there was no money to gamble with. Third, for a school that prided itself on providing a balanced liberal arts education, the enterprise seemed to favor music over academic subjects. Moreover, Spence feared the effect of dignifying "the singers themselves," which could result not only in the "dissipation" of their minds but the inflation of their egos.[58] Fourth, removing the students from their daily discipline and studies would not only interrupt but might terminate their academic careers. (This proved prophetic: America Robinson was the only Fisk student among the original Jubilee Singers to graduate, in 1875; the others received their degrees posthumously, in 1978—a century after they disbanded.) And finally, isolating the students from a Christian environment might adversely affect their piety.

Spence had little basis for estimating the success of such a venture, given the dearth of African American vocalists on the concert stage—or any stage, for that matter. If there *was* to be a touring group, Spence felt that the AMA's official sponsorship was indispensable. This would make it easier to target audiences who were in sympathy with Fisk's social and religious goals. His letter to Cravath continued:

On the other hand it is said that we must have money & God has given us a gift of music that we ought to use.

As to myself I have said and thought I was in favor of it, regarding it as a thing for the summer vacations and not for a year's work, as Mr W. [White] thinks it would need to be if successful. *I should have but little anxiety as to their singing.* They do sing admirably and Mr W. would make the matter succeed if success were possible. I am not so sure as to the financial question. Should the concert fees pay the actual expenses it would be all I should expect. Then an agent would need to follow them up or go with them and plead the cause in a short address in connection with the concert stating the condition and wants of the school. Mr W. might do that perhaps in addition to his singing, but someone would need to go to individuals.

You from your stand point could judge better in many respects than we here. *I wish the experiment could be tried without too much expense.* But one thing I think would be essential, that it should have the endorsement of the A.M.A.

I have thought too of the state of Tennessee. I am sure could the colored people hear the students sing it would inspire them with new courage for their race and desire to educate their children, and no doubt it would bring us students. As to these latter we have no guarantee for the future. We have no A.M.A. or other schools to point to us. Indeed there are very few schools in the state of any kind. It is a very destitute field. Could concerts be given at central points and talks be made to the people I am sure it would do good.

May we be guided in this, and in all things.

Yours in this good cause
A. K. Spence[59]

It wasn't financially practical to fund a jubilee group to sing in Tennessee for the purpose of student recruitment. In the South, White observed, it was difficult to attract black audiences, for "colored people, outside of two or three large places, know little of such things and do not appreciate these sufficiently to attend."[60] Furthermore most blacks wouldn't be able to afford tuition. For the venture to succeed the troupe would have to head north, as John Hutchinson had suggested, but Spence's logistical worries were valid: finding concert halls, restaurants, and overnight accommodations that would admit blacks would be daunting. Having White alone shoulder the responsibilities of rehearsals, travel arrangements, venues, and solicitation of donations was beyond imagination.

While Spence, his faculty, and the AMA continued to debate the merits of a tour, White spent the summer producing a series of trial concerts in the South and lobbying concerned parents for permission to take their students on tour. In the end, Cravath's approval was irrelevant, for White had already made up his mind to "make the trial trip at all hazards," as he defiantly wrote to his brother-in-law.[61] It was with mixed emotions—hope, anxiety, fear, excitement, dread, pride—that White and his group of ten singers struck out on the first leg of their journey north on 6 October 1871. The traveling band consisted of Ella Sheppard, Jennie Jackson, Maggie Porter, Minnie Tate, Eliza Walker, Phoebe Anderson, Benjamin Holmes, Thomas Rutling, Greene Evans, and Isaac Dickerson, as well as their white governess, Mary F. Wells, and her eight-year-old black ward, Georgie Wells. White had drained the school treasury of all but one dollar, borrowed what he could, and used his own savings to launch the enterprise.[62] They left behind a very worried school principal, who expressed his concern in a letter to Cravath: "Hope we may not starve. . . . What shall we do if we ever get out of money and he cant send us any?"—a very definite possibility that loomed unremittingly before them.[63]

Branding the Jubilee Singers

The success of the Jubilee Singers was the result of perseverance, strategy, and dumb luck. White's initial challenge was to make the public care about a ragtag group of black students of all sizes and skin tones, ranging in age from fourteen to twenty, clothed in items borrowed from their white teachers in Nashville, doing their best not to feel overwhelmed in environments far from friends and family.

Counting on sympathetic audiences, White followed the old route of the Underground Railroad to Ohio, a state that both White and Ella Sheppard had once called home. Upon arriving in a new town, he had the troupe—which as yet had no official name—sing some spirituals and hymns at praise meetings in local churches to arouse interest in the upcoming concert, but in concert halls the singers adhered to the white repertory they had been rehearsing for years. Audience response among whites was underwhelming. Sometimes only twenty people showed up, forcing White to beg for train fare so that the group could move on.[64] Black audiences were another story: highly appreciative but financially disadvantaged. Nonetheless the Jubilee Singers always stopped at black institutions. Just weeks into their tour, for example, they sang at a black Baptist church in Yellow Springs, Ohio, and at Wilberforce University in nearby Xenia. Performing for black audiences was part of the singers' mission from the outset, as was their insistence that blacks be admitted to their concerts regardless of venue. As Fisk chronicler J. B. T. Marsh wrote, "Those were days in which anything well done by a colored man was an inspiration to all the rest of his race to whose knowledge it came."[65]

Lack of organization, insufficient seed money, and caste prejudice intensified the students' already considerable discomfort. White was overextended, acting as musical director (rehearsing the singers—although Sheppard sometimes relieved him—and deciding which songs to sing), advance agent (hiring concert halls, making and distributing advertisements, renting a piano), business manager (socializing with potential benefactors, securing the endorsement of local officials, making travel and hotel arrangements, writing progress reports to Fisk and the AMA), treasurer (paying bills, selling and taking concert tickets, accounting for concert receipts), and chaperone. Unless something changed, the enterprise was doomed to failure.

Crafting a Public Image

Over the course of three grueling months on the road White made several key decisions that collectively led to a dramatic reversal of fortune. First, at Cravath's urging he arranged for the students to sing some spirituals at the National Council of Congregational Churches in Oberlin on 16 November 1871.[66] If they could win over the Congregationalists—the AMA's core membership—then the AMA might finally endorse (and financially support) the troupe. Amid a tired and indifferent crowd the students sang the spiritual "Steal Away," capturing the delegates' ears, hearts, and money—$131, to be exact, far exceeding previous profits. Although no endorsement materialized, two AMA officers who were present did arrange for an advance agent to assist the overtaxed White.[67] Among the listeners impressed by the singers was the Reverend Thomas Kinnicut Beecher, brother of Harriet Beecher Stowe, who invited the students to sing at his church in Elmira, New York. More importantly, he urged his brother Henry Ward Beecher, the most famous minister in America, to host them at his church in Brooklyn. That one strategic visit to Oberlin netted the troupe an advance agent, a powerful patron, some cash, and a much-needed boost in morale.

A second key decision was to christen the troupe. Since leaving Nashville to go north, the students went by a variety of descriptive names: "colored Christian singers," "a band of negro minstrels" (with "minstrel" sometimes implying "singer" and other times "blackface performer"), "colored students from Fisk University." Their ambiguous identity resulted in a confused public. In late November 1871, after a night of intense prayer, George White announced that the singers would henceforth be known as the Jubilee Singers. The multivalence of the word "jubilee" in American culture gave their name particular potency. White picked it in reference to the Jewish year of jubilee, or emancipation, described in Leviticus 25. "The dignity of the name appealed to us," recalled Ella Sheppard. "At our usual family worship that morning there was great rejoicing."[68] As "Jubilee Singers" they were framed as noble ex-slaves rising in triumph above their past of oppression. But the word "jubilee" had additional resonances. The United States was also the product of an emancipation, and the word marked not only public celebrations and anniversaries (e.g., Fourth of July jubilees, peace jubilees to commemorate the end of a war) but also institutional anniversaries (e.g., church and school jubilees to commemorate the year of founding). An official name facilitated advertising and publicity—at least for the few short months when the Fisk students were the only "Jubilee Singers" in America. The name also helped them articulate their message: freedom may have been granted by governmental decree but it was won by education, which in turn enabled self-determination.

A third key decision was White's inspiration to raise money for a building instead of an endowment. An endowment was nebulous, but a building would be a visible return on investment, one that would remain as generations of students came and went.[69]

Despite small audiences and meager financial returns in the initial weeks of their tour, the students garnered some praise for their singing, particularly when they performed spirituals. This prompted White's fourth key decision: to incorporate spirituals into concert programs. This change in programming took place gradually. Initially the troupe reserved a spiritual or two for an encore at the end of a concert, but toward the end of November, shortly after the students became Jubilee Singers, they began inserting a spiritual or two into the main program. "Roll, Jordan, Roll" and "Turn Back Pharaoh's Army," for example, were given during the second part of their concert in Mansfield, Ohio, on 29 November 1871.[70]

"Our sufferings and the demand of the public changed this order," Ella Sheppard recalled. "A program of nineteen numbers, only two or three of which were slave songs, was inverted. To recall and to learn of each other the slave songs demanded much mental labor, and to prepare them for public singing required much rehearsing."[71] This perhaps explains why the shift was gradual and not sudden: the Jubilee Singers' repertory of spirituals wasn't large enough to sustain a full program.[72] From late November to early January, their concerts continued to feature only two or three spirituals, although not always the same ones. As the troupe struggled to survive financially on its tour, it seems the singers were also learning, arranging, and rehearsing new jubilee songs.

A typical program from winter 1872 reveals that only five of fifteen items were songs from the white tradition (nos. 1, 4 in the first part; nos. 1, 3, 4 in the second):[73]

AMERICAN MISSIONARY ASSOCIATION CONCERT,
BY THE JUBILEE SINGERS.

of Fisk University, Nashville, Tenn.

Under the direction of GEO. L. WHITE, Treas. of the University.

Tuesday Eve., March 19, 1872.

PROGRAMME.
Part I.
1. Opening Anthem, With Lord's Prayer.
2. "O, the Rocks and the Mountains shall all flee away."
3. "O Lord! have mercy on me—Or sooner in the morning."
4. Song.—The Temperance medley,—I. P. Dickerson.
5. O Redeemed, Redeemed!
6. "Did'nt [sic] my Lord deliver Daniel?—and why not every man?"
7. "I'm travelling to the grave."—Jennie Jackson.
8. "Go Down Moses."
Statement by Rev. G. D. Pike, District Secretary of Am. Missionary Association.

Part II.
1. Duet and Chorus.—"Songs of Summer."
2. "Steal away, Steal away to Jesus."
3. Song.—"The Old Man Dreams."—Minnie Tate.
4. Vocal Medley. Messrs. Rutling, Holmes, Dickerson and Evans.
5. My Lord says there's room enough.
6. "I'm a Rolling through an unfriendly world."
7. "O, my good Lord! keep me from sinking down."

Just as the Hutchinson family championed American-made music, the Jubilee Singers were becoming champions of their own brand of native song, spirituals.

Patronage

Spirituals may have delighted their listeners, but the Jubilee Singers had to convert delight into money. This required sizable audiences, which in turn required influential individual and institutional patrons. The singers acquired both when they arrived in New York City.

When the Jubilee Singers met Henry Ward Beecher (1813–1887) in late December 1871, he was at the height of his career and influence. The fifty-eight-year-old "Hercules of American Protestantism" had been guiding the Plymouth Congregational Church in Brooklyn Heights for twenty-four years.[74] He was the best-paid preacher in Brooklyn—indeed in the country, with a salary of $20,000 annually exclusive of miscellaneous income. His lectures attracted crowds, his endorsements sold overcoats and other products, and his movements were scrupulously recorded in the press, especially by his hometown newspaper, the *Brooklyn Eagle*, which ran a regular column titled "Beecheriana."[75]

His social magnetism was fueled by a generous nature and a healthy sense of humor. His homey sermons, which favored common sense over dogma, were compelling for their rhetorical power. "Though Brooklyn claimed him as her own," recalled General William T. Sherman, "Henry Ward Beecher was too large a man for any single locality. He was essentially a national man grasping all the thoughts and feelings of a continent."[76] Indeed, churchgoers throughout America followed him, through his sermons reprinted in newspapers everywhere, his lectures throughout the North and West, and his steady stream of articles, essays, and books.

His was not an intellectual but an artistic, extravagant, and impulsive disposition, fed by an intense love of the natural world. "He stored his mind more by observation than by study or reflection," remarked Oliver Wendell Holmes. "I do not think he ever did reflect; he felt."[77] Beecher's emotionalism infused the music program at Plymouth as well. Under his guidance congregational singing supplanted the choir as the sole source of vocal music during worship. Beecher defined a hymn as "a lyrical discourse to the feelings"—a discourse that his parishioners came to embrace enthusiastically.[78] He was squarely in the "people's song" vein of Lowell Mason, George Frederick Root, and William Bradbury.

Beecher was also a lifelong activist, whose list of causes included temperance, labor reform, the expansion of public education, and civil rights for various ethnic groups on the social fringe. He regularly made Plymouth Church available for concerts that promoted such agendas, and in 1850 had even hosted the Hutchinson Family Singers, who attracted an audience of a thousand people.[79] Beecher's emotional temperament, social advocacy, gifts as a public speaker, national profile, and love of simple, direct congregational hymnody made Plymouth Church an ideal venue for introducing the Jubilee Singers to Brooklyn and New York society. (Brooklyn and "New York," meaning Manhattan, were independent cities until 1898.) Beecher later recalled their debut:

One of the things that I cherish with pride [is that the Jubilee Singers] took their start from Plymouth Church lecture room. Oh, those days after the war! My brother Thomas wrote to me that his jubilee band were trying to sing their way to the East and see if they could not raise a little money, and urged me to look after them. They called on me. There was not a mixed blood among them; they were as black as midnight, every one of them. [Beecher was wrong on both counts.] I said: "I do not know whether the folks will bear it or not, but come round on Friday night, at the prayer meeting, and I will give you a chance."[80]

The Jubilee Singers worked their magic at the prayer meeting that Friday, 22 December 1871. "It was as still as death," recalled Beecher. "They sang two pieces. Tears were trickling from a great many eyes. They sang three pieces, and they burst out into a perfect enthusiasm of applause; and when they had sung four and five pieces my people rose up in mass and said, 'These folk must sing in the church.'" And so they did: first on Sunday morning, and again on Wednesday evening, when the church was crammed with people who had paid fifty cents apiece to hear the students.[81] The Jubilee Singers finally had their massive audience: Plymouth Church seated twenty-seven hundred people.

Beecher took every opportunity to promote the students and introduce them to influential citizens—sometimes to his own disadvantage, as on a night in February 1872, when Beecher was scheduled to give a lecture in Hartford, Connecticut, on the same night that the Jubilee Singers were scheduled to sing. The advance ticket sales of the Jubilee Singers greatly outstripped those of Beecher. Ever the practical man, Beecher deferred his engagement and went to hear the Jubilee Singers. That night the troupe took in $1,209 in ticket sales, and an additional $500 in cash donations and valuables as the result of an appeal Beecher made at the concert.[82] If the sales figure is accurate, and assuming a typical ticket price of fifty cents, close to twenty-four hundred people heard the Jubilee Singers that night.

When Beecher made his first lecture tour through the South, in 1879, the first institution he visited was Fisk University. The four hundred students who turned out to hear his talk knew that they owed their access to a Fisk education in no small measure to Beecher's promotion of the Jubilee Singers.[83]

Beecher was so vocal about the Jubilee Singers in December 1871 that the AMA, headquartered in New York, would have risked the censure of its constituents if it continued to ignore the troupe. The *American Missionary* magazine printed an unqualified endorsement of them in January 1872, and White finally got the formal support he had asked for months ago. An AMA district secretary named Gustavus Dorman Pike (1831–1885) volunteered his services as business manager; he had become interested in the singers when they sang for Thomas K. Beecher's church in Elmira. By March the AMA relieved Pike of his regular duties so that he could work full-time for the Jubilee enterprise. Pike, who lived in Brooklyn and whose collecting field for donations covered the New York metropolitan areas and Connecticut, proved adept at converting his extensive contacts into patrons. He also instituted the last major change that would mold the Jubilee Singers' public image: now that they were singing primarily spirituals, their performances would be "services of song" rather than "concerts."

The Service of Song

Pike's first challenge as business manager was to convince the "better class of people"—white Christians of "taste and character"—that it was not unbecoming "to rush in crowds to a paid concert given by negroes." Pike recalled, "The first thing done after the arrival of the Singers at New York was to make it *popular* to attend their concerts."[84] Noticing that the Jubilees didn't lack for audience members when they sang as part of a church service but that concert hall audiences were modest, Pike decided to bring church to the concert stage.

The service of song had its roots in the evangelical institutional practices of the first half of the century, which included prayer meeting revivals, camp meetings, the Sunday school movement, and the Young Men's Christian Association (founded in London in 1844 and introduced to the United States in 1851, in Boston).[85] There was an insatiable need for simple, interdenominational songbooks to support all of this worship. Lowell Mason was one of many composers who complied: *The Hallelujah* (1854), for example, was meant for "the *service of song* in the house of the Lord" (title page; my italics). In 1871 Eben Tourjée (cofounder of the New England Conservatory of Music in 1867, and at the time head of Boston's YMCA) began leading "services of praise" throughout New England, which were "religious meetings devoted almost entirely to song."[86] This increasingly populist type of religious song, typified by Joseph Philbrick Webster's popular "Sweet By and By" (1868), prepared the way for the flowering of gospel hymnody in the 1870s.

Gospel hymnodist and singer Philip Phillips (1834–1895) spearheaded another development: the use of the sacred solo in worship. He began conducting services of song at Sunday school conventions and YMCA meetings,[87] and was the first to make a career of solo evangelistic singing. Although today his hymns are largely forgotten, his repertory was highly influential at the time and overlapped significantly with that of the Jubilee Singers: both sang selections from Bradbury's *Esther*, as well as songs by Stephen Foster, Henry Russell, and the Hutchinsons.

The Jubilee Singers' services of song, then, fit into a well-established mold of communicating a religious message in oratory and song. They debuted the format in New Haven, Connecticut, in February 1872. As Pike explained, "the Singers conduct the service of song, while I, in company with one or two others, if volunteers are found, occupy the remaining time in speaking of the Freedmen's work at the South. This plan is pursued, not because it is of more interest than a praise meeting, but because people may hear excellent singing till the world's end, and know nothing of the missions, or the wants of the perishing in consequence." Pike, a devout Christian, was discomfited by the idea that the singers were entertainers: "We were out to promote the cause of Missions, not like an organ-grinder, to gain a livelihood."[88]

Over time the format for the service of song became streamlined, with White or Pike (and eventually one of the male Jubilee Singers) opening the service with a summary of the AMA's causes and a history of Fisk University. The service of song had two parts, and pleas for donations were reiterated at intermission. There was usually an appeal printed in the program as well, and beginning in 1873, audience members could buy a whole book about the Jubilee Singers that was at once missionary propaganda, a romantic narrative of their adventures, and an anthology of the words and music to their spirituals.[89]

Concluding Thoughts

History suggests that the Jubilee Singers of 1872 (see figure 2.5) would have quickly drowned in obscurity had they not sung spirituals. By singing spirituals, the troupe presented to the public a new kind of people's song that not only matched the century's zeitgeist of emotionalism, nativism, and naturalism but also resembled the more recent gospel hymnody found in services of song. Spirituals were songs that lived in the hearts of people—George Frederick Root's definition of musical excellence.

But even with spirituals, the Jubilee Singers might not have succeeded without the imprimatur of the most powerful preacher in America and the sponsorship of the AMA, which opened doors to venues and patrons. For the religiously minded white middle class, presenting jubilee concerts as services of song accompanied by religious oratory removed the stigma associated with attending a theatrical entertainment. For former abolitionists, the concerts offered living proof that their cause had been a righteous one.

FIGURE 2.5. The Jubilee Singers, early 1872. *Seated left to right*: Minnie Tate, Greene Evans, Jennie Jackson, Ella Sheppard, Benjamin Holmes, Eliza Walker. *Standing*: Isaac Dickerson, Maggie Porter, Thomas Rutling. Courtesy of Fisk University, John Hope and Aurelia E. Franklin Library, Special Collections, Julius Rosenwald Archive.

When Spence recalled that "the real value" of the spirituals was unrecognized when the students first sang slave songs privately for their white teachers, he meant cultural value. Even after the Jubilee Singers began touring, Spence insisted on including spirituals in worship on the Fisk campus, and he remained a lifelong proponent of the songs. For White, on the other hand, the spirituals had a different kind of value. They were folk songs that could be improved with standard English instead of dialect, with four-part harmony, and with expressive devices. There's no doubt that he admired them as music—he devoted his life to bringing them before the public—but they also unavoidably represented the literal fortunes of the university. For the Jubilee Singers the spirituals had personal value; ironically, their education—their pathway to social improvement—caused them to distance themselves in public from the material and expressive culture of slavery. Over the course of the Jubilee Singers' careers they came to revalue spirituals as they experienced them through the opinions of their white audiences, the appreciation of their black audiences, and the stories they shared among themselves.

It was to Spence's credit that he recognized the potential for the Jubilee Singers to inspire black audiences. Performing regularly for black institutions remained central to their mission, and the singers refused to perform in any venue unless blacks were admitted to all portions of the house, challenging the usual practice of segregating blacks in the gallery, or top balcony. In fact, a Boston correspondent covering a concert in Baltimore remarked, "the most notable feature of the concert, which was given in the best hall in the city, was the selling of reserved seats to colored people—a thing unprecedented in the history of Baltimore."[90]

Although the Hutchinson family sang spirituals in their concerts before the Fisk students did, there was nothing exceptional in seeing and hearing white New Englanders sing yet another type of people's song. However, with the emergence of black jubilee singers, the public decided that whites literally paled in comparison. As late as the 1920s Mary Church Terrell (1863–1954) wrote, "Of course, white people can never learn to sing [spirituals], as the descendants of the group who composed them do. There seems to be something the matter with the vocal cords of white people, when they try to imitate colored people, while singing the Spirituals. They just 'haven't got em,' in the language of the street. Every time I have heard white choirs trying their best to sing the Spirituals, I have felt sorry for them."[91] Seeing and hearing the Jubilee Singers, on the other hand, was another matter altogether. Their "native" songs, combined with their status as ex-slaves, their youth, and their innocence, became the ingredients of a romantic tale of physical survival and religious righteousness. Even so, the favor of white audiences couldn't be taken for granted; the spirituals had to be conceived in a way that elicited profound sympathy without alienating those who had never heard such music. This was the task facing George White as he translated the folk spiritual into a new sound and method of performance, known as the concert spiritual.

CHAPTER 3

The Fisk Concert Spiritual

Bringing spirituals from riverboats, fields, praise houses, and camp meetings onto the concert stage required considerable musical and cultural translation. It meant converting participatory experiences into presentational performances for discerning audiences, and improvisatory compositions into standardized musical works. Impeccable preparation was essential, for a host of variables could detract from even the best performance, including the venue (size, acoustics, sight lines, lighting), audience demographics (political, religious, and racial attitudes), the oratory preceding the music (prone to being overly long), the number of performers (often diminished by sickness), performers' dress and demeanor, and even weather (which could adversely affect inside temperatures).

George White's challenge in arranging the spirituals was to preserve their idiosyncrasies within a recognizable musical framework, striking a balance between the familiar and the novel. He needed to ensure that the emotional quality of the singing would be admired and not derided as caricature. Only then would these songs touch the heart, and the pocketbook.

How might a sympathetic white northerner experience a service of song by the Jubilee Singers for the first time? Since the essence of spirituals was in their performance, it's helpful to imagine the details of a typical concert like the following, which is based on quotes from numerous contemporaneous sources:

> "This feeling of yours should tend to make us good and determined to raise ourselves in the estimation of men and God—this excellent aid to render us men and women as you yourselves are. We are touched with your kindness and concern for slavery in Africa, and ask that God will grant you your reward, and that at last He will say, 'Well done, good and faithful servant, inasmuch as you have done it to one of the least of these you have done it unto me.'" We all applauded and I glanced discreetly over my neighbor's shoulder as he pulled out his watch: just eight o'clock. We had been listening

to a half hour of oratory, first from a white missionary who talked about the importance of elevating the freedmen through religion and education, then from one of the male Jubilee Singers. The singers were seated at the rear of the chancel. I strained in vain to see their faces.

There was a strong feeling of anticipation in the large sanctuary. Every corner and side aisle accommodated the overflow, and in spite of the cold winter evening there were people hovering outside at the doors and windows. It seemed as though most of Newark had crowded into the church, for fifty cents was a small price to pay to hear something so novel and at the same time support a worthy cause. Conspicuously absent was the proprietor of the Continental Hotel, who had refused the singers admittance upon discovering that they were not blacked-up performers but came by their skin color naturally! Those assembled here tonight seemed intent on atoning for this embarrassing abuse.

As the applause died down the singers arose and moved forward to the front of the chancel. Plainly and unassumingly dressed, they were a variety of ages and heights and hues. Standing shoulder to shoulder in a semi-circle—women on the left, men on the right—they began singing without ceremony. "Steal away. . . ." It was magical! The words floated out slowly—an exquisite, barely audible plea. Then a repetition—"steal away"—slightly louder, fuller in harmony, more insistent. And yet another—"steal away to Jesus"—a command this time, sung loudly and forcefully in precise unison. "Steal away, steal away home"—softer again, lingering on this last word, so that the idea of home reverberated in our souls, as we felt what this word might mean now to these children of the plantation. And suddenly a whisper: "I hain't got long to stay here."

Surely I was listening to the voices of angels. The singers seemed to be in their own world, unaware of the audience. Time melted away, and I hardly knew whether I was in or out of the body. Immediately after the final note died away came the first words of the Lord's Prayer, chanted to perfection through to the Amen. It seemed sacrilegious to assault the ensuing stillness with applause. I heard muffled sobs around me and realized that tears were streaming down my own cheeks. Rather than wait the students began a weird slave hymn with a completely different character, a spirited song about turning back Pharaoh's army. As single words jumped out at us with sudden force, people around me laughed in surprise. The language was grotesque: "Gwine to write to Massa Jesus, to send some valiant soldier . . ." Who would sit down and write Jesus a letter? But the singers, with their erect postures and focused gazes, their full and confident voices, their unwavering sincerity, won us over. When they came to the "drowning" of old Pharaoh's army, oh! what a double fortissimo they gave that word, and what intense satisfaction they conveyed at his demise! I could not help but think of the proprietor of the Continental Hotel at that point, and surely the singers were thinking likewise!

This time we couldn't refrain from applauding, long and enthusiastically. The students looked slightly embarrassed, and as the applause did not abate, one of the women—the one who played piano later on, Ella Sheppard—stole a glance at their white director, who was seated behind them barely visible in the corner. He must have given her a little signal, because the group gave the song again!

At its conclusion all but one of the students retired to their seats. The program identified the singer who remained as Jennie Jackson. She was black as midnight, and I could barely make out her handsome features. She seemed small and defenseless until she opened her mouth and a full voice spilled forth, without accompaniment of any kind, "You may bury me in the east, you may bury me in the west, but I'll hear that trumpet sound in the morning." It was a wild, delicious melody—a wail of pathos. Where did such sounds come from? How could one voice contain so much rapture and solemnity at the same time? What peculiar music, the very embodiment of African heart-music!

More slave hymns followed, each one a revelation, and then suddenly it was the interval. One of the white gentlemen onstage came forward and announced that if we were willing to part with another twenty-four cents, we could take home a booklet of these unique slave hymns. Although I bought one I thought to myself, "These songs would fall flat were I to attempt them myself."[1]

Despite White's use of Euro-American elements in his arrangements, white audiences obviously heard something beyond their realm of experience that they identified as *African* in the Jubilee Singers' spirituals. The extravagant descriptors they applied to the spirituals—"wild," "delicious," "grotesque," "heart music"—embodied Romanticism's celebration of nature and the primitive. Musical scores, newspaper reviews, and anecdotal evidence identify the ingredients that gave the concert spiritual such power that an entertainment industry copied, parodied, exploited, and developed jubilee song over the next two decades.

Writers of an Oral Tradition

The American Missionary Association (AMA) capitalized on the spectacular success of the Jubilee Singers in New York and New England by publishing a slim volume of twenty-four spirituals called *Jubilee Songs, as Sung by the Jubilee Singers* (New York: Biglow and Main) in March 1872. Consisting of the words and music to the spirituals in the Fisk repertory, it's the most comprehensive source of White's arrangements. Unlike *Slave Songs of the United States* (1867), *Jubilee Songs* was not meant to document a dying tradition but rather to meet—and heighten—public demand for spirituals. The songbooks were sold during concerts and by mail order for twenty-four cents. They were so popular that only months later a second, enlarged volume of sixty-one jubilee songs was published, titled *Jubilee Songs: Complete.*[2]

Given that spirituals didn't become the Jubilee Singers' core concert repertory until January 1872, the work of transcribing and printing the twenty-four spirituals in *Jubilee Songs* was accomplished in at most two months. Unfortunately the personnel involved were together in New York at that time, so there's no written correspondence to document the publication's genesis,[3] and no explanation as to why a musician with no connection whatsoever to Fisk University was chosen to notate the spirituals.

That person was Theodore Frelinghuysen Seward (1835–1902), great-grandson of Colonel John Seward, an American Revolutionary leader and second cousin to William Henry Seward, who had been Abraham Lincoln's secretary of state (1861–1869). Lineage aside, Seward's musical career fit the AMA profile. He had studied with Lowell Mason, George Frederick Root, and Thomas Hastings, and like those musicians had published a variety of song collections in the "musical and moral edification" mold, with which White had long been acquainted.[4] He was editor in the 1860s of two New York–based periodicals, the *Musical Pioneer* and the *Musical Gazette* (resigning from the latter in 1872). He met Liszt and heard the papal choir on a six-month trip abroad in 1869, and when he finally settled down in New Jersey with his family in 1870, he worked as music director of the public schools in East Orange, as well as organist at two churches—and even hosted a visit by the Jubilee Singers.[5]

Dena Epstein speculated that the AMA hired Seward because of his association with the music publisher Biglow and Main, which took over publication of the *Musical Gazette* from Mason Brothers at the end of 1869 during Seward's editorship. The AMA probably approached Biglow and Main to publish *Jubilee Songs* because of the firm's long association with evangelical groups, and the publisher might have recommended Seward for the task of transcribing the spirituals.[6] Neither George White nor Ella Sheppard had time for such work (and it's doubtful White had the expertise). Two years later when White's health declined, Seward began a formal affiliation with the Jubilee Singers as assistant director.

The compilers of *Jubilee Songs* were completely ignorant of the history and documentation of antebellum folk spirituals. E. M. Cravath admitted as much in his introduction, writing that "neither the words or the music have ever before been published, or even reduced to written form, at least, to the knowledge of the Jubilee Singers." Seward later amended Cravath's statement in a footnote:

> "I'm traveling to the grave," and "Keep me from sinking down," were taken down at a concert [of the Jubilee Singers], after the other pieces were in the hands of the printer, and this introduction prepared; and before it was known that they had been previously written by Mr. Robbins Battell, and published, with pianoforte accompaniment, by Messrs. Oliver Ditson & Co., of Boston.—T.F.S.

Battell collected and arranged these two spirituals, and Gustave Stoeckel composed the sophisticated piano accompaniment; both men were connected with Yale University.[7] Seemingly unaware of the work done in the Sea Islands, the Fisk managers instead acknowledged the work of a member of the Connecticut legislature and a noted philanthropist who contributed to the AMA, who happened to reside in Pike's canvassing area.[8] Acknowledging Battell was good politics, but it underscored White's and Cravath's ignorance of the recent history of spirituals.

A good many white New Yorkers and Brooklynites knew more about slave songs than the Fisk managers, being familiar with "Go Down, Moses," "Roll, Jordan, Roll," and "Turn Back Pharaoh's Army," among others. The Reverend Theodore Cuyler named these three spirituals in an 1872 letter to the *New York Tribune*, and a John Davidson of New York wrote to Cravath shortly after the publication of *Jubilee Songs* to let him know that "Room Enough" and "Turn Back Pharaoh's Army" had been sung for the past two years by the Hutchinson family singers. "I know it from the fact that I heard the Hutchinsons sing them, & afterwards bought the songs at Pond's Music Store," he related, before helpfully advising Cravath that "the song 'Many Thousands Gone' you will find [in] 'Slave songs of the United States' . . . containing a large collection of just such style of pieces as the Jubilee Singers sing."[9] Seward's first public acknowledgment of *Slave Songs* occurred nearly at the end of his tenure with the Jubilee Singers. An undated program from their tour of Germany (ca. 1877–1878) lists a slave melody titled "My Father How Long," absent from all editions of *Jubilee*

Songs through 1886 but present in *Slave Songs*. The note about the song in the program, attributed to "Col. P. H. Higginson" (the initials are incorrect), is an almost verbatim quotation of Thomas Wentworth Higginson's remarks on the spiritual in *Slave Songs*.[10]

Despite his ignorance of slave songs, Seward assured the public in his preface to *Jubilee Songs* that "the music herein is entirely correct. It was taken down from the singing of the band, during repeated interviews held for the purpose, and no line or phrase was introduced that did not receive full indorsement from the singers." Seward's self-assurance invited criticism from knowledgeable contemporaneous music critics, Jubilee singer Thomas Rutling, and later from turn-of-the-century folklorists as well as modern scholars, who charged that the transcriptions were inaccurate, sometimes grossly so.[11]

Seward's inexperience with spirituals, and folk music generally, could explain many of the reputed inaccuracies. But his idea of "accuracy" may not have been the same as that of his critics. Unlike the editors of *Slave Songs*, for example, who were trying to create a *descriptive* record of songs and performance practice before they disappeared, Seward's goal was to create a *prescriptive* musical score that would enable audiences to sing these spirituals at home—in the same manner as the Jubilee Singers. Therefore the assertion that his scores are "entirely correct" should be taken in the spirit of a sales pitch. Even if Seward had wanted to notate microtonal variations in pitch and complicated embellishments, for example, such notational intricacies would have discouraged home users.

Inaccuracies in the transcriptions might have resulted from Seward's use of John Curwen's Tonic Sol-fa system, a solmization method popular in Britain and used especially in Sunday schools, public schools, and amateur choral societies.[12] In using a "movable-*do*" as opposed to a "fixed-*do*" system, the method gives primacy to tonality. The system was especially practical for vocal music: singers didn't have to worry about whether there were three sharps or six flats as long as they could identify pitches and intervals. Rhythm was denoted by a system of barlines, colons, and commas that marked strong and weak beats. Silence was indicated by a vacant space that was visually proportionate to the length of silence. For example, "Steal Away" (see example 3.3 for musical score) would begin like this:

KEY F

| d:– | .d | l d:– | | m:– | .m | l m:– | |
| Steal | a- | way, | | Steal | a- | way, | |

D and *m* stand for *do* and *mi*. The colon precedes a weak beat, the dash continues a note through another beat (or part of a beat), the period divides the beat in half, the short vertical line indicates a secondary accent, whereas the large vertical line marks measures. Although major works like Handel's *Messiah* appeared in Tonic Sol-fa notation, it's hard to imagine this method adequately representing melodic and rhythmic nuance—which spirituals had in abundance. (Standard notation, also inadequate, at least provides a wider range of options.) Seward, a proselytizer of Tonic Sol-fa in America, used it to transcribe some spirituals before writing them in conventional notation for publication—an extra step of translation that had the potential of introducing further inaccuracies.[13]

Even so, Seward's transcriptions have real value. Read as a record of his own ideologies and concerns—a white male Protestant, an arbiter of taste in music publications, a church musician in the Lowell Mason mold, an educator and Tonic Sol-fa advocate, an abolitionist with no experience of African American culture—they yield important clues about musical style and the Jubilee Singers' performances.

• • •

Ella Sheppard and Thomas Rutling were the only two Jubilee Singers to leave behind published transcriptions of spirituals. Seward enlisted Sheppard's aid in transcribing when he became assistant director in the fall of 1874. In diary entries from summer 1875, Sheppard wrote that she "took down" the following spirituals for Seward: "We'll Overtake the Army," "Wait a Little While," "Don't You Grieve after Me," "The Angels Changed My Name," "He Rose from the Dead," "Stand Still," "Move Along," and "A Happy New Year."[14] All of these songs were new additions to J. B. T. Marsh's 1875 chronicle of the Jubilee Singers, although Sheppard received no acknowledgment.

Rutling (1854–1915), the most celebrated tenor of the original Fisk Jubilee Singers, waited some thirty years to publish his transcriptions. After the original troupe disbanded in 1878 he remained abroad, finally settling in Harrogate, North Yorkshire, England. There he taught singing, gave concerts (mostly at churches in Manchester and Birmingham), and lectured about spirituals and slave life in the South. Around 1907 he published his life story, *Tom: An Autobiography*.[15] Modeled on the Pike and Marsh narratives of the Jubilee Singers, the book concludes with "Negro Melodies"—thirty-one spirituals plus the Lord's Prayer. Rutling believed that one of his duties was to "revise some of the songs of my enslaved ancestors, because the musician (all due respect to him) who took down the melodies from the singing of the Jubilee Singers, made so many errors in many of them that the singers did not recognize their own songs."[16] Nonetheless Rutling's scores disclose few major differences from Seward's. Most of the spirituals Rutling transcribed were those he'd sung the longest, having been in the early repertory of the Jubilee Singers. Of Rutling's thirty-one spirituals, sixteen match Seward's transcriptions either exactly or with the difference of one pitch, one word, or one phrase.[17] Of the remaining fifteen, only six (about one fifth of the total) differ in melody, harmony, rhythm, and expression to an extent that one might not recognize them in Seward's transcription.[18] Unfortunately Rutling muddied his own waters by adding piano accompaniments to spirituals that the Jubilees had sung unaccompanied, so that "the English people will not only understand the melodies better, but will be able to sing them."[19] His piano accompaniments are clumsy and rudimentary. His revisions to melody, however—especially in those six spirituals—provide an enlightening complement to Seward.

Rutling was born a slave in 1854 about twenty miles outside of Nashville. He shared with Ella Sheppard the traumatic experience of having a mother sold away. As a culture bearer whose later musical training followed the Euro-American "people's song" tradition, Rutling had the upper hand over Seward in evaluating the transcriptions in *Jubilee Songs*. But Rutling's transcriptions were published almost thirty years after the Jubilee Singers disbanded, whereas Seward's transcriptions had immediacy on their side. Did Seward's exact mistakes recede in Rutling's memory over time? Did Rutling's notated revisions adequately convey what he heard in his memory? The answers to these questions seem less significant than the types of corrections that Rutling made, all of which point to a more folk-inflected performance practice than Seward's transcriptions suggest.

Arrangements and Performance Practice

It seems that George White never wrote down his arrangements. His working method likely came straight from Lowell Mason's theoretical introductions to the teaching of vocal music: learn a spiritual from the singer by ear, work out an arrangement in his head, and then teach each voice section (soprano, alto, tenor, bass) its part by rote. During a lengthy period of trial and error White would refine every element of the performance. "In rehearsals," wrote Mary Spence, "his indomitable will never rested until the effect he wished was produced. Sometimes he tried plan after plan, covering days, perhaps weeks, before the results satisfied him." White "believed not only that the 'Jubilee Songs' expressed the highest possible spiritual fervor, but that they were capable of receiving the highest possible culture."[20] What exactly that meant can be deduced from musical analysis and descriptions of performances.

Melody, Harmony, and Texture

Most of White's arrangements rely on the triadic harmonies of Euro-American church hymns and SATB arrangement of voices, familiar from hymns and popular song. There's virtually an exclusive reliance on root position chords as well as on tonic, dominant, and subdominant harmonies; an almost complete absence of passing tones; and occasional open fifths and parallel voice leading.[21] The lack of harmonic inventiveness suggests that the spirituals enchanted white audiences in spite of, not because of, their harmony.

Texture proved an effective foil not only to harmonic monotony but to the burden of listening to a short melody repeated numerous times in the course of one song. What facilitated participatory folk performance in a praise house could quickly induce boredom in a concert hall. In the spiritual "I Ain't Got Weary Yet," to pick an extreme example, the refrain and the verse share an identical eight-measure melody, so that listeners heard eleven statements of the same melody over the course of three verses (given that the chorus is repeated each time). Listeners didn't hear the same texture, however. Although the opening refrain was sung by the whole choir in SATB harmony, the verse changed textures every two measures (see example 3.1):

Solo call
SATB response
soprano-alto call
SATB response

Further variations could be introduced by having the solos and duets rotate among different singers and voice parts. The tenors' brief counter-melody in measure three of the chorus also provides contrast.

Variation of harmonic texture wasn't an option in the case of unharmonized spirituals. Of the sixty-one spirituals published in 1872, twenty-one (about a third) consist of melody only, and several more contain just a few measures of harmony—in fact, a minority are entirely SATB. Although the entire ensemble sang some of the unharmonized spirituals in unison (e.g., "Didn't My Lord Deliver Daniel"), more often such songs were rendered by one of the troupe's powerful soloists: Maggie Porter, Jennie Jackson, Thomas Rutling, or Frederick Loudin. The potential to incorporate elements of folk performance resided in solos, as the transcription of "The General Roll" suggests.

Seward's transcription of "The General Roll" is interesting for its three-note melismas on the words "there" and "Oh" (see example 3.2A). Melismas, in which several pitches are sung to one syllable, are a type of melodic embellishment

No. 68.   I ain't got weary yet.

And I ain't got weary yet, And I ain't got weary yet; Been

down in the val-ley so long, And I ain't got wea-ry yet.

SOLO.   CHORUS.

1. Been praying for the sinner so long, And I ain't got weary yet;

DUET.   D. C.

Been praying for the sinner so long, And I ain't got weary yet.

2 Been praying for the mourner so long, &c.

3 Been going to the sitting-up so long, &c.

187

EXAMPLE 3.1. "I Ain't Got Weary Yet" illustrates ways in which textural variation prevents monotony in a highly repetitive tune. From Marsh, *Story of the Jubilee Singers* (1886), 187.

common in folk performance but uncommon in the published Fisk arrangements; only twelve of the sixty-one transcriptions in *Jubilee Songs: Complete* of 1872 contain a three- or four-note melisma.[22] Melismas are challenging to notate as someone is singing, because they can fly by so quickly that individual pitches are hard to discern. Seward's rendering of the melody on the word "there" hints at this difficulty, for his melisma begins on a neighboring tone and then skips upward, possibly "erasing" intermediary pitches that were in fact sung. Rutling's arrangement, however, "fills in" Seward's melodic outline with a four-note melisma that turns around the starting note (see example 3.2*B*); its stepwise motion is much more believable musically. Although Seward's score contains no tempo marking, Rutling specifies a moderately slow tempo, andante. Whereas the dotted rhythms of Seward's score give it a martial quality on the page, Rutling's melismatic melody seems more leisurely and suggests rubato. If any of the Jubilee Singers' repertory recalled the wails and chants described in after-hours worship among blacks at antebellum camp meetings, it was likely unaccompanied spirituals like "The General Roll," which freed the singer from the tyranny of synchronization that governed the SATB ensemble textures.

Jeannette Robinson Murphy (1865–1946), who grew up in a slaveholding family on a plantation in Louisville, Kentucky, was a keen observer and performer of African American songs and folktales. Her book *Southern Thoughts for Northern Thinkers*, self-published in 1904, contains a fascinating section titled "The Survival of African Music in America." Murphy found the melodies

EXAMPLE 3.2*A*. "The General Roll" as notated by Seward seems to outline a decoration on the word "there." Reset from [Seward], *Jubilee Songs: Complete* (1872b), 53.

EXAMPLE 3.2*B*. Rutling's arrangement furnishes a stepwise melisma on "there" and a smaller skip to the resting pitch, showing one way the melody could be embellished. Reset from Rutling, *Tom*, 37.

in *Jubilee Songs* to be genuine, but asserted that the notation was of no help in making the songs sound "authentic":

> For the uninitiated student of the future there is little or no instruction given, and the white singer in attempting to learn them will make poor work at their mastery; for how is he . . . to know that it is bad form not to break every law of musical phrasing and notation? What is there to show him that he must make his voice exceedingly nasal and undulating; that around every prominent note he must place a variety of small notes, called "trimmings," and that he must sing tones not found in our scale; that he must on no account leave one note until he has the next one well under control?[23]

Although Murphy was describing folk rather than concert performance, her instruction to sing with an "undulating" voice and to add "trimmings," or melismas, corroborates Rutling's efforts to make "The General Roll" more characteristic of the way it was actually sung.

Dynamics, Tempo, Vocal Intensity

White used various expressive devices to heighten the drama of the spirituals. An iconic example is "Steal Away," which opened almost every program and became the Jubilee Singers' signature song. It was Thomas Rutling's favorite spiritual (and his transcription matches Seward's in every detail). Seward's score, from the first edition of *Jubilee Songs*, begins characteristically with the refrain (see example 3.3). The furtive aspect of the phrase "steal away" is reinforced by a soft dynamic and the fermatas (a lengthening of duration) at the end of each iteration of that phrase in the first line; the song unfolds slowly and haltingly, by one-measure increments, and then "steal away home" flashes suddenly and brightly, before the soft dynamic returns as the refrain ends. By contrast the verses paint the thunder of the Lord's call in loud unison melody; the rhythm becomes more urgent (and, one imagines, slightly faster), unimpeded by fermatas until the end of the phrase—the word "soul" in the last line. The softness returns and the singers linger on the word "long"—the last fermata—before the verse concludes. Mary Spence's firsthand account of the performance reveals the effect of the dynamics:

> The basis of [White's] tone coloring was one note, the very first of every concert, the opening whisper of "Steal away to Jesus." Exquisite in quality, full of the deepest feeling, so exceedingly soft that it could hardly be heard, yet because of its absolute purity carrying to the farthest part of any large hall, it commanded the attention of every audience. As the tone floated out a little

EXAMPLE 3.3. Seward's transcription of "Steal Away." The fermatas on the syllable "way" and the word "home" throughout the first two lines create a halting sensation. From [Seward], *Jubilee Songs* (1872a), 28; courtesy of Emory University Libraries.

louder, clearer, rose to the tremendous *crescendo* of "My Lord Calls Me," and diminished again into exquisite *pianissimo* sweetness, the most critical enemy was conquered.[24]

A British reviewer also commented on "the softest pianissimo" of the beginning, which then "gradually welled out in a strong volume of sound" before dying away. He concluded, "Without the artful aid of instrumental accompaniments these colored singers held their audience by a chain of sympathy that a Jenny Lind could not have better forged."[25]

Another description confirms the arrangement as given in *Jubilee Songs*, and also reveals the tempo:

> It was sung slowly; the first chords came floating on our senses . . . followed by the unison of phrase, "Steal away—to Jesus," delivered with exquisite precision of time and accent; then came the soft chords, and bold unison again, followed by the touching throbbing cadence, "I hain't got long to stay here"; next follows the loud, lofty trumpet call in unison, "My Lord calls me, the trumpet sounds it in my soul; I hain't got long to stay here." . . . We hear again those beautiful chords delivered with double pianissimo, whispering to the soul, "Steal away to Jesus."[26]

To achieve the Jubilee Singers' famous pianissimo, Mary Spence recalled, White "used to tell the singers to put into the tone the intensity that they would give to the most forcible one that they could sing, and yet to make it as soft as they possibly could." One way he illustrated this idea was to say, "If a tiger should step behind you, you would not hear the fall of his foot, yet all the strength of the tiger would be in that tread."[27] As late as the 1930s White's practice sessions remained vivid in the memory of eighty-one-year-old Jubilee soprano Maggie Porter Cole:

> Mr White, who never did things by halves, is standing before us. Ella Sheppard is at the organ as we go over and over a single passage, 'till Mr White at last says "good," and we know that it is perfect, that we have caught his idea. Perhaps it was simply an accent upon a single word; sometimes it was simply to breathe that word, so soft and pure one might think it the voice of angels.[28]

"We sometimes found him too exacting," recalled singer Georgia Gordon Taylor, "but we who are left know too well that our success was through the rigid training received at his hand."[29]

If soft dynamics enchanted the listeners of "Steal Away," the opposite end of the dynamic spectrum was at work in "Turn Back Pharaoh's Army." The score has no dynamic markings, but a reviewer wrote that the Jubilee Singers sang the chorus with such spirit, "such grand crescendos, with such bright sforzandos" and "such a will the 'turning back of Pharaoh's army,' that we thought they would have no force to spare for the last verse." But the Jubilees proved their mettle: "When they came to the '*drowning* of old Pharaoh's army,' oh! What a double fortissimo they gave! And *such* a fortissimo it was, not an overstrained, dissonant clattering shout, . . . but a fortissimo as pure and true as it was strong."[30] Given that most scores in *Jubilee Songs* don't contain expressive markings other than fermatas, such descriptions of performances are invaluable in understanding the Jubilee Singers' performance practice.

Pitch

Pitch is defined by frequency, and the placement of a note on a musical staff indicates a specific frequency, or an absolute pitch. In his introduction to *Slave Songs of the United States* William Allen bemoaned the slurred tones, slides, melismas, and other melodic ornaments he heard, which make folk performance notoriously difficult to notate accurately. If melismas were a carryover of folk practice in the Fisk spirituals, as in "The General Roll," then perhaps there were other ways in which pitch was obscured, as Allen mentions. This seems to be the case with "Roll, Jordan, Roll"—the only arrangement that was ever rearranged for a succeeding edition of *Jubilee Songs*.

Example 3.4*A* shows the original arrangement from 1872, and *B* shows its revision from 1875, which stood in all remaining editions. There were three important changes in the revision: the men delay their entrance until the second measure and sing an upward slide (depicting the "roll" of the river) before joining the unison; there are two pitches instead of one on the word "die" in line 2; and there are three-note melismas (instead of one pitch) on the words "ought" and "in" in lines 3 and 4, respectively.

The rare amendments to the scores in *Jubilee Songs* were small—the addition of a double barline or a da capo sign, for example. Why "Roll, Jordan, Roll" was changed so extensively can be answered only with an educated guess. In the fall of 1874—shortly before the revision was published—the Jubilee Singers acquired a new bass singer named Frederick Loudin. At the time of his audition he was married, approaching thirty years of age, and living in Memphis, where he worked at a church teaching music, playing the organ, and leading the choir; he never was enrolled at Fisk. His deep, resonant voice startled people with its magnificence. A person who was present when he sang at a gathering of Jubilee Singers for the first time wrote, "Mr. Seward said there were few such voices black or white. . . . Mr. White asked if I did not think he had 'struck oil.'"[31] His

EXAMPLE 3.4A. Seward's original version of "Roll, Jordan, Roll." From [Seward], *Jubilee Songs* (1872a), 9; courtesy of Emory University Libraries.

EXAMPLE 3.4B. The revised score, first published in 1875, with slides and melismas. From Marsh, *Story of the Jubilee Singers* (1886), 131.

big voice and stage charisma made him an immediate celebrity, and reviewers seldom missed an opportunity to single out his extraordinary powers. Given that Loudin's arrival and the revisions to the score happened at about the same time, and that the most radical revision concerned the bass part, his influence seems probable. "Roll, Jordan, Roll" was an audience favorite that remained in the original Jubilee Singers' repertory for their entire existence. It wasn't the only spiritual that had a "roll"—the bass part of "I'm a-Rolling" undulated in what one reviewer described as an arpeggio movement, naming the superb Loudin as the source[32]—and in his transcription Thomas Rutling added a melismatic turn in the bass, illustrative of a roll. As for the addition of melismas, perhaps the editors took the opportunity to make the score more accurately reflect actual performance practice, as long as a new plate had to be made for printing.

The earliest recording of "Roll, Jordan, Roll" by a Fisk troupe dates from 1909.[33] Despite the fact that it was sung by a male quartet rather than a mixed chorus and was thirty-one years removed from the disbanding of the original Jubilee Singers, the recording is nonetheless a rich source of information about performance practice from the 1870s. The leader of the troupe, John Wesley Work II (1873–1925), was a Fisk graduate (class of 1895) and a professor of Latin and history who also directed jubilee troupes at Fisk. Although "forty years have naturally made some changes in the rendition of certain songs," he wrote in 1911, these were "not so marked . . . as is sometimes supposed."[34] He singled out as primary changes the use of close chords (barbershop style) and the development of new harmonies (e.g., diminished chords) and arrangements. Nonetheless Jubilee singing at Fisk was a conservative tradition. The original Jubilee Singers were still revered in the early twentieth century, and Ella Sheppard Moore even helped Work train a group of singers for an appearance at an AMA meeting in 1898.[35] There was a direct line of transmission through Sheppard from the original Jubilee Singers to Work's 1909 quartet.

It's not surprising, then, that the 1909 recording of "Roll, Jordan, Roll" resembles Seward's original transcription (see example 3.4A; website recording 3.1). Although the harmony is modified to fit male voices, the original chord progressions remain intact. And yet the recording displays a less absolute approach to pitch than the notation prescribes. For example, on the D♭ in measure 3 (on the word "roll") there are microtonal variations in pitch—not because of the singers' inability to achieve precise intonation, which is evident elsewhere in the recording, but probably because this pitch is characteristically ambiguous. Seward's transcription even hints at this: in measure 3 the D is lowered but in measure 4 it's natural, even though both pitches resolve upward to E♭. It's tempting to conclude that the original Jubilee Singers likewise didn't tune that pitch precisely, or that Seward was unable to render a pitch that was vexatious in its ambiguity.

Although none of the early Fisk recordings display the famous bass roll, Jim Europe's Singing Serenaders / Four Harmony Kings sing the roll on a 1919 recording that uses an alternative melody of the spiritual (see website recording 3.2). It's a slow slide, starting somewhere around B♭ and ending a minor seventh above, on A♭. A 1926 recording by the Spiritual Singers, singing the same melody as the Fisks, also uses a roll.[36] The slide attracts the ear immediately and propels the song forward.

Recordings also suggest another type of pitch ambiguity in this spiritual: portamento, or connecting two pitches separated by an interval with a vocal slur. What appears as two discrete pitches in notation may have been connected by a slide in performance, as it was on the Fisk quartet's 1909 recording between the syllables "Jor–dan" (m. 3) and on the word "die" (m. 6), which was revised in the later score to be sung over two pitches instead of one. The latter example is reminiscent of Jeannette Robinson Murphy's admonition that the singer of black folk music "must be very careful to divide many of his monosyllabic words into two syllables, placing a forcible accent on the last one."[37]

Rhythm, Asymmetry

In his preface to *Jubilee Songs* Seward notes that spirituals are differentiated from "conventional" melodies by their rhythm, "which is often complicated, and sometimes strikingly original." Although this is as specific as he gets, rhythmic challenges typically associated with folk spirituals include rhythmic swing, off-beat prosodic accents, densely syncopated passages, and asymmetrical phrasing.

An article in *Dwight's Journal of Music*, a highbrow periodical of the time, pronounced "Didn't My Lord Deliver Daniel" (see example 3.5) "the most difficult of all for anyone save a Southern negro to sing—difficult on account of its incomprehensible rhythm."[38] In this unaccompanied melody, sung in unison by the ensemble, a combination of irregular line lengths, continuous cadences, and dense syncopation create an ongoing feeling of instability.

In most of his transcriptions Seward printed one or two verses underneath the melody and placed the additional verses in stanzas at the end, believing that even though "in some of the verses the syllables do not correspond exactly to the notes in the music," the singer could easily adapt them to the melody. But the varying line lengths in each verse of "Daniel" made this impractical. Very few of the corresponding lines in the different verses are the same length; in verse 2, for example, the third line ("And every star disappear") is four syllables

No. 10. Didn't my Lord deliver Daniel.

Sung in Unison.

Did-n't my Lord de-liv-er Dan-iel, D'liver

Dan-iel, d'liver Dan-iel, Did-n't my Lord de-liv-er

1ST VERSE.

Dan-iel, And why not a ev-e-ry man? He de-

liv-er'd Dan-iel from the li-on's den, Jo-nah from the

bel-ly of the whale, And the He-brew children from the

fie-ry fur-nace, And why not ev-e-ry man?

Did-n't my Lord de-liv-er Dan-iel. D'liver

Dan-iel, d'liver Dan-iel, Did-n't my Lord de-liv-er

* Go on without pause, leaving out two beats of the measure.

134

EXAMPLE 3.5. "Didn't My Lord Deliver Daniel" presented Seward with a set of notational challenges that included rhythm, meter, text setting, and phrasing. First published in [Seward], *Jubilee Songs* (1872a); reproduced from Marsh, *Story of the Jubilee Singers* (1886), 134–35 (continued on next page).

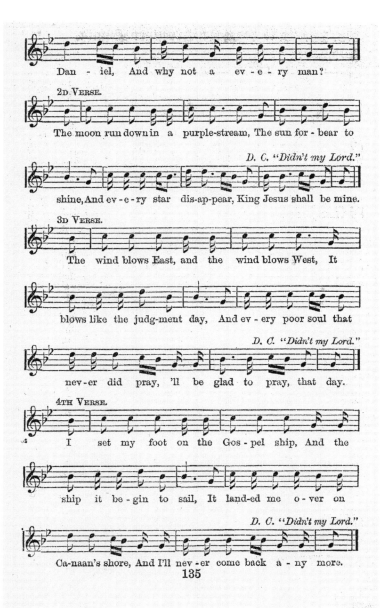

135

EXAMPLE 3.5. Continued.

shorter than the third line in verse 1 ("And the Hebrew children from the fiery furnace"). For this reason Seward wrote out the melody to every verse with text underlay, so that the score occupies two full pages instead of the typical whole or half page.

The text underlay was also a boon on account of the lively tempo. In the words of one reviewer, to sing this spiritual one "must first get the easy quick tongue of the Negro race."[39] This probably alluded to the elision of the first two syllables of "deliver," which were sung on one short note in measure 2 ("dli"), in contrast to measure 1, where each syllable gets its own note. The word "every," normally pronounced as two syllables, is notated as three emphatic syllables, each with its own pitch (m. 7). Although there is one syllable sung to one pitch for most of the song, sometimes one syllable is sung to two pitches (e.g., "star," "-pear," and "shall" in v. 3). The absence of a predictable pattern keeps the novice singer off guard.

The continuous cadences further contribute to this feeling of instability, as the footnote in the score suggests. Rather than bringing the first verse to a rest with four full beats (which would be typical of a Euro-American hymn), the first verse ends with an eighth note, after which the singer should "go on without pause, leaving out two beats of the measure," as Seward's footnote reads. The chorus continues directly from the verse, with barely time for a breath. If one is tapping time, as audience members may have been, the four-beat pattern is suddenly disrupted with a two-beat measure. Murphy elaborated on this practice, commenting that the uninitiated singer "might be tempted, in the *ignorance* of his twentieth-century education, to take breath whenever he came to the end of a line or verse! But this he should never do. By some mysterious power, to be learned only from the negro, he should carry over his breath from line to line and from verse to verse, even at the risk of bursting a blood vessel."[40] A Brooklyn reviewer concluded that "Daniel" was "a most odd arrangement of music and words." "One could not keep from laughing right out when the verse came in."[41] The Reverend George H. Griffin of Milford, Connecticut, likewise found that "many of the 'resolutions' of chords [meaning cadences] are abrupt and startling."[42] Other spirituals in *Jubilee Songs* characterized by a continuous cadence include "I'm a Rolling," "O Redeemed," "Old Ship of Zion," and "Turn Back Pharaoh's Army."

Asymmetry could also manifest in overall form. The balanced phrases so common in church hymns and popular song, wherein a phrase of four measures is answered by a phrase of the same length, were absent in the spiritual "Oh! Sinner Man." Its refrain begins with a five-measure phrase answered by a four-measure phrase. Such occurrences are rare in *Jubilee Songs*, and Seward notes in his preface that there are but "few cases of what theorists call *mis-form*." It's to Seward's credit that he preserved these examples of "mis-form" instead of making them "conform to the 'higher law' of perfect rhythmic flow," as he says elsewhere in his preface. Such "mis-form," or asymmetry, was much more common in actual folk practice, according to Zora Neale Hurston. "Asymmetry is a definite feature of Negro art," she wrote, and the "abrupt and unexpected changes" in key and time made the music difficult for white people to follow. "There is always rhythm, but it is the rhythm of segments. Each unit has a rhythm of its own, but when the whole is assembled it is lacking in symmetry."[43]

Mode

Each spiritual in *Jubilee Songs* is given a key signature, implying a major or minor mode. Not all the pitches of a major or minor scale are always present, however; many of the melodies consist of only five tones (see chap. 1). "Steal Away" is obviously in a major key as transcribed (see example 3.3): the melody outlines an F-major triad in the first three measures, and the harmony uses the leading tone. Other spirituals, especially those written without accompaniment, are more tonally ambiguous (which might explain why they were left unharmonized). The key signature of "I Ain't Going to Die No More" (see example 3.6), for example, is D major, and the melody seems to play along initially, landing on the "keynote" of D at the end of the first phrase—the word "glad" in measure 3. Furthermore, the five pitches used—D-E-F♯-A-B—suggest a "pentatonic" scale with D as the tonic. But the final note of the refrain (and of the verse that follows) is E, not D, which is the territory of E (natural) minor. Why then is there a C♯ in the key signature? If the song is in D major, the C♯ could make sense, but C♯ isn't present in E minor, and in any case there isn't a C♯ to be found in the melody. Without harmony, a gapped scale melody doesn't have to commit to a key. Many nineteenth-century reporters found this worthy of comment, noting, for example, that the Fisk Jubilee Singers "would swing from natural to minor keys and back."[44]

In evaluating Seward's transcriptions, it's worth keeping in mind that he was trained to hear every song in terms of major or minor tonality, and that tonality governed his interpretation of pitches as he wrote them down. In his preface to *Jubilee Songs* he ruminated on whether the frequency of gapped scales among the spirituals was "a peculiar language of nature, or a simpler alphabet than the ordinary diatonic scale, in which the uncultivated mind finds its easiest expression." In this last supposition he succumbed to the racialized thinking

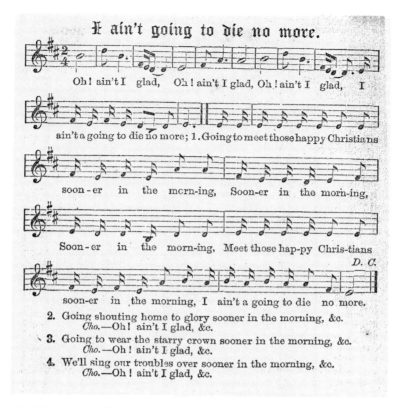

EXAMPLE 3.6. An illustration of the tonal ambiguity that can result from a five-tone gapped-scale unharmonized melody. From Pike, *The Jubilee Singers*, 211.

of his era, for gapped scales are found in the melodies of art, traditional, and popular musics around the world.

Declamation

"In their most plaintive or most impassioned songs, the words are so distinctly enunciated," wrote a reviewer of the Jubilee Singers. "Both the pronunciation and articulation of the language are more perfect than we almost ever hear, and put to shame our most highly trained and artistic singers, whether public or private."[45] With rare exceptions, the singers used standard English in the spirituals: the use of dialect was considered inappropriate for ambassadors of an educational institution, and it could have invited a comparison with blackface minstrelsy—something Spence had feared from the outset.

In becoming experts at declamation the singers were again guided by the precepts of Lowell Mason, whose singing texts provided exhaustive rules on pronunciation (e.g., "The definite article [t-h-e-] should never receive the sound of thee") and elocution, which should always sound natural.[46] Consummate declamation was useless, however, unless the message of the text was expressed with conviction. On this topic Mason was adamant: singers should attend to both pitches and words, and "grasp the spirit of both (the music always being subordinate to the emotional character of the poetry), and make them his own; he should make an entire surrender of himself to his work, throw his whole soul into the performance, and produce a living song, which shall draw out and intensify the feelings of those who hear."[47] In this George White was Mason's devoted disciple. Mary Spence remembered one occasion "when Mr. White was drilling his singers, they were singing along without seeming to think much about what they were saying, when, from the distant point where he was accustomed to stand, he thundered forth in tones which almost frightened them, *'Do you believe that?'"*[48]

Even the extent of the Jubilee Singers' education and their rigorous drilling were not enough "to shake off the old pronunciations," however, according to original Jubilee Singer Maggie Porter Cole. As a Boston audience member affirmed, "They have the real plantation 'twang.'"[49]

Contrasting the Concert Spiritual and the Folk Spiritual

The concert spiritual as designed by George White shared several basic features with the folk spiritual, among them form, call and response, gapped-scale melodies, duple meter, and lyrics. Writing about folk spirituals in the preface to *Jubilee Songs*, Seward maintained that "the power is chiefly in the songs themselves." But the "song itself" didn't exist outside of performance. Every sounding of a spiritual was unique, the result of an improvisatory practice in which words, melody, tempo, harmony, number of participants, and dynamics were changeable according to the occasion. Distinguishing the folk spiritual from the concert spiritual, then, means distinguishing between two modes of performance.

Because folk performance was participatory, everyone was welcome to join in whether or not they could carry a tune. It didn't even matter if everyone sang the same words, because there was no one "correct" set of lyrics. The participants were their own audience and had no one else to please. Concert spirituals, on the other hand, relied on trained voices that blended perfectly and moved in synchronicity. The extensive rehearsal required to achieve this ideal removed the spontaneity and improvisation of folk performance (and over time conditioned audiences to expect a high degree of refinement at jubilee concerts). The goal was to display the artistic merit of the music through standardized performances that could be replicated countless times.

To this end, White created in concert spirituals dramatic miniatures that swept up listeners in their dynamic shadings, alterations in tempo, variations of texture, and other expressive devices. Execution required controlled, modulated vocal production, as opposed to the full-throated, intense singing typical of folk performance. Singers of folk spirituals expressed their emotion in bodily movement, swaying to the music, dancing in a ring, stomping, clapping, or patting parts of their body, with the percussive sounds often forming cross rhythms with the singing. In contrast the Jubilee Singers stood still onstage, letting their faces convey the emotions they felt as they sang.

Folk spirituals were sometimes harmonized spontaneously in performance; other times people sang variations of the melody simultaneously, creating a thick, heterophonic texture. The texture of the Fisk spirituals was always transparent, marked by a homophonic SATB texture or a precise unison melody.

Perhaps most obviously, there were differing preferences of sound ideal. The folk performance of spirituals is characterized by what Olly Wilson has termed a heterogeneous sound ideal: a texture in which individual voices can be readily identified.[50] The Fisk Jubilee Singers acquired a reputation for the opposite: a homogeneous sound ideal, or perfect blending. "Not one voice was even to be heard as distinct from the others in the *ensemble* singing," boasted Mary Spence. "The whole nature of the singers was in control, the most difficult control of all."[51] Others agreed: "The charm of their music does not depend upon individual voices. In their singing the voices are so beautifully blended that individuality is nearly lost."[52]

In some respects there was overlap between folk and concert performance practice. The improvisatory melismas, slides, swoops, calls, moans, and interjections that created a heterogeneous sound ideal in folk performance made occasional guest appearances in concert spirituals, but they were carefully controlled and used in moderation. The same applied to pitch. In concert spirituals pitch accuracy was paramount, whereas in folk spirituals pitches were more approximate. Despite this, there was the D♭ in the 1909 recording of "Roll, Jordan, Roll" that wasn't quite a D♭—perhaps an exception that proved the rule.

Reception

Thousands of people heard the Fisk spirituals in January, February, and March of 1872, in New York, New Jersey, Connecticut, Massachusetts, Vermont, New Hampshire, Maine, Rhode Island, and Washington, DC. The students returned to Nashville in April for a brief respite before resuming their tour, this time through Illinois and neighboring states. By May they had sent $20,000 to Fisk and inspired the formation of other groups of black jubilee singers. The rhetoric surrounding the spirituals in this earliest phase of the Jubilee Singers' career proved resistant to change during the ensuing decade-long "jubilee craze."

Sympathetic Responses

The Jubilee Singers were still refining their sound during their first campaign. In their very earliest performances their nervousness onstage was palpable, their borrowed clothing from the teachers at Fisk ill-fitting, their demeanor uncertain. They were homesick and fatigued, geographic and cultural foreigners tasked with ensuring a brighter future for their fellow students in Nashville. If they were initially dubious about singing their spirituals for outsiders, public acclaim boosted their confidence until it seemed that the spirituals sustained them onstage. Former white abolitionists who were now advocates for black self-reliance were predisposed to admire the Jubilee Singers, their songs, and their mission—for the three were inseparable.

"The leading feature" of the Jubilee Singers' concerts, noted the *New York Evening Post*, "is in the strange and weird negro melodies of a religious order which are sung by the freedmen of the South."[53] As Henry Ward Beecher explained, the Jubilee Singers "make their mark by giving the spirituals and plantation hymns as only *they* can sing them who know how to keep time to a master's whip"[54]—a statement that peppered the publicity for the singers' residency in Boston in March 1872 and beyond. Slavery gave the spirituals the stamp of authenticity, and it became the primary marketing strategy, even though some of the students had been born free.[55]

One of the most widely quoted responses to the Jubilee Singers was a letter to the *New York Tribune* that the Reverend Theodore Cuyler (1822–1909) wrote after hosting the troupe at his Lafayette Avenue Church in Brooklyn, the largest Presbyterian church in the United States.[56] Titled "Our Native Music—The Jubilee Singers" and printed 19 January 1872, the letter is a glossary of paradigmatic reactions to the singers and their spirituals. Cuyler points out that he had never seen a "*cultivated* Brooklyn assemblage so *moved* and *melted* under the *magnetism* of the music before. The *wild melodies* of these *emancipated slaves* touched the fount of *tears*" (my italics). Framing the students as ex-slaves allowed him to portray the melodies as "wild," as remnants of an (African) uncultivated past that a Fisk education was presumably rectifying. The music's magnetism seems to have been fueled in part by one of the most enduring novels of slavery in American history, Harriet Beecher Stowe's *Uncle Tom's Cabin* (1852). As Cuyler writes, "one might imagine himself in the veritable Uncle Tom's cabin of the 'old dispensation.'" His invocation of Uncle Tom, the noble, long-suffering Christian slave, was a sentimental nod to a fictional character many Americans regarded as real.

Cuyler walks a fine line between attesting to the singers' skill and praising them for the inherent musical qualities of their race: "The harmony of these children of nature and their musical execution were beyond the reach of art"—a statement in celebration of primitivism. And yet in the next sentence he pays tribute to their training: "Their wonderful skill was put to the severest test when they attempted 'Home, Sweet Home' before auditors who had heard those same household words from the lips of Jenny Lind and Parepa [Euphrosyne Parepa-Rosa]"—two of the century's most popular operatic sopranos. But again, it is imagination that feeds the emotional reaction to the music: "Yet these emancipated bondwomen—now that they know what the word home signifies—rendered that dear old song with a power and pathos never surpassed." This contrast between past and present—enslaved and emancipated, homelessness and rootedness—is strengthened by Cuyler's reference to the singers' repertory of "weird and plaintive hymns sung in the dark days of bondage" and, one sentence later, "their rich, plaintive voices." The immediate repetition of the word "plaintive" associates the spirituals with suffering (which W. E. B. Du Bois reinforced in his 1903 book *The Souls of Black Folk*), with slavery, with the past.

Past and present are brought into higher relief when Cuyler describes Jennie Jackson's solo performance of "I'll Hear the Trumpet Sound," in which he mixes biblical allusions with African attributes. He refers to Jackson not by name but by appearance: a "young negress." In pronouncing her "exceedingly 'black [referring to original sin] yet comely [having received the grace of God],'" a phrase from the Song of Solomon (1:5) in the Old Testament, he acknowledges her Christianity. The key to Cuyler's attraction to the spirituals is the phrase "the very embodiment of African heart-music," for he recognizes the spirituals as the product of lived social experience. As much as Cuyler may have admired the words and tunes, for him the spirituals gained their ultimate power through their transmission by black African bodies that had been redeemed by God's grace.

Cuyler did admire the melodies, however, describing the spiritual Jackson sang as "wild yet most delicious." The contradiction here, delicious in spite of being wild, echoes that in his physical description of Jackson (black yet comely), revealing the common need to qualify admiration of black bodies and black culture. Cuyler's use of the adjective "delicious," linked so closely to his characterization of Jackson as the "embodiment of African heart-music," calls to mind Kyla Wazana Tompkins's metaphor of white ingestion of blackness, of black bodies as "food" to be consumed. Blackness is put *in* (as in singing the spirituals) as opposed to put *on* (as in blackface minstrelsy). As Tompkins demonstrates in her perceptive book *Racial Indigestion*, "the fantasy of a body's edibility does not mean that the body will always go down smoothly"; black bodies and subjects, specifically, "stick in the throat of the (white) body politic."[57] This helps explain why Cuyler's enthusiasm for the singers is always tempered with reminders of black difference.

Returning to the spirituals, Cuyler calls them the "genuine soul music of the slave-cabins before the Lord led his 'children out of the land of Egypt, out of the house of bondage,'" declaring that "we have long enough had its coarse caricature in corked-faces," referring to blackface minstrelsy. In another allusion to the old dispensation, Cuyler draws a parallel between the slaves and the captive Israelites in Egypt, the slaveowner and pharaoh—a common trope in the lyrics of spirituals and by this time well-established in abolitionist rhetoric. Although the term "soul music" again bypasses the role of hard work in preparing the spirituals for performance, it also acknowledges that blacks have a spiritual dimension. For a people combatting the stereotype of savagery, this was a significant declaration.

In summary, Cuyler's comparative approach in articulating the power of the spirituals rests on a number of binaries: past and present, slavery and freedom, primitive (driven by emotion) and cultivated (driven by intellect). His equivocation reflects white anxiety about black bodies and black song, encompassing both desire and aversion.

Other reviews echoed and extended Cuyler's response. For example, the *Daily National Republican* (Washington, DC) referred to the Jubilee Singers' "pathos and plaintiveness." The *New York Evening Post*, quoted by the *Memphis Daily Appeal*, suggested that the spirituals were at once physically seductive, religious, and exotic: "These negro verifiers sometimes strike a real poetic chord among much that is semi-barbaric. . . . The harps, the crowns, the trumpet calls, the glassy sea and the crystal gates all appeal at once to their rather sensuous sense of the beautiful." The writer found these "pious rhapsodies" to be beautiful, weird, strange, curious, peculiar, and original, but was unsure whether the lyrics qualified as "poetry," putting the term in quotation marks.[58] Such descriptors were replicated in newspaper after newspaper, in advertisement after advertisement, in address after address in services of song. Although in the first half of 1872 the Jubilees toured no farther south than Washington, DC, reports of their success were reprinted in newspapers of the Deep South, especially in the singers' home state of Tennessee. In Washington they sang for an ailing William G. Brownlow (then senator from Tennessee, who had been governor when the Fisk school was founded); for a host of religious and political dignitaries at Lincoln Hall; and for President Grant at the White House.[59] The dignitaries, Cuyler's letter, the reviews—all were featured prominently in Pike's and Marsh's narratives of the Jubilee Singers and in their publicity. Rhetoric about the Jubilees became entrenched, predisposing new audiences to hear the Jubilee Singers the way their critics had.

Critical Responses

Not surprisingly, there were those who resisted the Jubilee enterprise, dismissing outright the idea of black performers on the concert stage, deeming the spirituals unworthy of serious attention, or denouncing the singers' mission. The following review managed both disparagement and (tepid) praise in one paragraph:

> These young people sing the old camp-meeting, Methodist, and plantation songs of the Southern States. The singing itself is rude; the songs are, from an art standard, almost barbarous, the words deal with holy things with a freedom that borders on irreverence, if not blasphemy, and yet, because the melody and the words come from the heart, and because they are genuine, unaffected, simple, homely and direct, they take people captive. It is the rude unwritten music of an untutored race, born of that nervous frenzy miscalled religious ecstasy, and giving expression to a low order of devotional and musical feeling. We do not find the melody very much superior to the poetry. Both rise from the same source and attain about the same art elevation.[60]

The spirituals took people "captive" (as if against their will); their "magnetism," in Cuyler's words, made people "melt" and weep. Even the singers themselves succumbed, singing "as if they couldn't help it."[61] Whether these emotional responses were deemed appropriate or repellant depended on the listener's standpoint. For the *Sun* reviewer in the foregoing extract, the music was debased because it stemmed from a wild, "nervous frenzy" instead of authentic religious ecstasy. However, the "genuine, unaffected" quality of the songs mitigated the so-called blasphemous lyrics and almost barbarous melodies.

The management came in for its share of criticism as well. There were those who felt that the Jubilee business had "milked enough money out of Brooklyn," using the "emancipation dodge, the ex-slave dodge, the university dodge, and the education and missionary dodge." (The writer said that for Fisk to call itself a university at this time was "simply cheek, or worse," and he had a point. Although Fisk's university department was organized in 1869, it had no students until 1871, when 4 were admitted. In 1872 only 8 out of 257 students were in the college.)[62] Others found white patrons and managers who spoke at concerts—often at length and sometimes in numbers—tedious and superfluous: "There was nothing that was not already in print before our eyes, and, indeed, there was nothing necessary to be said or read. 'Story,—God bless you, I have none to tell, sir.' The nine singers told their own story, by their appearance and their songs, far better than any one else could tell it for them."[63] Pike conceded that on occasion the speeches were too "elaborate" but argued against omitting them, asserting that the Jubilees were not *showmen*."[64] This highlighted a basic tension in the Jubilee enterprise, for White, devout as he was, had trained the students to be performers. Such criticisms receded as a few of the male singers became the primary spokesmen at concerts, telling their stories in both oratory and song. Perceptive critics also sometimes found fault with the content of the speeches, as when Theodore Seward "took the fallacious ground that because the music sung by the negroes was effective, therefore it was necessarily good music."[65]

Race prejudice, always present, was more explicit in some reactions. The Jubilee Singers' first full concert at Henry Ward Beecher's church was poorly reviewed the next morning by the *New York Herald* under the headline "Beecher's Negro Minstrels," and the illustrated newspaper *Day's Doings* printed an illustration of the singers onstage with an inattentive white audience accompanied by the caption "Rev. Henry Ward Beecher as the manager of a Negro minstrel troupe . . . Wednesday, Jan. 3, 1872."[66] Pike took the view that there was no such thing as bad publicity, however. Long after the troupe dissolved, singer Maggie Porter Cole remembered, "the victory was ours," for after that successful concert "the New York Herald thereafter called us 'Mr. Beecher's nigger minstrels,' which served us well as an advertisement."[67]

What Audiences Heard

Since most white northerners had no aural model for interpreting the spirituals, they compared them to music they knew: popular songs, art songs, minstrel songs with a plantation theme, British folk songs, and church hymns. The spiritual was an outsider to all of these musical realms, a rule breaker—indeed, the song form without rules. A New York reviewer, likening spirituals to "the Folk songs of northern Europe," observed that "they contain progressions and phrases scarcely allowable by the rules of musical grammar."[68] (It was to pre-emptively defend against such comments that Seward wrote in his preface to *Jubilee Songs* that whatever "irregularities" did exist "invariably conform to the 'higher law' of perfect rhythmic flow" and that the pentatonic scale belonged to the ancient Greeks.) The reviewer concluded that despite their unruliness the spirituals "touch the heart with their tenderness, while at the same time they amuse by their grotesqueness."

What made the music amusing and grotesque? Sometimes audiences laughed because the melody or the rhythm startled them—their expectations were suddenly countered by a violation of "the rules of musical grammar," as in "Didn't My Lord Deliver Daniel." Sometimes it was on account of the direct and forceful language of the lyrics: "The crudities of thought and the boldness of imagery displayed in their hymns often provoke a smile," wrote a reviewer in 1874 of another jubilee troupe, the Tennesseans. "It is difficult to say whether tears or laughter are the proper response. The fact is, both are given at every concert."[69] Sometimes the differentiation of verses by substituting only one word for another was amusing to those bred on the hymns of Charles Wesley and Isaac Watts.

The internal refrains found in so many spirituals could also provoke bewildered laughter: "A part of the oddity of these plantation tunes [i.e., spirituals] plainly arises from the constant interruption of the flow of the verse by the refrain, which comes in with tremendous unction at the end of each line. These quaint little ditties coolly hold in suspense a sentence dis-severed almost between subject and verb. A favorite song runs thus":

I heard a rumbling in the sky—	Waiting on the Lord.
Oh, then I thought my end was nigh—	Waiting on the Lord.[70]

Whereas in folk performance the internal refrain was a communal rejoinder in a musical dialogue, in concert performance it more obviously disrupted a sentence or thought.

Concluding Thoughts

The architect of the Jubilee Singers' sound was almost never singled out by reviewers. A rare acknowledgment of George White's achievement came from a fellow musician, who wrote that "the singing of these strangers is so natural that it does not at once strike us how much of true art is in it, and how careful and discriminating has been the training bestowed upon them by their accomplished instructor and leader, who, though retiring from public notice, deserves great praise."[71] This was also a rare acknowledgment of the singers' hard work, for it was more usually assumed that those of African heritage were inherently musical.

The Fisk concert spiritual encapsulated both artistic and social contradictions. In the language of the time, the music was premodern yet cultivated. It conformed to the higher laws of music, but it could not be completely disciplined. It threatened loss of sensory control, but in the name of religious rapture. In this it had an analog in some of the original songs of the Hutchinson Family Singers, particularly a famous performance of "Get Off the Track" in 1844. In this song about emancipation, the singers described an engine called the "Liberator" mowing down anything standing in its way. "They forgot their harmony," shouting as if they were about to witness a terrible railroad catastrophe, according to Nathaniel Peabody Rogers (1794–1846), editor and founder of the pioneer antislavery newspaper *Herald of Freedom*. "It was life—it was nature, transcending the musical staff. . . . It was the cry of the people, into which their over-wrought and illimitable music had *degenerated* and it was glorious to witness them alighting down again from their wild flight into the current of song, like so many swans upon the river from which they had soared. . . . They transcended the very province of mere music."[72]

For Rogers, the power of that performance derived from the disintegration of the rules of harmony, rhythm, and vocal timbre into a kind of sonic catastrophe that became a metaphor for the impending collision in the narrative; the subsequent restoration of consonant harmonies, sweetness of voice, and regulated rhythm represented the order that would reign once the country agreed to end slavery. As self-educated Americans from rural New Hampshire who wrote their own "simple" (sometimes referred to in the press as "primitive") songs, as passionate performers who could inspire transcendent experiences by combining social and musical "transgressions" that broke the laws of performance, the Hutchinsons created an uneasiness in their audiences similar to that described by those who heard the Fisk Jubilee Singers.

If any one word summarized the musical translation of folk spirituals into concert performance, it was perhaps "discipline." Pitches, rhythms, enunciation, intonation, tempos, articulations, lyrics—all were rehearsed, perfected, synchronized. And yet as anyone who has tried to discipline something knows, total discipline is an elusive goal. So it was with the spirituals, whose melodies did not always submit to key signatures, whose form could not always be balanced, whose lyrics didn't always make "sense," whose singers kept traces of their southern accents and raw vocal timbres. Just as the audience lost discipline in succumbing to the music, so did the singers. Facial expressions, small gestures, and vocal timbres communicated the depth of feeling in their singing. The "folk" survived in these concert arrangements and performances, disciplined by but not quite contained in art music aesthetics. Like the Hutchinsons' "Get Off the Track," the unruliness of "nature" was always balanced by the rules of civilization.

Slavery conferred authenticity upon the Fisk concert spirituals, from the perspective of a white northern public raised on literary rather than aural images of plantation life. To listen to the Fisk Jubilee Singers was to take a sonic journey to distant times and places. It was both an exotic adventure and a colonial encounter, rendered safe by white guideposts (harmony, tonality, meter, the Jubilee management). The travelers could bring home artifacts between the covers of *Jubilee Songs* and re-create the music at home in an emerging appropriative act.

CHAPTER 4

Innovators, Imitators, and a Jubilee Industry

The Jubilee Singers' 1872 spring tour culminated in several appearances at Patrick Gilmore's World's Peace Jubilee in Boston, which celebrated the end of the Franco-Prussian War with twenty thousand choristers, some two thousand instrumentalists, and three weeks of mammoth concerts dominated by European classical music (17 June–4 July). Although the Fisk Jubilee Singers sang spirituals in three of the main concerts, their most conspicuous performance was "The Battle Hymn of the Republic" on Saturday, 22 June. Joining them were the Hyers sisters, a chorus of some one hundred fifty African Americans, and the distinguished festival orchestra. After a long orchestral concert of German and Austrian music (with Johann Strauss II leading his own "Neu-Wien" waltz) and a spectacular "Star-Spangled Banner" featuring a soloist, the full chorus, the orchestra, the military bands, and a cannon, the Hyers sisters began to sing "The Battle Hymn." Their two verses were barely audible. Although several reviewers attributed this to the uncomfortably high key of E♭ (a perfect fourth higher than normally performed), a more likely explanation for the "small" sound of these accomplished classical vocalists was the giant orchestra and even more gigantic hall (which had generated numerous complaints about acoustics during the festival)—and perhaps even the cannon shots still ringing in people's ears. The Jubilee Singers were to sing the third verse. Outnumbering the Hyers sisters by five to one, their voices were said to be heard in every corner. The crowd and musicians erupted in cheers of "the Jubilees forever!" and threw up their handkerchiefs and hats, while Strauss waved his violin in excitement. Gilmore brought the Jubilee Singers onto the stage with him and had them repeat their verse as an encore, to an equally enthusiastic ovation.[1]

The glow from "The Battle Hymn" remained with the Jubilees the next day, when they were slated to sing two spirituals on a program by the festival chorus, orchestra, and soloists that included Mendelssohn's "He, Watching over Israel," Rossini's "Inflammatus," and Schubert's "Ave Maria." As the concert neared its end, the chorus and orchestra began the well-loved hymn "Nearer, My God, to Thee," and the audience joined in. Then the Jubilee Singers took the stage with "Swing Low, Sweet Chariot," which the crowd greeted with an enthusiasm that "almost, if not quite, equaled any of the obstreperous demonstrations [against the singers] that were so prevalent during the preceding week," according to the *Boston Daily Globe*. The second, unidentified spiritual was received "with a still larger share of plaudits and excitement," which the singers rewarded by singing "Roll, Jordan, Roll." Additional encores were demanded, but none was given.[2] Handel's "Hallelujah Chorus" brought the concert to a close.

The largest crowds at the Peace Jubilee numbered close to sixty thousand, and the festival received national newspaper coverage. Although the Jubilee Singers didn't attract extraordinary attention from journalists, they made an indelible impression on those who heard them. Their appearance at the Peace Jubilee was the culmination of nine months of touring. In October 1871 they had been a motley group of students, dressed in cast-off clothes from their teachers, lacking overcoats and boots for the northern winters, plagued by stage fright and the insecurity of not knowing how their next train ticket or meal would materialize. They returned to Nashville in May 1872 as the Jubilee Singers, ambassadors of the AMA, well dressed and newly confident, with accolades following liberally in their wake—and with $20,000 for their school. The Jubilee Singers and their concert spirituals were well on their way to becoming a phenomenon.

■ ■ ■

As audiences took note of the Jubilee Singers, so did aspiring African American performers. In the fall of 1872, George White traveled to several New York towns to investigate the Canaan Jubilee Singers, a private enterprise that was trying to ride the coattails of the Fisk students' success. In his opinion the group's renditions of spirituals were "in the rough—the rudest & least musical I have ever heard . . . without any grip at all." The Canaan Jubilees boasted earnings of $43,000 by that time—an impossibly large amount, given that the Fisk Jubilees had earned just upwards of $20,000. Although they claimed this money was for their "colored brethren" and, moreover, *everyone* who needed an education, they were not affiliated with an institution. White, vexed with this bogus competition, wrote, "They get what favor they do get because people think they are the Fisk J.S. I have no fear of their doing much but they ought to be prevented from humbugging the people if possible."[3]

For the time being, the greatest threat posed by groups like the Canaans was that audiences might mistake the imitators for the imitated. Because they appeared in the same towns and cities as the Fisks, White worried that such unscrupulous rivals would destroy the goodwill that his students had established. As it happened, the Jubilee Singers finished 1872 without serious competition. But the new year brought a better class of rivals as well as more imitators, thereby sowing the seeds of a jubilee entertainment industry. As jubilee singers began to saturate the cultural marketplace, variety and blackface minstrel performers inevitably made them the objects of parody. Innovators, imitators, and parodists all contributed to the jubilee industry, not necessarily by the quality of their performances but by their eventual ubiquity. The jubilee troupes that entered the field in 1873 and 1874 enlarged the repertory of spirituals circulating in the public domain and introduced new standards of performance.

Innovators

The Fisk Jubilee Singers (it was now necessary to qualify them with their school name) had several advantages over their competitors: having had years to prepare, being first on the scene, originality, and the backing of a powerful missionary organization. Successful rivals would have to give audiences something different, and in 1873 two groups did just that: the Hampton Institute Singers and the Tennesseans.

The Hampton Institute Singers

The first significant rival of the Fisk Jubilee Singers was, in a sense, its mirror image. The Hampton Institute Singers, like the Fisks, sang for an institution in desperate need of money. But this small school in Hampton, Virginia, differed from Fisk by promoting an industrial rather than a liberal arts education. Just as Fisk University's educational philosophy was reflected in the sound of its Jubilee Singers, so was Hampton's in the singing of its student troupe.

HAMPTON'S EDUCATIONAL PHILOSOPHY Hampton Institute owed its existence to Samuel Chapman Armstrong (1839–1893). Raised by missionary parents in Honolulu, Hawaii, he learned from them the values of elevating and protecting an "inferior" race through education and evangelism. His father, who served as minister of public instruction of the Hawaiian Kingdom, was instrumental in establishing a manual-labor model among the higher schools throughout the islands. Armstrong, whose youth was passed largely outdoors, grew up hale, hearty, independent, and irreverent—and these qualities endured as he matured.

Armstrong came to the mainland in 1860 to complete his education at Williams College in Massachusetts, where he acquired an appreciation for the importance of social service. Although he was an abolitionist, he joined the army upon graduating in 1862 not out of any "burning patriotism" or "special interest in the cause of the slave" but because his friends were doing it, and because he had the temperament of a soldier.[4]

He applied for a command of colored troops, passed the examination, and in December 1863 became lieutenant colonel of six companies of the Ninth Regiment, United States Colored Troops, in Benedict, Maryland. He relished the work, and while serving in Benedict was appointed president of a military school for black soldiers operated by five women from Boston. His letters suggest that from this time on he began to treat the abolitionist cause more thoughtfully. Armstrong mustered out of the military in 1865 at the rank of brevet-brigadier general; the following year he was appointed bureau agent for the Freedmen's Bureau at Fortress (today called Fort) Monroe in Hampton, Virginia, with responsibility for supervising the schools in more than ten counties on the Virginia Peninsula.

Settled in 1610, Hampton was connected to the earliest Africans in America, who were brought to nearby Jamestown in 1619 as indentured servants. The antebellum slave culture that developed in the region was unusual. Surrounded on three sides by water, Hampton furnished a variety of sea-related livelihoods as well as craft professions; soil exhaustion had diminished the importance of agriculture by the mid-1800s. This meant that African Americans had access to a greater diversity of work than in plantation economies. There were 201 free blacks (many of them mulatto) in Hampton's Elizabeth City County in 1860, some of whom owned property, and they mixed freely with whites. As a result, an African American social elite of literate community leaders emerged before the war. (Although education of blacks was against Virginia law, it took place informally and went unchallenged as long as there were no negative repercussions.) At the same time there were 2,417 slaves in the county, and they lived lives of destitution, despite the relative leniency of their owners.

The Union Army occupied Fortress Monroe early in the war. It was there, in May 1861, that General Benjamin Butler made his ingenious declaration that slaves were "contrabands of war." Faced with three escapees applying for sanctuary, he reasoned that since they were property, he could seize them to prevent their use by the enemy in waging war. Before long Fortress Monroe was deluged with black refugees, who quickly outnumbered the white population. They became laborers for the troops, suspended between freedom and slavery.[5]

It was against this backdrop that Armstrong began to plan for a school in Hampton in 1867. Within a three-mile radius were seven thousand freedmen, "camping in squalid fashion"—the failed result of the Union Army's inability to cope with the overwhelming number of black refugees who arrived at Fortress Monroe during the war.[6] On 1 April 1868 the Hampton School opened under Armstrong's direction (a year shy of his thirtieth birthday), with fifteen students from Hampton's black elite families and five teachers.[7] Two years later the Assembly of Virginia voted to incorporate the school as the Hampton Normal and Agricultural Institute.

Influenced by his father's work among the Hawaiians, Armstrong imposed a curriculum favoring manual and technical instruction: men would become skilled laborers, and the articles they made would be sold for the benefit of Hampton and freedmen's education. The students would farm, and the crops would feed the school. The male students would work as printers, painters, carpenters, coopers (crafters of casks and buckets), shoemakers, janitors, clerks, mail carriers, waiters, police, and guards.[8] The female students would learn to cook, sew, clean, and manage a household. This philosophy of industrial education was new in the 1860s, and it quickly became controversial. Critics of the "Hampton Idea" believed that it reinforced the subordination of blacks in society, whereas proponents found it pragmatic. (As Robert Engs recounts, black minister William Roscoe Davis spoke for many freedmen when he said that the idea of teaching work habits to a people who had spent their lives as slaves was "the height of foolishness.")[9]

In Armstrong's mind, his system had finer shades of gray. He regarded blacks as slovenly and indifferent, but improvable: labor would teach discipline, industry, and self-respect. To this end, he had his male students learn to make every article possible from wood and iron. Specialization was undesirable because it would elevate the object at the expense of the real lesson: that labor was a "moral force." For the same reason, girls learned to play the piano through exercises, not tunes. This philosophy was the foundation of Armstrong's own education. Labor was reinforced with religious instruction and mandatory chapel attendance; as at Fisk, all students were urged to become Christians. Whereas the AMA viewed slaves as victims, Armstrong—without endorsing it—saw slavery as a logical result of blacks' inherent laziness and immorality, traits that could be offset by industry and discipline.[10] Despite his "benevolent" racism, Armstrong seems to have been beloved by most of his students. His most famous protégé, Booker T. Washington, applied Armstrong's educational model at Tuskegee Institute, which he founded in 1881 after graduating from Hampton.

Notwithstanding their fundamentally different educational philosophies, the Hampton and Fisk schools—and most of the white-sponsored schools for blacks at that time—were linked by their professed goals of racial uplift and self-determination, as well as by a common pool of donors and advisers. There was considerable interaction among their leaders. In fact two of Fisk's founders were on Hampton's Board of Trustees: E. P. Smith and E. M. Cravath. Cravath's tenure ran from 1870 to 1877, which virtually paralleled the original Jubilee Singers' tours (1871–1878) and overlapped with the first two years of his term as president of Fisk University.

ORGANIZING THE HAMPTON INSTITUTE SINGERS According to Hampton teacher Helen W. Ludlow (white; 1840–1924), the idea of using the students' "wonderful musical talents for the good of their people had for years been a favorite one" with Armstrong, but he lacked a suitable leader.[11] Perhaps his determination was renewed upon hearing the Fisk Jubilee Singers at the High Street Church in Lowell, Massachusetts, in spring 1872, where Armstrong gave the opening address,[12] for that summer he hired Thomas P. Fenner (white) to teach music at Hampton and to organize a choir of singers. Their goal would be to raise Virginia Hall, a dormitory for the female students.

Fenner (1829–1912) was born in Providence, Rhode Island. A singer and violinist, he helped Eben Tourjée establish the New England Conservatory of Music in 1867. As it happened, Tourjée was superintendent of the massive choir at Gilmore's Peace Jubilee in Boston. It's possible that Fenner attended the jubilee, and even heard the Fisk Jubilee Singers sing, before arriving in Hampton that September with his wife and daughters.[13]

Even with his formal music training and the Fisk Jubilee Singers as a model, Fenner was at a considerable disadvantage in starting a singing troupe to represent Hampton. George White had spent almost four years finding and training the best voices in the student body before heading north; Fenner had less than six months to become acquainted with his students, learn and arrange their spirituals, teach them repertory, and turn them into singers who could hold their own next to the famed Fisk Jubilee Singers.

Armstrong gave Fenner a helping hand by personally recruiting many of the singers, from both within and outside of the school. Any outsider who consented to sing had to enroll as a Hampton student. Armstrong discovered singer Sallie Davis, for example, in a Norfolk, Virginia, classroom. Davis recalled the first time she met Armstrong:

> Our teacher made us stand and sing for him when he visited our class one day in Norfolk. He told her he was going to send some students from the Hampton School to sing and get money to help finish a new building to be called Virginia Hall. . . . He needed more good singers to join the band and the school. . . .

What was my surprise when he said, "I should like to have that little girl go."
... He then approached my parents and my father, having heard of Hampton's
power for good, readily consented. .... I became at once a Hampton student
and a Hampton singer.[14]

The original Hampton Institute Singers numbered seventeen, almost double the
number of the initial Fisk troupe (see web table 4.1 for personnel). The theory
was safety in numbers: given the students' lack of performing experience, the
extra voices might camouflage vocal deficiencies. The singers left Hampton on
a cold, rainy evening on 13 February 1873, a year and four months after the Fisk
Singers launched their first tour.[15]

Like the Fisk Jubilee Singers, who at the time boasted exceptional voices in
Maggie Porter, Jennie Jackson, and Thomas Rutling, Hampton also had its stars.
Joseph Towe quickly distinguished himself as the troupe's "shout leader":

Many an audience was carried away by his improvisations and wild refrains,
as he seemed to lose sight of all before him in the visions of the "Great Getting up Mornin'." He was a genius in his way, and representative, as he was,
of the "old time Negro," he had a good head for books too, and a very earnest
desire for his own improvement and his people's. .... Returning to complete
his school course, as all the Hampton Singers did, he graduated with an honor.
His Commencement essay was on the old slave music: in the middle of it he
electrified all his hearers by breaking into an unexpected musical illustration
of his subject.[16]

Robert Hamilton was in some ways the "Ella Sheppard" of the Hampton
troupe—a reliable assistant to Fenner, an ongoing advocate of spirituals, and a
vocal coach for later troupes. He was born a slave in Louisiana and was freed
by the Union Army. At Hampton he learned tailoring and ran the industrial
department (which made the students' school uniforms and work suits) for
seven years after graduating in 1877. At that same time "he also had charge of
the music," according to his alumni report, "drilling the choir, and teaching
singing to the entire school—especially keeping up the old 'Plantation Songs'"
(meaning spirituals). He continued with this work after graduation. In 1884 he
led and sang in a quartet of male jubilee singers that toured on behalf of Tuskegee Institute (later Tuskegee University). In the summers of 1886 and 1887 he
directed a company of student singers associated with Norfolk Mission College
(Virginia), and in 1887 he joined Booker T. Washington full-time at Tuskegee
Institute, where he became a teacher and director of their choir.[17]

Another impressive soloist was James Monroe Waddy; in fact, he was the only
one of the original Hampton singers to perform professionally after graduating.

Waddy's wife reported that the couple sang with a Chautauqua choir in 1876 under the direction of a "Mr. Bliss" and "traveled through the Northern and New England States and Canada." In 1878, she wrote, "we sailed for Liverpool and spent three years abroad, visiting all the cities and towns of importance in England, Scotland and Ireland." According to Waddy's alumni report, they traveled with a "colored troupe, giving concerts for themselves in England and on the Continent." Although Grace McLean Waddy returned home in 1881, her husband "wandered," and it isn't clear whether they remained married.[18] In the 1880s Waddy turned up several times in Boston, performing with Marie Selika and Wallace King in Sam Lucas's Colored Ideals in fall 1880, and giving a series of Sunday night concerts at the skating rink in 1885. He sang with Slavin's *Uncle Tom's Cabin* troupe in 1878 and was also one of only four black men credited with playing the role of Uncle Tom on stage as of 1891.[19]

Sallie Davis, James Waddy, and Hampton singer Joseph Mebane reunited after the original Hampton troupe dissolved and sang with an independent company known as the Virginia Choristers, who toured in 1876. The troupe was disowned by Hampton Institute, which had no confidence in its management and disapproved of singing for personal profit.[20]

THE HAMPTONS' FIRST TOUR Whereas the Fisk Jubilee Singers had taken to the road with a borrowed sum of $100 and the clothes on their backs, the Hamptons left home with concert and travel wardrobes, a $500 donation, and the goodwill of the Jubilee Singers' audiences to smooth their way. At the same time, they faced their own set of uncertainties: perhaps audiences had tired of jubilee songs, perhaps donors were depleted, perhaps listeners would judge the singing of the Hampton students to be inferior to that of the Fisks. In a "preemptive strike" against such possibilities, the Hamptons began their tour in Washington, DC, where they sang for President Grant (as had the Jubilee Singers before them)—the most esteemed audience the country could provide. Buoyed by that success the Hamptons headed for Philadelphia, New York City, and Massachusetts, where they were patronized by many of the same religious leaders who had welcomed the Fisk Jubilee Singers.[21]

Religious leaders didn't immediately endorse the Hampton singers, however; their reluctance seemed to be fueled by fear that the students, and even General Armstrong, weren't Christians. Fortunately Helen Ludlow, who was traveling with the Hampton troupe as teacher and girls' chaperone and was herself a minister's daughter, found a solution. Upon arrival in New York in March 1873, Ludlow invited a number of clergymen and their wives to a private concert. The select audience was so impressed that the ministers made a number of resolutions to support the university and its singers. "These resolutions with the signatures in fac-simile, printed on all our programmes, became a passport to churches and public interest all through the North," remembered Ludlow.[22]

The Hampton students had a challenging life on the road. They faced the same prejudice that had barred the Fisk students from hotels. They studied their schoolbooks all day on trains, then had lessons and recitations once they reached a boarding house. They lugged heavy trunks of programs and books for sale, as well as extra clothing for seasonal weather. They did all of this without expectation of remuneration. (By 1873 the Fisk singers each received a salary that significantly exceeded that of white teachers at Fisk, although their contracts set explicit limits on their public and personal behavior.)[23]

The Hamptons never adopted an official name. Known variously as the Hampton Institute Singers, the Hampton Students, and the Hampton Colored Students, they billed their songs as "Negro spirituals," "cabin and plantation songs," or simply "the quaint melodies of the Negro race." Their publicity played up authenticity: "Go and hear the Cabin and Plantation Melodies sung in their Original Style!"[24] They avoided the term "jubilee," perhaps to avoid confusion with the Fisks. Although the Hampton singers styled their concerts on the service-of-song model like the Fisks, they did not use that term in their advertisements. General Armstrong, who traveled with them as much as he was able, delivered the appeal for donations. In his absence, Thomas Fenner or singer Robert Hamilton spoke.

In March 1873 the Hamptons arrived in New York after only one month of touring. The Fisk Jubilee Singers had preceded them in January, advertising new singers and "many new and touching songs." The Fisks' ads signaled a new boldness: "This is the year of Jubilee! We will sing the new song. The Lord has set his people free! We will sing the new song." They proudly recorded the amount of money they had earned and named the influential patrons they had acquired.[25] The troupe was beginning its farewell tour—on 12 April they were sailing to Great Britain, leaving the home field wide open for their competitors. After a brief tour of the Northeast the Fisks returned in March to New York, where the Hampton and Fisk students found themselves in the same place at the same time.

The Jubilee Singers attended the Hamptons' fifth performance at Steinway Hall and afterward went to greet the Hampton students in the anteroom. They were reunited once again "at the farewell concert of the Fisk Singers, who were on the eve of their departure for Europe," recalled Helen Ludlow, "and they enjoyed a social sing together before exchanging their good-bys and good wishes."[26] Both Theodore Cuyler and Henry Ward Beecher opened their Brooklyn churches to the Hamptons for performances on 31 March and 5 April, respectively, while the Jubilee Singers performed at Brooklyn's Academy of Music on 8 April. Other ministers who had helped introduce the Jubilees did the same for the Hamptons. If the Jubilee Singers hadn't been leaving the country to cultivate new donors abroad, this overlap might have caused some rancor between the two troupes, but their relationship seems to have been mutually supportive. (Even so, it was a delicate one. A year later, Armstrong wrote to the AMA for permission to send the Hamptons to England; when consulted, G. D. Pike put a damper on the idea by estimating that the Hamptons might get half the amount of money they would earn at home. Pike was reluctant to discourage the enterprise outright, however, fearing that his motivation could be misread as an attempt to exclude competitors.)[27]

The publication of *Jubilee Songs* allowed the Hampton students to select spirituals that in 1873 were "entirely new and fresh, never having been sung in the North."[28] A program from a 23 May 1873 concert at Tremont Temple in Boston consisted of:

"Oh, the Heaven Is Shining" (with "Hail, Hail, Hail")
"Don't You View That Ship Come Sailing?"
"Yonder Comes My Jesus, Hallelu"
"Gideon's Band, Or Milk-White Horses"
"Oh, the Fountain Lies Open"
"In Search of Liberty"
"Peter, Go Ring Dem Bells"
"Bow Low, I Know You Want Religion"
"The Gospel Train Is Coming"
"So Will I Go into Yonder World"
"I'm Hunting for a Home"
"In Dat Great Getting Up Mornin'"[29]

Just two days earlier in the same hall the Hamptons had sung thirteen different songs, and they advertised eleven more new titles for the next day's concert; at the very least they had an active repertory of over thirty spirituals.

PERFORMANCE STYLE The Fisk and the Hampton singers performed the contrasting ideologies of their respective institutions on the concert stage. The Fisk students, as representatives of a liberal arts institution, performed "cultivation." The Hampton students, representing the manual arts, were "less cultured than their predecessors" but gave performances that were even "more characteristic" of actual slave songs, according to a report in *Dwight's Journal of Music*.[30] For example, they used dialect liberally. Their "Swing Low, Sweet Chariot" (see example 4.1), which shared a title with the Fisk spiritual but had a different melody and words, was sung to a "humming accompaniment, suggestive of the rhythmic moaning which was such a peculiar characteristic of the slave prayer meeting."[31] One New York reviewer pronounced their singing "very guttural."[32] The apparent improvisations of "shout leader" Joseph Towe transported performer and audience alike, suggesting that Fenner's arrangements and the Hamptons' performances were closer to a folk aesthetic than were those of the Fisk students.

Fenner arranged and notated the Hampton spirituals, and his preface to their first publication in 1874 is worth quoting in full. Unlike Theodore Seward and George White, Fenner took a distinctly folkloristic interest in this music:

The slave music of the South presents a field for research and study very extensive and rich, and one which has been scarcely more than entered upon.

There are evidently, I think, two legitimate methods of treating this music: either to render it in its absolute, rude simplicity, or to develop it without destroying its original characteristics; the only proper field for such development being in the harmony.

Practical experience shows the necessity, in some cases, of making compensation for its loss in being transplanted. Half its effectiveness, in its home, depends upon accompaniments which can be carried away only in memory. The inspiration of numbers; the overpowering chorus, covering defects; the swaying of the body; the rhythmical stamping of the feet; and all the wild enthusiasm of the negro camp-meeting—these evidently can not be transported to the boards of a public performance. To secure variety and do justice to the music, I have, therefore, treated it by both methods. The most characteristic of the songs are left entirely or nearly untouched. On the other hand, the improvement which a careful bringing out of the various parts has effected in such pieces as "*Some o' dese Mornin's*," "*Bright Sparkles in de Churchyard*," "*Dust an' Ashes*," and "*The Church ob God*," which seem especially susceptible to such development, suggests possibilities of making more than has ever yet been made out of this slave music.

Another obstacle to its rendering is the fact that tones are frequently employed which we have no musical characters to represent. Such, for example, is that which I have indicated as nearly as possible by the flat seventh, in "*Great Camp-meetin'*," "*Hard Trials*," and others. These tones are variable in pitch ranging through an entire interval on different occasions, according to the inspiration of the singer. They are rarely discordant, and often add a charm to

EXAMPLE 4.1. "Swing Low, Sweet Chariot," as arranged by Fenner in 1874 for the Hampton Institute Singers. The observation that this was sung to a humming accompaniment underscores one of the deficiencies of scores as sources for performance practice. From Armstrong and Ludlow, *Hampton and Its Students*, 179.

the performance. It is of course impossible to explain them in words, and to those who wish to sing them, the best advice is that most useful in learning to pronounce a foreign language: *Study all the rules you please; then—go listen to a native.*

One reason for publishing this slave music is, that it is rapidly passing away. It may be that this people which has developed such a wonderful musical sense in its degradation will, in its maturity, produce a composer who could bring a music of the future out of this music of the past. At present, however, the freedmen have an unfortunate inclination to despise it, as a vestige of slavery; those who learned it in the old time, when it was the natural outpouring of their sorrows and longings, are dying off, and if efforts are not made for its preservation, the country will soon have lost this wonderful music of bondage.[33]

For a classically trained musician, Fenner shows unusual sensitivity to performance context. Like George White, he recognized that folk spirituals could not simply be transplanted from the camp meeting to the concert stage: functional, participatory music was not necessarily interesting for audiences to listen to. Yet he also evinces a desire to portray spirituals in as characteristic a manner as possible, by leaving them largely "untouched." Those spirituals that he lists as benefiting from "improvement," like "Some o' Dese Mornin's" (see example 4.2), anticipate the jubilee gospel quartets of the twentieth century in the independence of parts, which echo or base one another—a style familiar in white gospel hymns of the time. In "Mornin's" Fenner achieves a rich texture by splitting the voices into six and sometimes seven parts, a hallmark of his arranging style. On the repetition of the chorus, which he writes out (not shown in the example), the first altos sustain a high E♭ until the closing cadence (the last two measures). This provides an anchor for all the moving parts and creates tension before the voices reunite in a homophonic resolution. Fenner also "improved" what he called the "more characteristic" (i.e., simpler) songs with passing tones in the harmony. In general, the Hampton arrangements have a busier and denser texture than the Fisk spirituals, allowing for a heterogeneous sound ideal.

Whereas Seward professed his 1872 transcriptions to be "entirely correct," Fenner—like the editors of *Slave Songs* before him—admitted defeat in trying to identify certain pitches and explained that his choice to notate flat seventh scale degrees, for example, was meant as a compromise (compare to the flat seventh in "Roll, Jordan, Roll," example 3.4). An interesting example of this is "A Great Camp Meeting in the Promised Land" (see example 4.3), which was recorded by a Fisk Jubilee Quartet in 1916 and by an independent group called the Southland Jubilee Singers in 1921.[34] (See web recordings 4.1, 4.2.) The Fisk Jubilee Singers added it to their published jubilee songs in J. B. T. Marsh's 1881 narrative, taking

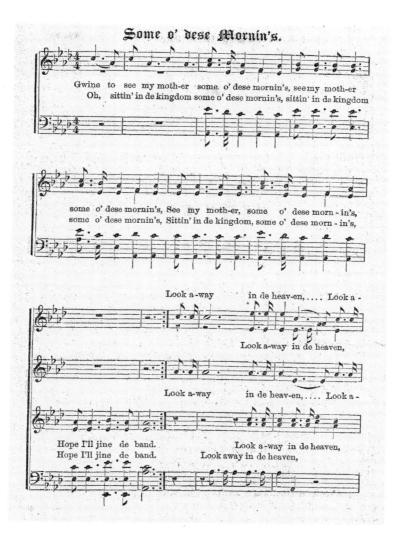

EXAMPLE 4.2. Excerpt from "Some o' Dese Mornin's," which Fenner "improved" by creating a dense texture to mask the simplicity (especially repetitiveness) of the folk spiritual. From Armstrong and Ludlow, *Hampton and Its Students*, 190.

EXAMPLE 4.3. Pitches outside the diatonic scale frustrated transcribers from William Allen to Seward to Fenner. A lowered seventh scale degree appears in the last two measures of the first page of this Hampton spiritual, on the words "Gwine" and "mourn." Pitch is further obscured in the next measure, on "tire," which has both a lowered seventh and a grace note. From Armstrong and Ludlow, *Hampton and Its Students*, 222.

EXAMPLE 4.3. Continued.

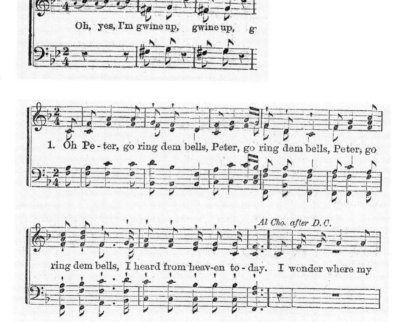

EXAMPLE 4.4. The expressive markings in Fenner's transcriptions point toward a folk performance style. *A*: The grace notes in the first two measures of "Gwine Up" suggest ambiguity of pitch. *B*: The marcato markings in the chorus to "Peter, Go Ring Dem Bells" designate emphasis and a percussive way of singing. From Armstrong and Ludlow, *Hampton and Its Students*, 216, 174.

the arrangement from the Hamptons' anthology (with attribution); the song was performed by George White's independent group of Fisk singers in 1882, which he reorganized after the original group disbanded. It's instructive to compare these two recordings with Fenner's score. Both recordings begin at a quicker pace but slow the tempo dramatically at the chorus ("Gwine to mourn . . ."), resuming the original tempo in the last two measures. The Fisk quartet sings the chorus almost exactly as notated by Fenner (with allowances for register in the harmony, since it's all male), with an absolute flat seventh. The Southland Jubilee Singers, however, demonstrate the kinds of problems Fenner probably faced. The soloist who sings the chorus starts on C (the words "gwine to") instead of E♭; on the word "mourn" he slides up, almost to E natural (see example 4.3). The word "tire," pronounced as one syllable by the Fisks, is two distinct syllables (ti-yer), and there is a melisma instead of a grace note on that word. In addition, the rhythm throughout swings more than the notation indicates; for example, the internal refrain of the verse—"don't you get weary"—is often anticipated rather than sung exactly on the first beat of the measure.

Shout leader Joseph Towe took the solo calls when the Hamptons performed this song. The contrast between the expressive solos and the exuberant responses sung by the large choir (as opposed to the small groups on the recordings) must have been exhilarating.[35]

In general, Fenner's scores notate folk traits by way of accents, grace notes, and flatted pitches. He uses grace notes more liberally and suggestively than Seward; in example 4.4A, for example, the graces suggest that the first three iterations of "B♭" are varied in rhythm and pitch. Finally, many of Fenner's scores contain accents to indicate a percussive vocal effect—another trait common in folk performance of spirituals (see example 4.4B). In the end Fenner, in contrast to Seward, admits the inadequacy of notation and admonishes readers to go listen to native singers.

There's no evidence that George White was motivated to preserve the spirituals in concert or in written form because they were rapidly passing away; certainly he had deep respect for the music, but economic profit was his driving force. Although Fenner too had an economic mandate, he seemed genuinely concerned with preservation, much like the editors of *Slave Songs*. In fact, Fenner often prefaces a song score with a description of its origin or manner of performance (the explanation in example 4.3 comes from bass singer Joseph Towe); such descriptions are rare in the Fisk transcriptions.

Fenner's arrangements and the Hamptons' performance style, then, represented an innovation in the arranged concert spiritual rather than a direct imitation of the Fisk Jubilee Singers. One might argue that the Hamptons used dialect and retained folk aesthetics because Fenner didn't have time to purge his singers of these habits in only six months; perhaps he was trying to turn a disadvantage into an advantage. But Fenner's remarks in his preface to the transcriptions suggest genuine pride in the songs as originally sung. Fenner harmonized only those spirituals that he believed were "susceptible" of development; the "most characteristic" songs were left (almost) untouched. In the greater retention of folk traits, Fenner and his singers—whether intentionally or not—gave audiences an alternative to the more cultivated performance style of the Fisk Jubilee Singers.

■ ■ ■

The Hampton troupe toured for almost a year. After spending the summer of 1873 in the Berkshires resting and rehearsing, they began their concert season in September to enthusiastic crowds and good financial returns. Their season was abbreviated, however, by the nationwide financial panic induced by the failure of the investment banking concern Jay Cooke and Co. A domino chain of collapses—the closing of the New York Stock Exchange for ten days, the failure of banks and factories—meant that the previously steady stream of charitable donations dried to a trickle. The Hamptons kept touring, but they worked harder for diminishing returns.

By the time the Hampton singers returned to New York in November 1873, the *Times* declined to review them, deciding that "their efforts have so often received attention that they do not require notice at present."[36] Despite friendly audiences, the financial panic proved fatal to their tour, and they disbanded at year's end, bringing back to Hampton $10,000 for the building of Virginia Hall. (This was admittedly a large sum, but by contrast, the Jubilee Singers earned twice that amount in less time during their first tour, which was completed before the panic.) Armstrong, in the habit of staring down adversity, pared the troupe, devised a new strategy, and put them back on the road again a month later.

The new plan—to tour the West and Canada, where there would be untapped audiences—could have been highly successful with proper planning. Instead it was a disaster. Not anticipating Canada's short but hot summers, the Hamptons arrived just as city dwellers were heading south to lakes and rivers. The next major destination, Chicago, was still recovering from the great fire of late 1871. The Hamptons' advance agent had them push farther west, through Illinois, Wisconsin, and Iowa, where they encountered a grasshopper plague that intensified the already devastating consequences of the financial panic. The students returned to the Berkshires for the summer disheartened, exhausted, and in poor health. Their performances may not have reaped the desired financial rewards, but they had spread spirituals far and wide. They concluded this second season of touring with a return to Hampton at Christmastime 1874.

There would be one more campaign, in 1875. A troupe of some ten students toured for about a year. Fenner left Hampton in 1875, and for the rest of the century the university sent out quartets and quintets assembled for short-term tours.[37] Hampton deserves greater recognition for the important role it played in enlarging the soundscape and repertory of jubilee song in the early 1870s.[38] Certainly popular entertainers took notice (see chap. 6).

The Tennesseans

In January 1874 John Wesley Donavin (1833–1893), a white Methodist layman from Delaware, Ohio, launched a singing tour with nine young people to raise money for a new building at Central Tennessee College in Nashville (see personnel in web table 4.2).[39] Central Tennessee, established by the Missionary Society of the Methodist Episcopal Church (aided by the Freedmen's Bureau) and chartered in 1866, opened in temporary buildings but moved to a permanent site in 1868. John Braden, a Union Army chaplain, directed the school from 1870 until 1900 on the Fisk model, with an emphasis on teacher and professional training, and instruction in vocal music. Unlike Fisk, however, slave melodies were the foundation of the music program; only later was "white" repertory—Sunday school songs, church hymns, and instrumental music—introduced.[40]

Donavin had a flair for business, vocal music, and politics—a handy skill set for the director of a black singing group at the time. In the 1860s he sang with a quartet and directed a large male glee club while running a grocery store; he eventually engaged with a range of successful business ventures. As Marvin Latimer Jr. notes, he was an abolitionist "particularly known for . . . his concern for the disenfranchised poor specifically, especially former African-American slaves."[41]

A NEW KIND OF "AUTHENTICITY" The original Tennesseans offered "slave-cabin concerts," described in this February 1874 advertisement:

> They sing with wonderful power and effect the GENUINE, RELIGIOUS MELODIES OF THE PLANTATION, just as they have known them from childhood, or have learned them from the lips of the "Old Aunties" in the lowly cabins of the South. The music of these singers is as original, quaint, and touching as the songs themselves. It is THE WONDERFUL UNWRITTEN MUSIC of our country, and our only characteristic National Music.[42]

Authenticity, religion, and nativism were already standard emphases of the Fisk and Hampton publicity machines. Although the Hamptons advertised "slave cabin songs," the Tennesseans went a step further, calling their performances "slave cabin concerts." Theirs was not a "service of song" but a naturalistic representation of slave life, as descended from the lips of the "old aunties": the nurturing caregivers who were stereotyped as mammies in minstrelsy, and later in film. The songs were "religious," part of the female domestic sphere rather than the arena of "wild" and "primitive" worship.

This advertisement is also interesting because it uses oral transmission as a selling point. Although the troupe eventually published broadsides (large inexpensive flyers with song lyrics) and songsters (with and without musical scores), in these early years they did not. Audiences who wanted to appreciate the elusive songs of the Tennesseans would have to return in person again and again to hear them.

Puff pieces were designed to attract the demographic that appreciated populist music from the past:

There are thousands of people in [Chicago] to whom there are no songs like the old songs. Those lovers of old-fashioned music will undoubtedly go and hear the Tennesseans. There are very many enthusiastic devotees of music, who will avail themselves of this opportunity to study a class of music composed without art, preserved without any system of musical notation, and attributable to no known composers. There is a host of habitual concert-goers who will be glad to descend from operatic heights to the vales of humble, unpretentious song. And they will go to hear the Tennesseans. There are many people who will hail a really enjoyable sacred concert, and these will go to hear the Tennesseans.[43]

The ad covered all the bases: nostalgia for the rural past, populism, and religion.

Donavin was well aware that the Tennesseans were taking to the road "on the very heels of the great panic."[44] Clever marketing was essential, and so too were strategic tour routes. Rather than revisit the eastern venues depleted by the Fisk and Hampton troupes, the Tennesseans initially stayed mostly in the west, beginning in Nashville and proceeding north to Ohio and then to Wisconsin, heading east for their first major tour only in 1876–1877.[45] (They eventually toured throughout the east, north, and west.) Although the Fisk Jubilee Singers were in Great Britain when the Tennesseans started out, the Jubilees were hardly forgotten thanks to numerous weekly if not daily press reports of their successes abroad. They were still the yardstick of success for any jubilee troupe.

THE ARRANGEMENTS Initially the Tennesseans' repertory consisted of about forty-five spirituals, many of which had already been introduced by the Hamptons and the Fisks. A small number of their arrangements survive in an undated broadside and two songsters (ca. 1882 and ca. 1884) with identical contents. The songsters contain music and lyrics to "Rise! Shine! And Give God the Glory"; "Steal Away to Jesus"; "Good News! The Chariot Is a Coming"; "We'll Camp a Little While in the Wilderness"; "Swing Low, Sweet Chariot"; and "There's a Meetin' Here To-night," as well as the lyrics to "History of Jonah and the Whale" as sung by J. T. Washington, the troupe's "shouting tenor."[46] All but two of these songs ("We'll Camp" and "Jonah") were in the Fisk repertory at the time.

The Tennesseans' repertory grew to comprise at least 166 spirituals that were largely distinct from those performed by the Fisk and Hampton troupes (see web table 4.3 for a repertory list), as were their arrangements. In the cases of overlap, the Tennesseans' arrangements differed from the Fisks' or Hamptons' by a change in key, minor textural alterations (e.g., duet vs. unison), or more abundant expressive markings. The Tennesseans' expressive markings were notably elaborate compared to other published concert spirituals and would be incongruous even in parlor music of the time, with such phrases as *allegro ma non troppo* and *adagio religioso* for tempo, and *afflito* or *crescendo e incalcendo poco a poco* for expression.

Some if not all of the Tennesseans' arrangements ("I've Been Redeemed," "Rise! Shine! And Give God the Glory") were made by their bass singer, Leroy (L. N. D.) Pickett, who was credited as arranger on the broadside but not in the songbooks. These seem to be the earliest examples of concert spirituals arranged by an African American. Pickett was a multi-instrumentalist, a composer of parlor songs, and an orchestrator. In addition to serving as the group's organist he also played violin, cornet, and xylophone. The biography of this extraordinarily talented musician remains frustratingly obscure.[47]

The broadside score of "Rise! Shine!" (see example 4.5) reveals some interesting differences from the spiritual as sung by the Jubilee Singers, titled "Rise and Shine," first printed in Marsh's *Story of the Jubilee Singers* in 1875 (217–18). Pickett's score begins with the verse rather than the chorus (Seward preserved the folk trait of starting with the chorus); the tempo is marked allegro (the Fisk version has no tempo indicated); and the lyrics differ. Most important is the direction in the Tennesseans' score to sing "in staccato style" in the chorus; a rest between the words "rise" and "shine" facilitates this. The Fisk version, in the absence of rests and performance directions, implies a legato articulation. As a result, at least on the page, the Tennesseans' spiritual seems to have much more personality than the Fisk version. The percussive quality is also more consistent with folk performance, resembling that found in Fenner's arrangement of "Peter, Go Ring Dem Bells" (see example 4.4B).

EXAMPLE 4.5. "Rise! Shine! And Give God the Glory" as sung by the Tennesseans is one of the earliest examples of a concert spiritual arranged by and credited to an African American. Undated broadside, "Songs of the Tennesseans," courtesy of Center for Popular Music, Middle Tennessee State University, Murfreesboro.

Like the Hamptons, the Tennesseans seemed to offer a folk-inflected performance style that allowed for improvisation. A Chicago reviewer observed that "the distinction of parts [i.e., SATB], though made by the troupe, is not very clearly defined throughout, the songs consisting mostly of the peculiar camp-meeting melodies, which are sung in chorus, and each individual member intoning his or her voice to the harmony adds to it as seems most effective at the moment." This suggests not only improvisation but a layered, possibly heterophonic but definitely heterogeneous texture. Of the "stirring" chorus that closed the concert the writer observed: While singing, "the troupe shook each other by the hand, and danced in a sort of religious phrenzy."[48] (The song may have been "Goodbye, Brother"—a spiritual found both in *Slave Songs of the United States* and in the Fisk anthologies; the Jubilees often sang it to close their concerts.) Another article noted the interactive nature of the concerts: "They sing with more spirit and 'power,' when encouraged by a full house, than when singing to a small audience."[49] The Tennesseans may have pleased audiences, but they failed to impress George White. When searching for singers to refresh the Fisks in October 1874, White wrote: "We could do nothing at all with such singers as comprise the 'Tennesseans' without months of drill"[50]—an apparent confirmation of the Tennesseans' lack of cultivation and discipline.

For their part, the Tennesseans tried to lure singers away from Fisk that same month, just before their northern tour.[51] A few years later in 1878, Fisk president E. M. Cravath coveted one of the Tennesseans when illness debilitated the Jubilee Singers' leading sopranos. AMA official E. P. Gilbert reported to Cravath: "The Central Tennessee people have a company formed to go North, of which Miss Patti Ewing is the leading Singer. They hesitate about going, and yet hold on to her, so that we cannot interfere to get her."[52] Maneuverings like these illustrate the increasing professionalization and profitability of jubilee singing, such that management recruited talented singers without requiring them to enroll as students.

LATER INCARNATIONS AND IMPACT   The original Tennesseans raised $18,000 over three years for the erection of a building for Central Tennessee College.[53] After that they toured under the auspices of the Freedmen's Aid Society for three years, then reorganized as a private enterprise under J. W. Donavin's management. Figure 4.1 shows the company as of 1878. The Tennesseans toured for ten months out of the year, typically playing 256 engagements. Since the company regularly received more invitations to perform than they had time for (in the 1880–1881 season they had to refuse 163 requests), Donavin created two companies for the 1881–1882 season: Donavin's Original Tennesseans and

FIGURE 4.1. Although this poster is undated, Donavin's troupe would have made its fifth annual tour in 1878. Pictured here are *(from top, moving clockwise)* Leroy N. D. Pickett, who arranged some of the spirituals; Bella Sayler, Delia Scott, F. A. Stewart, J. A. Coleman, W. E. Thompson, Jasper Washington, Bertha Heathcock, and Jennie Robinson. Manager J. W. Donavin is in the middle. Library of Congress, minstrel poster collection.

Donavin's Famous Tennesseans, each troupe having nine singers. Donavin was careful to point out that there was no first or second, no good or bad—both companies were equal in merit.[54] (George White had similarly tried to meet demand by creating two companies of Fisk Jubilee Singers in fall 1872, but the plan proved financially unsustainable.)

Before the split into two companies, twenty-eight vocalists had cycled through the original Tennesseans, owing to "sickness, marriage, and various other reasons."[55] With the creation of a second company, it becomes difficult to trace the Tennesseans' career with accuracy. Not only were newspapers lax in reporting names of troupes and singers, but rival troupes purposely cultivated confusion by using similar names, such as the Tennessee Jubilee Singers, Tennessean Jubilee Singers, Tennessee Cabin Singers, and the like. Even the Fisk Jubilee Singers were sometimes referred to by their state of origin, so that "Tennessee" became a metonym for slave song in the public imagination. This put the original Tennesseans, like the Fisks before them, on the defensive. "Beware of the many imitators," warned the Tennesseans' 1883–1884 songster, in capital letters.

For these reasons it's difficult to say how long the Tennesseans performed. As Marvin Latimer Jr. notes, from about 1880 the Tennesseans relied less on spirituals in favor of cultivated vocal and instrumental music.[56] Pickett remained acting musical director until 1886, when he became musical director of the Wilberforce Concert Company. According to minstrel Ike Simond, the troupe was still touring in 1891 when Simond wrote his memoir. There's an advertisement for the "Original Tennessean Jubilee Singers" as part of a concert and lecture course for the 1895–1896 season sponsored by the Wichita Lyceum Association, and a notice of a Tennesseans troupe singing jubilee melodies in January 1896 in Wellington, Kansas; a February 1896 article notes that the Original Tennessean Jubilee Singers are "in the twentieth year of their success,"[57] which coincides with the year (1876) that the troupe began performing independently of Central Tennessee College. No notices appear after 1896. The Tennesseans were the longest-lived continuously performing jubilee troupe to emerge in the immediate aftermath of the Fisks' initial success and were among the earliest to sustain a performing career independent of an educational institution. Even as they expanded their repertory to other genres, they never abandoned spirituals.

. . .

Like the Hamptons, the Tennesseans brought a new repertory of spirituals before the public. The Tennesseans' initial success derived from their folkloric performances. Like the Hamptons they had a shouter, they contextualized their spirituals in concert through stories, and their singing style featured gritty timbres, bodily movement, heterophony, and some improvisation. If individual Fisk and Hampton singers helped arrange their spirituals, their contributions remained unacknowledged, in contrast to the Tennesseans' Leroy Pickett. The Tennesseans' innovations, combined with the high quality of their performances and Donavin's astute management, set the troupe apart in the jubilee marketplace and attracted even those listeners who had already heard the Jubilee Singers.

Naturally, the Tennesseans matured over time. By 1875 reviews began to shift their emphasis from authenticity to musical excellence. One reviewer quoted a gentleman who said, "If they were white, they could all get first-class positions as vocalists." To this the tenor of the troupe reportedly remarked, "That gentleman would be almost handsome if he were black!" Concluded the reviewer, "The only distinction we see between the Tennesseans and an extra good troupe of white singers is, that the Tennesseans appear to have retained their modesty, while professional singers among our own race seldom do for as long a time."[58]

Imitators

Although the Fisk Jubilee Singers were in England from May 1873 until May 1874, their memory was kept alive stateside through newspaper reports of their triumphs and through sales of *Jubilee Songs*. Having set the standard for all who followed in their wake, they did their part to popularize spirituals even in absentia, and they remained the standard against which all others were judged. No one could rival the Fisks on their own terms. The Hamptons and Tennesseans didn't even try, opting instead for more folk-inflected identities. Other troupes competed by imitating the sound and business model of the Fisks, with varying degrees of success. The imitators may not have contributed to the evolving style of spirituals in concert performance, but they played an important role in establishing a jubilee industry.

The Hyers Sisters

As African American singers of art music, Anna Madah (1855–1925) and Emma Louise Hyers (1857–1899) had little competition when they began their concert career in the 1860s.[59] Raised in Sacramento, California, they received private classical training in voice and piano and made their debut at the ages of twelve and ten, performing with their parents as a family act at the Metropolitan Theater in Sacramento.[60] Over the next several years they performed locally, honing their skills and attracting admirers. Under the management of their father, Samuel, they began a cross-country tour in 1871 that would take them to New York and Boston, where they intended to further their musical education.

The sisters experienced an ambivalent reception in the East. The timing of their arrival in 1872 was overshadowed by the newly celebrated Fisk Jubilee Singers, as demonstrated by their joint performance at the World's Peace Jubilee described at the beginning of this chapter. Rather than go it alone, the Hyers sisters partnered with tenor Wallace King and Luca brothers John and Alexander of the Luca Family Singers to form a Grand Colored Operatic

Concert Troupe. Despite winning praise for its artistry, the troupe played to extremely small audiences during the first half of 1873. At a June concert in Reading, Pennsylvania, there was a meager audience, despite the reviewer's unqualified praise for the sisters' execution of "gems" from the "masters" of Straus, Balfe, Flotow, Verdi, and others. In Wilmington, Delaware, that same month they delayed the start of their concert at the Opera House to wait for an audience. "The number of persons in the hall not exceeding fifty, the most of whom were in the gallery, it was announced . . . that there were not enough present to warrant . . . proceeding with the performance," and those who had come received refunds. Even black audiences seemed apathetic; the *New York Sun* noted that "only a handful" of blacks were present for a March concert, with most of the applause coming from the white audience. The *Brooklyn Eagle* offered a forthright explanation for the sparse attendance: "The fact is these vocalists are too much above the popular style of camp meeting songs of the Jubilee singers to attract the church people, and not artistic enough to suit the patrons of fashionable concerts."[61]

The Hyers sisters had little choice but to accede to the demands of the marketplace. By the second half of 1873 they had added spirituals to their repertory, joining the swelling ranks of jubilee singers. Brooklynites gave the sisters and their expanded repertory a warm reception during two weeks at the end of September and beginning of October 1873. The Hyers sisters' initial advertising was (likely intentionally) misleading and seemed to reflect some disquiet over their new direction:

JUBILEE-SINGERS.
THE HYER SISTERS,
OF THE SOUTH (Colored),
Assisted by Jubilee Singers, will
Give a concert at
SIMPSON M.E. CHURCH.[62]

"South" and "Colored" guaranteed authenticity, and "Jubilee Singers" was meant to confuse patrons aware of the Fisk and Hampton students' relationship with Beecher's Plymouth Church. The following *Brooklyn Eagle* puff piece attempts to promote the sisters as part of the jubilee phenomenon:

People who have a taste for what is known as "Jubilee singing" will have another and, perhaps for a long time, a final opportunity of hearing it to-night at the Simpson M. E. Church. The programme includes the Southern music which has in recent years attracted attention and curiosity when illustrated by actual Southern singers. The "Ethiopian minstrelsy," long offered as genuine, was a bald counterfeit. Just about the time the counterfeit began to lose favor, the real began to find it. Hence the popularity of Jubilee singers here and abroad. Several of them to-night will assist the Hyer sisters, whose performances have heretofore been heard in Brooklyn with marked approval.[63]

The Hyers sisters quickly discarded their initial tentativeness and fully embraced jubilee singing. The day after their concert the *Eagle* declared, "some of those present thought it superior to that of the Jubilee Singers." By the end of the month they proudly billed themselves as "the Hyers Sisters (colored) and Jubilee Singers of California," claiming that their musical abilities were "equal, if not superior, to the celebrated Jubilee Singers or Hampden [*sic*] Students."[64]

Success followed them into 1874. In June they won rave reviews for a concert of art and jubilee songs in Vermont, the reviewer proclaiming the first vocal piece, from the cultivated tradition, "an elocutionary as well as vocal triumph." In praising the jubilee singing he wrote:

No one can wonder any longer at the unexampled success which has attended the jubilee singers in this country and in Europe. Steal Away, Judgment Day, Nobody knows what trouble I see, Lord; I'm a rolling, Mary and Martha, and Swing low, sweet chariot, cannot be described. The jubilee singing must be heard to be appreciated.[65]

"Jubilee singers" was now an established category of performers, and spirituals had become popular music.

The "Jubilee Singers" appearing with the Hyers sisters were tenor Wallace King, baritone John Luca, and pianist Alexander C. Taylor, all three of whom had been performing with the sisters since late 1871.[66] Exactly which spirituals the sisters sang remains unknown; the few existing reviews name the art music selections but refer only generically to the "jubilee songs" and the sisters' vocal excellence.

In order to sustain their careers, the Hyers sisters became occasional jubilee singers, imitating the groups who were drawing the larger crowds in the East. Like the Fisk Jubilee Singers, they had begun by performing cultivated music, but gained financial success only when they sang "the music of their race." By refusing to endorse the Hyers sisters' programming of art song, white America "forced them back upon the resources of their folk tradition," as Berndt Ostendorf has written—a move that assumed all black people shared one tradition.[67] The sisters went on to play an important role as popularizers of the spiritual, upholding the highest musical standards in all their repertory. In addition to their concerts, in the late 1870s they incorporated spirituals into their popular music dramas with social and political themes rooted in black experience (see chap. 7).

Other Imitators

Many of the jubilee troupes that materialized in 1873–1874 received little press coverage; at best a stray program or poster survives in archives. It was one thing to sing on behalf of a black school sponsored by a powerful missionary organization; it was quite another to sing on behalf of a little-known organization in a far-away southern town. Whereas the management of the Fisks, Hamptons, Tennesseans, and Hyers sisters worked tirelessly to promote their enterprises, smaller troupes, lacking such resources, often couldn't even pay for a two-line concert announcement in the local paper or for printed programs. The lack of coverage by black newspapers also contributed to the invisibility of the poorer troupes, for black newspapers weren't a significant source of information about entertainers until the late 1870s, once freed slaves had become literate in large numbers. Even then, many black newspapers were victims of short life spans and poor preservation. The richest surviving sources regarding entertainment cover the period 1887 and beyond, just as the jubilee phenomenon was fading—for example the *New York Age* (1887), *Indianapolis Freeman* (1883), and *Chicago Defender* (1905).

Consequently, little is known about many of the rival troupes, a good number of which foundered after short careers. Some were legitimate, others were con artists. The Freedmen from the First Baptist Church in Richmond, Virginia, for example, traded on a superficial similarity to the Fisk Jubilee Singers to attract audiences. Conducted by a Mr. C. H. Osborn, their program at Boston's Tremont Temple in June 1873 featured about fifteen men and women singing some "Southern merits," although apparently jubilee songs were in scarce evidence. The *Boston Daily Globe* was not impressed, noting that there were "few of the pieces in which the colored people excel, the programme being made up of anthems and concerted pieces familiar to all church choirs 'up North.'"[68] The reviewer's comment suggests that the singers didn't know their "musical place"—a criticism that had dogged the Hyers sisters when they first came east.

The following overview briefly introduces the legitimate jubilee groups that are known to have emerged in 1873 and 1874.

SHAW JUBILEE SINGERS Shaw Collegiate Institute (Raleigh, North Carolina) was a Baptist institution for the education of freedmen founded by the Reverend Henry Martin Tupper (white), who served as its president from 1865 until his death in 1893. The school began in temporary quarters; the institute was formalized in 1870, and in 1875 it was renamed Shaw University, with a curriculum similar to that of Fisk.[69] The Shaw Jubilee Singers, sometimes referred to as the North Carolina Colored Vocalists, were short-lived, touring the Northeast and Canada from August to December of 1873. The troupe consisted of thirteen male and female students who were preparing to become teachers in the South, and were accompanied by Tupper as well an unidentified music teacher. Two puff items from Vermont compared them favorably with the Fisk Jubilee Singers.[70]

WILMINGTON JUBILEE SINGERS "Hamptons Eclipsed," claimed the ad. "The Jubilee Singers, under the leadership of Prof. Payne, of Howard University, Washington, D.C., will give a grand concert for the benefit of the 2d M. E. Church" at the Music Hall on 25 March 1874. "Native Warblers from the banks of the Suwanee, Santee and Pearl, in their glorious soul-stirring Melodies, rendered with all the native pathos peculiar to this music loving and gifted race."[71] The Wilmington Jubilee Singers, who numbered between ten and twelve, were an independent troupe purportedly from the "Normal School" in Wilmington, North Carolina; they seem to have organized at the beginning of 1874.[72] ("Prof. Payne" isn't mentioned in any other notices and remains unidentified.) Until 1876 their concerts consisted of jubilee songs and costumed tableaus of slave life that were in no way caricatures, as their publicity took care to point out. Henry Ward Beecher, who had given a helping hand to several jubilee groups, did the same for the Wilmingtons.[73] Although jubilee singing remained a mainstay, in 1876 some of their entertainments took on the flavor of a variety show, the likely influence of having toured with a production of *Uncle Tom's Cabin* (see chap. 8, and web table 4.4).

NEW ORLEANS JUBILEE SINGERS Confusingly, the New Orleans Jubilee Singers were named not for their place of origin—Petersburg, Virginia—but rather for the object of their charity. Most of what is known about them is contained in Lynn Abbott's article on the New Orleans University Singers (a different, later group that actually was from New Orleans).[74] The New Orleans Jubilee Singers toured from 1873 through 1877, singing in churches from Virginia to southern Michigan, throughout New England, in eastern Canada, and by 1877 throughout the Deep South. Their leader was the Reverend Joseph Pollard, an African American, who was ordained in the African Methodist Episcopal Church and sang bass with the troupe. They numbered six members at most, and the women sometimes appeared alone as a quartet. Pollard intended to donate the troupe's earnings to various charitable enterprises benefitting the freedmen of New Orleans, but it isn't clear whether this actually happened. They did donate to charitable causes, however, principally the churches in which they sang. They published a booklet of spirituals in 1876 consisting of lyrics only; about two-thirds of the songs were in the Fisk repertory, although over time their repertory of spirituals seemed to diversify (see web table 4.4, Biographical Dictionary of Jubilee Troupes). Pollard may have been the first black leader of a group of jubilee singers, and his troupe was the earliest, or one of the earliest, troupes to tour without institutional sponsorship. Their concerts followed the Fisk model of mostly spirituals, with a hymn and parlor song or two in each part.

JACKSON JUBILEE SINGERS   In 1874 a group of five men and five women billing themselves the "the Famous Colored Jubilee Singers" from Jackson University, Jackson, Tennessee, appeared on the scene. Apparently the school never existed and the singers were from New York, although they seemingly staged a legitimate entertainment. Of their performance at a Presbyterian church in Brooklyn on 15 December 1874 the *Brooklyn Eagle* wrote, "the staging elicited loud plaudits from the numerous audience, and the lengthy programme was thoroughly enjoyed by all present."[75]

The troupe clearly meant to confuse concertgoers in their advertisements, which promised the "famous colored jubilee singers" without further identification, as the Hyers sisters had done. The inclusion of a program for the Jackson Jubilee Singers in the AMA Archives dated only Tuesday, 17 November [1874] shows that the parent organization was keeping an eye on Fisk's competitors.[76] The program's description of the Jacksons' concert was probably more elaborate than what was delivered: the staging consisted of tableaux that recreated "southern scenes and incidents of days gone by," such as "the glorious old-time Colored camp Meetings in the far South in former years" and the "magnolia groves and cotton fields of the Sunny South." The singers were described as "Native Warblers! From the banks of the Suwanee, Santee and Pearl [identical to the wording in the Wilmington Jubilee Singers' ad]. . . . Formerly Slaves, they give the best and truest picture of Slave Life on the Plantations of the Far South." Their claim to "authenticity" emulated that of the Tennesseans.

The Jacksons' program was unusual in having three parts rather than two (which explains the *Eagle* describing it as "lengthy"):

PART FIRST.

1—I CUM FOR TO TELL YOU 'BOUT HOW I CUM ALONG.

2—GWINE TO BE A MEETIN' HERE TO NIGHT.

3—SHINE ALONG, (de Spirit is de Ingineer.)

4—ALL DEM DAYS DUN GONE.

5—GWINE TO RIDE UP IN DE CHARIOT. [Seward 1872a]

6—BEEN LISTENING ALL DE NIGHT LONG. [Seward 1872a]

7—OLD SATAN TRIED FOR TO TEMPT MY MIND.

8—YOU BETTAH DUN HUMBLE YESELF.

PART SECOND.

9—WAY DOWN UPON THE SUWANEE RIVER, (by request) [Stephen Foster, 1851]

10—I'LL HEAR DE TRUMPET SOUND IN DE MORNIN'. [Seward 1872a]

11—PETER, GO RING DEM BELLS. [Fenner 1874]

12—BRETHREN DON'T GET WEARY. [Fenner 1874]

13—ROLL, JORDAN, ROLL. [Seward 1872a]

14—SWING LOW, SWEET CHARIOT. [Seward 1872a; Fenner 1874]

PART THIRD.

15—TURN BACK PHARAOH'S ARMY. [Seward 1872a]

16—MARY AND MARTHA HAVE JUST GONE ALONG. [Seward 1872b]

17—THE LITTLE OCTOROON. [George Frederick Root, 1866]

18—GO DOWN MOSES. [Seward 1872a]

19—I WANT TO DIE LIKE A LAZARUS DIED.

20—ALL I WANT IS A LITTLE MORE FAITH. [Seward 1872a]

Of these eighteen spirituals (two of the pieces being prewar parlor songs), seven may have been new to the public. The remainder had already been performed by the Fisk and Hampton troupes and printed in their song books (as indicated by the sources in brackets).

In the years immediately after the Civil War, concert promotion was in a state of transition. Before the war, artists achieved success through a combination of luck and endorsements by well-chosen patrons. After the war artists began to hire managers to arrange their tours and publicity, although patron endorsements still played a vital role.[77] The Jacksons' attempt to pass themselves off as the Fisk Jubilee Singers extended to their cooptation of Fisk testimonials as well, which selectively quoted Henry Ward Beecher's 1872 letter to James Redpath ("The Jubilee Singers will charm any audience, they make their mark by giving the plantation hymns as only *they* can sing them").[78] Such deception frustrated George White and the Fisk Jubilee Singers, as it did Beecher, who announced an appearance by the Fisk singers at his church in early 1875 with these words: "We have coming to us the Jubilee Singers. A spurious band stole their name and their recommendations, among others mine, and went around the country swindling the people. This is not the bogus: this is the genuine gold."[79] Imitators forced the Jubilee Singers to doubly assert their authenticity: first as genuine ex-slaves, and second as the original Jubilee Singers.

The Jacksons also tried to ride the coattails of the Tennesseans, prompting a "Caution to the Public" from manager J. W. Donavin, who warned of a singing band using the Tennesseans' name and claiming to be from Jackson, Tennessee. "This same band," wrote Donavin, "was organized in New York, and assumed the name of Famous Jubilee Singers, converting to their use complimentary notices from Henry W. Beecher, President Grant, and others."[80]

The Jackson Jubilee Singers seems to have lasted only a year, although their chameleonlike identity makes them hard to track. Their program claims it is their "last season"—but "first and last" was perhaps more accurate. Around the turn of the century a new Jackson Jubilee troupe, founded by Robert G. Jackson (1880–1929), toured the Chautauqua circuit, but it had no connection to its 1870s namesake.[81]

THE OLD ORIGINAL NORTH CAROLINIANS The North Carolinians toured from at least 1874 to May 1877 and perhaps later; the only notices located are from midwestern newspapers. A review dated 19 August 1874 claimed that they "will not compare with the Tennesseans in culture and training," although which "Tennesseans" isn't clear. "With one or two exceptions" the singers were "elderly persons, and taken right from the plantations," giving "a more accurate representation of the musical negro race than if they had been more thoroughly trained."[82] Another writer confirmed that the voices were uncultivated but pointed out that their earnestness won them "frequent and hearty applause" from full houses over two nights.[83] A year of touring (and perhaps an infusion of new singers) apparently improved them, for in September 1875 a reviewer claimed, "Mr. Johnson, as a basso, has few superiors anywhere, while the lady next to him . . . had as sweet a soprano voice as we ever heard."[84]

The troupe was managed by Professor T. H. Brand (white), a sometime composer of parlor songs and the principal of the Madison (Wisconsin) Vocal Academy and Music Institute from at least 1868 to 1874. According to the U.S. Census he was born about 1837 and from at least 1870 to 1880 listed Dane, Wisconsin (just outside of Madison), as his home, with the occupation of "music leader."[85] Brand may not have been with the troupe at its outset. As a program from the second half of 1876 or early 1877 claims, the troupe of "five gentlemen and five ladies" was founded "over three years ago" (around 1874) by "the far-famed revival singer, Aunty Chloe, of Wilmington, N.C., since which time they have been traveling in the Western States" (see figure 4.2). This program for their "third annual tour" acknowledges the troupe's debt to "Aunt Chloe" for many of the songs they sing. Its announcement that "Prof. T. H. Brand" is engaged to manage them suggests a recently established relationship, although

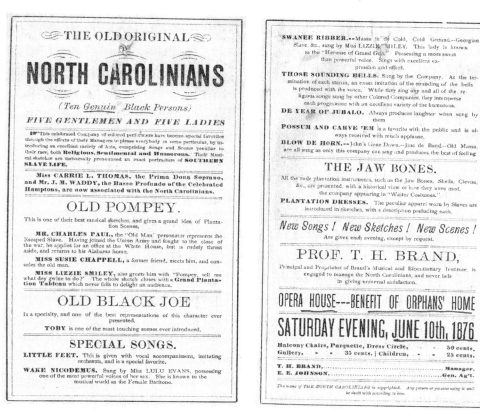

FIGURE 4.2. The first two pages of a four-page program for an 1876 entertainment by the North Carolinians. The troupe sang dignified renditions of spirituals as well as parlor songs; the jaw bones, plantation costumes, and sketches were the influence of minstrelsy. Courtesy of the Chemung County Historical Society, Elmira, New York.

there's evidence he was with them as early as 1875.[86] Interestingly, the second page of their program gives notice that "the name THE NORTH CAROLINIANS is copyrighted."

The third annual tour also featured the engagement of two jubilee singers with former connections to the Hampton Institute Singers: Carrie L. Thomas, billed as the prima donna soprano (a former student in Philadelphia of Elizabeth Taylor Greenfield), and James M. Waddy, the Hamptons' basso profundo. The troupe also celebrated the powerful voice of their singer Lizzie Smiley, who appeared in sketches and sang solos. Although the program shown in figure 4.2 resembles that of a minstrel show more than a jubilee concert, it does note that "while they sing any and all of the religious songs sung by other Colored Companies, they intersperse each programme with an excellent variety of the humorous."

The troupe sang for many charities but had a rocky road while traveling, dogged by the Ku Klux Klan. They apparently dissolved in late 1877; by the 1880s manager Brand had moved on to other musical pursuits.

SHEPPARD'S COLORED JUBILEE SINGERS Sheppard's Jubilee Singers formed in 1874, according to an 1883 program announcing that the group had been in existence for nine years.[87] The director, Andrew Sheppard, was said to have been thirty years a slave, "formerly the property of Gen. Robert E. Lee, at Arlington, Va., emancipated by Abraham Lincoln's Great Proclamation of Freedom." His troupe, also former slaves, "make no pretentions as to musical abilities, they being unable to read or write"—a claim that exploits their "authenticity."[88] Sheppard joined Pollard as a pioneer black director of a jubilee troupe. The troupe maintained its existence by walking the line between jubilee concertizing and variety performance (see chap. 8 for more on their later performances).

Concluding Thoughts

By 1873 a jubilee entertainment industry was taking shape, with the Fisks, Hamptons, and Tennesseans as its pillars. Innovative groups like the Hamptons and Tennesseans, who adopted the Fisks' business model but forged their own distinctive sounds and repertories, were essential to this new industry's prosperity and eventual maturation. So too were the imitators, whose ever-increasing presence helped establish new norms, especially in the adoption of minstrel elements in their entertainments, veering away from the Fisks' and the Hamptons' service-of-song model. Jubilee groups continued to multiply like sparrows, as the New York Clipper phrased it, for the rest of the decade and into the early 1880s.[89] Table 4.1 lists in rough chronological order groups that formed between 1871 and 1890 according to best evidence; further details about these groups can be found in the "Biographical Dictionary of Jubilee Groups" (see website table 4.4). Inconsistent spellings, name changes, and deliberate attempts to confuse the public complicate their identification as well as description of their career trajectories.

Religion greased the machinery of the earliest jubilee troupes. Missionary organizations sponsored them, ministers promoted them, and as a result white audiences largely accepted them. In 1873 the Methodists broke the American Missionary Association's initial stranglehold on jubilee singing. Before long

TABLE 4.1. Jubilee groups in rough chronological order of formation

1871

Fisk Jubilee Singers (original), representing Fisk University, Nashville, TN, and the American Missionary Association

1872

Canaan Jubilee Singers, independent

1873

Carolina Singers

(Donavin's) Tennesseans, representing Central Tennessee College, Nashville, TN; independent from 1876

Hampton Institute Singers, representing Hampton Institute, Hampton, VA

Hyers Sisters (various troupes), independent

Jubilee Singers, representing Shaw Collegiate Institute, Raleigh, NC

National Jubilee Singers, independent?

New Orleans Jubilee Singers, independent

1874

Jackson Jubilee Singers, independent

Jubilee Singers of Virginia, independent?

Old Original North Carolinians, independent

Sheppard's Jubilee Singers, independent

Wayland Seminary Jubilee Singers (also known briefly as Jubilee Singers of Virginia); representing Wayland Seminary (Baptist), Washington, DC

Wilmington Jubilee Singers, independent

1875

Centennial Jubilee Singers, representing Storer College, WV (also known as Gatewood's Jubilees and Harper's Ferry Jubilee Singers)

Juvenile Jubilee Singers (a generic name)

Nashville Jubilee Singers (a generic name used by several troupes)

Tennessee Jubilee Singers (a generic name used by several troupes)

1876

Alabama Jubilee Singers, independent

Arlington Jubilee Singers, independent

Centennialites, independent

(Coleman's) Louisiana Jubilee Singers, independent

Duncan's Old Dominion Slave Troupe, independent

Georgia Jubilee Singers, independent

Louisiana Jubilee Singers, independent

New Orleans University Singers (or University Singers of New Orleans, New Orleans Jubilee Singers, New Orleans Centennial Singers), representing La Teche Orphans' Home, New Orleans, LA

TABLE 4.1. Continued

North Carolina Jubilee Singers, independent
Richmond Jubilee Singers, independent (possibly same as Louisiana Jubilee
    Singers)
Slavin's (Georgia) Jubilee Singers, independent
Southern Jubilee Singers, independent
Virginia Choristers (also used the names National Sable Quintet of Jubilee
    Singers; Sable Quintette Club), independent offshoot of Hampton Institute
    Singers
Virginia Jubilee Singers (likely a generic name), independent

1877
Great Sable Quartet, with Slave Troupe, independent
Hopkins Colored Troubadours (also used the name Savannah Jubilee
    Singers), independent
Kentucky Jubilee Singers, independent
Maryland Jubilee Singers, independent
Old Tennessee Jubilee Singers, independent
Southern Jubilee Singers, began with *Uncle Tom's Cabin*, became independent
Southern Warblers, independent?
Virginia Choristers, independent

1878
Crescent Jubilee Singers, independent
Troubadour Negro Quartette, independent

1879
Canadian Jubilee Singers, independent
Charleston Jubilee Serenaders, independent
Fisk Jubilee Singers (George White director), independent
Home Jubilee Singers

1880
Ideal Colored Troubadours (also Ideal Jubilee Singers, Ideal Colored
    Company), independent
Indianians, independent

1881
Memphis University Students/Singers, independent
Norfolk Jubilee Singers, independent
Slayton's Jubilee Singers, independent, sponsored by Slayton Lyceum Bureau
Stewart-Wilberforce Concert Company

TABLE 4.1. Continued

1882

Fisk Jubilee Singers (Frederick Loudin, director), independent
Fisk Jubilee Singers (initially Maggie Porter Cole, then Charles Mumford, director), independent
Olympian Colored Male Quartette, independent
Pine Jubilee Singers, Hampton College, Hampton, VA
(Thearle's) Original Nashville Students, independent

1883

Glazier's Jubilee Singers / Glazier's Carolinians, independent
Walker Quintet, independent

1884

Canadian Jubilee Singers, independent
Texas Jubilee Singers, independent
Tuskegee Institute Quartet, Tuskegee Institute, Tuskegee, AL
Virginia and Texas Jubilee Singers, independent (consolidation of the two troupes)
Zion Jubilee Singers (also known as Rossville Jubilee Singers), representing Zion Church, Rossville, Staten Island, NY

1885

Excelsior Jubilee Singers, representing Christian Bible College, New Castle, KY

Note: Groups are alphabetized by year for convenience. Some of these groups were short-lived, but many had careers of a decade or even three decades (in various incarnations), as did, for example, the Fisk Jubilee Singers, Hamptons, Tennesseans, Nashville Students, New Orleans Jubilee Singers, and Sheppard's Jubilee Singers. Some groups toured mainly abroad (e.g., White's as well as Loudin's Fisk Jubilee Singers). See web table 4.4, Biographical Dictionary of Jubilee Concert Troupes, for more on these and other troupes through the turn of the century.

singers who had belonged to institutional groups struck out on their own, and unaffiliated troupes sang for their own profit, led by such entrepreneurs as Samuel Hyers, Joseph Pollard, and Andrew Sheppard.

The term "jubilee song" gradually became a convention, so that by 1873–1874 the public understood "jubilee singer" as a category of performer signifying young adult black performers of spirituals. Spirituals became the first mass market music to have originated in black experience. With the Fisks having so thoroughly covered Ohio and the northeast on their tours, succeeding troupes toured the west: Michigan, Wisconsin, Minnesota, and even Iowa. The Tennessee Jubilee Singers under Lew Johnson had successful tours of California in 1876 and 1877, appearing in Sacramento, Oakland, San Francisco, and Los Angeles.

Jubilee song was transmitted far and wide. Although groups from Tennessee or Virginia might perform in their hometowns, the southern limit for most touring groups in the 1870s was Maryland or Washington, DC. By the 1880s, however, troupes were expanding their routes to Texas, Missouri, Kansas, and points west, largely thanks to lyceum bureaus.

The lyceum movement began in New England in the 1820s offering lectures as a means of adult education, and it quickly spread throughout the nation. In the late 1860s centralized bureaus were formed to market performers to local lyceum committees, which might include YMCAs, local lecture courses, women's clubs, church clubs, and the like. By "leasing" performers to local committees, the central bureaus encouraged them to embrace new marketing strategies and new categories of performers.[90] In 1875 lyceum bureaus started including jubilee troupes on their rosters, as lyceums devoted greater shares of their programming to entertainment.

James Redpath, whose Boston Lyceum Bureau (est. 1868) was one of the most preeminent, organized a Musical Department in 1872, and in 1875 the Redpath Lyceum Bureau became the first lyceum to include African American entertainers in its annual series when it signed the Hyers sisters. They were the only black presence on the season's slate. They weren't a main attraction but rather sang their ballads and jubilee songs either after the lecturer had spoken or as the third part of an evening of vocal music by white companies. Other musical offerings included European opera singer Teresa Titiens supported by the Strakosch Concert Company and Patrick Gilmore's Grand Military Band.[91]

Before long other bureaus followed suit. Henry L. Slayton's Lyceum Bureau, founded in Chicago in 1874, presented the Louisiana Jubilee Singers in its 1877–1878 season, as well as the Hutchinson Family Singers. In 1881 Slayton even founded his own black concert company: Slayton's Colored Ideals. Redpath's Lyceum Bureau signed the Original Nashville Students, another jubilee company, in the 1880s. The Nashville Students was the first music troupe to appear in Wood River, Idaho, in 1884 under the bureau's auspices, and it was hoped that if successful, then other "first-class organizations" would follow.[92] George White used Williams' Lecture and Musical Bureau (founded 1869, Boston) to manage his reconstituted troupe of Fisk Jubilee Singers in 1880.[93]

Lyceum bureaus expanded the reach of jubilee troupes while lightening the load of their managers. At the same time they conferred status on the jubilee troupes, who appeared in series that also featured the leading European and American luminaries of the time. Patrick Gilmore's National Peace Jubilee had provided an opportunity for ordinary Americans to perform next to top European talent, and in a sense, as Sara Lampert notes, Redpath continued Gilmore's project, "establishing a longstanding corporate structure to solicit and facilitate the professional careers of rising native talent alongside those of established celebrities."[94] It was, in effect, an assault on America's longstanding sense of artistic inferiority in relation to Europe.

Chautauquas, also like Gilmore's jubilees, juxtaposed celebrities with local talent. The Chautauqua movement began as a training school for Sunday school teachers at Lake Chautauqua, New York, in August 1874. Over time it expanded beyond Sunday school to a general education enterprise, much in the manner of a lyceum, and many jubilee groups appeared under Chautauqua auspices. In fact in August 1880 George White's independent Fisk Jubilee Singers sang at the National Sunday School Assembly at Chautauqua with a chorus of three hundred, an orchestra, and various soloists, one of whom was the famous gospel hymnodist Philip Phillips, whose service of song was a model for the original Fisk students' musical programs.[95] By late century and into the early twentieth, Chautauquas were one of the major venues for the presentation of jubilee song.

The jubilee industry had all of the competitive pressures of the broader entertainment marketplace. Managers competed with each other for singers and for audiences. Troupes exploited each other, appropriating repertory and even endorsements, so that managers felt compelled to protect their brand. Private groups were formed. Entrepreneurial blacks became troupe managers and arrangers. "Jubilee singer" became a new, viable career. As the jubilee marketplace grew, it splintered, with some groups stressing their cultivation (performing with lyceums and Chautauquas) and others exploiting the white public's fascination with slave life (in slave cabin concerts). Regardless of which route a troupe took—and many troupes took both—"authenticity" and "preservation" became their watchwords.

White listeners uncritically equated authenticity with lack of formal training and the lived experience of slavery. As Jon Cruz points out, this was partly a reaction to a central tenet of Transcendentalist thought: that "nature harbored truth and that social conventions tended to obscure rather than reveal" it. The "romantic response to modernity enabled some to detach authenticity from its older moorings in traditional religious thought," leading to such concepts as the "noble Savage."[96] Jubilee singers represented one such formulation in the idealized slave, who as a "child of nature" was a fount of religious and emotional inspiration, and whose music offered a direct line to the heart, bypassing the brain and to a certain degree social convention. Jubilee troupes like the Hamptons communicated "authenticity" in a musical style that adopted aspects of folk performance. Troupes like the Tennesseans and North Carolinians, however, marketed "authenticity" in ethnographic renderings of the slave cabin and plantation, with costumes, props, and instruments like the bones—appropriating the tools of minstrelsy in an attempt to prove their own genuineness.

Even the Fisk Jubilee Singers, who began their career trying to avoid associations with slavery by singing white repertory, were forced to trade in the imagery of slavery to succeed, as were the Hyers sisters. The public embrace of spirituals had the unfortunate consequence of constraining black performers who wanted to perform classical music from the white tradition, forcing them to conform to white Americans' newly emerging understanding of what black music was.

The idea that blacks were natural musicians, and that music was the only "art" that they came by naturally, had long been received opinion among whites. Jubilee singing became a primary signifier of slavery in the public consciousness, and the racialization of spirituals became more deeply entrenched. As jubilee troupes marketed their authenticity, the purported representation of black life by white minstrels in blackface came to be seen as counterfeit, and audiences expressed a preference for minstrels who were genuinely black. Two primary associations attached to spirituals as a result of jubilee groups' marketing and programming: the southern plantation and the camp meeting. Just as these powerful songs were being released for all to enjoy, they became another vehicle of containment for the African Americans who performed them onstage.

Spirituals for the Masses

CHAPTER 5

The Minstrel Show Gets Religion

Nothing was sacred when it came to blackface performance, including religion.[1] Before the Civil War, religious topics surfaced in occasional pokes at cults and fads. There were parodies of the celebrated preacher Henry Ward Beecher, malaprop-laden stump speeches by "backwoods preachers," burlesques of the Shaking Quakers' contortions,[2] and secular songs featuring cameos by biblical characters (e.g., Dan Emmett's popular social satire "Jordan Is a Hard Road to Travel," in which David and Goliath materialize for no obvious reason).[3]

After the war, however, blackface performers found in religion a steady stream of subject matter tailor-made for comedic treatment, owing to several broad trends. One was the journalistic writing about black spirituals. White northerners who had streamed to Port Royal, South Carolina, during the war published descriptions of the black religious practices they encountered there, with particular emphasis on the ring shout and its spiritual fervor, manifested as bodily movement and "weird chanting." Such literary descriptions were supplemented on a small scale by the Hutchinson family, who had started singing spirituals in their concerts. These developments coincided with an emerging nostalgia among conservative, older-generation whites for the old-time Methodist camp meeting—where whites had "shouted" every bit as energetically as blacks. That nostalgia was in part a reaction to the modernizing reforms that were turning camp meetings into big business. By the 1870s, for example, the impromptu camp meeting in the wilderness was more likely a scheduled event at a large, permanent campground that had its own railway station, permanent cabins instead of tents, admission fees, and nearby commercial services such as restaurants, stores, and a post office. (An "enterprising showman" even beseeched the *New York Clipper* to publish a list of camp meetings with their dates and locations, so he could schedule his sideshows next door and poach the audience.) Camp meetings were incipient resorts, with the attendant social "problems" abhorred by the strictly religious: drinking, gambling, and males consorting with females.[4] Both interest in slave music and longing for the pre-modern camp meeting were embedded within a burgeoning postwar nostalgia, whether the object of longing was the "simple and happy plantation days of the sunny South," rural life in general, or the "home" idealized in the songs of Stephen Foster and others. The "beautiful land" celebrated in so many gospel hymns and spirituals also played into this sentiment.

Three songs nicely illustrate the postwar phenomenon of religious parody in its infancy and its evolution toward slave-themed entertainment: "Carry the News! We Are All Surrounded" (1870), "Rock'a My Soul" (1871), and "Contraband Children" (1872). Performed initially by whites in blackface, these songs replicate the musical style of black folk spirituals in their parody of a camp meeting. The story of "Carry the News" in particular shows how blackface entertainers were already drawing on musical styles and themes loosely related to those of spirituals, and how the public easily confused newly created popular songs with traditional folk songs. When the vogue of jubilee singing began to spread a few years later, minstrelsy was primed for a convergence and eventual merger with jubilee song. As black minstrel entertainers multiplied, white minstrels increasingly found that they had to cede their plantation-themed material to them.

"Carry the News"

"Carry the News! We Are All Surrounded" was created, developed, and performed by three white males: blackface comedians Walter Bray and Charley Howard wrote the music and lyrics, respectively, and Eddie Fox—violinist and orchestra leader for Simmons and Slocum's Minstrels—made the arrangement.

Howard's lyrics are a nonsensical mix of sacred and secular imagery. In the first two verses, "Martha wept and Mary cried" because "the good old man [massa? Lincoln?] has gone and died," abandoning his "darkies" as he answers the call of "Gabriel's trumpet." Verse 3, a non sequitur, is pure minstrel silliness: Adam and Eve climb a tree to get a better look at God, Eve steals an apple, and Adam gets stung by a bumblebee.[5] The melody has only four pitches—B♭, C, D, and G—and is characterized by numerous leaps of a third. The verse is highly repetitive, consisting of a two-measure statement (a) answered by the two-measure internal refrain "we're all surrounded" (b), with the whole ab phrase repeated four times to comprise a sixteen-measure verse (see example 5.1). Summarizing the form as ||:abababab:|| underscores the song's reliance on direct repetition.

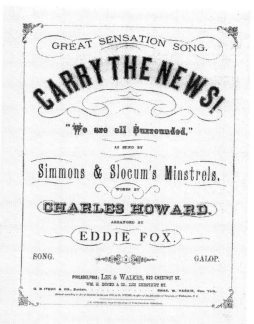

EXAMPLE 5.1. "Carry the News" (1870), a white minstrel parody of a black camp meeting spiritual. Courtesy of Lester S. Levy Collection of Sheet Music, Sheridan Libraries, Johns Hopkins University.

The musical relationship of "Carry the News" to the folk spiritual is located in its repetitive form, gapped scale, and modal harmony. Whereas the verse melody is accompanied by the expected tonic, dominant, and subdominant harmonies, the chorus surprises with modal progressions: it begins on the subdominant rather than the tonic (leading listeners to expect a change of key), then moves to the submediant and back to the subdominant before ending on the tonic. Furthermore, the sheet music renders the chorus as solo melody—perhaps as a matter of publishing economy—rather than the four-part close harmony that typified refrains of popular songs; in performance it was likely sung by several voices. A lively dance relieves the monotony of the verses and follows the formula of all minstrel songs, whose dance breaks were more stylistically similar to one other than to their "host" melodies. Indeed, the dance in "Carry the News" bears little relation to the vocal music, using all seven pitches of the scale, a chromatic passing tone, and tonic-dominant harmony exclusively.

Little is known about the composer, Walter Bray (born Baker; d. 25 February 1891, Fort Worth, Texas). He seems to have begun his long career in blackface comedy and dialect songs in the 1860s, working primarily as an independent performer in minstrelsy and variety from Boston to New Orleans to San Francisco. Of the ten songs composed by Bray on deposit at the Library of Congress, "Carry the News" is the earliest, and the only one with lyrics credited to another person: Virginia native Charley Howard (1826–1895). Howard began his career at the age of ten with a concert troupe that appeared in barns and churches throughout the South.[6] In maturity his fame rested on his realistic (at least to white audiences) portrayals of the "old darkie," perhaps informed by firsthand experiences during his formative years.

"Carry the News" became an immediate audience favorite upon its introduction by Simmons and Slocum's Minstrels on 29 August 1870. Lew Simmons (1838–1911) and E. N. "Ned" Slocum (1836–1895) were former members of Carncross and Dixie's Minstrels, Philadelphia's revered resident minstrel troupe, but an altercation with their managers caused the duo to resign and erect their own hall—the Arch Street Opera House. On opening night nearly eighteen hundred people crowded the new theater to see what the renegades had to offer. The curtains opened to reveal seventeen men in black pants and coats with white vests. On the left spectators saw the vocal soloists and a quartet; on the right, the principal instrumentalists (violins, clarinets, cornets, and double bass). In the middle was interlocutor Ned Slocum, flanked by endmen Lew Simmons (tambo) and Willis P. "Billy" Sweatnam (bones). After an overture, an opening chorus, and three solo songs, Simmons sang "Carry the News," and a hit was born.[7] Audience demand kept the song in their repertory throughout the

1870–1871 season and propelled it into print: Philadelphia publisher R. Wittig published a sheet music edition in November 1870 with Simmons and Slocum on the front cover, and three additional arrangements followed in short order.[8]

Simmons may have introduced the song, but Welch, Hughes, and White's Minstrels transformed it into a cultural phenomenon at the end of 1870. The troupe leaders were Fayette Welch (born Patrick Walsh, 1838–1892; referred to as both Welch and Welsh in newspapers), Arthur "Archie" Hughes (1830–1881), and Cool White (born John Hodges, 1821–1891). They settled into the Brooklyn Opera House the first week of November 1870 for a run of several months. Exactly how Welch learned the song remains unknown, but he had ample opportunity. Perhaps he heard it when he and Walter Bray were paired as endmen in Allen and Pettingill's Minstrels in June 1870,[9] or perhaps he learned it from J. W. McAndrews, one of many variety performers that Welch and his partners hired every couple of weeks to refresh their show at the Brooklyn Opera House. McAndrews (born in Richmond, Virginia; 1831–1899), famous for his convincing impersonations of blacks, had performed "Carry the News" to good reviews in a variety show in Pittsburgh in September.[10] Or maybe Welch and his cohort saw Lew Simmons perform the song in Philadelphia; Welch later joined Simmons's troupe, and given the frequency with which performers quit and joined new troupes, Simmons and Welch may have known (of) each other before 1870.

In any case, Welch and his minstrels transformed "Carry the News" into a plantation sketch that closed the first part of their show. The first-part finale of a minstrel show was a transcendent moment, with all the performers and musicians engaged in extended singing, dancing, and comic business. What better context for energetic performance than a camp meeting scene? The finale was "given with the greatest applause" beginning the week of 12 December 1870. Nothing else could follow it—other than two or three repetitions every night. The *Brooklyn Eagle* declared it "one of the very best acts that has ever been put upon the stage," even better than Bryant's Minstrels' popular walk-around "Shoo Fly," which had become a classic in its own right.[11] The *New York Clipper* singled out Welch's and Hughes's impersonations of the "old Darkie" and the "Aunty," respectively. Newspaper notices began touting Bray's four-month-old song as traditional folk music:

A hit [has been] made in the old plantation refrain of "Carry the News to Mary." It is sung in the real old Virginia style, and brings down the house nightly.[12]

The Brooklyn Opera House has now the right of bragging on the inauguration of a minstrel sensation which may run through the country as "Shoo Fly" has done. We refer to the performance of the old camp-meeting refrain of "Carry the News to Mary," which is *encored* again and again nightly at Welch, White and Hughes' Opera House. . . . The singing, together with the growing excitement of the refrain, is enthusiastically applauded. "Carry the News to Mary," alone, draws hundreds to hear it sung.[13]

Endman Lew Simmons had presented "Carry the News" as a comic song, but Welch and company reinvented it as a camp meeting refrain, which along with their "authentic" delineations of plantation slaves gave audiences an entertaining glimpse into the unfettered religious life of southern blacks, who shouted, danced, sang, and strummed the banjo, with laughs and clowning galore. The centrality of this song to the entire show's success was underscored by advertisements that began to feature the song title—sometimes conspicuously (see figure 5.1A) and other times more subtly (see figure 5.1B).

Given the fervor surrounding "Carry the News"—nurtured by performers, audiences, and publicity agents alike—it isn't surprising that the song traveled across the East River and into Bryant's Opera House in New York in February 1871. Other minstrel troupes wrote to Welch asking for a copy of the act, and "Carry the News" journeyed westward. Manning's Minstrels performed it in Chicago from Welch's manuscript, and veteran minstrel Billy Emerson carried the news in a whimsical dance at Maguire's Opera House in San Francisco. (Emerson, it seems, isolated the dance from the sketch and gave it a life of its own. One newspaper observed that "Carry the News" was "now played at every ball by [Louis] Ballenberg," the famous impresario and future cofounder of the Cincinnati Grand Orchestra in 1872.)[14] Meanwhile Welch, Hughes, and White were forced to take their minstrel show—including "Carry the News"—on the road during February, March, and April while the Brooklyn Opera House closed for remodeling. As a result of these many borrowings and road tours the song, barely six months old, had spread to theaters across the nation by the beginning of 1871.[15] In 1872 Billy Emerson's California Minstrels were performing the sketch as the finale to the first part of their show.[16] The various sheet music editions brought the song into countless parlors as well. In short, "Carry the News" was transmitted formally through its manuscript as well as informally, through adaptation (as in the case of Emerson), as summarized in figure 5.2.

Even though Welch's group apparently dropped the song upon their return to the Brooklyn Opera House in April 1871 in favor of a complete change of program, the public continued to identify the song with them. For example, a *Brooklyn Eagle* article describing the theft of the troupe's wigs, costumes, and props bore the headline "Carry the News to Mary" (10 May 1871). The song had

```
            BROOKLYN OPERA HOUSE,
            BROOKLYN OPERA HOUSE,
            BROOKLYN OPERA HOUSE,
            BROOKLYN OPERA HOUSE,
    JUNCTION OF FULTON AND FLATBUSH AVES,
    JUNCTION OF FULTON AND FLATBUSH AVES,
              THE TOWN TALK,
              THE TOWN TALK,
              THE TOWN TALK,
              THE TOWN TALK,
                  CARRY
                  CARRY
                  CARRY
                  CARRY
                   THE
                   THE
                   THE
                   THE
                  NEWS
                  NEWS
                  NEWS
                  NEWS
                   TO '
                   TO
                   TO
                   TO
                  MARY
                  MARY
                  MARY
                  MARY
         CARRY THE NEWS TO MARY,
         CARRY THE NEWS TO MARY,
         CARRY THE NEWS TO MARY,
         CARRY THE NEWS TO MARY,
WELCH,
WELCH,
WELCH,
WELCH,
                HUGHES,
                HUGHES,
                HUGHES,
                HUGHES,
                        & WHITE'S
                        & WHITE'S
                        & WHITE'S
                        & WHITE'S
        GREAT ORIGINAL SENSATION,
        GREAT ORIGINAL SENSATION,
        GREAT ORIGINAL SENSATION,
        GREAT ORIGINAL SENSATION,
            CARRY THE NEWS
            CARRY THE NEWS
            CARRY THE NEWS
            CARRY THE NEWS
               TO  MARY.
               TO  MARY.
               TO  MARY.
               TO  MARY.
        THE GREATEST HIT EVER MADE.
        THE GREATEST HIT EVER MADE.
        THE GREATEST HIT EVER MADE.
        THE GREATEST HIT EVER MADE.
```

FIGURE 5.1A. Excerpt from an advertisement for Welch, Hughes, and White's Minstrels in the *Brooklyn Eagle*, 17 Dec. 1870. The layout highlights the song's importance in attracting the public to the show, which featured a minstrel first part and variety acts in the second part.

BROOKLYN OPERA HOUSE.
Junction of Fulton and Flatbush aves.
A HAPPY NEW YEAR TO ALL!
"CARRY THE NEWS TO MARY."
WE STILL LIVE.
"CARRY THE NEWS TO MARY,"
AND
LET THE ECHO BE HEARD
IN THE FAR WEST
THAT
WELCH, HUGHES & WHITE'S
B R O O K L Y N   M I N S T R E L S .
STILL REMAIN
at their post, firmly established as a
PERMANENT BROOKLYN INSTITUTION,
CONDUCTED BY
BROOKLYN CITIZENS,
whose interests are identified with
T H E   G R O W T H   O F   B R O O K L Y N .
"CARRY THE NEWS TO MARY"
THAT
WELCH, HUGHES & WHITE
Have faithfully performed all promises made to the pub-
lic at the commencement of the season,
"CARRY THE NEWS TO MARY"
That in honor of the coming year
WELCH, HUGHES & WHITE'S
BROOKLYN MINSTRELS
Will give
TWO PERFORMANCES
M O N D A Y , January 2, 1871.
One in the
AFTERNOON at 2 ½ o'clock,
On which occasion they will introduce
WILLIS COBB,
Withy his Troupe of Trained
DOGS, GOATS AND MONKEYS,
The Screaming
HOLIDAY PANTOMIME
"THE SLIPPERY BOYS AND LIVELY POLICEMAN."
And their
Great Original Sensation
"CARRY THE NEWS TO MARY,"
Which has created the Greatest Furor ever known in the
Annals of Minstrelsy.
Orders for this great sensation are received daily from
THE LEADING MINSTREL TROUPES of the country.
This Great Original Sensation was performed
IN CHICAGO,
BY MANNING'S MINSTRELS,
"THE STAR TROUPE OF THE WEST,"
AT "MANNING'S OPERA HOUSE,"
Late DEARBORN'S THEATRE,"
From our Manuscript.
On Christmas Day, and has created there a sensation
UNPARALLELED IN THE HISTORY OF MINSTREL-
SY IN THE WEST.
"CARRY THE NEWS TO MARY,"
That after
SIXTEEN WEEKS' TRIUMPHANT SUCCESS,
WELCH, HUGHES & WHITE
Respectfully announce their intention of remaining at the
BROOKLYN OPERA HOUSE.

FIGURE 5.1B. Excerpt from an advertisement for Welch, Hughes, and White's Minstrels in the *Brooklyn Eagle*, 31 Dec. 1870. "Carry the News" appears throughout the ad as an "internal refrain"—a nineteenth-century version of subliminal advertising.

1870
Lew Simmons, Aug., Philadelphia
McAndrews, Sept., Pittsburgh
Manning's Minstrels, Dec., Chicago

Early 1871
Bryant's Opera House, Feb., New York
Billy Emerson dance, Feb., San Francisco

Sheet music published Nov. 1870 (Bray & Howard)
PLANTATION SKETCH:
Welch, Hughes, and White, Dec. 1870, Brooklyn
Welch, Hughes, and White tour Feb.–April 1871

Later 1871
Variety finale, June, Cincinnati
Simmons & Slocum, Sept., Philadelphia
Kelly & Leon, Sept., New York
Charley Howard, Sept., San Francisco
Georgia Minstrels, Nov.–Dec., Ohio

1872–73
Variety, Feb., Brooklyn
Emerson's Calif. Minstrels, June 1872
Walter Bray, Sept., Cincinnati
Johnny Weaver, variety, Oct., Cincinnati
Carroll Boys, Jan. 1873, Chicago

FIGURE 5.2. Overview of those who helped carry the news, with ultimate destinations.

taken on a life of its own. It turned up as the finale to a variety bill in Cincinnati in June 1871 and brought the first part of two different minstrel shows to a close in September 1871: Simmons and Slocum's in Philadelphia (which may have been Welch's influence, since he performed with them after his troupe disbanded at the end of the 1870–1871 season), and Kelly and Leon's Minstrels at Lina Edwin's Theatre in New York. The song's lyricist, Charley Howard, also sang it that fall at the Alhambra Theatre in San Francisco.[17]

About a year after Welch introduced "Carry the News," an African American minstrel troupe called the Georgia Minstrels performed it. Black minstrel troupes started touring in the 1860s, although financial instability and racism frequently made for short-term careers. The Georgia Minstrels, formed in fall 1866, were the first troupe to have an enduring presence, aided by the fact that their manager, Charles B. Hicks (ca. 1840–1902), was light-skinned and able to pass for white. There were numerous troupes calling themselves "Georgia"—in fact Hicks had traveled with Brooker and Clayton's Georgia Minstrels just the year before—and over time the name was used so widely that "the Georgias" became a generic term for African American minstrels, much as "Tennesse-ans" had for jubilee singers in the 1870s.[18] By the mid-1870s there were at least twenty-eight companies of African American minstrels, perhaps more.[19]

The programs of Hicks's Georgia Minstrels were devoid of camp meeting themes in the 1860s, but once white troupes began performing imitations of camp meeting songs like "Carry the News," the Georgias followed suit. In November and December 1871 they programmed "Carry the News to Mary"—just weeks before Henry Ward Beecher introduced the Fisk Jubilee Singers to New York metropolitan audiences.[20] Wrote one reviewer, "The jubilee song by Jimmy Grace, 'Down in Carolina,' was immensely applauded, while the audience were almost carried away with the song, 'Carry the News to Mary.'"[21] The 1871–1872 season was a turning point for black minstrels. By programming "Carry the News" and other "jubilee material" (discussed later), audiences came to perceive them as the cultural owners of plantation material. As a result there was a gradual changing of the guard, with white minstrels ceding portrayal of slave life to "the genuine article."

A sampling of performances from the 1872–1873 season illustrates the song's continued popularity, which happened to coincide with the Fisk Jubilee Singers' rising fame:

Variety show at Hooley's Opera House, Brooklyn, February 1872 [unnamed performer]
Finale to first part, [Billy] Emerson's California Minstrels, Chicago, June 1872 [Welch, Hughes, and White had dissolved, and Fayette Welch was now a member of Emerson's company]
Walter Bray, performing with Rice's Minstrels, Melodion Hall, Cincinnati, Sept. 1872
Johnny Weaver, Race Street Varieties in Cincinnati, October 1872
The Carroll boys, Globe Theatre, Chicago, January 1873 [Dick Carroll][22]

Both the song and the sketch versions were performed regularly for over two years—by which time popular songs directly modeled on spirituals ("commercial spirituals") were beginning to emerge as a genre (see chap. 6). "Carry the News" had an afterlife as well. McAndrews was still singing it in 1879, and the lyrics were printed in minstrel and variety songsters until at least 1881.[23] According to the *Boston Globe* of 11 June 1882, the African American piano prodigy Thomas "Blind Tom" Wiggins (1849–1908) played "We Are All Surrounded" (the song's subtitle) in concert.

"Rock'a My Soul"

Whereas "Carry the News" imitated the style of a camp meeting hymn, Fred Cartee's "Rock'a My Soul," published in 1871, had more concrete links to slave song. A folk spiritual titled "Rock o' My Soul" appeared in Allen, Ware, and Garrison's *Slave Songs of the United States*, which was republished in a second edition that same year and may have contributed to the spiritual's popularity.[24] But the spiritual could have been widely known despite *Slave Songs*. (A relative of the tune from Playford's *Dancing Master* of 1651 was familiar and circulated in Anglo-American folk traditions.)[25] It was one of only twenty songs in *Slave Songs* (out of 136) collected in the northern seaboard slave states of Delaware, Maryland, Virginia, and North Carolina. It could have easily traveled northward from that region, or perhaps it already existed in the North but wasn't documented. Nothing is known of Cartee. The spiritual was in the repertory of the Tennesseans circa 1874–1875, and the Fisk Jubilee Singers used the tune for "Come Down, Angels," which they added to their repertory circa 1877.[26]

As notated in Allen's collection (see example 5.2A), the song consists only of a chorus with two sets of words. Cartee used a variant of that melody (see example 5.2B), adding a piano harmonization that reveals his inexperience. The penultimate pitch of E rather than D is a misprint, judging from the piano introduction, which ends the same way but with an octave jump from D to D.

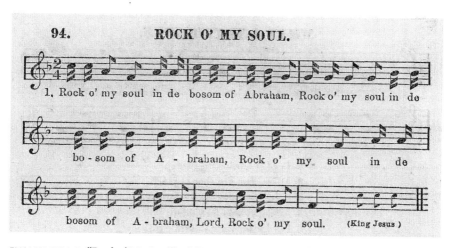

EXAMPLE 5.2A. "Rock o' My Soul," a folk spiritual collected in Allen, Ware, and Garrison's *Slave Songs of the United States* (1867). Courtesy of Rare Book Collection, Wilson Special Collections Library, UNC–Chapel Hill.

EXAMPLE 5.2B. Chorus of Cartee's "Rock'a My Soul," which is more similar in rhythm than melody to the version in *Slave Songs*. Music Division, Library of Congress.

That large leap in the vocal part suggests an upward slide or cry, typical of folk performance. Cartee added a newly composed verse in the form of abab' (where b is an internal refrain and b' represents the same words with a different melody). Cartee's lyrics loosely resemble those of a folk spiritual ("A little longer here below . . . an' a home to glory I muss go") except for the second verse, which reveals its minstrel roots ("I went to de circus an' dey wouldn't let me in . . . An' I paid half a dollar for a big glass of gin"). According to the cover of the sheet music, the song was performed by the white song and dance team of (George) Powers and (Carroll) Johnson, blackface minstrel Harry Bloodgood (white; born Carlos Mauran, 1845–1886), and Charley Howard—the lyricist for "Carry the News."

The difference in the spelling between "rock'a" in Cartee's song and "rock o' " in the folk spiritual is probably insignificant, as they sound the same. The apostrophe in the folk spiritual suggests a contraction, so that the full version would be "rock of my soul." In Cartee's song the "a" is spelled as a filler syllable, recalling Jeannette Robinson Murphy's admonition for the singer of black folk music to divide one-syllable words into two (see chap. 3). Interpreting "rock" as a verb, it might suggest the rocking and cradling of the soul in Abraham's bosom, or the rocking movements of a ring shout.[27] It's a safe guess that a minstrel performance of Cartee's song would have featured rocking shouters, much as earlier performers had impersonated Shaking Quakers.

"Contraband Children"

Commercial songs about contrabands had a burst of popularity between 1861 and 1865 because of the Civil War. Most were dialect songs for blackface performance and depicted happy-go-lucky emancipated slaves. Veteran minstrel Frank Dumont (white) reminisced in 1915 about General Benjamin Butler's coining of the term "contrabands of war":

> The papers took up the phrase, and in fact everybody talked about it, and the word "Contraband" crept into our conversation. The minstrels were quick to attach the word to songs, nigger acts and speeches. "The Happy Contraband," "Contraband From Dixie," "Contraband's Lament," "Contraband Children," "Contraband's Adventures" and "Contraband Brothers" appeared on all programs, and furnished subjects for all kinds of songs and dances.[28]

As minstrels began turning to plantation themes in the early 1870s, contraband songs made a brief comeback. In 1872 the white song and dance team of (William H.) Delehanty and (Thomas M.) Hengler jumped on the contrabandwagon with "Contraband Children" (New York: C. H. Ditson), in which the contrabands find refuge not with General Butler but with God's heavenly army (see example 5.3). The song features a repetitive verse structure of abab'—the same as Cartee's "Rock'a My Soul"—and a gapped-scale melody (written by Frank L. Martyn, who worked as an orchestra leader in variety halls). The lyrics by Hengler combine phrases and images from spirituals ("sweet chariots flying," "get home

EXAMPLE 5.3. Excerpt of "Contraband Children," music by Frank Martyn and lyrics by Thomas Hengler. Both the melody and the lyrics index folk spirituals. Music Division, Library of Congress.

byn by," "wear a golden crown") with minstrel stereotypes of blacks ("cut de pidgeon wing," molasses pouring down, "old massa").

Delehanty, like many minstrels, was of Irish extraction; he was born in Albany, New York, on 25 September 1846 to Irish parents. His partner, Hengler (born Slattery), was born in Cashel, Ireland, in 1844, although his parents brought him to the United States when he was three months old, and the family eventually settled in Albany. Presumably Delehanty and Hengler met each

EXAMPLE 5.3. Continued.

other as boys; they both debuted at Albany's Green Street Theatre—Hengler around the age of ten and Delehanty around the age of twelve. They began their professional careers in different minstrel troupes, but in 1866 Delehanty (who was a talented bones player and worked as an endman) and Hengler both joined Dingess and Green's Minstrels in Champaign, Illinois, putting together a song and dance act that quickly attracted attention. Although they performed in blackface, Delehanty and Hengler appeared in variety rather than minstrel shows for most of their career; in the 1870s they were a regular presence at Tony Pastor's Opera-House, Wood's Museum, and Brooklyn's Olympic Theatre.[29]

FIGURE 5.3. Sheet music cover to "Happy Hottentots," showing Delehanty and Hengler in a variety of whiteface and blackface scenes. In this song the duo pranced to an "exotic" minor-mode tune (a common musical trope for "Africa") and proclaimed "I'm a happy Hottentot"—happy because life consisted of picking buchu leaves (presented as the African equivalent to cotton), singing, and dancing the whole day and night through. Music Division, Library of Congress.

"Contraband Children" seems to have been conceived as a dance number much like "Carry the News to Mary." It differs from "Mary" in that the song's characters are slaves, thereby combining two trends: imitations of camp meeting songs and contraband songs. "Contraband Children" pointed the way toward future popular songs that drew an explicit connection between slave life and spirituals. Later songs by Delehanty and Hengler, for example, are obvious responses to the increasing prominence of jubilee singers and spirituals: their song "Jubilee Singers" (ca. 1875) announces, "We're the jubileers, and we come from Tennessee,"[30] and Delehanty's "Sing Low, Sweet Children" (ca. 1874) seems to have been a contrafactum (new words to an existing melody) of the Fisks' popular spiritual "Swing Low, Sweet Chariot."[31]

Delehanty and Hengler's overall repertory was divided between sentimental and comic songs, and between whiteface and blackface performance (see figure 5.3). Delehanty attributed the duo's success to keeping current with popular taste, originality, respectability, and policing pomposity: "we must be alert to novelties in keeping with '*the spirit of the times*,' always ready and apt to '*shoot folly as it flies*,' representing pictures of the past and present, *Negro life as it was and is*."[32] Delehanty and Hengler's commercial spirituals were certainly in the "spirit of the times," although they hardly represented "Negro life as it was and is."

Concluding Thoughts

"Carry the News" (1870), "Rock'a My Soul" (1871), and "Contraband Children" (1872) are all early specimens of songs intended to recall the old-fashioned camp meeting. They were associated initially with a coterie of white performers—most of them already celebrated for their "realistic" portrayals of slaves—who were beginning to develop a specialty of burlesquing black religion: Charley Howard, Walter Bray, Lew Simmons, J. W. McAndrews, Fayette Welch, Harry Bloodgood, Billy Emerson, William Delehanty, and Thomas Hengler. But "Carry the News" transcended the realm of white performance when the Georgia Minstrels added it to their repertory of plantation "jubilee" specialties in 1871.

Although "Carry the News" preceded widespread awareness of spirituals by way of jubilee troupes, its deliberate imitation of camp meeting songs forecast the symbiotic relationship that would develop between spirituals and popular song over the course of the 1870s:

1. *Cross fertilization*. In the intensely competitive entertainment sphere, performers copied or co-opted each other's material as a matter of course.

(The weekly entertainment newspaper *New York Clipper* frequently printed cards from entertainers asserting that theirs was the only true version of a song, or that another entertainer had used it without permission—reliable evidence of a song's profit potential.) The theatrical community was small and entertainers intermingled, traveling extensively, changing troupes frequently, belonging to the same social clubs and civic groups, and keeping careful tabs on their competition. Borrowing took place across generic boundaries (e.g., minstrel to variety to instrumental music) and across racial boundaries.

2. *Development.* A popular song could be expanded into a theatrical sketch through the addition of dances, scenery, characters, and spoken dialogue. In this way, "Carry the News" went from song to extravaganza. Development could also go in the opposite direction, by paring the song down to instrumental music, as in Billy Emerson's dance, Blind Tom's piano solo, and instrumental arrangements for society dances.

3. *Purported authenticity.* Not surprisingly, the past depicted in these three songs was distorted by an idealized nostalgic lens and the racial politics of their present. That didn't deter performers from asserting the songs' authenticity, through newspaper advertisements, programs, posters, and puff pieces (laudatory "reviews" written by a troupe's agent before the actual performance). "Carry the News," a newly composed popular song, was re-branded as "an old camp-meeting refrain" shortly after its introduction. Its musical characteristics (gapped scale, repetition, modal chord progressions) may have supported that claim, but the lyrics did not. "Rock'a My Soul," on the other hand, used the melody of an actual folk spiritual. The claim to authenticity was the bedrock of success for many black minstrel troupes in the late 1870s and early 1880s, just as it was for jubilee troupes. The blurring of boundaries between the folk, the popular, and concert music only intensified as time went on.

4. *Publishing.* Publication reinforced all of the foregoing processes, expanding audiences beyond those who patronized minstrel and variety halls by putting sheet music in the family parlor for instrumentalists (especially women and children) of all abilities, and songsters and broadsides in the hands of those who had only their voices. The covers of sheet music also served as reminders of the premium placed on performers, for it was their reputation that sold the song, not the composer's. Consequently Simmons and Slocum graced the cover of "Carry the News," and Delehanty and Hengler did the same on "Contraband Children."

George White chose the name "jubilee" for his singers because of the word's widespread religious and political currency. In 1871, before the Fisk Jubilee Singers equated spirituals with "jubilee song," the Georgia Minstrels used "jubilee" to describe high-energy songs about plantation life, as noted earlier regarding Jim Grace's "Down in Carolina." Some six months after that performance the Georgias performed "Jubilee Carolina" at Lina Edwin's Theatre in New York, a "refrain and chorus" that was "an echo of the African camp-meeting." It was encored three times on opening night and nightly thereafter, and it was singled out for its excellence in a review that found the entire entertainment otherwise mediocre.[33] In another six months (January 1873) they gave a sketch called "Jubilee Echoes" as the grand first-part finale, written expressly for them by white minstrel/songwriter/playwright Frank Dumont (1848–1919), who at the time was a member of Duprez and Benedict's Minstrels.[34] Plantation jubilees and walk-arounds, as well as camp meeting jubilee frolics, became standard components of Georgian entertainments in the 1870s.

Although this book compartmentalizes the histories of jubilee groups and minstrels for the sake of narrative simplicity, it's worth pausing to remember that when Billy Emerson danced "Carry the News" in San Francisco, the Hyers sisters were singing their art songs just a few blocks away. And when the Fisk Jubilee Singers performed in New York at various times in 1872, the Georgia Minstrels were often in town at the same time. Performers on each side of the minstrel-jubilee divide certainly knew of each other, and some of them would go on to become collaborators. As a result, "jubilee" took on additional resonances, among them the use of spirituals as a model for popular songs: commercial spirituals.

CHAPTER 6

Commercial Spirituals

The rise of student jubilee troupes offered minstrels a new opportunity for bur-lesque. The trickle of camp meeting parodies introduced by minstrels in 1870 converged with new parodies of jubilee singers and their spirituals, forming a tributary of religiously influenced popular music that dominated minstrelsy and variety for close to a decade. In jubilee troupes blackface minstrels found a new target to add to their list of politicians, celebrities, operas, plays, religious fads, and other caricature-worthy topics of the day.

By 1875, black and white entertainers alike were singing and composing popular songs that drew on the musical form and lyrical imagery of traditional spirituals, or "commercial spirituals." (Many black jubilee groups would even incorporate such songs into their programs.) Scholars have tended to dismiss these songs as ersatz versions of folk and concert spirituals. Sam Dennison, in his book *Scandalize My Name: Black Imagery in American Popular Music* (1982), expressed contempt for popular songs modeled on spirituals, arguing that in the hands of commercial songwriters "the unquestioned sincerity of the spiritual's cry from the depths of the black soul became a tawdry, derisory desecration of the original; all the sublime expression of the black's innermost being was transformed into a ridiculous triviality that was in every sense as degrading to the imitator as to the imitated."[1] Dennison focused on textual analysis and rarely discussed performance; on that ground it's easy to sympathize with him and reject these songs as unworthy of serious attention. As these songs amassed over time, however, they came to constitute a substantial, self-conscious category that transmitted to listeners the idea, if not the ideals, of spirituals. To ignore them would be to ignore the foundation of an entertainment industry in which blacks played vital roles—as performers, composers, and managers—for the first time in the history of the nation. The very shortcomings that have led most scholars to dismiss commercial spirituals—their irreverence toward religion, their apparent deracination from black folk culture, their perpetuation of black stereotypes—can be qualified in important ways by attention to performance context. A commercial spiritual could have different cultural resonance depending on the performer, venue, and audience.

Defining the Commercial Spiritual

What were commercial spirituals? Although many scholars have called attention to popular songs based on spirituals, there's been no comprehensive definition or even satisfactory label for this type of song. Dennison called them "pseudo-spirituals," declaring that "the term does not convey adequately the contempt which the form merits." Charles Hamm called them "minstrel-spirituals," Robert Toll "religious songs," and Eileen Southern described them without labeling them.[2] Toll's term is misleading, as the songs weren't created for or typically used in religious contexts. Hamm's is too restrictive, because the songs were found in a wide variety of entertainments beyond minstrelsy—even concerts by legitimate jubilee troupes. Dennison's use of "pseudo" highlights what the songs are not (i.e., real spirituals). Typical contemporaneous labels were "plantation songs and choruses," "Negro songs," "jubilee" or "colored camp-meeting" songs, and "end songs" or "comic songs" (indicating their function within the minstrel show)—each of which could refer to any number of styles at the time.

The challenge of naming this song category is made more difficult by the wide variation of lyrical content and performance styles, from the virulently racist to the earnest. Nonetheless, all commercial spirituals have three fundamental commonalities. First, the songs were written for personal financial profit and mass market appeal, attributed to a composer, and usually published. Second, although the lyrics typically display minstrel humor and stereotypes, they index traditional spirituals through idiomatic words and phrases (e.g., "golden chariot," "Gabriel's trumpet," "gospel train/raft/ship," "hallelujah") and themes (getting to heaven, judgment day). Third, most commercial spirituals bear at least a superficial musical resemblance to folk spirituals, most commonly manifested in internal refrains, call and response, and gapped-scale melodies. The term "commercial spiritual" may usefully be posed as a counterpart to the terms "folk/traditional spiritual" and "concert spiritual" in a way that draws attention to their various originating creative impulses, social functions, performance styles and venues, and modes of transmission (see table 6.1).

Many commercial spirituals were published only in songsters and as broadsides, not in sheet music editions. Songsters were one of the cheapest and most widespread methods of disseminating popular songs in the nineteenth century, and people of all social classes purchased them. Postbellum songsters were

TABLE 6.1. Comparison of folk, concert, and commercial spirituals

	Folk spiritual	Concert spiritual	Commercial spiritual
Performance mode	Communal, participatory	Presentational, for discerning audiences (concert stage, churches)	Presentational, for mass entertainments (variety, minstrelsy, plays, concerts)
Social function	Psychological survival, worship, work, private entertainment, lullaby, conveying coded messages	Fundraising, entertainment, education, racial uplift, religious edification, professional livelihood, cultural preservation	Professional livelihood, entertainment
Creators	Anonymous	Arrangers, usually known and credited	Composers, lyricists, and publishers, known and credited
Transmission	Orally transmitted	Primarily printed and sold in broadsides, songsters, anthologies, and sheet music; some oral transmission	Primarily printed and sold in broadsides, songsters, anthologies, and sheet music; some oral transmission
Audience	Black cultural insiders / participants	Primarily white middle- and upper-class Protestants outside of the South, though also performed in black churches	Undifferentiated mass market, white and black

pocketbooks (standard sizes were four by six or five by seven inches) printed on cheap paper, issued to advertise the latest hits (e.g., *James Bland and Mannie Friend's "In the Evening by the Moonlight" Songster*, 1881), anthologize songs associated with a specific performer (e.g., *Callender's Georgia Minstrels Songster*, 1878), or promote songs of the day (e.g., *The Vocalist's Favorite Songster*, 1885). Manufacturers sometimes issued songsters to advertise their products, sandwiching a few songs in between product endorsements (e.g., Merchant's Gargling Oil's *Nick Roberts-Gardner Two-Ring Circus Songster*). Postbellum songsters often had hand-colored illustrations on the cover, whereas sheet music covers of the 1870s and 1880s were black and white. The songsters typically ranged in length from about thirty to over one hundred songs and cost anywhere from a dime to forty cents accordingly. Although they sometimes included musical scores, jokes, skits, or monologues, most consisted only of song lyrics.

Songsters aren't a statistically reliable gauge of a song's popularity, since they were often assembled along arbitrary guidelines. One common formula was to place several of the latest hit songs in the opening pages, followed by titles chosen from a publisher's alphabetical catalogue, so that the contents stopped abruptly at N or P or T once the remaining pages had been filled. Even so, the most popular songs were anthologized widely, which is why Pete Devonear's "Dar's a Meeting Here Tonight," James Bland's "In the Morning by the Bright Light," and Will S. Hays's "Keep in de Middle ob de Road"—all of them commercial spirituals—are familiar titles in songster indexes.

Commercial spirituals began to crystallize as a genre between 1873 and 1875, peaking in popularity in the early 1880s. In the early 1870s a commercial spiritual could be performed for up to three years before being published as sheet music, likely because the new genre hadn't yet proved its worth to publishers, for whom a run of sheet music represented a higher financial outlay and risk than a songster. For example, the lyrics to Pete Devonear's "Den I Hope We'll Join de Band" appeared in *The Ham-Town Students Songster* in 1875, but the song wasn't published as sheet music until 1878. Between 1873, when the publication of commercial spirituals becomes easier to trace, and 1886, some 270 commercial spirituals were published.[3] Over half of this number were published by the end of 1881. By the late 1880s programming and publishing of these songs diminished as blackface minstrel acts declined in popularity and new popular styles emerged.

By the 1890s jubilee groups and spirituals were considered old-fashioned, as was blackface minstrelsy. Although publishers continued to issue new commercial spirituals, from 1890 onward the songs assumed the musical style of ragtime and Tin Pan Alley, with contemporary harmonies (especially diminished chords), expanded forms, temporary modulations within verses and choruses, and more sophisticated arrangements. Nevertheless, vestiges of commercial spirituals lingered into the 1930s and 1940s (a well-known example being Cole Porter's "Blow, Gabriel, Blow" from *Anything Goes*, 1934). Meanwhile, many of the commercial spirituals that had found special favor with audiences in the 1870s and 1880s passed into oral tradition—finally earning by legitimate means the label that publicists had originally asserted: folk music (see chap. 8).

Commercial spirituals came in different varieties. Dennison, the only scholar who has dealt with them at length, divides them into lyrical categories: camp meeting songs, which are hortatory messages delivered by a preacher figure; tocsins, which threaten punishment for sinning; and salvation songs, which anticipate the glory of an afterlife free of hatred and prejudice.[4] (Scholars sometimes use similar categories to classify traditional spirituals.) A more thoroughgoing understanding of commercial spirituals can be achieved by categorizing them instead by compositional model--parody, folk song, or popular song (although admittedly the lines of demarcation are not always clear)--and considering performative intent.

Parody

Broadly speaking, all commercial spirituals can be considered parodies, by virtue of their musical and textual allusion to traditional spirituals. In a stricter sense, however, a parody has a direct relationship with a traditional spiritual in at least one of three ways: (1) the lyrics of a traditional spiritual are set to a new melody, (2) new lyrics are set to a traditional melody (a contrafactum), or (3) a specific performance practice of culture bearers is parodied (e.g., the Hamtown Students' parodies of student jubilee groups, discussed later in this chapter). Parodies seem to have been most numerous in the mid-1870s and were one of the earliest types of commercial spirituals—an almost ready-made and immediate commentary on the public attention lavished on jubilee troupes.

Folk Song as Model

Commercial spirituals based on folk song emulate traditional spirituals through specific musical elements, including call and response, internal refrains, repetitive form, gapped scales (with descending thirds), prosodic syncopation (avoidance of four-square marching hymn style), flexible approach to pitch (indicated in scores by melismas, grace notes, and altered pitches), and filler phrases instead of silence. Less frequent folk traits include asymmetrical phrases (e.g., an opening phrase of three measures and an answering phrase of four measures), modulations that don't return to the home key (e.g., a song beginning in major but ending in minor), and continuous cadences. Like all popular songs but unlike traditional spirituals, printed commercial spirituals begin with the verse rather than the chorus—although there's no way of knowing if this format was practiced in performance.

Most commercial spirituals—about three-fourths—were modeled on folk song, which provided not only a style and structure for commercial spirituals but a compositional method as well. Eileen Southern noted that black songwriters often composed by mixing new and old, borrowing a preexisting slave-song melody for the chorus and adding a newly composed verse. In fact, white composers such as Will S. Hays used this process as well; like parody, this compositional practice had been employed since the inception of blackface performance (and is common in many traditions around the world). If folk spirituals were often pastiches—patched together from various repetitions, refrains, and choruses, or "sung to pieces" in the words of George Pullen Jackson[5]—it stands to reason that their descendants in the popular realm would be similarly constructed. Rather than *imitating* a folk composition, these self-taught composers were in a sense *extending* the folk process of composition to commercial songs. Black—and many white—songwriters used folk song as the basis of a new popular music because their musical knowledge, and often that of their audience, sprang from folk practice; in this sense, commercial spirituals were a logical development in a compositional continuum that gave rise to folk song on the plantation, jubilee song on the concert stage, and popular song in theatrical entertainments.

Popular Song as Model

About a fifth of commercial spirituals have a more tenuous relationship to folk spirituals. Conceived as typical verse-chorus popular songs, they invoke spirituals variously through a random formulaic phrase, a hybrid musical style combining a folklike chorus (e.g., using call and response) with a standard verse style, or simply through assertion (e.g., the label "jubilee song" on the cover). For example, the white composer M. H. Rosenfeld, writing under the pen name F. Belasco, combined a folk-flavored verse and a popular-style chorus in his 1884 hit "Hush Little Baby, Don't You Cry."[6]

. . .

That popular composers purposefully emulated traditional spirituals in terms of style, form, and/or lyrics is confirmed as much by what is absent as what is present: triple and compound meters, ballads (with their strophic form and coherent narratives), through-composed songs, and expanded forms—all of which were commonplace in popular song more generally but inconsistent with the style of traditional spirituals. Whereas songs like "Carry the News" had folklike qualities that were meant to recall old-fashioned camp meetings (see chap. 5), commercial spirituals showed the direct influence of the Fisks and other jubilee singers, through song titles that were identical to those of traditional spirituals, direct references to jubilee singers in lyrics, and melodies co-opted from traditional spirituals.

Profiles in Parody

As with traditional spirituals, printed music can provide a starting point for understanding commercial spirituals, but any credible interpretation must rest on how they were performed and how audiences heard them. Unfortunately, the abundant reportage on minstrel and variety shows in contemporaneous periodicals rarely describes the performance and reception of counterfeit jubileers and their songs. Understanding a commercial spiritual from the 1870s or 1880s, then, necessitates summoning a wide range of sources and applying some imagination.

"Gospel Train"

In December 1873 famed (white) blackface minstrel Dan Bryant sang "Get Aboard, Little Children" in Part First of Bryant's Minstrels show. (Later on troupe member Nelse Seymour sang it in Bryant's stead.) The title was a line from the refrain of "Gospel Train," a spiritual that had been published in the Fisk singers' *Jubilee Songs* of 1872 and was already popular in their repertory.[7] The 13 December 1873 issue of the *New York Clipper* noted that "Get Aboard" was "comically rendered" by Bryant, and indeed on Bryant's programs the song is labeled either a "comic" or a "coal" ditty (see figure 6.1); its placement on the December program provided an emotional respite from the sentimental songs "Hard Times Come Again No More" and "Touch the Harp Gently."

Given that "Get Aboard" was a common alternative title to "Gospel Train," and assuming that Bryant was indeed singing a parody, how might the song have sounded? In the absence of contemporaneous descriptions and sheet music, a 1917 recording titled "De Gospel Train Am Coming" by the white performer Harry C. Browne with the Peerless Quartet suggests some ways in which Bryant and other minstrel troupes may have presented "Get Aboard" in the late 1800s.

Browne's recordings are among the few surviving aural links to postwar minstrel repertory and performance. His career spanned the twilight years of the nineteenth-century minstrel show and the birth of the recording industry in the 1890s and early 1900s. Born in Massachusetts, he grew up singing minstrel songs and playing the banjo; between 1916 and 1920 he recorded many minstrel standards at the request of Columbia Record Company.[8]

Browne's "Gospel Train" orients the song with a snippet of minstrel dialogue. Speakers 1 and 2 are endmen characters, as revealed by their malapropisms and exaggerated dialect, and the conductor functions as interlocutor:

> SPEAKER 1 (*SOUTHERN DRAWL*): Say, boy, ain't that train comin' pretty soon?
> SPEAKER 2 (*SOUTHERN DRAWL*): Mm-hmm. The man said it'll be along right soon now. Dar he is now! Maybe he's gonna make a denouncement.
> CONDUCTOR (*SHOUTING, STANDARD ENGLISH*): The Hallelujah Express, making four stops: Peace, Glory, Contentment, and Happiness, due in one minute on track number 1! Stand back everybody, . . . no crowdin', there's room for all.

FIGURE 6.1. Bryant's Minstrels performed "Get Aboard, Little Children" in the first part of their program in early 1874. MS Thr 556, folder 272, Houghton Library, Harvard University.

A train whistle blows, the orchestra—with Browne's banjo prominent—plays a short introduction, and then Browne begins to sing (see web recording 6.1). The lyrics are identical to those of "Gospel Train" by the Fisk Jubilee Singers, and the rhythm closely matches the Fisk score. But Browne's parody differs in its minor mode, melodic contour, and the use of instrumental accompaniment (compare example 6.1A, B). His rendition trades on its identification with the traditional spiritual, sounding at once recognizable and original.[9]

Using Browne's recording as well as what is known about minstrel show conventions and Bryant as a performer, it's possible to make some inferences about the music and performance style of Bryant's "Get on Board" in the 1870s. Like Browne, Bryant was a celebrated banjo player and renowned comic who, as one fan recalled, "not trusting in costumes, vocalists or dancing alone, … gave performances in which innocent, though noisy fun brightened all three."[10] Given Bryant's energy and comic ingenuity, and the longstanding popularity in minstrelsy of human imitations of locomotives, a scenario for "Get on Board" could have gone something like this:

> *A replica of a train engine and passenger car are wheeled onstage. The conductor calls, "All aboard," and the whistle blows. Passengers shove their way onto the train, hang out of car windows ("there's room for many-a more," claims the refrain), do pratfalls, drop luggage, and perform other comic stage business. Train chugs and whistles abound, conductors call, and passengers yell. Bryant's lively banjo gradually emerges out of this cacophony, and as the hubbub dies down he launches into the verse, singing in the minstrel version of black dialect. The troupe animates the call and response between soloist and chorus with cries to "get aboard," "hurry," "don't be late." The passengers join in on the refrain. Bones, banjo, and tambourine keep the momentum going, and the interludes of verses are enlivened by dancing and a bones solo. The act concludes with two rousing choruses.*

Although it's impossible to state definitively that Bryant's and other minstrel troupes performed "Get Aboard" as a parody, Browne's recording of "Gospel Train," combined with what is known about Bryant as a performer and about minstrel humor generally from contemporaneous prompt books, reviews, and photographs, conjure up a convincing scenario.

It's certainly jarring from today's perspective to visualize a white minstrel in blackface singing a broad parody of a spiritual. But if Bryant wanted to acknowledge the jubilee craze, his only real avenue in 1873 was comedy. White theater audiences increasingly craved "authenticity" in minstrel portrayals of slave life and judged white performers of "plantation" material more severely in comparison to those who had no need of blacking up, such as the revered Fisk Jubilee Singers and emerging black minstrels like the Georgias. (The Hutchinson Family was an exception; their politics and early embrace of spirituals gave credence to their performances, as discussed in chap. 2.) For performers of all backgrounds, however, comedy and the (presumably) original lyrics and/ or tune of a song parody also served a purpose beyond mere entertainment. Minstrel careers were commonly sustained on the basis of a distinctive song or act (e.g., Billy Kersands inserting billiard balls into his cavernous mouth, or Fayette Welch's sketch of "Carry the News"). In a profession based on pretense (men dressing as women, whites blackening their faces, performers assuming all sorts of ethnic accents, burlesques of plays and operas), an original element allowed the performer to "own" the material. In inventing a new tune to a spiritual—or new words to an old tune—white performers could assert "ownership" of a song that originated outside their own tradition.

From Hampton to Hamtown: Faux Jubilee Singers

The popularity of black jubilee groups guaranteed that minstrel and variety performers would burlesque them. If the Fisk Jubilee Singers' "Gospel Train" was an argument for equality,[11] the minstrels' train traveled the well-worn tracks of racial caricature. In entering the ranks of the lampooned, the student jubilee singers joined an august company that included the Hutchinson Family, Swedish diva Christina Nilsson (minstrelized as "Kneelson"), Sarah Bernhardt ("Sarah Heart-Burn"), politicians, preachers, and lecturers on the lyceum circuit. Burlesques of celebrities generally mocked the self-important attitudes of managers, publicity agents, reviewers, audiences, and occasionally the performers themselves.[12] Parodies would crop up shortly after jubilee singers came to town. For example, the appearances of the Fisk Jubilee Singers in Philadelphia at the end of January and again in February 1873 were acknowledged with a burlesque by Frank Moran's Minstrels (white) at the end of February, in which Billy Manning (ca. 1834–1876), Frank Moran (1827–1898), and James Unsworth (1835–1875) "occupied the most prominent parts."[13] The Carolina Singers, who also sang spirituals in late January 1873 in Philadelphia, were lampooned by Simmons and Slocum's Minstrels.[14] In February 1874 Chicago audiences could hear the beloved Tennesseans and their spirituals as well as their paler parodists appearing with Arlington, Cotton, and Kemble's Minstrels (troupe members

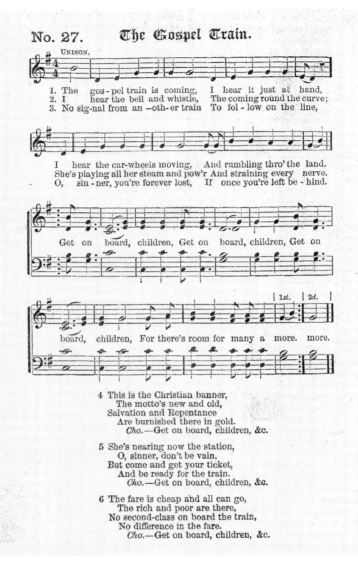

EXAMPLE 6.1A. "The Gospel Train" as transcribed in spring 1872 by Theodore Seward for *Jubilee Songs: Complete*. Reprinted from Marsh, *Story of the Jubilee Singers* (1886), 150.

EXAMPLE 6.1B. Verse and chorus of "De Gospel Train" from the singing of Harry C. Browne on *Early Minstrel Songs*. The instrumental accompaniment consisted of trumpet, clarinet, perhaps trombone, and Browne on banjo. Transcribed by the author.

Charley Walters, J. W. Morton, Billy Arlington, and William Courtwright).[15] No jubilee troupe of repute was spared.

In addition to the student singers, the white management had its share of minstrel mockery, as suggested by a performance at Boston's Howard Athenæum in 1872.[16] On that evening the white faux jubilee entertainers donning blackface were James H. Budworth (1831–1875), a blackface comedian who excelled at impersonating famous thespians, and Bob Hart (born James M. Sutherland, 1834–1888), a baritone who began his career as a ballad singer in minstrel shows. Hart's experience as a Methodist preacher made him "one of the best speech makers in the profession," according to nineteenth-century theater impresario and historian T. Allston Brown. His stump speech "was just such an oration as a pompous darkie, better stocked with words than judgment, might shoot off at an assemblage of terrified hearers. It was purely an original effort, differing in toto from the average burlesque address of the minstrel stage."[17] A burlesque jubilee concert playing to these performers' strengths might begin by lampooning the lengthy prefatory speeches or, more cuttingly, by portraying the singers as puppets of white entrepreneurs. (After all, the *New York Herald* had characterized the Jubilee Singers as Henry Ward "Beecher's Negro Minstrels," as noted in chap. 3.) The following scenario, adapted from an actual stump speech, offers one conceivable caricature:

> Hart and Budworth take the stage in blackface and formal attire. Hart introduces his jubilee singers, impersonating the long-winded missionary G. D. Pike or bass singer and future minister Isaac Dickerson, who sometimes spoke on behalf of the Fisk troupe. He addresses the audience in character with a self-important, malaprop-laden plea for funds on behalf of the American Missionary Association: "Brudders, Fellow Brudders, and Bretheren Brudders: I have been invited to address dis meeting dis evening by de American Commissionary Desociation. I arrived in your beautiful city about ten minutes ago; I would hab been here sooner if I had got here before. Before proceeding I desire dat de hall door shall be locked, and a collection taken up to defray de expenses ob de singers. You all know dat we hab just gone through an era of incongruous and imperceptible conglomeration and dat will eventually terminate in de disfranchisement of periodical imbecility." The speech drags on for another couple of minutes, finally giving way to a contrafactum of "Swing Low, Sweet Chariot" sung with mock gravity, followed by a lively popular song featuring dance, comic business, and banjo accompaniment.[18]

The only known description of a burlesque performance suggests that burlesque jubileers targeted the manner of performance rather than the spirituals themselves. The following anecdote, discovered by Doug Seroff, dates from one of the Fisk Jubilee Singers' tours of England and concerns their signature spiritual "Steal Away," which audiences celebrated for its barely audible beginning that gradually swelled into a robust declamation (see chap. 3). As Fisk singer Mabel Lewis Imes describes it: "There was a time in London when they impersonated each one of us at a place for minstrels. They had 'Steal Away' and when they came to the soft parts, they just opened their mouths, you couldn't hear a sound. It was really funny."[19] A group of freed slaves treating their folk songs as art music seems to have been a ready-made, irresistible joke to minstrels, whose comedy thrived on puncturing pretension. Fisk musical performances furnished liberal potential for exaggeration. For example, in their spiritual "I'm a-Rolling" the Fisk singers depicted the "roll" in the lyrics with an "arpeggio movement of the bass" and performed a "lingual roll"—including a "trill of the r"—on some of the words, the protracted r "giving more than ordinary expression to the meaning conveyed in the song."[20] One can imagine minstrels replicating the trilled r, neatly embedding in that single extended consonant a sarcastic comment on the stiff elocutions of formal theater diction and upper-class speech.

Although initially jubilee parodies were local and topical, by late 1874 into 1875 jubilee troupes had developed a national profile, and consequently burlesque jubilee troupes started to become permanent, generic acts in many minstrel and variety shows, both white and black. The most enduring were the "Hamtown" groups, who were known variously as the Hamtown Students, Hamptown Students, Original Colored Hamtown Students, and Hamtown Quartette/Quintette/Sextette. "Hamtown" was the quintessential minstrel pun; with its layered associations, it could lead to a wide variety of interpretations, of which even the most serious was susceptible to minstrel humor. Besides the overt reference to Hampton, the name also alluded to the "curse of Ham" (Genesis 9:22–25), which equated punishment with slavery and had been an accepted justification among Christians for the oppression of blacks since the sixteenth century; the phrase was used abundantly in postbellum literature, song, and conversation. "Hamtown" also had gustatory implications: after possum, ham was the meat most stereotypically associated with African Americans in the South. (Black minstrel Henry Hart underscored this relationship in his end song "Good Sweet Ham": the first two verses extol ham's many virtues, then verse three begins: "Now my song is almost ended, / And you all know who dis darkey am, / For the boys have all nicknam'd me, / By them calling me sweet old ham".)[21] The term *hamfatter* was applied to minstrels who rubbed ham fat on their face to remove the cork that darkened their skin; shortened to *ham* it connoted lower-class variety performers, especially those who were excessively theatrical.[22] Groups in the Hamtown mold continued to perform until 1882–1883. Over time "Hamtown" became a generic name for a burlesque jubilee act, prompting some performers to adopt different names altogether, such as the Bogtown Quartette or the California Quartette.

WHITE HAMTOWN GROUPS The *Ham-Town Students Songster* is the most informative source on white Hamtown groups. Although this iteration of Hamtown Students wasn't the first Hamtown act, it was perhaps the most successful; group leader E. D. Gooding's claim that "from the first night the Ham-towns were pronounced a hit" was no exaggeration.[23] The group seems to have formed in early 1875, when Gooding performed with a white Hamtown troupe that debuted on a variety bill at the Olympic Theatre in New York. Gooding was a veteran minstrel who had begun performing in the 1850s. Billed in newspaper advertisements as "the colored Hampton Students," the troupe consisted of Gooding, Billy Gray, James Sanford (who had already burlesqued the Fisks in

1873), and Charles Wilson.[24] "Who first conceived the idea of burlesquing the famous Hampton Students I do not know," admits Gooding in the songster introduction; "were I possessed of that knowledge I would most undoubtedly give him credit for it."

When Sanford and Wilson, who had been performing as a duo since 1873, left the Hamtown Students circa 1875 in order to honor engagements in other cities, they were replaced by tenors Sam Holdsworth and William Courtright—who already had experience impersonating Donavin's Tennesseans with Arlington, Cotton, and Kemble's Minstrels in 1874. After Courtright and Gray left, bass singer G. W. H. Griffin and song-and-dance artist John Gilbert (who had partnered with Courtright ca. 1871–1872) stepped in. This troupe—Gooding, Griffin, Gilbert, and Holdsworth—far surpassed the lifespan of earlier burlesque jubilee troupes, beginning with their performance at the Olympic on 23 August 1875 and continuing throughout the eight-month season.[25] As their photograph shows (see figure 6.2), Gooding and Griffin's quartet presented themselves as minstrels, with kinky wigs, blackened faces, lips outlined in white, and formal attire complete with the white gloves that reflected minstrelsy's attempts at refinement. (Postwar minstrelsy was in the midst of a rebranding effort as middle-class family entertainment, suitable not only for men but for women and children as well.) The Hamtown act was a manifestation of the male quartet tradition within minstrelsy; the choruses of solo songs in the first part had been rendered in four-part harmony since the late 1840s in imitation of the Hutchinsons and other singing families, and by the 1850s male quartets were a free-standing and permanent feature on minstrel programs.[26]

Of the forty-one songs in the *Ham-Town Students Songster*, thirteen are traditional spirituals and ten are commercial spirituals. The remainder are evergreen antebellum songs (e.g., "Home Again," Old Folks at Home," "Stop Dat Knocking") and current hits (e.g., "Flewy, Flewy," "Dashing Female Swell"). Fourteen songs are printed with musical scores. The influence of legitimate jubilee singers on this Hamtown repertory is unmistakable. Several of the Hamtown songs come from the Fisk Jubilee Singers, such as "I'm a-Rolling," "Nobody Knows the Trouble I See, Lord" (which uses the Fisk, not the Hampton, melody), and "Turn Back Pharaoh's Army." They are faithful copies of the Fisk arrangements first transcribed by Seward in 1872, with the exception of a minor correction or two in note duration or pitch in the harmony.

Two of the songs have connections to the Tennesseans, the group formed on behalf of Central Tennessee College in Nashville in 1873: "Do You Think I'd Make a Soldier?" and "There's a Meetin' Here To-night"—not surprising given that two Hamtown troupe members had a history of burlesquing the Tennes-

FIGURE 6.2. *From left*: Gooding, Gilbert, Holdsworth, and Griffin as the Hamtown Students, with the aid of blackface and wigs. MS Thr 556, folder 77, Houghton Library, Harvard University.

seans. The first song went by the title "Rise! Shine! And Give God the Glory" in the undated broadside "Songs of the Tennesseans," arranged by their bass singer Leroy Pickett. The third verse begins "We are climbing Jacob's ladder, ladder"—a phrase that later became the title most people know today. For all their strong resemblances, the Tennesseans' and Hamtown versions are in different keys, have different time signatures (2/4 and 4/4), and differ in important textual phrases. The connections between the Tennesseans' and Hamtown versions of "There's a Meetin' Here To-night" are more evident. The Tennesseans were performing this song during their 1874–1875 season, and their version was identifiable by a verse that begins "Shadrach, Meschach, and Abednego," which does not appear in the Fisk and (later) Hampton versions but does match the Hamtown songster (which gives only lyrics for this spiritual).[27] Although the Hamtown songster prints five verses to the Tennesseans' four (there wasn't room on the printed page for more), the lyrics of each conform to the other in every other respect. The only spiritual in the songster that comes from the Hampton

Institute Singers' repertory seems to be "De Ole Sheep Done Know de Road"; the words match the Hampton spiritual as printed in Armstrong and Ludlow (1874) almost identically, and the Fisks didn't perform it. (A similar version of the spiritual exists in Gullah culture.)[28]

The connection to the Hampton Students is stronger, however, in the Hamtown songster's commercial spirituals. "Run, Mary, Run" as sung by the Hamtown Students, for example, is a contrafactum of the spiritual sung by the Hamptons, with new words by E. D. Gooding. (Original music is consistently credited in the songster, so it's safe to assume the Hamtowns sang the traditional melody.) It serves as a useful model for how the minstrels parodied traditional spirituals. In this case the song begins with a few lines of traditional lyrics, underscoring its relation to the spiritual, but then segues into new lyrics. The italicized lines are of Gooding's composing:

> SOLO.—Fire in de East, and a fire in de West,
> CHORUS.—I know de oder world am not like dis,
> SOLO.—Bound to burn de wilderness;
> CHORUS.—I know de oder world am not like dis,
> SOLO.—*When the world am coming to an end,*
> CHORUS.—I know de oder world am not like dis,
> SOLO.—*All good niggers will den ascend,*
> CHORUS.—I know de oder world am not like dis.
>   GEN'L CHO.—Run, Mary, run,—run, Mary run,
>   Oh run, Mary run;
>   I know de oder world am not like dis.
>
> SOLO.—Jordan's ribber am de ribber to cross,
> CHORUS.—I know de oder world am not like dis,
> SOLO.—*Nigger's foot slip, and den he's lost;*
> CHORUS.—I know de oder world am not like dis,
> SOLO.—*When de good ship Zion do set sail,*
> CHORUS.—I know de oder world am not like dis,
> SOLO.—*Hang on niggers to my coat-tail,*
> CHORUS.—I know de oder world am not like dis.
>   GEN'L CHO.—Run, Mary, run, etc.
>
> SOLO.—*De wedder's hot whar de debbil resides,*
> CHORUS.—I know de oder world am not like dis,
> SOLO.—*You get no ice-cream dar besides;*
> CHORUS.—I know de oder world am not like dis,
> SOLO.—*So all you sinners, do as you oughter,*
> CHORUS.—I know de oder world am not like dis,

SOLO.—*And you go to heaven and you drink ice-water,*
CHORUS.—I know de oder world am not like dis.
    GEN'L CHO.—Run, Mary, run, etc.[29]

Gooding transformed this traditional spiritual about Judgment Day, a plea to "let God's children hab some rest," into a racist editorial. The narrator, who voices a white perspective, suggests that "niggers" (a word never found in folk spirituals) are helpless and can get to heaven only through white intervention (by riding a white person's coattails). The trivializing, childish metaphors for heaven in verse three—ice cream and ice water—prosaically rather than poetically extinguish the fires of judgment. Gooding's lyrics change the authorial voice from that of agent in the traditional spiritual to that of subject. The lack of identification between the parodist and the object of parody, magnified by belittling language, is common in commercial spirituals, facilitating disdainful and derogatory humor through an act of distancing. And yet the chorus remains unchanged, perhaps giving the singers an opportunity to display their vocal skills while reminding audiences that this is a genuine slave song.

"'A' for Adam" differs from the other contrafacta in that its new verses are topical rather than parodic. The chorus is borrowed literally from the spiritual (famed for its lyric "Humble, humble, humble yourself, for de bell done ring"), but all the verses are newly composed on the model of a category or counting song, with only tenuous religious overtones (see example 6.2):

1. A for Adam, de berry man dat eat de apple, sin began. (*chorus*)
2. B for Brooklyn, de city of sin, spect dey don't want any scandal agin. (*chorus*)
3. C for Chicago, of the terrible fire, spect dey'll git to heaven, but dey never git no higher. (*chorus*)

The second verse ("B for Brooklyn") alludes to the very public trial of Henry Ward Beecher, the early patron of the Fisks and other jubilee groups. Beecher's extramarital affair with a female congregant was front-page news every day in papers across the country in 1875—the year this songster was published—but it was particularly relevant to those who patronized Hooley's Opera House in Brooklyn, which was also home to Beecher's Plymouth Church. The third verse ("C for Chicago") refers to the great Chicago fire of 1871, which occurred at the beginning of the Fisk Jubilee Singers' first tour. The Jubilees donated their meager proceeds from a concert in Chillicothe, Ohio, to the Chicago fire victims—a remarkable act of charity given their own tenuous finances at the time. Although the Hamtown song as printed in the book has only three

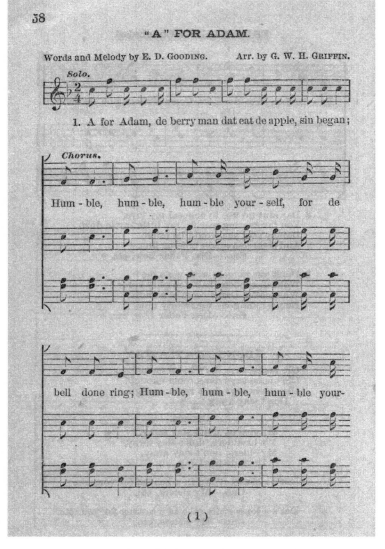

EXAMPLE 6.2. Excerpt from "'A' for Adam," which parodies the spiritual "Humble Yourself," also known as "Live-a Humble" in F. J. Work, *New Jubilee Songs*, 4–5. The very short verse melody is Gooding's, but the chorus is traditional in words and melody. From *Ham-Town Students Songster*, TCS 89 box 14, folder 276, Houghton Library, Harvard University.

verses (having taken up two full pages), the performers surely went through the alphabet and extemporized additional verses about current events.

Although Gooding and Griffin's Hamtown Students appeared in variety shows, other Hamtown quartets appeared in minstrel shows, either in the olio or in the second half along with the other specialty acts—banjo solos, songs and dances, stump speeches, acrobatics, female impersonations, and the like. By the Hamtowns' very position in the program, then, audiences were predisposed to see them as a comic novelty. At the New Park Theatre in Brooklyn, white minstrels Sam Devere, Luke Schoolcraft, George H. Coes, and Harry Macarthy presented a sketch called "The American Rifle Team" in which they impersonated bumbling colored troops in military dress during target practice, then quickly changed costume to become the Hamtown Students.[30] It's doubtful that the Hamtown acts burlesqued individual jubilee singers; they more likely poked fun at the general convention of jubilee singing. This accorded with the public's perception of jubilee groups as collectives rather than groups of individuals; in reviews the singers were frequently referred to by their gender, height, and degree of darkness (in the manner of slave advertisements) instead of, or in addition to, their names.

Not every Hamtown group appeared in formal attire. As legitimate jubilee troupes strove to distinguish themselves in an ever more competitive environment, some of them performed in plantation costumes and tableaus, and some even added comic sketches to their programs. As did the jubilee singers, so did the minstrels. In 1877, for example, a white Ham Town Student troupe with Harry Bloodgood's Minstrels appeared "at each and every entertainment in their great and original Burlesque on the Hampton Students, . . . with appropriate costumes and introducing all the latest Camp-Meeting Hymns and movements peculiar to that class," according to a playbill.[31] (By this time the Hampton students—who never dressed in plantation costume—had stopped touring regularly, yet the Hampton name seems to have become a metonym for jubilee singers of all stylistic persuasions.) The "Jubilee Singers" who appeared with Sheridan and Mack's Specialty Combination were punningly billed as "off-colored" and sang contrafacta of spirituals, judging from the titles of the four songs listed on their playbill (see figure 6.3).

If Hamtown was a burlesque act, what is to be made of the traditional spirituals in the *Ham-Town Students Songster*? Were they included in an effort to confer legitimacy on their commercial counterparts? Or did Gooding's white quartet perform noncomic arrangements of spirituals? The minstrel mask would have severely undercut any serious performance. Another possibility is that the quartet alternated serious and comic renditions, exploiting the juxtaposition of tradi-

SHERIDAN & MACK'S
Specialty Combination!

PROGRAMME.

Grand selection from Le Cocq's Opera,

GIROFLE, GIROFLA.

By J. B. DONIKER AND ORCHESTRA.

The performance to commence with the laughable Comedy, entitled,

THE MIMIQUES!

Or, A DRESS REHEARSAL.

Mrs. Launcelot Whirligig......................................Miss Rosa Leigh
Mrs. Columbus Babrooster.................................Miss Alicia Jourdan
Miss Pauline Belknap......................................Miss Blanche Corelli
Lillie...Miss Carrie Boshell
Dionysius Duffy...J. D. Kelly
Columbus Babrooster..J. W. Mack
Prof. Wienauski...J. B. Donniker
Raphael Crayon..D. J. Waters
Michael Fogarty (a cop)..Geo. Percy
John (a stage struck servant)..................................J. F. Sheridan

During the Comedy the following original Songs, Duetts, Trios, Quartettes, Musical and Dialogue Specialties will be introduced:

"THEY STOLE MY CHILD AWAY."

Opening...Chorus

THE BERGER FAMILY OF BELL-RINGERS ECLIPSED!

"MUSIC IN THE AIR,"..Trio
Misses Corelli, Jourdan and Leigh.

CONCERTINA SOLO...J. D. KELLY

By request, the great hit,

REGULAR ARMY, OH!...............SHERIDAN & MACK

BALLAD...Miss ROSA LEIGH

Messrs. KELLY, MACK, WATERS AND SHERIDAN,

The (off) Colored

JUBILEE SINGERS,

IN THEIR CAMP MEETING SONGS.

1..Held a camp meeting in de Swamp
2...Ain't dem hard trials
3...............................Pick up de little lamb put it in your bosom
4...Don't get weary get home by'me by

MISS BLANCHE CORELLI

The accomplished queen of song.

POOTY KATRINA.........................SHERIDAN & MACK

VIOLIN SOLO, "Seventh Air," De Beriot . . J. B. DONNIKER
Miss BLANCHE CORELLI, Accompanyist.

FIGURE 6.3. Playbill excerpt for Sheridan and Mack's Specialty Combination featuring the "(Off) Colored Jubilee Singers," a Hamtown-style act, circa 1876. This entertainment was essentially a variety show with some minstrel elements. MS Thr 556, folder 574, Houghton Library, Harvard University.

tional song and its parody for humorous effect, or even for the sake of variety. With little contemporaneous commentary available, it's impossible to know how, or if, traditional spirituals played a consistent role in Hamtown performance.

BLACK HAMTOWN ACTS   Black Hamtown acts emerged in the season after the white Hamtowns debuted. Callender's Georgia Minstrels offered "jubilee chantings" by their own Hamtown Students (see figure 6.4), usually featuring Pete Devonear and Dick Little, among other rotating members. Callender's Hamtowns were renamed the Georgian Students circa 1877 but otherwise were a constant on programs. The Hamtowns/Georgians seem to have given non-comic renditions of traditional spirituals. For example, a reviewer for a black newspaper wrote of an 1877 performance in New Orleans, "We take pleasure also in complimenting the Hamtown students . . . for the correct, yet odd, style of hymn singing without accompaniment. These four form an excellent quartette, seldom surpassed among minstrels."[32] When J. H. Haverly (white) bought Callender's Georgia Minstrels in 1878, an element of parody took hold: "four performers sang as the Hamtown Quartet, and four others immediately caricatured their performances as the Bogtown Quartet."[33] This kind of caricature remained a regular feature of the Haverly-produced entertainments through 1883, with occasional variations on the name of the parodists, such as the Blackville Jubilee Singers.[34]

James Bland, one of minstrelsy's towering talents, also fell in with Hamtown-style parodies. Circa 1878 he stage-managed and starred with his own short-lived minstrel troupe named the Black Diamonds. The second part of the program featured the Black Diamond Quartette (William Hunt, Hosey MacKey, John Cisco, and John Johnson) performing "jubilee songs, chantings and refrains."[35]

Commercial Spirituals Sung by the Georgia Minstrels

By 1875 the once struggling Georgia Minstrels had been around for ten years and were finally beginning to establish a reputation that would make them one of the premier U.S. minstrel troupes. Like the Fisk Jubilee Singers, who found success after largely forsaking songs from the "white" tradition for their "native" spirituals, the Georgias' turn to slave-themed songs, dances, and humor propelled their popularity. Whereas in 1872 the plantation was an infrequent reference in their shows, by 1874 it permeated their entertainments, as Eileen Southern first suggested.[36] As with the Fisks, the about-face was driven by the enthusiasm of white audiences for material they considered the authentic domain of black performers. Wrote one reviewer of the Georgias' plantation

CALLENDER'S GEORGIA MINSTRELS.

CHARLES CALLENDER..Manager
R. G. LITTLE..Stage Manager

PROGRAMME—PART FIRST.

Tambos..........Moore and Devonear   Bones..........Grace and McIntosh
Interlocutor—Wm. Morris

Overture...Callender's Georgia Minstrels
Keep dem Lamp a Burning...J Grace
Little...S Jones
Run Home, Levi..P Devonear
As they Greet Me at the Door...W Morris
Linda Burke..N Moore
Are you Tired of Me, Darling..T Chestnut
Angel Gabriel...W Kersands
Beneath the Maple by the Mill...R G Little

Concluding with the Ludicrous Finale, entitled

THE GINGER BLUES.

Gen. (Black) man and his Skilled Recruits.

PART SECOND

THE DASHING BELLE.
W. E. LYLE, in Artistic Female Portraiture.

THE PEDESTAL CLOG,
W. ALLEN, Champion of the World.
Danced on a surface 15 inches square, 4 feet high.

THE HAMTOWN STUDENTS.
MORRIS, JONES, DEVONEAR, LITTLE.

Essence,   -   -   -   -   -   Kersands

Concluding with a genuine and characteristic Plantation Jubilee Walk-around,

Holiday on the Old Plantation.

Uncle Ike Simpson		............W Morris
Aunty Susan Simpson		............J Grace
Estella	their	............W Lyle
Philla Jane Della	daughters	............T McIntosh
Rufus		............P Devonear
Thad	their sons	............T Chestnut
Nat		............Young Kersands
Brother Joe Marcus		............Neale Moore
Sam Lyons	Visitors	............Dick Little
J W Marcus, Jr		............W Allen
Peter Vandgrass' Cotillon Band		............Orchestra

Concluding with a Grand Tableau.

Published at the Office of THE DAILY CRITIC, 511 Ninth Street Northwest.

FIGURE 6.4. Program circa 1883 for Callender's Georgia Minstrels featuring the Hamtown Students: William Morris, Sam Jones, Pete Devonear, and Richard G. (Dick) Little. The first part features three commercial spirituals: "Keep Dem Lamp a Burning" (the internal refrain of Jacob Sawyer's "Hand Me Down Dem Golden Shoes"), "Run Home, Levi" composed and performed by Devonear, and "Angel Gabriel" by James Stewart, performed by Billy Kersands. MS Thr 556, folder 295, Houghton Library, Harvard University.

songs and sketches, "Those who give them appear to have been there, and to know all about it."[37] Whether reviews were laudatory, critical, or indifferent, the fact remained that the Georgians were "unmistakable gentlemen of color, and their pranks *quite different from the gyrations of the burnt cork fraternity*" (my italics).[38] Before black minstrels arrived on the scene, white audiences in the north especially had considered white men in blackface to be the genuine representation of slave culture, but they now transferred their loyalty to black minstrels, some of whom blacked up and others of whom did not.

After four weeks of daily performances in Boston in March and April 1875, the Georgia Minstrels had played to over 40,000 people (Beethoven Hall, where they were in residence, seated 1,526), prompting the *Boston Globe* to invite them to locate permanently in the city. Noted the *Globe*, "Ladies and gentlemen of the best society patronize these unique entertainments of the genuine darkies from down South."[39] At least in urban environments the Georgias played to audiences of some socioeconomic diversity, the most sophisticated of whom were as likely to flock to the Boston Theatre for the renowned actor Edwin Booth's portrayal of Richard III as they were to visit Beethoven Hall for Pete Devonear singing "Dar's a Meetin' Here Tonight." Black Americans joined them: when the Georgias played Hamlin's Theatre in Chicago in 1879, "the colored population turned out in full force to welcome their friends." That audience especially relished the first part of the program, and "encored again and again the camp-meeting ballads, which were capitally rendered, conspicuous among them being Sam Lucas' 'Golden Raft' and James Bland's 'Golden Slippers'"—both commercial spirituals.[40] The Georgias' publicity trumpeted endorsements by abolitionist William Lloyd Garrison ("nothing offensive to eye or ear"), P. T. Barnum, the well-known American singer of art music Clara Louise Kellogg, and other notables.[41]

During March 1875, the Georgia Minstrels and the Fisk Jubilee Singers had almost identical itineraries, appearing in New York and Boston at the same time. Newspaper reviews and advertisements for the two groups were often contiguous, inviting a comparison that was increasingly inescapable as slave-themed entertainments multiplied.

Georgia Minstrel shows from 1875 to 1880 featured two commercial spirituals in the first part. Not all commercial spirituals were created equal. Although black composers could and did write commercial spirituals that were just as offensive as those of whites, and although white composers wrote songs in varying degrees of derogation, in performance the same song could take on different overtones depending on who performed it. Four commercial spirituals that were regularly programmed by the Georgias—two by black composers and two by white composers—illustrate ways of thinking about songs in this genre and their meaning.

PETE DEVONEAR: "DAR'S A MEETING HERE TONIGHT" "Dar's a Meeting Here Tonight" by Pete Devonear (see figure 6.5) is possibly the earliest commercial spiritual composed by an African American. Devonear—who played tambourine on the end, sang, and played banjo—introduced it during the Georgia Minstrels' summer season at Hooley's Opera House, Brooklyn, in 1874.[42]

Virtually nothing is known of Devonear's biography. He joined Barney Hicks's Georgia Minstrels in 1871 (after Hicks returned from England) and stayed with that company through various permutations and proprietors (Callender, Haverly, Frohman). After 1884 his name disappears from minstrel programs and newspaper advertisements, although his song "Keep a Movin'" was published in 1885 (J. R. Bell, Kansas City), and in 1899 he was the dedicatee of James T. Williams's song "Down on the Farm," suggesting he was still alive at the time. "Dar's a Meeting Here Tonight," the most celebrated of the five songs credited to him, was singled out for excellence time and again in reviews and deemed an "already famous" song when the Georgia Minstrels concluded their Boston run in April 1875.[43] It was an almost constant presence in the first part from August 1874 through 1875, and it stayed in Devonear's active repertory until at least 1880. A sheet music edition of Devonear's song appeared in 1875 in both piano-vocal and guitar-vocal arrangements, and it was anthologized in at least six songsters between 1878 and 1882.[44]

Devonear's commercial spiritual incorporates the chorus of the traditional spiritual "There's a Meeting Here Tonight" (see example 6.3, from the singing of the Tennesseans) and the continuous flow of folk performance between the verse and chorus ("Get you ready, there's a"). Although he retains the internal refrain used in the traditional spiritual, he writes new verses featuring the kinds of caricatures expected in endman humor (the "yaller gal," "two overseers to one little nigger") and uses the typical double verse form of minstrel songs, ||:abab':|| (see example 6.4).

Given the large number of spirituals circulating at this time, why did Devonear choose to base his first composition on "There's a Meeting Here Tonight"? It was probably one of Devonear's favorites, and its various social resonances made it a fortuitous choice. The spiritual played an important role in conveying coded information in slave culture. Ex-slave William Henry Robinson (1848–1923) recalled in his autobiography that "in order to notify slaves on other farms when there was going to be a meeting they would sing this song, and the slaves would understand what it meant. White people would think

FIGURE 6.5. Illustration of Pete Devonear from the sheet music to his composition "Run Home, Levi" (Boston: White, Smith, 1878). Music Division, Library of Congress.

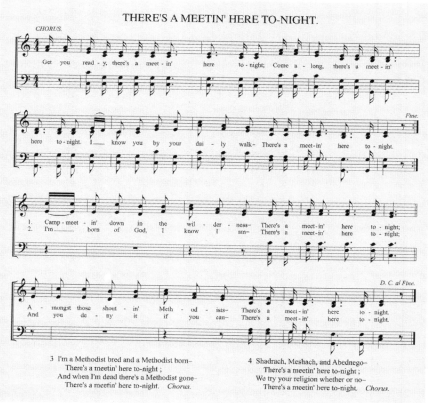

EXAMPLE 6.3. A transcription of the Tennesseans' version of the traditional spiritual "There's a Meetin' Here To-night," from *Selections of Plantation Songs as Sung by Donavin's Famous Tennesseans.*

EXAMPLE 6.4. Pete Devonear's commercial spiritual, "Dar's a Meeting Here Tonight" (1875). Music Division, Library of Congress.

they were only singing for amusement."[45] It also seems to have been known by a wide range of African Americans and, through the jubilee singers, by many white audiences. Two versions of the traditional spiritual appeared in Allen, Ware, and Garrison's *Slave Songs of the United States* (no. 11), and the Tennesseans, the Jackson Jubilee Singers, and the Fisks, among others, all sang it.[46] The traditional lyrics appear in *The Ham-Town Students Songster*—perhaps the strongest evidence of the spiritual's popularity. The lyrics cohered with

EXAMPLE 6.4. Continued; see also p. 172.

minstrelsy's longstanding interest in religion and postwar fixation with camp meetings as a representation of slave culture, and the upbeat lyrics and tempo were ideal for dancing.

SAM LUCAS: "CARVE DAT POSSUM" Lucas had his name attached as composer or lyricist to at least fifty-four published songs, twenty-one of which were commercial spirituals.[47] Lucas's commercial spirituals, like Devonear's, exhibit strong folk traits.

EXAMPLE 6.4. Continued.

Lucas (see figure 6.6) was born into slavery on 7 August, most likely in 1840, on a plantation in Romney, Hampshire County, Virginia. His parents, who belonged to Samuel Cockerill, were freed upon Cockerill's death one or two years after Lucas was born. The family then moved to southern Ohio, settling in Washington Court House, where Sam was raised. This small rural town (which many sources erroneously cite as his birthplace) is located in Fayette County, home to two heavily used routes on the Underground Railroad. After about five years in secondary school, Lucas apprenticed to a barber—an occupation that

FIGURE 6.6. Sam Lucas, from a poster for C. H. Smith's Double Mammoth Uncle Tom's Cabin Company. Courtesy of the Historical Society of Pennsylvania, theater posters collection, V6-0494.

would sustain him in lean times as he began his theatrical career.[48] He started performing in amateur minstrel shows in Wilmington, Ohio, before moving on to more prestigious jobs in Cincinnati. Lucas interrupted his burgeoning theatrical career in order to serve in the U.S. Colored Infantry.[49] From 29 March to 4 October 1865 Private Lucas worked at the hospital at Fortress Monroe— three years before Samuel Armstrong founded the Hampton Institute. In 1870 at the advanced age of thirty, he began working steadily and professionally as a minstrel. (Most minstrels began their careers as children.) In July 1873 Lucas joined Charles Callender's Georgia Minstrels as a ballad singer and general performer, later graduating to endman on bones. He performed with the troupe through 1875—the year his first compositions were published. By the time he left, his pleasing tenor, comic ingenuity, and flair for dramatic roles had made him an audience favorite.

"Carve Dat Possum" is the first song for which Lucas claimed sole authorship; it was published as sheet music in 1875. Although the secular content of this song would seem to exclude it from the category of commercial spiritual, the tune of the verse belongs to the slave spiritual "Go Down, Moses" and the chorus, while deviating from the melody of "Moses," nonetheless reproduces its familiar refrain "Let my people go," substituting the words "carve him to de heart" (see example 6.5). The traditional spiritual and its commercial cousin are identical in structure except for the double verse of "Possum."

"Carve Dat Possum" was the subject of a public feud between Lucas and Henry Hart, a violinist and minstrel manager with whom Lucas had worked. (They cowrote the hit song "Daffney, Do You Love Me," which was also published in 1875.) Lucas placed an ad in the *New York Clipper* (4 Sept. 1875) to refute the charge that Lucas had appropriated Hart's songs, one of them being "Carve Dat Possum." "This Hart has a good deal of cool impudence, which is rather refreshing this hot weather," wrote Lucas. "The words of 'Carve Dat Possum,' which H. Hart also has the effrontery to claim, were written by a lad in Kentucky; the music has long been sung in many colored churches." According to the cover of the sheet music, however, "the Author of Words and Music" to this "Original Song and Chorus" was Sam Lucas. Lucas and Hart's dispute, whether genuine or fabricated for publicity, confirms that Lucas intentionally borrowed the tune of a spiritual for his secular song. It also demonstrates a longstanding knowledge of black sacred music, most likely fostered by his mother, whom Lucas remembered as singing religious songs during his childhood.[50] Like many entertainers of the day, Lucas claimed the authenticity of tradition and original authorship in the same breath.

"Carve Dat Possum" was embraced by both black and white performers, who sang it on minstrel and variety stages into the 1880s. Another indicator of its early popularity is a Hamtown Students parody arranged by G. W. H. Griffin, with new words by E. D. Gooding. Although Gooding retained the internal refrain "carve him to the heart," Griffin changed the key from minor to major, retaining enough of the melodic contour that the song was recognizable. The Hamtown "Possum," then, is a parody that signifies upon a secular minstrel song that itself signifies upon a spiritual—the kind of musical punning that had long

EXAMPLE 6.5. First half of the chorus to Sam Lucas's "Carve Dat Possum" (1875); the second half is identical. Music Division, Library of Congress.

been at the heart of minstrel performance. Harry C. Browne recorded Lucas's version in 1917, and white old-time musician Uncle Dave Macon (1870–1952) recorded a song by that name in 1927 that shares little with Lucas's original composition other than the possum theme and the internal refrain—the melody, in major, is altered significantly.[51]

Although "Carve Dat Possum" had nothing whatsoever to do with spiritual matters, the melody transmitted the *sound* of spirituals—in this case, the historically significant spiritual "Go Down, Moses," the first to be published in print. Lucas's first composition was a notable example of how a commercial secular song could popularize spirituals—or reflect their popularity—without explicit textual reference to the traditional genre.

WILL S. HAYS: "ANGELS MEET ME AT THE CROSS ROADS" Given the talented songwriters within their own ranks, the Georgia Minstrels had no need to program a commercial spiritual by an outside composer, especially one who was white. But hit songs can't be ignored, and Will S. Hays's "Angels Meet Me at the Cross Roads" was one of the greatest hits of 1875.[52]

William Shakespeare Hays (1837–1907) was a southerner from Louisville, Kentucky. He began writing songs in 1853 and didn't stop until over three hundred titles later, which sold some twenty million copies over the course of his career. Five of his songs were greatest hits in 1871, 1872, 1875, and 1878 (two that year), and three of those five were commercial spirituals. During the Civil War, Hays served as a war correspondent for the *Louisville Courier* and commanded a transport on the Mississippi—pursuits that ended abruptly in 1862, when Union General Benjamin Butler imprisoned him for writing seditious songs. After the war he focused largely on comic and slavery-themed songs, which were popular among minstrel entertainers. (Fisk tenor Thomas Rutling sang one of these, "Little Sam," in a school entertainment in 1867, discussed in chap. 2.)[53]

Although Hays didn't write many commercial spirituals, two of them— "Angels Meet Me at the Cross Roads" (1875) and "Keep in de Middle ob de Road" (1878)—were among the best-known commercial spirituals ever written, performed by both black and white entertainers alike. "Angels," as published in the 1875 sheet music edition, had no possums or yaller gals, unlike Devonear's and Lucas's songs that year. The first verse set the tone: "Come down, Gabriel, blow your horn, / Call me home in de early morn; / Send de chariot down dis way, / Come and haul me home to stay."

Despite the lyrics, the song didn't resemble a folk spiritual musically. The melody was essentially that of "Zip Coon," also known as "Turkey in the Straw"—which Hays also recycled in the choruses to his songs "Don't Forget Me, Hannah" (1875) and "Roll Out! Heave Dat Cotton" (1877). (He was hardly the only composer to borrow this melody; for example, white composer/minstrel Hughey Docherty employed it in the refrain of his 1884 commercial spiritual "Put on de Golden Crown.")

The song inspired numerous parodies, as well as an answer song by Frank Bristow called "Keep Move-a-lin Along" (with words by Hays). Of course song titles on playbills don't always indicate which lyrics minstrels sang. The version of "Angels" that Billy Kersands sang with Callender's Georgia Minstrels a few years later put the verses in a different order and used a new second verse: "What kind shoes is those them angels wear, / That they walk up yonder, up in the air? / Stand by the gate till I hear angels knock, / Then I'll drop al my nickles [*sic*] in the missionary box."[54] The first line is related to the popular spiritual "What Kind of Shoes You Gwine to Wear," and the reference to the missionary box comes from verse 3 of Hays's "Angels." T. M. Hengler (white) also sang an altered version that reversed the first two lines of Hays's introductory verse, which he completed with his own original lyrics: "Make haste darkies, don't you wait, /

'Case you all may lose dem keys to de gate."[55] Many other white minstrels also sang the same version as Hengler.

JAMES STEWART: "ANGEL GABRIEL" One more commercial spiritual joined "Angels, Meet Me" among the hit songs of 1875, and like the first line of Hays's song it too invoked Gabriel in its message of crossing over into heaven. "Angel Gabriel" by white composer James Stewart and white lyricist and minstrel Frank Dumont was marketed as an end song "as sung by Callender's Jubilee Minstrels."[56] (At the beginning of 1875 Callender formed a second troupe of black minstrels in addition to the Georgias and chose the name to capitalize on the jubilee singing craze. Lew Johnson's Original Tennessee Jubilee Singers, formed in 1877, was another contribution to the already bewildering array of minstrel troupes with "Tennessee" and "Jubilee" in their name.) A specialty of Billy Kersands, who also sang "Angels Meet Me," the song was a staple on programs by Haverly's Colored Minstrels in the 1880s, and many other troupes sang it as well. Harry C. Browne recorded it in 1916, and the song survives today in old-time and bluegrass traditions.[57]

Stewart (1842–1884) wrote at least a hundred songs but only one commercial spiritual, and it turned out to be his greatest hit. His life had several tragic parallels with that of Stephen Foster: although Stewart was born in Detroit, his parents were born in Foster's native city of Pittsburgh; both composers were musically precocious at an early age; both lived in Cincinnati (Foster only for a short time, Stewart in the last four years of his life); both were the foremost songwriters of their day; and both died premature deaths resulting from long dissipation.[58]

"Angel Gabriel" is an infectious tune with the flavor of a folk spiritual. Although its G-minor melody uses every diatonic scale degree except E♭ (employing both F♯ and F natural), the liberal doses of minor-third intervals give it a pentatonic flavor. The chorus, which begins in relative major, is written in four parts in the manner of a gospel hymn, with the lower voices echoing the lead (see example 6.6; see also web recording 6.2). The schottische rhythm (which singers undoubtedly altered liberally in performance, as Browne's recording suggests) was a common dance rhythm in minstrel songs of the time. In the hands of Callender's premier comic, Billy Kersands, this end song was a ready-made opportunity for humorous vocal delivery, gesture, and dance.

Stewart had an ongoing relationship with black minstrels in the 1870s and was an early influence on the noted black songwriter Gussie Davis.[59] He arranged Henry Hart's 1873 song "Good Sweet Ham"; wrote "Old Massa's Dead" (1876) for Charles (Barney) Hicks, whose name and affiliation with the Original

EXAMPLE 6.6. Chorus to James Stewart's "Angel Gabriel" (1875). Music Division, Library of Congress.

Georgia Minstrels is prominently displayed on the cover of the sheet music; and wrote "The Flower of Tennessee" (1878) for Callender's Georgia Minstrels. Minstrels both black and white would perform a good hit song regardless of its composer's race, although the color line caused "the song" to be a fluid concept. As the foregoing examples demonstrate, just as performances of folk spirituals were unique, so were performances of commercial spirituals, in which different performers' decisions regarding lyrics, dialect, tempo, instrumentation, and performance style could result in dissimilar renderings of the same song.

Concluding Thoughts

Although the early student jubilee troupes distanced themselves from blackface minstrelsy through dress, comportment, and musical style, minstrel and variety shows became one of the most reliable barometers of their popularity. There was nothing unique in this, since minstrels had a tradition of spoofing everything from classical drama to operas to famous actors, political and religious figures, scandals, and fads. When jubilee singers came along, their earliest parodists were, not surprisingly, white performers.

The burlesque of spirituals was progressive, evolving over four stages. The earliest stage was characterized by a one-to-one relationship between a jubilee troupe and its parody, with white performers in blackface impersonating specific jubilee troupes and singing contrafacta, a time-honored compositional method among minstrels. Such acts began in mid-1872 but remained ephemeral through 1874, materializing when a jubilee troupe came to town and vanishing shortly thereafter. The second stage involved black minstrels composing their own contrafacta of spirituals, as Pete Devonear and Sam Lucas did in 1874. The third stage consisted of the establishment of white Hamtown acts in 1875, featuring both traditional and commercial spirituals in blackface. With their long-running Hamtown Student Singers, Gooding and Griffin converted what had been brief, topical burlesques into a near-permanent fixture on variety and minstrel programs, parodying the phenomenon of jubilee singing rather than any one group. The final stage was the formation of similarly generic black Hamtown acts in 1876. The Georgia Minstrels, at least, appear to have sung noncomic renditions of spirituals in the guise of the Hamtown or Georgian students, which they later parodied as the Bogtown Quartette. Over time, then, faux jubileers developed from an ephemeral to a sustained presence on minstrel and variety bills, singing both traditional and commercial spirituals.

This development went hand in hand with the turn toward plantation themes in minstrelsy, which began in white shows but quickly became the province of black performers, whom white audiences considered to be the living representations of the southern slave, no matter their individual life circumstances. White performers certainly continued to perform commercial spirituals and plantation-themed sketches, but black troupes built their shows around them through the 1880s and on occasion into the 1890s. In fact, black performers chasing commercial success were stuck on a theatrical plantation, whose sets of cotton fields, cabins, and rolling rivers followed them around the country.

Dennison wrote of commercial spirituals that "the songs speak for themselves; no great perspicacity is needed to discern the racism in them."[60] As this chapter attempts to show, however, the songs don't speak for themselves—in fact, no song does. Commercial spirituals had complicated social lives that offer perspective on how black entertainers in particular made use of folk material as they navigated the shoals of popular entertainment. For example, many black performers in the 1870s were illiterate and/or musically illiterate. Raised with the norm of orally transmitted and communally created expressive culture, they borrowed tunes and texts freely. They taught their songs to the orchestra by standing on the stage and humming, or else they spent several dollars to hire an arranger to make scores for the instrumentalists.[61] (Devonear likely used the former method; Lucas used the latter, which could explain in part why Lucas's songs were published more quickly after they were performed.)

It's understandable that Dennison saw the commercial spiritual as a new "gimmick" that "represented a fresh point of departure in [the commercial songsmith's] slander of the black," but an examination of the social contexts in which such songs operated points to additional dimensions.[62] First, commercial spirituals extended a preexisting trajectory of religious burlesque that included camp meeting songs. Second, even though some white performers used commercial spirituals as a vehicle for racist commentary, some black performers capitalized on the genre for their own ends. Third, meaning could be altered in performance; for example, when black minstrels performed commercial spirituals for black audiences they likely deployed "Africanist cultural inflections" to add layers of allusion and commentary that only insiders could appreciate and decode, as Brenda Gottschild suggests.[63] Moreover, the complex relationships between white and black performers, and between performers and their audiences, often included liberal doses of admiration and respect, which is obscured when focusing solely on song lyrics.

Dennison admits more nuance into his analysis in asserting that some songwriters of commercial spirituals attempted to capture "authentic" black folk music, but his argument rests on the cover illustration of the sheet music. The more "textually serious" songs, he observes, have a dignified illustration or none at all, whereas the more insulting songs have grotesque caricatures.[64] Cover illustrations were usually conceived by the publisher, however, not the songwriter or performer, and they didn't necessarily correspond to the way a particular song was performed. A popular song like "Angels Meet Me at the Cross Roads," for example, was performed by all manner of entertainers, using different arrangements and performance practices that conveyed varied attitudes and interpretations—white and black (with or without blackface), minstrel and variety, young and old, male (more likely) but also female (e.g., the popular Charlotte Crabtree, known as Lotta). Cover illustrations and printed music couldn't reflect how performers changed words, adapted tunes, and changed the degree to which a song was comic or serious.

In embodying racial stereotypes and caricatures, black minstrel performers were in essence required to perform their own invisibility, as Stephanie Dunson powerfully phrases it.[65] Considering commercial spirituals as an extension of that axiom, and considering that black performers had no choice but to inhabit racist caricatures onstage, why did Pete Devonear, Sam Lucas, James Bland, Fred Lyons, and others contribute new songs to the genre?

- Published commercial spirituals provided additional income and contributed to a performer's reputation, especially when other minstrels adopted their compositions for performance. (If black performers were going to be forced to burlesque black music and performance practice, they might as well profit from it.)
- Composing their own commercial spirituals gave black performers a measure of control over their material, even if they ultimately had to conform to stereotype.
- Some black composers used the composition of commercial spirituals as an escape route from minstrelsy. Sam Lucas, for example, was intent on a legitimate stage career and determined to sever his connections to the minstrel show. After achieving popularity with a number of commercial spirituals and other stereotypical minstrel songs, he went on to perform character songs, sentimental songs, and other nonracialized popular songs from the late 1880s on.[66] Jacob Sawyer is another black composer who wrote the requisite commercial spirituals but who ultimately composed in the style of cultivated parlor music.

Judging from the few reviews of black minstrels performing for largely black audiences, it's evident that black audiences especially appreciated hearing tunes from black culture, and their enthusiastic embrace of these songs' reception invigorated black performers in the highly interactive theatrical environment of the time. Admiration was by no means universal, however, especially among educated black audiences. Robert Moton, who after graduating from Hampton Institute in 1890 served in the administration there and then succeeded Booker T. Washington as president of Tuskegee Institute in 1915, wrote in his autobiography about attending Robinson's Circus in Farmville, Virginia, around 1878:

> I remember the animals, of which I had only seen pictures before, and also the ring performances—fancy riding, antics of the clowns, and so forth. At the close of the main performance a concert was announced and my last ten cents was paid for it. Some twenty or thirty men with faces blackened appeared in a semicircle with banjos, tambourines, and the like. The stories they told and the performances they gave were indeed most interesting to me, but I remember how shocked I was when they sang, "Wear dem Golden Slippers to Walk dem Golden Streets," two men dancing to the tune exactly as it was sung by the people in the Negro churches of my community. This song was as sacred to me as "Nearer, My God, to Thee" or "Old Hundred." I felt that these white men were making fun, not only of our colour and of our songs, but also of our religion. It took three years of training at Hampton Institute to bring me to the point of being willing to sing Negro songs in the presence of white people. White minstrels with black faces have done more than any other single agency to lower the tone of Negro music and cause the Negro to despise his own songs.[67]

Moton's trauma at hearing his sacred melodies used as a means for blackface humor echoes Dennison's sentiments about commercial spirituals. To read commercial spirituals as multifaceted and historically significant is not to deny that they could inflict psychological and social violence. That it took Moton three years to overcome his reluctance to share the music he loved with white audiences, after he had witnessed white performers disrespect that music and the culture it represented, underscores the complexities of class, education, and religiosity that underlay blacks' complex and varied reactions to commercial spirituals in the nineteenth century.

CHAPTER 7

Spirituals in Uncle Tom Shows, Melodramas, and Spectacles

A rainy night in Boston, spring 1876. The truck that paraded Uncle Tom's little log house with its smoking chimney through the city all week long had accomplished its goal: crowds thronged the theater. Most everyone in the audience had read the novel and seen the play several times before (it had been staged off and on in Boston for over twenty years!) but it didn't matter—every performance was a little different, and the sets were so grand and the cast so large, it was impossible to take it all in during one viewing. Fifty cents bought something for everyone: a moral story that the most ardent critics of the theater could not condemn. (Everyone knew that even Harriet Beecher Stowe, who had never set foot in a theater before she wrote Uncle Tom's Cabin, *finally acknowledged its salutary potential.) An Uncle Tom so realistic you'd swear he'd been plucked right out of old Kentucky, and so pathetic that his very presence brought tears to your eyes. (Who could be immune to Shelby's final plea: "Oh! dear Uncle Tom! do wake—do speak once more! Look up! Here's Master George—your own little Master George. Don't you know me?") And Little Eva floating up to the portals of Heaven! (Each of us ladies carried a dainty kerchief that night, which over the course of the performance passed through all stages of moisture, until it became as wet as the pavements outside.) Spectacular scenery—my favorite was the maze of bobbing ice floes during Eliza's treacherous escape across the Ohio River. The sassy, blackfaced Topsy, whose gleeful "Golly, ain't I wicked?" drew shouts of agreement from the audience as she sang her famous song and danced a breakdown. A virtuoso black banjoist with the fingers of Paganini. Sentimental songs, which supplied a good dose of emotion in case the acting didn't. And a spectacular plantation scene along the Mississippi River featuring over a hundred real black folk picking cotton, along with—and this is what I'd come to see—jubilee singers singing songs of the African race!*[1]

Uncle Tom's Cabin was adapted for the stage before the serial publication of the story in the abolitionist newspaper *National Era* was completed, and before it appeared in book form.[2] The immediate and spectacular success of the novel, published in March 1852, prompted numerous other attempts at dramatization by a variety of authors but never by Stowe herself. *UTC* (as it became known in advertisements) became a staple of theaters—urban and rural, legitimate and makeshift—well into the twentieth century. "Poor old Uncle Tom doesn't get much of a chance to rest in his grave," a *New York Times* writer commented sardonically, "even though all the Uncle Toms have . . . joined the Freedmen's Bureau."[3]

As theater historian Harry Birdoff and others have pointed out, stage adaptations of *Uncle Tom's Cabin* were folk plays that defied easy categorization. Different versions survive today in script form, but *UTC* onstage *lived* in oral transmission, retaining its topicality long after the Civil War through interpolations of characters, jokes, songs, specialty acts, and even plot points that reflected local tastes and the latest fads. Although the earliest *UTC* productions were earnest melodramas featuring orchestral interludes and songs that portrayed a character's personality (the original definition of "melodrama"),[4] the proliferation of Tom companies and the ensuing efforts to outdo one another contributed to the play's transformation into a sensational, multifaceted entertainment by the 1870s and 1880s. The *UTC* productions of this later era were melodramas in the sense that most people understand the term today—dramatic plays with exaggerated characterizations that play (or prey) on the emotions—and they often bore only superficial resemblance to Stowe's novel. The original political message was gradually overwhelmed by specialty dancers, magicians, animal menageries (bloodhounds, donkeys, Shetland ponies, even alligators), and other novelty acts as various productions absorbed influences from farce, burlesque, pantomime, minstrelsy, variety, and circus. In short, as Birdoff observes, *Uncle Tom's Cabin* on stage, like the beloved character of Topsy, "just grow'd."[5] Among this menagerie of specialty acts were jubilee singers, one of the few interpolations with dramatic if not strictly historical legitimacy, since jubilee groups didn't exist until well after the war. Debuting in 1876, their presence quickly became mandatory, not only in productions of *Uncle Tom's Cabin* but in other plays and stage entertainments as well.

The timing was auspicious. By 1876 jubilee singing had been prospering for over three years, with no sign of abatement. (On 1 January of that year the fruit of the Fisk Jubilee Singers' labors became a national news story when General Clinton B. Fisk presided over the dedication of Fisk University's new

Jubilee Hall, raised with the singers' donations.)[6] Nostalgia for plantation days before the war also fueled interest in jubilee singers and spirituals. Callender's Georgia Minstrels, who had been touring for ten years, and Callender's new Jubilee Minstrels were beginning to find success with their plantation-themed shows, which included "slave and jubilee songs." And as the previous chapter demonstrates, a commercial spirituals industry was already thriving in minstrel and variety shows.

Furthermore, 1876 was the centennial year, and the United States was in a self-congratulatory mood. The Centennial Exhibition in Philadelphia, which ran from 10 May to 10 November, displayed the progress Americans had made in agriculture and industry to some 10 million visitors from home and abroad.[7] Those who passed through the Main Exhibition Building could see what black schools of the South had contributed. Hampton Institute was the only black school sponsored by the American Missionary Association to have its own exhibit; the fourteen others (including Fisk, whose Jubilee Singers were in Europe at the time) exhibited collectively. Whereas the Fisk Jubilee Singers were represented by an oil painting of the troupe (made in England by artist Edmund Havell), Hampton sent photographs, bound volumes of manuscript examinations, a file of the periodical *Southern Workman* published by the Hampton Institute, copies of Armstrong and Ludlow's *Hampton and Its Students* with Thomas Fenner's *Cabin and Plantation Songs*, and a map of West Virginia, Virginia, and North Carolina that showed where Hampton graduates were teaching. In addition, Joseph B. Towe, one of the original Hampton student singers (class of 1875), who had written an essay titled "Old Time Music" illustrated with songs by the school, was advertised to "be in attendance upon the articles exhibited and ready to answer questions about them."[8] Hampton was poised to display not only the progress of African Americans but the role of spirituals in facilitating that progress.

Many of the millions who visited the Centennial Exhibition in Philadelphia went on to visit neighboring cities, which translated into good business for northern theaters in general and *Uncle Tom's Cabin* productions in particular. Despite a certain discomfort in reviving the play to commemorate the centennial—"so that, presumably, we may be chastened by remembrance of things that most people would be glad to forget," as one one journalist complained[9]—New York theaters in particular benefited, for the city was "full of rural visitors . . . to whom the subject is so well known and so strongly interesting."[10] As the *New York Clipper* noted in November, just before the Philadelphia exhibition closed, "The trials and tribulations of the colored race, as exemplified in the alleged checkered career of 'Uncle Tom,'" brought "thousands to tiers at the Grand Opera-house; . . . to the Centennial pilgrim may the credit be awarded," who was "bound to take in all the sights and marvels of this great city."[11]

It was amid this incipient jubilee mania, a growing nostalgia for the Old South, and the dawn of centennial fever that the "colored Georgia Jubilee Singers" made their debut in *Uncle Tom's Cabin* starring Mr. and Mrs. G. C. Howard (white) in a three-week run at the Bowery Theatre in New York, in February 1876.[12]

The Origin of Jubilee Singers in Tom Shows

Some independent jubilee groups attempted to distinguish themselves from the Fisk Jubilee Singers by giving a theatrical slant to their performances. The Wilmington Jubilee Singers, for example, lent their "slave songs of the South" an air of verisimilitude with tableaus and costumes of slavery days, with the intent of giving "portraits, not caricatures, of the slave as he was" (see also chaps. 4 and 8). Their ads promised a "beautiful illustration of a slave camp meeting; a good time on the old plantation; Uncle Tom and Aunt Chloe on a holiday; life among the lowly of the Far South."[13] These scenes reveal the unmistakable influence of Harriet Beecher Stowe's *Uncle Tom's Cabin* (Uncle Tom and Aunt Chloe being characters in the novel, and "life among the lowly" the book's subtitle) and also extend the imagery of cabins and old aunties that the Tennesseans had used in their advertisements (chap. 4). The reviewer of the Wilmingtons' May performance at Henry Ward Beecher's Plymouth Church noted that only one of the twelve performers (seven females, five males) had received "anything like a technical education in music":

> But every one of them is gifted not only with the musical temperament of his race, but also with extraordinary vocal powers to give that gift singular effect. . . . Their voices have a strange sympathetic mellowness, while their evident feeling of the power of their own singing increases the sympathy of the audience. Their presentation of certain pictures of Southern life are admirable illustrations of the slaves in ante-war times; and their whole entertainment is quaint, exciting and even instructive.[14]

For some white audience members, then, the costumes, scenery, and settings were not just entertaining but ethnographic. In 1876 the Howards extended this concept by incorporating jubilee singers and scenes of plantation life into their stage play of *Uncle Tom's Cabin*.

The marital union in 1844 of actors George Cunnibell Howard (1815–1887) and Caroline Emily Fox (1829–1908) was the beginning of a theatrical dynasty.

Their first production of *Uncle Tom's Cabin* in Troy, New York, in 1852 featured three generations of their combined families and marked their beginning as "Tommers"—actors who devoted an entire career to the play. Although their extended family of performers eventually dispersed, for the next thirty-five years the names of Mr. and Mrs. G. C. Howard were synonymous with the roles of St. Clare and Topsy; and for almost a decade their daughter, Cordelia, was the personification of Eva. Caroline Howard's cousin, George L. Aiken (1830–1876), dramatized Stowe's novel for the troupe and also inaugurated the role of George Harris. Aiken's version became the most popular and frequently performed of the century.[15]

By January 1876 *UTC* productions had been playing for almost twenty-five years, and the Tom arena was more crowded than ever. The Howards gained an edge on their competitors and, as Thomas Riis notes, "changed the face of *Uncle Tom's Cabin* productions" for the next twenty-five years, by introducing jubilee singers and spirituals to their melodrama.[16] The first troupe they worked with, the Georgia Jubilee Singers, was managed by John H. Slavin (white) and became known as Slavin's Georgia Jubilee Singers. Until this time, the advertised "plantation songs and dances" in the play were white compositions with a minstrel flavor. The verisimilitude promised by the addition of genuine African American songs, singers, instrumentalists, dancers, and supernumeraries (e.g., "field hands" working on the plantation who didn't speak or sing) revived white audience interest in this well-worn story. Since jubilee troupes and Tom productions shared audiences from the same geographical areas (the North, stretching west to California), it was a natural fit.[17]

The Howards' decision to include jubilee singers in *UTC* was artistically and economically shrewd. Not only did the Wilmington Jubilee Singers turn up in a rival *UTC* company just two weeks later, but by March there were so many *UTC* productions sporting jubilee singers that Slavin printed a notice in the *New York Clipper* reminding the public that the Georgia Colored Singers "were the FIRST that appeared in UNCLE TOM'S CABIN," and warned theater managers against "unscrupulous parties who represent themselves as the Original Georgia Colored Singers."[18] Within the year there were even jubilee singers in West Coast productions.[19]

The Howards' itinerary in 1876 gives some idea of their influence and the ability of a jubilee troupe to make a living with a Tom show. From 15 February to 11 March they played the Bowery Theatre in New York followed by the Brooklyn Academy of Music and the Brooklyn Theatre. They moved to Boston in April and May, where they played the Boston Theatre and the Boston Museum, before returning to New York for a three-week run at the Park Theatre. Over the summer, when most city theaters were deserted, Slavin's troupe of Georgias would go on the road as a concert organization, and then rejoin a Tom troupe in the fall. By November 1876 they were back in New York for a five-week run at the Grand Opera-House.[20]

They gave performances Monday through Saturday nights, adding matinees on Wednesday and Saturday, and the jubilee singers customarily gave a "sacred concert" (so called to sidestep the prohibition against entertainments on the Christian Sabbath) on Sunday evenings. Although attendance records aren't available, long runs indicate healthy attendance, and most of these theaters were large ones: the Bowery seated 4,000, the Boston Theatre 3,140, the Grand Opera-House 2,000 (plus accommodation for 1,500 standing). Conservatively speaking, if 800 people saw the show five times per week, then 100,000 people (some of them repeat attendees) saw the show over those twenty-five weeks; in likelihood the number was larger (allowing for matinees and the large crowds that the newspapers claimed). And this was just one production, in one year. Considering that large cities might host several productions of *UTC* in a year, and smaller towns at least once a year, the impact of this play—and of its jubilee singers—becomes evident.

The Role of Black Singers in Tom Shows

Jubilee troupes were among the three or four attractions consistently singled out in *UTC* advertisements and publicity blurbs through the 1890s. As their presence became a convention, one Tom show even distinguished itself from the competition by proclaiming, "No 'jubilee singers,' No 'slaves before the war,' No 'shouters.'"[21] How were spirituals presented in Tom shows, and what effect did they have on audiences? Because of the paucity of descriptive evidence, this question must be answered by piecing together clues from various productions.

Howard Productions

In 1876 George Howard reconstructed, or "perfected" as he termed it, Aiken's script. Among his several revisions was the insertion of a band of singing slaves (i.e., jubilee singers), although he specified no song titles. Programs, reviews, and advertisements, however, name some of the spirituals in Howard's productions from 1876 and note that they were refreshed periodically.[22]

The jubilee singers appeared mostly at the beginning and ending of scenes, as relevant to the plot. In a functional sense, their singing masked the noise of scene changes. In an artistic sense, their singing set the mood and provided emotional commentary on the action. In response to audience acclaim, the Howards' production expanded the jubilee singers' role to other types of song, causing one critic to grumble, "Though they are dragged into it without motive they sing very well, and so long as they confine their vocalization to characteristic negro songs their presence is sanctioned by the canons of art. But it is just as inconsistent for slaves to be indulging in classical music [songs from the white cultivated tradition] as for philanthropists to be giving greenbacks to fugitive slaves years before greenbacks were thought of."[23] This was the very opinion that the Hyers sisters encountered when they tried to sing art music upon their arrival in the East (chap. 4).

The action begins with George Shelby regretfully settling his debt with the slave trader Haley by giving him his trusted slave Tom (played by a white actor in blackface, as were all the speaking parts for black characters circa 1876) and little Harry, the child of his wife's servant, Eliza.[24] The next scene, in which Uncle Tom and Aunt Chloe learn of Tom's sad fate, concludes with the jubilee singers slowly crossing and then exiting the stage singing the spiritual "Is Massa Gwine to Sell Us Today?," whose funereal echoes drift from the wings (see example 7.1). The singing of "Gospel Train" (also known as "Get on Board, Children") adds urgency to the next incident: Eliza's escape with Harry across the treacherous ice floes of the Ohio River.

The locale then changes to the plantation of St. Clare in Louisiana. The slave troupe sings a sentimental parlor song about the sunny South in the background. During Uncle Tom's trip with Haley down the Mississippi to New Orleans, he had saved a little white girl—Eva—who fell into the water as the rush of passengers disembarked from the steamboat. St. Clare gratifies his daughter's immediate attachment to her savior by buying Tom. Eva's character is distilled in these few lines from the first scene in act 2:

ST. CLARE: I say, what do you think, Pussy? Which do you like the best—to live as they do at your uncle's, up in Vermont, or to have a house-full of servants, as we do?

EVA: Oh! of course our way is the pleasantest.

ST. CLARE: [Patting her head.] Why so?

EVA: Because it makes so many more round you to love, you know.

Eva has also heard Tom sing—"about the new Jerusalem, and bright angels, and the land of Canaan." St. Clare comments, "I dare say, it's better than the opera, isn't it?" and Eva answers, "Yes; and he's going to teach them to me."[25]

Also present on the plantation is St. Clare's sickly, selfish wife, Marie, and his northern cousin Ophelia, who oversees the household and for whom St. Clare

EXAMPLE 7.1. "Is Master Going to Sell Us To-morrow," a staple of *UTC* productions in the 1870s, arranged by Robert H. Hamilton, an original Hampton Institute Singer and the first director of the Hampton Choir at the school (1880–1886). The *UTC* productions called it "Is Massa Gwine to Sell Us Today?" and may have used a different arrangement. Reprinted from *Jubilee and Plantation Songs*, 51.

has brought a present: a little slave girl named Topsy. She is Eva's opposite in every way: black, energetic, mischievous, uneducated, unworldly, wily—qualities that she proceeds to celebrate in G. C. Howard's famous song and dance "I'se So Wicked." Ophelia's interrogation reveals that Topsy has no idea where she came from and gives rise to her famous speculation, "I spect I growed. Don't think nobody never made me."

The remaining scenes in act 2 shift briefly back and forth between Kentucky and Ohio. George, Eliza, and Harry are reunited but still pursued and become engaged in a gunfight. Uncle Tom pleads with St. Clare to avoid alcohol, and Eva pleads with Topsy to be good. The jubilee singers are temporarily absent, to return in act 3.

The first scene in act 3 foreshadows Eva's death; the script calls for Uncle Tom and Eva to sing of the New Jerusalem in the Methodist hymn "I See a Band of Spirits Bright" (which Stowe included in the novel). Eva, knowing she is not long for this world, pleads with her father to free his slaves after she is gone. By scene 3, her death is imminent. In an 1878 staging by Jarrett and Palmer (discussed in the next section), Eva reclines on a couch surrounded by her family, and the slaves kneel outside the house, softly and solemnly singing the spiritual "Steal Away" as the scene opens (see figure 7.1). The emotional power of this tableau resides chiefly in the music. "As the spirit of the child wings its flight the slaves sing 'Tell Me Where My Eva's Gone,' and then, as the curtain descends," the (white) gospel hymn "In the Sweet Bye and Bye," wrote a reviewer in the *New York Clipper*. The audience demanded two repetitions of the music.[26]

We next discover that Topsy, in possession of a lock of Eva's hair, is only half as wicked as she used to be, and that St. Clare is a broken man. He tells Tom of his promise to free him, and Ophelia offers to take Topsy to Vermont, which she gleefully accepts. The joy is short-lived, however, when Tom breaks the news to Ophelia that St. Clare has been killed. As his body is brought in and placed on the sofa, the singing band of slaves follows. St. Clare has just enough strength to regret that he has not signed Tom's freedom papers, and then expires to the strains of Stephen Foster's "Massa's in de Cold, Cold Ground" as the curtain descends.

St. Clare's death brings Uncle Tom to the auction block in New Orleans, which is the setting as act 4 opens. (Some productions used this opportunity for minstrel business, in which slaves showed their talents to prospective buyers by singing, dancing, and playing instruments.) The evil Legree buys Tom. Scene 2 jumps to Vermont, where Topsy has completed her conversion to goodness, and Ophelia attracts the attention of the widower Deacon Perry. The next scene—scene 3—is the one that audiences from the late 1870s on learned to anticipate.

The curtain opens onto a "marvelously realistic" plantation scene, populated by one hundred "genuine" blacks—male and female, young and old—on a cotton plantation in full bloom as a steamer floats on the Mississippi River in the background (see figure 7.2). "The dusky field hands are hard at work, and in the foreground a group of male and female figures are chanting an old camp-meeting melody" such as "Ole Sheep Know the Road" or "Children Don't Get Weary" (both of them spirituals).

FIGURE 7.1. Eva's death scene from William A. Brady's (white) lavish production of *Uncle Tom's Cabin*, circa 1901. The tableau is similar to that in late-1870s productions. The spiritual originally associated with this scene was "Steal Away." Photograph by Byron. From the Harmount's Uncle Tom's Cabin Company collection in the Jerome Lawrence and Robert E. Lee Theatre Research Institute of the Ohio State University Libraries.

Their bodies rock to and fro, the cadence of their song rises and falls, now swelling out loudly in a grand burst of melody, and then dying away in a soft refrain, like the whisper of the night winds through a grove of palms. Behind these stretches a long expanse of the Mississippi river, forming a picture in which the idea of distance is admirably conveyed to the eye. As the moon comes up and its light floods the river and gleams on the islands dotted here and there, a band of colored melodists arrive on a raft with the traditional banjo, tambo and jawbone. All hands gather together, and soon the stage is filled with colored men and women, the latter decked out with parti-colored turbans, and the men in all manner of nondescript attire. As the music begins they all strike out into a wild chorus.[27]

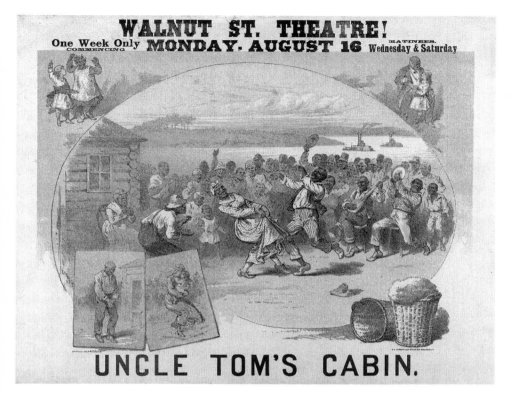

FIGURE 7.2. Plantation scene from an *Uncle Tom's Cabin* production at the Walnut Street Theatre, Philadelphia, starring Mrs. G. C. Howard as Topsy. The jubilee singers were joined by one hundred black singers, dancers, instrumentalists, and supernumeraries for what was in essence a minstrel plantation sketch ("Dramatic," *New York Clipper*, 14 Aug. 1880: 166; ad, *Times* [Philadelphia, PA], 20 Aug. 1880: 3). Courtesy of the Historical Society of Pennsylvania, theater posters collection, V6-0506.

A plantation festival unfolds. At the center of the stage is banjoist Warren Griffin, who plays "The Little Old Log Cabin in the Lane" with one hand while causing "the banjo to oscillate like the pendulum of a clock."[28] (Rival productions featured banjo virtuoso Horace Weston.) Weston's solos give way to dances accompanied by a side-splitting "African orchestra" of "former slaves" playing the jawbone, banjo, fiddle, and "congo tambo" in one of "the most laughable" plantation scenes ever presented:[29]

> The darkies begin by dancing a regular sort of a breakdown, to the music of
> "Carve Dat Possum" [a commercial spiritual by Sam Lucas; see chap. 6], sung

by all hands. You never saw such a wild scene, hands and feet all going as fast as they can. Some of the women got so excited that they just jumped straight up and down, while the men cut pigeon wings. Two of the men, with the most pronounced negro features, acted exactly like monkeys; they stuck their lips out till they looked like telescopes; it seemed as though there was no end to them, and then they wagged their jaws till they looked like a quivering black mist. You can imagine nothing more grotesque.[30]

Suddenly, however, the frenzy ceases, and "one voice is heard chanting a few lines, and then again the voices blend together in harmony. A spirit of frenzy seems to take possession of all. They leap, dance, grimace, wave their arms, keep time with their bodies to the music, or spin around like Eastern dervishes"[31] in a crude imitation of a ring shout. ("Five times the curtain was rung up on this weird scene, and it seemed as though the audience was as wild as the darkies.")[32]

According to one reviewer it was a scene so magnificent that "by itself [it would] repay a visit to the theatre."[33] Audiences delighted in the "abandon" of the dancing, the "barbaric charm" of the singing, and the "verisimilitude" that "no trained body of white supernumeraries could have possibly given."[34]

The festive atmosphere is interrupted by a horn, and Tom enters, to reveal the true nature of Legree's plantation: a vale of shadows and darkness. He expresses his anguish through the sentimental plantation song "The Old Home Ain't What It Used to Be" (Charles A. White's 1872 answer song to Stephen Foster's "Old Folks at Home") and sustains himself with a lock of Eva's hair and a silver dollar he wears around his neck, which George Shelby had given him. When Tom refuses Legree's command to whip a female slave, Legree orders that same punishment for Tom: "Flog him within an inch of his life!" This horrific scene concludes—incongruously—with the return of the slaves, who according to the prompt book "introduce their songs, shouts—banjo solos, dances &c."

Act 4 opens with Legree showing signs of a conscience; Eva's hair, which had been sustaining Tom as the whip descended on him, had reminded Legree of his own mother. Meanwhile, George Shelby has recovered his financial equilibrium and has come to New Orleans to repurchase Tom. Lawyer Marks takes him to Legree's plantation. Legree's hatred of Tom has extinguished the embers of tenderness that had flared briefly in him, and he strikes Tom, who is carried off by the slaves just as Shelby arrives. Legree will not take five or even ten thousand dollars for Tom, and the two men fight. Shelby kills Legree, and the slaves have another body to carry off.

The fourth scene belongs to Uncle Tom. He is on his deathbed, and the slaves sing, "I've got the victory, the Lord has given it to me," probably a hymn. George pleads with Tom to wake up and recognize him. Tom obeys and dies a happy man. The slaves sing the famous hymn "Nearer My God to Thee" as the stage transforms into the final tableau (as described in the prompt book): "Gorgeous clouds, tinted with sunlight.—EVA, robed in white, is discovered on the back of a milk-white dove, with expanded wings, as if just soaring upward.—Her hands are extended in benediction over UNCLE TOM who [is] kneeling and gazing up to her." The slaves sing, slowly and reverently, "Swing Low, Sweet Chariot," until the curtain falls.

Other Productions

In 1878 the white impresarios Henry C. Jarrett and Harry David Palmer commissioned a new script for a Tom show from George Fawcett Rowe.[35] Rowe kept the singing band of slaves and even expanded the scene with Uncle Tom and Aunt Chloe in the cabin to include a praise meeting, creating an opportunity to sing the one spiritual named by title in the script: "Sweet Canaan" (act 1, scene 2), which the Fisks had been singing since 1873. (This was a significant addition, for the Howards' production in a sense denied Tom's blackness by giving him only white-composed songs to sing, the spirituals being reserved for the jubilee singers. This was understandable, given that Tom was typically played by white actors in blackface.)

Jarrett and Palmer had produced the sensational hit of 1866, *The Black Crook*—a derivative melodrama that they inflated with songs, "transformation scenes" (in which, for example, a cave was transformed into a fairyland in front of the audience's eyes), and female ballet dancers in skin-colored tights. Thanks to the combination of spectacle and seminudity the show ran for over a year and was revived many times in the following decade. Jarrett and Palmer approached *Uncle Tom's Cabin* in a similarly spectacular vein. They were managing Booth's Theatre in New York in 1878 and had been looking for a show they could take to England. They settled on *UTC*, to capitalize on the great success of jubilee and minstrel singers in Britain, and the ongoing fascination with plantation life among the British. They set sail in August 1878 with a full complement of African Americans, after trying out their new production in New York, Philadelphia, and Washington, DC, to enthusiastic crowds.[36]

Unlike the Howards, Jarrett and Palmer offered *two* bands of jubilee singers. Whereas the Howards staged their great plantation festival in act 4, scene 3, Jarrett and Palmer (using Rowe's script) added a second festival in act 5, on Legree's plantation, "during which Sarah Washington, camp-meeting 'shouter' from Richmond, Va., led the chorus in several pleasing hymns."[37] This double dose of plantation hilarity also revived songs and dances from the antebellum minstrel era, such as "Dan Tucker," "Nelly Bly," and "Dandy Jim."[38]

Jarrett and Palmer's Tom show foreshadowed the explosion of "monster" productions in the 1880s: Barnum-style extravaganzas with casts of hundreds. In 1879 there were at least 49 known traveling *UTC* companies; by 1899 there were about 490. "The play was the bread and butter of the profession," wrote Harry Birdoff. "When other means of subsistence failed, actors metamorphosed themselves into Tom troupes."[39] White producer Jay Rial's 1880 Tom show featured bloodhounds and trick donkeys, and his menagerie only expanded over the years.[40] C. H. Smith, following the model of P. T. Barnum's and J. A. Bailey's combination of circuses in 1881 (two shows for the price of one), brought out C. H. Smith's Ideal Double Mammoth Uncle Tom's Cabin Company that same year—with two Topsies, two Markses, and the now requisite animal menagerie.[41] Subsequent combination companies varied these formulas. But it was the Howard and the Jarrett and Palmer productions that created the model of using jubilee singers and spirituals in Tom shows.

The Spirituals of *Uncle Tom's Cabin*

Spirituals in Tom shows fulfilled two dramatic functions: they expressed mourning (e.g., in separation and death scenes) and represented plantation life (e.g., work songs while picking cotton, ring shouts). Table 7.1 is a preliminary list of twenty-one spirituals that appeared in *UTC* productions from 1876 to 1879.

"Is Massa Gwine to Sell Us Today?" (see example 7.1) seems to have been considered essential to the productions using a jubilee troupe; the Howards first introduced the song in 1876, Poole and Donnelly retained it in their 1877 production (possibly because it was in the repertory of the Virginia Jubilee Singers, whom they had hired), and two other jubilee troupes sang it in different productions. Although it bears the musical hallmarks of a spiritual, the lyrics offer unusually specific descriptions of earthly circumstances as opposed to more typical metaphoric language—a narrative quality well suited to advancing the plot of *Uncle Tom's Cabin*. As Henry Krehbiel observes, antebellum spirituals with specific references to servitude are rare, and this one was an anomaly.[42] Its earliest published arrangement—in *Jubilee and Plantation Songs* (1887)—was by Robert H. Hamilton, an original Hampton Institute Singer and later a choir director at Hampton, the leader of the Norfolk Jubilee Singers, and an eventual choir director at Tuskegee Institute.

The only other spirituals in table 7.1 that were common to different *UTC* productions were "Gospel Train," "Steal Away," and "Swing Low, Sweet Chariot,"

TABLE 7.1 Spirituals in Uncle Tom shows, 1876–1879

Spiritual and source reference	Troupe	Performance
Children, Don't Get Weary (Fenner 1874: My Bretheren, Don't Get Weary)	Virginia Jubilee Singers	Gilmore's Holliday St. Theatre, Baltimore, 7 Jan. 1877[a]
Gospel Train (Git on Board) (Seward 1872)	Slavin's Georgia Jubilee Singers	Grand Opera House, New York, Oct. 1876[b]
	Tennessee Jubilee Singers	Academy of Music [New Orleans], 14 Jan. 1877[c]
	Virginia Jubilee Singers & Louisiana Troubadour Cabin Singers	Grand Opera House, New York, 5 Nov. 1877[d]
Gwine Up (Fenner 1874)	"	"
Hail! Hail! (Fenner 1874)	Slavin's Georgia Jubilee Singers	
Hard Trials (Fenner 1874)	Tennessee Jubilee Singers	Academy of Music [New Orleans], 14 Jan. 1877[c]
He Is the Lily of the Valley (Seward 1872b)	"	"
I'm So Glad (Seward 1872b)	"	"
Inching Along (Pike 1875)	Sam Lucas, as Uncle Tom	Michigan-Ave. Baptist Church, Chicago, 1 Sept. 1879[e]
Is Massa Gwine to Sell Us Today? (Jubilee & Plantation Songs, 1887: Is Master Going to Sell Us To-morrow?)	Slavin's Georgia Jubilee Singers	Grand Opera House, New York, Oct. 1876[b] Boston Museum, 8 May 1876[f]
	Virginia Jubilee Singers & Louisiana Troubadour Cabin Singers	Grand Opera House, New York, 5 Nov. 1877[d]
	Jubilee Singers	Booth's Theatre, 23 Feb. 1878[g]
	"	Michigan-Ave. Baptist Church, Chicago, 1 Sept. 1879[e]
John Saw de Number (Fenner 1874)	Slavin's Georgia Jubilee Singers	Grand Opera House, New York, Oct. 1876[b]
Jus Come from de Fountain (Seward 1872a)	"	"
De King Exited, Oh! Daniel	"	"
Oh Lord! Dese Bones of Mine [possibly commercial spiritual]	"	"

TABLE 7.1 Continued.

Spiritual and source reference	Troupe	Performance
Ole Brother Noah	"	"
Ole Sheep Know de Road (Fenner 1874)	"	"
Peter, Go Ring Dem Bells (Fenner 1874)	"	"
Rise, Shine, and Give God the Glory (Fenner 1874)	Tennessee Jubilee Singers	Academy of Music [New Orleans], 14 Jan. 1877[c]
Room Enough for All (Seward 1872a)	"	"
Steal Away (Seward 1872a)	Slavin's Georgia Jubilee Singers	Grand Opera House, New York, Oct. 1876[b]
	Tennessee Jubilee Singers	Academy of Music [New Orleans], 14 Jan. 1877[c]
	Virginia Jubilee Singers & Louisiana Troubadour Cabin Singers	Grand Opera House, New York, 5 Nov. 1877[d]
Sweet Canaan (Fenner 1874)	Unknown	Act 1, scene 2, in script by George F. Rowe for Jarrett & Palmer production, 1878
Swing Low, Sweet Chariot (two versions: Seward 1872a and Fenner 1874)	Slavin's Georgia Jubilee Singers	Grand Opera House, New York, Oct. 1876[b]
	Tennessee Jubilee Singers	Academy of Music [New Orleans], 14 Jan. 1877[c]

Note: Sources for spirituals are for reference only and aren't meant to imply a specific arrangement as performed in *UTC*.

[a] Ad, *Baltimore Sun*, 7 Jan. 1878. With the Howards.

[b] New York Herald, 1 Oct. 1876.

[c] Playbill, Harry Birdoff Collection, Harriet Beecher Stowe Center, Hartford, CT; http://www.iath.virginia.edu/utc/onstage/bills/tsbills8f.html.

[d] Odell, *Annals*, 10: 391; a Poole and Donnelly production.

[e] Ad, *Chicago Daily Tribune*, 31 Aug. 1879. This production, with Sam Lucas as Uncle Tom, advertised the Choir of the Michigan Avenue Baptist Church and "a strong force of the Original Jubilee Singers," who were not further identified but could have been Lucas's own troupe. "Inching Along" probably entered Lucas's repertory through the Hyers sisters, who programmed it in their 1876 jubilee concerts ("The Lyric Stage," *Boston Daily Globe*, 13 Mar. 1876: 5), and who themselves may have gotten it from the Fisk Jubilee Singers.

[f] Playbill, Billy Rose Theatre Collection, New York Public Library.

[g] Playbill, Harry Ransom Humanities Research Center, University of Texas at Austin; http://www.iath.virginia.edu/utc/onstage/bills4/oshrc09f.html.

a reflection of their immense popularity. "Gospel Train," for example, was introduced by the Fisk Jubilee Singers in 1873 and performed by the Hamptons that same year; the Tennesseans sang it in 1875; and it was one of the earliest spirituals to be parodied in a minstrel show, by Bryant's Minstrels in 1873 (see chap. 6). "Steal Away," the Fisk students' signature song, was probably the most well-known spiritual of the nineteenth century, introduced by them in 1872; before the Howards' interpolation it was performed regularly by the Hamptons, the Tennesseans, the Hutchinson family, and the Sheppard Jubilee Singers.

Judging from the spirituals in table 7.1, Tom show producers took a "greatest hits" approach when choosing spirituals for their shows. Of those twenty-one spirituals, nine (or possibly ten) were originally introduced by the Hamptons, whereas about eight came from the Fisk Jubilee Singers. The prevalence of Hampton repertory (which was performed by other troupes as well) is significant. The Hamptons' stronger folk orientation in performance and inclusion of shouting tenors (chap. 4) complemented *UTC*'s aesthetic.

As spirituals rejuvenated *UTC* onstage, the understanding of what constituted a spiritual—already complicated by the emergence of commercial spirituals—became even more confused. Terms like "shout," "plantation song," "slave hymn," and "chant" were used indiscriminately in programs and advertisements to refer to anything from a minstrel song to a Methodist hymn to a spiritual to a ring shout. Black audiences would have known the difference upon hearing the music, but white audiences (especially those lacking knowledge of southern culture) might well think "Old Black Joe" and "Steal Away" had a common musical heritage. A case in point is the commercial spiritual "Carve Dat Possum" (1875) by Sam Lucas, included as part of the plantation festival. Set to the tune of "Go Down, Moses," accompanied on the banjo, and performed on a large stage populated with crowds of slaves and the Mississippi River in the background, the song undoubtedly had the ring of traditional authenticity to some white listeners.

Tom Shows and Jubilee Troupes: A Symbiosis

Between 1876 and 1900 a large number of jubilee troupes appeared with Tom shows. Many—perhaps most—were anonymous bands of singers who appeared under the generic banner of "Colored Jubilee Singers" and were culled from local talent when traveling productions came to town. Others, like the Wilmington Jubilee Singers, had already been concertizing independently. For them and others like them, Tom shows were an economic lifeline, especially during the

1870s recession. The following troupes appeared with Tom shows (see website table 4.3, "Biographical Dictionary of Jubilee Troupes," for more information):

Alabama Jubilee Singers / Alabama Slave-Cabin Singers
Arlington Jubilee Singers
Blackville Jubilee Singers
Centennial Jubilee Singers
Georgia Slave Troupe
Invincible Plantation Jubilee Singers
Lew Johnson's Jubilee Singers
Macon [Georgia] University Quartet
Magnolia Jubilee Singers
Memphis University Students
New Orleans Jubilee Singers
Norfolk Jubilee Singers
Old Dominion Jubilee Singers
Sheppard's Jubilee Singers
Slavin's Georgia Jubilee Singers
South Carolina Jubilee Singers
Southern Jubilee Singers
Tennessee Jubilee Singers
Virginia Jubilee Singers
West Tennessee Colored Jubilee Singers
Wilmington Jubilee Singers

Many of these troupes had already been featuring sketches with costumes and scenery in their concert programs (e.g., Centennial Jubilee Singers, Tennessee Jubilee Singers, Wilmington Jubilee Singers). Others were assembled for a particular production and had no career independent of the play; some of them even changed their troupe name when they joined a new Tom organization. Jubilee singers customarily gave sacred concerts during their run in Tom shows, which not only advertised the show but also created a reputation for troupes that toured independently.

Slavin's Georgia Jubilee Singers appeared in *UTC* with the Howards for just over a year. The singers were reputed to have been former slaves in Louisiana, but little is known about their personnel.[43] When Slavin printed his notice in the *New York Clipper* reminding the public that his troupe was the first company of slave singers to ever sing in *UTC*, he claimed they had been organized three years before, which would be 1873.[44] If the Georgia Jubilee Singers had a career before they joined forces with the Howards in January 1876, however, it was an obscure one, for newspapers yield no trace of them. Nonetheless,

GRAND OPERA-HOUSE.
POOLE & DONNELLY. . . . Lessees and Managers.
THIS (SUNDAY) EVENING
GRAND——SACRED——CONCERT.
PROGRAMME.—PART I.
1. "Rise and Shine" (Gib God the glory).*
2. "Gwine to Be a Meeting Here To-night."*
3. "Going to Ride Up in the Chariot."*
4. "Our God Rules."
5. "Did Not Old Pharaoh Git Lost?"*
6. "Bathe in de River."*
7. Solo. "Waiting." . . . Miss Allen.
8. "Turn Back Pharaoh's Army."*
9. "O, Good Lord, Gib Me Dem Wings."*
10. "Wrestling Jacob."*
11. "Ye had Better Dun Humble Yeself."*
12. "I'm No Ways Tired."*
   WARREN GRIFFIN in his wonderful banjo performance.

PART II.
1. "Swing Low, Sweet Chariot."*
2. "Shine Along."*
3. "There's a Mighty Camp Meeting in the Promised Land."*
4. "Blessed Are Thy People."
5. "Ole-Time Religion."*
6. Solo. "Only Waiting." . . . Miss Allen.
7. "Joshua Fought the Battle Around Jericho."*
8. "I Come for to Tell You How I Come Along."*
9. "Hail, Hail."*
10. "Blow, Gabriel, Blow."*
11. "Don't You Want to be a Lover of the Lord?"*
   Admission, 25cts. Reserved, 50cts.

FIGURE 7.3. Program for a concert by Slavin's Georgia Jubilee Singers on 8 October 1876. The spirituals on the program, marked here with an asterisk, were likely used in *Uncle Tom's Cabin* at some point. From "Introductory Overture," *New York Clipper*, 21 Oct. 1876: 238.

the ten-member troupe had a repertory large enough to sustain Sunday night sacred concerts,[45] and a program from October 1876 reveals a full evening of spirituals in two parts, patterned on the Fisk model (see figure 7.3). By March Slavin advertised that the Georgias were available for independent bookings doing concerts, tableaus, and farces. Like the Fisks they too did charity work.[46]

The Georgia Jubilee Singers apparently broke with the Howards in March or April 1877. Slavin took his troupe on the road over the summer as a concert organization, billing them as Slavin's Cabin Singers. They then reorganized as a dramatic troupe for the 1877–1878 season, opening in September at the Leland Opera-house in Albany, NY—in *Uncle Tom's Cabin*.[47]

Meanwhile, the Howards formed an ongoing relationship with a new troupe: the Virginia Jubilee Singers, who had been touring independently as a concert troupe.[48] They appeared with the Howards in April 1877, although in May the Howards advertised the Old Dominion Jubilee Singers. By fall, however, the Virginias were a permanent fixture. In spring 1878 the Howards' *UTC* combination came under the management of John Pemberton Smith, a white southerner who enhanced the plantation scene with more realistic scenery, added black specialty artists, and aggressively publicized his company. His advertisements singled out Virginia Jubilee singers Sarah Green and Isaac Thompson, both of them camp meeting shouters from Richmond, Virginia; and Henry Duncan, a famous shouter from Lynchburg, Virginia.[49] In 1880 a newspaper notice named a "Miss Martin" as their leader."[50] Further details are elusive, especially given that there was also a Virginia Jubilee Singers troupe local to Boston, so that the name alone is insufficient for identifying troupe activities.

The Smith and the Slavin *UTC* combinations became rivals, each emphasizing the contributions of black performers in their publicity. The Smith production may have had celebrated shouters, but Slavin had stars of his own and the reputation of having managed the first jubilee troupe to appear in *UTC*. In February 1878, when his combination was offering two plays—*UTC* and *The Drunkard's Home*—Slavin announced a number of new "specialties." Among these were the splendid bass James M. Waddy, one of the original Hampton Institute Singers (see chap. 4); Alexander C. Taylor, who had been pianist with the Hyers sisters' concert companies from 1871 to 1877; and Isabella Miles, a "colored cantatrice."[51] Alex A. Luca was vocal director for the entire combination. (Luca, like Taylor, joined the Hyers sisters in 1871 and later served Callender's Georgia Minstrels as musical director and tenor. He remained with Slavin for a year.)[52] The Hamptons, the Hyers sisters, the Georgia Minstrels—all of these represented different experiences of spirituals along the folk–arranged–minstrel continuum that coalesced in Slavin's *UTC* combination—a cross-pollination rarely demonstrated in histories of African American music.

Slavin managed his *UTC* combination through early 1881 but then disappeared from mainstream newspapers. The Georgia Jubilee Singers continued to give both variety and jubilee performances, appearing with Anderson's *UTC* in 1882 and as a concert troupe through 1901, although whether these later iterations all descended from Slavin's troupe is impossible to determine.[53]

Other Plays with Jubilee Singers

After the success of jubilee singers in *Uncle Tom's Cabin*, other plays inevitably jumped on the jubilee bandwagon (see table 7.2). Jubilee singers spiced up older shows (*Kit*, *Octoroon*) or were a badge of currency for new shows. In southern-themed plays jubilee singers at least made historical sense, as in the derivative *Uncle Anthony! Or from the Parlor to the Cabin*, a companion play to *UTC* that debuted a month after the Georgia Jubilees joined the Howards. The star was Charley Howard, one of the early propagators of the commercial spiritual, and the group was the Southern Jubilee Singers.[54] Likewise, Dion Boucicault's *Octoroon* (1859) proved an obvious choice for an 1870s infusion of jubileers. This melodrama about miscegenation on a Louisiana plantation was a perennial audience favorite, and an October 1876 revival introduced "a troupe of negro singers" who "sang some of the popular jubilee plantation songs."[55] As with *UTC*, the jubilee singers became indispensable, and productions in the 1880s and 1890s continued to feature them.

TABLE 7.2. Other white theatrical productions using jubilee singers

1876

Little Nell and the Marchioness, by John Brougham (1814–1880; born Dublin, Ireland)
    A variety entertainment loosely disguised as a play (itself loosely based on Dickens's *Old Curiosity Shop*) with music. It premiered in 1867 with Lotta; her 1876 revival featured the Southern Jubilee Singers ("Dramatic," *New York Clipper*, 17 Aug. 1867: [6]; ad, Lotta, Park Theatre, *New York Times*, 26 Dec. 1876).

Octoroon, by Dion Boucicault (1820–1890; born Ireland)
    In 1876 a production at Ford's Opera House introduced a troupe of jubilee singers for "local effects" ("Amusements," *Evening Star* [Washington, DC], 9 Oct. 1876: 4). In the 1879–1880 season J. N. Gotthold's touring *Octoroon* production employed the Old Dominion Jubilee Singers. Although utilized as an adjunct rather than a leading feature of the play, audiences sometimes demanded of the jubileers four or five encores (*St. Louis Spirit* review quoted in "Amusements," *Wheeling [WV] Daily Intelligencer*, 13 Nov. 1879: 4).

Pique, by Augustin Daly (1838–1899; American)
    To celebrate its 195–200 performances (the play debuted 14 Dec. 1875), the Georgia Jubilee Singers appeared in "special entertainments" between acts (ad, *New York Times*, 19 June 1876).

Uncle Anthony! Or, from the Parlor to the Cabin, by George L. Stout, music by David Braham (1838–1905; born London)
    One of the earliest (if not the first) of the many *UTC* "companion plays" to incorporate jubilee singers. The "Original Southern Jubilee Singers" performed with Charles Howard as Uncle Anthony at the Eagle Theatre, where Braham was conductor of the orchestra and where Stout had served as stage manager (ad, *New York Times*, 24 Feb. 1876).

TABLE 7.2. Continued

1877

Zip; or, Point Lynne Light, by Frederick Marsden (1842–1888; American)

Marsden's first vehicle for Lotta debuted in 1873, but commercial spirituals weren't added until later. Lotta plays a young girl living with a lighthouse keeper. There is a villain who threatens to expose secrets, a lost mother, a restored fortune, and other melodramatic elements. Lotta survives it all while dancing and singing black composer James Bland's commercial spiritual "In the Morning by the Bright Light" (published 1879), among other popular songs.

1879

Musette, by Frederick Marsden (1842–1888; American)

Lotta had debuted in this 1874 vehicle playing a saucy girl who wreaks havoc in her English household with practical jokes and flirtations; the play was generally agreed to be wretched. In the 1879 revival Lotta introduced James Bland's commercial spiritual "Dem Golden Slippers"; she also reprised Bland's "In the Morning by the Bright Light." In the 1880s she interpolated Monroe Rosenfeld's (white) commercial spiritual "Hush Little Baby, Don't You Cry" (published 1884 under the name Belasco). ("Lotta Next Week," *Cincinnati Daily Star*, 27 Dec. 1879: 4; "Music and the Drama," *Rose Belford's Canadian Monthly and National Review* 17 [1880]: 444–46; "Lotta in Musette," *Chicago Tribune*, 17 March 1885.)

1882

The White Slave, by Bartley Campbell (1843–1888; American)

Productions in 1882 and throughout the 1880s featured "colored jubilee singers" who "made a hit," although they were rarely commented on in reviews or advertised prominently; top billing was reserved for the "rain storm of real water" and other special effects (e.g., "The White Slave," *Wheeling [WV] Daily Intelligencer*, 17 Oct. 1882; "Amusements," *St. Paul [MN] Daily Globe*, 10 Oct. 1884: 2). Later revivals in the 1890s through the early 1900s, on the other hand, used black jubilee singers as a selling point, as well as buck and wing dancers and pickaninnies (e.g., ad for Grand Opera House, *Morning Times* [Washington, DC]: 13; untitled article, *Norfolk [VA] Weekly News-Journal*, 31 Jan 1902: 10; "The White Slave," *Appeal* [St. Paul, MN], 7 Nov. 1903). An ad for Poll's Theater boasts "a group of colored plantation singers and dancers in the songs of long ago," feeding nostalgia for old-fashioned entertainment (*Evening Star* [Washington, DC], 25 Nov. 1917).

1883

Passion's Slave, by John A. Stevens (1844–1916; American)

Stevens appears to have written the original play in the 1870s, but it was a failure; this was a revision. Some productions featured a generic company of jubilee singers (e.g., "Grand Opera House," *Brooklyn Eagle*, 8 Apr. 1883), whereas others advertised distinguished troupes such as the Tennessee Jubilee Singers ("'Passion's Slave' at the Howard [Athenaeum]," *Boston Daily Globe*, 28 Dec. 1884).

TABLE 7.2. Continued

1887

Kit: The Arkansas Traveller (ca. 1868), by Edward Spencer (1834–1883; American) and
later revised by actor Frank S. Chanfrau (1824–1884; American)
The title role was originated by Chanfrau, and after his death his son kept the role alive
into the 1890s. The story is set in 1858 and concerns Kit Redding, an Arkansas farmer
whose wife and daughter are kidnapped. He moves to St. Louis, where he amasses a
fortune and succumbs to drink, and then ends up on a Mississippi steamboat with the
kidnapper, resulting in many adventures and a reunion with his grown daughter. It's not
clear when jubilee singers were first added to the production, but they appeared in 1887
and 1888 ("Musical and Dramatic Notes," *New York Clipper*, 23 June 1888: 234).

1888

Kentuck, by James J. McCloskey (1825–1913; born Canada)
Another "characteristic American drama" influenced by Boucicault. A family feud
and a horse race are at the center. At its 17 September performance at the Lee Theatre,
Brooklyn, "there were jubilee singers, who didn't sing very well," and "the orchestra
evinced a lack of rehearsal, even in the old plantation melodies." Nonetheless, the play
was "unquestionably popular" ("Lee Avenue Theater," *Brooklyn Eagle*, 18 Sept. 1888).

Putnam, the Iron Son of '76 (1845); later called *Old Put*, by Nathaniel Harrington Bannister
(1813–1847; American)
A revival of a military drama about the Revolutionary War ("Standard Museum," 2 Oct.
1888: 4). Its inclusion of jubilee singers and female soldiers was beyond historical logic.

1889

Held in Slavery, by Martin Hayden
The original title of this play was *A Boy Hero*; this was a "revivified and re-written"
version, in which Hayden acted the leading role of Julian, a young sailor. "The play
abounds in strong sensationalism, realism, sentiment, and pathos. In addition to the
regular cast, a corps of jubilee singers and dancers will be introduced to intensify the
realistic features" ("Amusements," *Washington Post*, 28 Apr. 1889).

1890

The Beautiful Slave, pastiche
"Announced as a new play, but in reality a jumble of nearly all the incidents in 'The
Octoroon,' 'The White Slave,' 'Fate,' and 'Uncle Tom's Cabin' . . . at Niblo's Garden April
27." There were "some clever jubilee songs, dances, etc. by a dozen or more colored
people" ("New York City," *New York Clipper*, 2 May 1891: 138).

1891

Shiloh, by Covier
A new military drama in five acts and seven tableaux that premiered in Philadelphia
in April, about two brothers separated at birth who reunite at the battle of Shiloh—one
fighting for the Union, the other for the Confederates. At the New National Theatre,
Washington, DC, week beginning 11 May. The plantation scene gave employment
to thirty jubilee singers and dancers (*Philadelphia Inquirer*, 19 April 1891: 12; ad,
"Amusements," *Washington Post*, 10 May 1891).

TABLE 7.2. Continued

1894

Down in Dixie, by Scott Marble (1847–1919; American)
    Debuted at Heuk's Opera House, Cincinnati, OH, 2 Sept., and went on to tour points
    south (Charleston, Nashville, Memphis, New Orleans). "Among the latest additions
    to the list of Southern plays," it featured songs by the Florida Quartette, who posed as
    cotton pickers ("New Plays," *New York Clipper*, 29 Sept. 1894: 475).

1895

On the Mississippi (1894), by William Haworth (1860–1920)
    Debuted in Baltimore on 10 Sept. 1894 with William and Cordelia McClain
    ("Maryland," *New York Clipper*, 15 Sept. 1894: 436) but no mention of jubilee
    singers. In spring 1895 it was produced in Chicago at McVicker's and in November
    at the Alhambra with "a pickaninny band and jubilee singers" rendering "the old
    plantation melodies," probably under the influence of shows like *South before the War*
    ("Alhambra—'On the Mississippi,'" *Chicago Daily Tribune*, 17 Nov. 1895). It toured for
    many seasons and had multiweek runs. The hero is plagued by the evil machinations
    of the Ku Klux Klan, though the tension is relieved by comic musical interludes and
    sensational effects (electric fireflies and croaking frogs in the Louisiana swamp, Mardi
    Gras costumes, mountain views) ("Coming to Theatres," *Washington Post*, 24 Dec.
    1896). See also Abbott and Seroff, *Out of Sight*, 347, 409, on "river" and "state" shows.

1902

My Kentucky Home, by Corse Payton (1867–1934; American)
    Military drama; debuted September in Brooklyn with Payton, known as "America's
    best bad actor," as a war correspondent and his wife, Etta Reed Payton, as the southern
    heroine in love with a northern soldier. The heroine's brother quarrels with the soldier
    and appears to murder him. There was the requisite "quaint old colored slave," and
    "a double quartet of colored jubilee singers" was engaged "to lend atmosphere to the
    plantation scenes" ("Corse Payton's," *Brooklyn Eagle*, 28 Sept. 1902).

The inclusion of jubilee singers in *The White Slave* (1882) and *Passion's Slave* (1883) was also historically appropriate. *The White Slave*, by Pennsylvania native Bartley Campbell, was regarded by some critics as an inferior revision of Boucicault's *Octoroon*, but audiences supported its many revivals through 1918. The story concerns a quadroon (later revealed to be white) who works on a Louisiana plantation before the war and whose master threatens her with a life of slavery in the fields unless she gratifies him sexually. Jubilee and plantation songs find a home in the opening tableau, titled "The Old Kentucky Home."[56]

In *The Passion's Slave*, which American playwright and actor John A. Stevens rewrote and produced in 1883,[57] "the hero has committed a crime in a moment of passion, and goes through three hours of repentance and atonement."[58] The play centers on the family of General Briscoe, who lives on a Louisiana plantation. The plot involves two rivals for the hand of the general's daughter, the murder of Briscoe's son, and one suitor framing the other for the crime. Unnamed jubilee singers were in the New York 1883 production, and the Tennessee Jubilee singers performed in an 1884 Boston production—perhaps the same group that was in *UTC* productions of 1877 (see table 7.1).[59] Reviews mention only that the jubilee singers appeared in several scenes and that the curtain rose to reveal them in song. Act 1 takes place in the environs of Fortress Monroe in Virginia—where the Hampton Institute was founded. The association of this place with jubilee singers and spirituals was already strong in the public's mind because of the famed Hampton student singers, and those who burlesqued them. The act centers on a dramatic confrontation between General Briscoe and his son, Walter, who had been banished from the household for a gambling debt two years previous and was now wrongly imprisoned for an imputed crime. It ends with Walter's death. Spirituals would have furnished a moving prologue and epilogue to this dramatic episode.

By contrast, the inclusion of jubilee singers in Nathaniel Harrington Bannister's military drama *Putnam, the Iron Son of '76* was beyond all historical logic. This play, which debuted in 1845, "is full of blue coats and red coats and Bunker Hill and everything Revolutionary."[60] Verisimilitude was obviously not a concern when it was revived in 1888, for the large cast included not only jubilee singers but female soldiers. *Old Put*, as it was then called, as well as other plays with jubilee singers from the late 1880s and 1890s, more likely presented commercial spirituals and coon songs (rag songs that took derogation of African Americans to new lows as Jim Crow escalated in the 1890s).

Then there was Lotta (Charlotte Crabtree, white, 1847–1924) and her musical plays. Born in New York City, she moved at the age of six to Grass Valley, California, where her parents ran a boarding house. There she fell under the tutelage of the infamous dancer Lola Montez (Elizabeth Rosanna Gilbert, 1821–1861), who taught Lotta to dance and sing in the gold fields' rowdy concert saloons. Lotta picked up the banjo and developed her vivacious, kittenish, and winsome stage persona, with just enough hint of the suggestive to please her male admirers without offending the public at large. She became a celebrity in variety halls, amusement parks, and theatrical productions.

In 1864 Lotta headed east, where her ultimate fame rested on a string of musical plays (among them *Musette, The Little Detective, Little Nell and the Marchioness, Zip*) that gave the red-haired diminutive beauty an excuse to sing (camp meeting songs were her specialty), do a clog dance, play a banjo solo, and otherwise charm audiences with her talents.[61] Camp meeting "jubilees" became her specialty, perhaps inspired by her appearance in 1876 as Topsy in *UTC*. That same year the Southern Jubilee Singers joined in the "great fair scene" of Lotta's vehicle *Little Nell and the Marchioness*, a drama based on Charles Dickens's *Old Curiosity Shop* that was merely a pretext for variety entertainment.[62] In both *Musette* and *Zip* Lotta and fellow actor Ed Marble sang James Bland's immensely popular "In the Morning by the Bright Light," a commercial spiritual about a camp meeting.

Spirituals in Black Plays and Environmental Spectacles

Hyers Sisters: Out of the Wilderness / Out of Bondage

Musical theater by and about African Americans was in its infancy in the 1870s, and the Hyers sisters and their concert/dramatic troupe were its progenitors. In August 1875 James Redpath and his Lyceum Bureau of Boston, the preeminent bureau in the country at the time, took over the Hyers sisters' management, refashioning them as a dramatic troupe. Redpath's was the first bureau to engage African American entertainers in its annual series, partnering with them off and on until about 1893.[63]

Initially the sisters sang their ballads and jubilee songs on lecture programs, following the speaker. In an effort to give them a more substantive vehicle, Redpath sought a writer for a music drama that the new Hyers sisters combination could perform. He settled on Joseph Bradford, whose credentials included an established literary reputation, liberal sympathies, and knowledge of black culture. Bradford (1843–1886; born William Randolph Hunter) was a white southerner who grew up in a slaveholding family on a plantation near Nashville, Tennessee, but fought for the Union during the Civil War. In 1871 he moved to Boston, where he worked as a journalist and playwright. On 20 March 1876 in Lynn, Massachusetts, the Hyers sisters combination premiered his play *Out of the Wilderness*, whose title was changed a month later to the less ambiguous *Out of Bondage*.

As Eileen Southern points out, Bradford was ultimately only one of the play's creators, for like *Uncle Tom's Cabin* the essence of the play was not in the words on the page but in the comic business, songs, dances, and improvisations created by the multitalented troupe—among them comedian/singer/composer/character actor Sam Lucas ("a whole team in himself," in the words of one reviewer), fresh from his stint with the Georgia Minstrels (see chap. 6).[64] A *Boston Globe* review of an August 1877 revival of the play encapsulates the plot and underscores the importance of performance to the play's success:

The Boston Theatre was opened last evening for a season of one week for the production of the drama, "Out of Bondage," written for and produced by the Hyers Sisters Combination and Sam Lucas, under the management of the Redpath Lyceum Bureau, Hathaway & Pond, proprietors. A very large audience assembled to witness the first performance and the entertainment proved eminently successful, the most generous applause being accorded throughout the four acts into which the piece is divided. The dialogue has little to commend it, except as serving to introduce the numerous melodies which make up the larger part of the entertainment, and to afford Miss Emma H. Hyers and Sam Lucas an opportunity to indulge in impudence to an unlimited degree in their characters of Kaloolah and Henry, two young darkeys of the traditional sort [meaning minstrelized characters]. In the first two acts the melodies common among the negroes before the war [i.e., spirituals] were introduced in great numbers, and the scenery, costumes and inimitable acting of Sam Lucas and Miss Emma gave an entirely new attraction to these quaint music compositions, which have generally been heard in the concert room without these accompaniments. The numbers contributed by Miss Emma and Miss Anna Hyers were rendered with excellent taste, and apparently the ladies have given much time to careful study since last season. The third and fourth acts bring the characters on in evening toilettes and in drawing-room scenes, as showing the advance in culture during five years at the North, and in both of these the musical selections are pleasingly varied and well rendered. A trained chorus assist the leading artists, who are, in addition to those already named, Mr. Wallace King, J. W. Luca, Mr. Z. A. Coleman, and Miss Dora Mayo, and incidental to the piece, the recently organized colored company, Captain C. F. A. Francis, appear, and execute a series of movements with excellent precision. The piece is finely put upon the stage, and an excellent orchestra under the baton of Mr. J. H. Wadsworth introduces a brilliant programme of entr'acte music. The same bill will be repeated each evening of this week and on Saturday afternoon, and offers an attraction of no slight degree to all lovers of the class of music for which this combination has already won a high and enviable reputation.[65]

The first act takes place in a cabin during slavery and centers on the preparation of a possum for a meal.[66] The second act depicts the arrival of the Union Army during the war and the ensuing emancipation. The youngsters Henry (Lucas), Kaloolah (Emma Louise Hyers), Prince (Wallace King), Narcisse (Anna Madah Hyers), and Jim (A. C. Taylor) decide to go North and seek their fortune; Uncle Eph (John W. Luca) and Aunt Naomi (May Daniels) stay behind. The third act takes place up North five years later. Uncle Eph and Aunt Naomi have come to visit and are amazed that the young people are educated and earning a living . . . by singing! The old couple does not at first recognize the northerners, who now speak in standard English and wear fine clothes. The drama concludes with a "concert" in the fourth act, in which Sam Lucas performs a ballad, the company sings "a higher class of music" accompanied by instrumentalists, and Jim has traded in the banjo for a piano.[67]

As might be expected, the first two acts, set during slavery, are dense with spirituals (see table 7.3)—there are twelve, three of which are commercial spirituals. By contrast the final act, featuring the emancipated northerners, comprises only white people's music. (Identification of songs relies on titles or first lines in the script; there are no scores.) This use of music as a metaphor for social advancement certainly resonated in the minds of all who were familiar with the student jubilee groups, and indeed with the performers themselves. At the same time, this metaphor reinforced the image of spirituals as rooted in a past time and place: in moving "out of bondage" the characters likewise moved out of its folkways, which included spirituals. As a result, the music drama paid homage to spirituals at the same time that it portrayed their irrelevance to social advancement.

As a play, *Out of Bondage* was little more than a skeletal framework on which the Hyers company hung the kind of songs, dance, and comedy for which they had already won recognition. Despite the undeniable influences of minstrelsy and Tom shows, its distinctive message of racial uplift and use of music as metaphor distinguished this important first step toward a black musical theater.

Elizabeth Hopkins: Peculiar Sam, or The Underground Railroad

Before Pauline Elizabeth Hopkins (1859–1930) wrote the novels and articles for which she is remembered today, she spent about a decade pursuing music and theater in Boston, where she was lauded as Boston's "Favorite Colored Soprano." Whether singing with her parents in the Hopkins Colored Troubadours or producing theater, Hopkins displayed an interest in "black empowerment politics," as Daphne Brooks has observed.[68] In 1879 she wrote *Peculiar Sam, or The Underground Railroad* as a vehicle for Sam Lucas. The production toured initially throughout the Midwest under the management of white minstrel proprietor Z. W. Sprague. Originally a four-act play, it premiered in Boston on 8 December 1879, having been shortened to three acts and retitled *The Slave's Escape, or, The Underground Railroad*.[69]

Although the play has the same theme as Bradford's and contains similar comic business, there are significant contrasts. Hopkins, who was only twenty when she wrote it, displayed more imagination and idealism in her plot. For example, her characters were not freed by the Union Army but took responsi-

TABLE 7.3. Folk and concert spirituals in *Out of Bondage* and *Peculiar Sam*

Song title	Out of Bondage (4 acts)	Peculiar Sam (4 acts)
Gwine Up	Act 1, p. 14	[Act 2, p. 136: This is in Hopkins's hand but is crossed out by someone else, who wrote in "Way over in Jordan"]
Carve Dat Possum (Sam Lucas, 1875)	Act 1 [Redpath program lists as incidental music]*	
Nobody Knows de Trouble I've Seen	Act 1, p. 18	
Gwine to Ride up in de Chariot	Act 1, p. 22	[Southern assigns this to act 3, p. 138, but there's no evidence for this in the facsimile script]
A Big Camp Meeting in the Promised Land	Act 1, p. 22	
Angels Meet Me at the Crossroads (Will S. Hays, 1875)	Act 2 [Redpath program lists as incidental music]*	
Peter, Go Ring Dem Bells	Act 2, p. 29	[Southern assigns this to the opening of act 2, where the direction is to "sing several choruses," but there's no evidence for this in the facsimile script]
Run Home, Levi (Pete Devonear, 1878)[a]	Act 2, p. 30	
Didn't My Lord Deliver Daniel?	Act 2, p. 36	
I'm a Rolling	Act 2	
Ef Ye Want to See Jesus	Act 2	
Oh, Wasn't Dat a Wide Riber (One More River to Cross)	Act 2 [Redpath program lists as incidental music]*	Act 3, p. 139 [added to script but not in playwright's hand]
I'll Hear the Trumpet Sound	Act 3	
When Shall I Get There?	Act 3 [Redpath program lists as incidental music]*	
Rocks and the Mountains		Act 2, p. 129 [not in playwright's hand]
Rise and Shine	Act 3 [Redpath program lists as incidental music]*	Act 2, p. 135 [not in playwright's hand]

TABLE 7.3. Continued

Steal Away	—	Act 2, p. 130 [not in playwright's hand]
Gospel Train	—	Act 2, p. 134 [not in playwright's hand]
Way over Jordan	—	Act 2, p. 136 [not in playwright's hand; see "Gwine Up" above]
Oh, Dem Golden Slippers (James Bland, 1879)	—	Act 4, p. 144 [not in playwright's hand]

Note: Titles of commercial spirituals are in italics. Songs are listed in order of appearance in *Out of Bondage* and are reproduced in part from Eileen Southern's compilation of music in these two plays, although there are some minor differences in my list.

* Asterisks denote an interpolation; otherwise the playwright indicated song titles in the script. See Southern, *African American Theater*, xxxiii–xxxv, and xxx–xxxii. Page numbers refer to her volume.

ª Southern identifies this as a commercial spiritual by Pete Devonear on the basis of the line "I don't want to stay here no longer" in the script. Devonear wrote the song for Sam Lucas; the earliest evidence of performance is by Devonear with Callender's Georgia Minstrels, 23 April 1877 (Program, Beethoven Hall, Boston, HTC, minstrel playbills). The song was published in 1878 (LC). The identifying lyric, however, could just as well come from the folk spiritual "Run to Jesus," which Frederick Douglass taught to the Fisk Jubilee Singers and was first published in Pike, *Singing Campaign for Ten Thousand Pounds*: "I don't expect to stay much longer here." Devonear was obviously referencing this.

bility for their own freedom by becoming fugitives. Their education and freedom prepared them for diverse professions—not just that of concert singer. In addition, Hopkins's experience as a musician led her to conceive her cast of characters in terms of voice part so that there was a balanced ensemble for the songs; she was also sensitive to the ways in which music might express the play's themes.

The action begins with slaves Pete (Sam Lucas), Pomp, and Sam dancing. This minstrel frivolity is cut short when Mammy enters and informs them that Virginia, the "plantation nightingale" and Pete's love, has just been forced into marriage up at the big house with Jim, an overseer who is essentially a black Legree. Virginia and Sam's sister, Juno, join the group in the cabin, and they plot their escape to Canada. Unlike in Bradford's play, Mammy goes with the young folk; there is no question of her staying behind. Jim makes an entrance, and he and Pete have a confrontation.

Act 2 opens with a chorus singing "The Rocks and the Mountains," the first spiritual identified in the script, as the travelers arrive at the first station on the Underground Railroad in the dark of night. The lyrics are appropriate to the action: "Oh, the rocks and the mountains shall all flee away, And you shall have a new hiding place that day."[70] The owner of the house, Caesar, is wary, but Sam assures him in coded language: "Look hyar uncle dar aint no use bein' uppish, kase de black clouds am risin'" (129). Sam then gives the password, the fugitives gain entrance, and they sing "Steal Away." Jim appears, and Sam tricks him out of a hundred dollars. Three more spirituals are sung: "Gospel Train"; "Rise and Shine"—an "old song" that comforts the nervous escapees by momentarily transporting them back to safety on the plantation (135); and another code song, "Way over Jordan," as they are about to resume their journey. (As table 7.3 indicates, most of the songs in Hopkins's manuscript were written in another, unidentified hand, so it's unclear who made these musical decisions.)

Act 3 also takes place at night, on a riverbank. The nervous travelers are considerably relieved to learn that Sam has drugged the "marser's" dogs, and they sing "One More River to Cross" as they ford the water on a raft.

Act 4 finds them in Canada after the war. Juno is a schoolteacher, Virginia is a singer, and Sam has been elected to Congress, having run his campaign from Cincinnati. Caesar has joined them and married Mammy. The only thing standing in the way of true happiness is the evil Jim—who is still married to Virginia. But he has since become "Mr. James Peters, Esq., D.D., attorney at law, at the Massachusetts bar, and declined overseer of the Magnolia plantation" (142). He admits his marriage to Virginia was a sham, clearing the way for Sam and Virginia's union and providing an occasion for singing and dancing. Although these modern youth speak in standard English, as in *Out of Bondage*, their plantation heritage isn't erased. They begin to dance the quadrille, which represents their newfound cultivation, but Hopkins writes these stage directions: "*Go through three or four figures lively, Juno, Mammy, and Caesar begin to get happy*." In getting happy, the dancers begin to display the kind of transcendent bodily movement that descended from black camp meetings and, before that, West African rituals. Sam rushes to the footlights and says directly to the audience: "Ladies and gentleman, I hope you will excuse me for laying aside the dignity of an elected M.C., and allow me to appear before you once more as peculiar Sam of the old underground railroad."

The play was given a second production in July 1880 in Boston's Oakland Garden under the title "The Slave's Escape" (it was also reported as "The Slave's Return"), although its integrity suffered. In June, Sam Lucas had withdrawn from the Hyers sisters ensemble to perform in Boston's Oakland Garden as interlocutor with Haverly's Colored Minstrels.[71] The minstrels performed in a large pavilion but presented their afterpiece on the adjoining lawn, "which was fitted up with scenery to represent a plantation in the old slavery days, with the planter's house, cotton-field, negro cabins, whipping-post, real bloodhounds, a mounted overseer and a numerous body of male and female negroes, who represented the slaves of the bygone era," according to a Boston correspondent to the *New York Clipper*. The plot elements comprised "the return of a runaway slave to his old home, his meeting with wife and children, the detection by the overseer, his refusal to whip the fugitive, and the enjoyment of his dusky brethren at his humane decision."[72] Sam Lucas played a generic "Uncle Tom," and it was noted that "this act" would continue the following week with "the aid of the Hopkins Colored Troubadours." Plantation scenes from earlier minstrel shows as well as Tom shows (in which Lucas had starred that year) were forerunners of this spectacle.

When the Hopkins troupe and the Hyers sisters arrived that next week of 5 July, they used the same plantation scene that Haverly's Georgia Minstrels had erected for their production of "The Slave's Escape." The *Clipper*'s Boston reporter, noting the play's similarity to *Out of Bondage*, described it this way:

> It is made entertaining by the singing of negro and camp-meeting songs by a numerous chorus and the excellent acting of Tony Williams, who, under the cognomen of Wm. Cummings, appeared as an aged uncle, Caesar, and Pete, his friend. Sam Lucas acted grotesquely and delivered a burlesque sermon in excellent style. Besides these, the other performers were W. A. Hopkins, Thos. Scottron, G. W. Paine, Fred Lyons, Mrs. S. A. and Miss P. E. Hopkins and Miss S. Williams. Between acts two and three Johnnie and Willie La Rue gave songs-and-dances, and at the close of the performance the plantation scene was reproduced on the lawn by Sam. Lucas and chorus; there was added since the previous representation an exciting and realistic race between the steamers Natchez and Robert E. Lee.[73]

Returning to the plantation after the characters had built new lives in Canada in act 3 certainly dampened, if it didn't drown, Hopkins's progressive message, and the spectacular race of the steamers diverted attention from the play's theme. Brooks notes that the musical "drew an attendance of 10,000 on the amusement park fairgrounds," but this figure surely describes the total number of visitors to the gardens on July 4, the national holiday, and not the number viewing Hopkins's play.[74] As a spectacle, the plantation scene on its own was a ringing success; at the end of his career, however, Sam Lucas wrote of *Peculiar Sam* that "the piece failed as the time was not propitious for producing such a play."[75]

Peculiar Sam clearly had more subtleties than audiences likely recognized—or ever got to see. In its original conception, Hopkins "remade the minstrel," as Martha Patterson phrased it, signifying "on the racist tropes of white minstrelsy" by having her characters use buffoonish behavior to thwart the overseer and achieve social mobility.[76] They didn't need the Union Army to free them, as it had in Bradford's play—they emancipated themselves. In Hopkins's conception, racial uplift didn't mean leaving behind the expressive culture of slavery but rather honoring it even as emancipated citizens. *Peculiar Sam* demonstrated the *function* of spirituals, as coded communication on the Underground Railroad, as an expression of hope, and as homage to home and roots; as such, spirituals were more integrated into the action and message of the play. In *Out of Bondage*, ironically, spirituals portrayed the state of being "in bondage" and were left behind with the bonds of slavery when the characters moved north. Both shows, however, utilized spirituals in the midst of action rather than relegating them to the opening and closing of scenes, as Tom shows did. Furthermore, whereas *Underground Railroad* ends with cultivated (white) music, a note at the end of Hopkins's script identifies James Bland's *O Dem Golden Slippers* as the music for the final "get happy" dance, so that musical drama ends with a commercial spiritual by a successful African American ringing in the playgoers' ears—a stronger expression of race pride than is found in the music concluding Bradford's play.

The Hyers Sisters, Sam Lucas, and Uncle Tom's Cabin

In 1879–1880 the Hyers' Sisters Combination, consisting of a double troupe of twenty white and black artists, and including Sam Lucas, staged a revolutionary version of *Uncle Tom's Cabin* in which all the black characters were played by blacks, and the white characters by whites. The troupe omitted the Vermont scenes, so that all the action took place in the South.[77] The reason for the cuts was probably length, but the decision further reinforced the identity of black Americans as southern slaves—ironic given the theme of the earlier *Out of Bondage*. Emma Louise Hyers played Topsy, Anna Madah played Cassy and Eliza, and Sam Lucas played Uncle Tom. Their premiere at the Euclid-Avenue Opera-House in Cleveland was an unqualified hit, with estimates of five hundred to a thousand people turned away at one matinee. Even if that was hyperbole, the troupe's claim that they were now booking only large halls was a distinct contrast to their more modest past.[78]

Hathaway and Pond, who succeeded Redpath as managers of his Lyceum Bureau, produced the Hyers sisters' *UTC* in March 1880, at the Gaiety Theatre in Boston.[79] The contents of the sacred concert they gave during their weeklong run are a good indication of the kind of plantation songs they offered in *UTC*. The three songs labeled "jubilee" were all recently composed commercial spirituals by African Americans who were members of the Hyers combination at that time: "I Must Go" (1880) by Fred Lyons, "Dese Bones" (1880) by George Scott, and Sam Lucas's "I'se Gwine in de Valley" (1879). The rest of the selections were white cultivated music.[80] The company went on to tour New England, giving concerts on off nights, and the "plantation melodies" (commercial spirituals) were praised as "one of the most attractive features of the evening."[81]

Environmental Spectacles and Plantation Shows

During the hot summer months city audiences fled stifling theaters for rooftop gardens, excursion boats, and parks, which became home in the late 1870s and 1880s to "environmental spectacles": lavish productions that re-created exotic locales with elaborate scenery, colossal casts, and dramatic, musical, and even circus-style elements. People thronged to reenactments of natural disasters and other breathtaking events; night after night they could relive, for example, the Chicago Fire of 1871, the Siege of Paris, or the eruption of Mount Vesuvius.

The Oakland Garden—where *Escape from Slavery* was performed—was one such summer "resort" in Boston. Twenty-five cents bought city residents a return ticket on a railway car plus admission to the park. The crowds were huge, since most city theaters closed for the summer. Hundreds of brilliantly colored Chinese lanterns—spectacular after dark—greeted visitors, who upon entering the garden encountered a spacious house, with broad piazzas on the upper story, a small stage where magicians performed, and a bandstand. There was a restaurant for refreshments (ice cream and cake, but no liquor), whose broad veranda hosted various musical entertainments. Beyond the restaurant was a miniature lake with an island, and beyond that was a small amusement park with rides.[82] The Oakland Garden frequently hosted jubilee troupes in "sacred concerts" on Sunday evenings, among an array of other entertainments.

In summer 1880 J. H. Haverly (white; 1837–1901) brought his "Gigantic Colored Minstrels" to the Oakland Garden for the largest and most spectacular all-black minstrel show ever mounted, in which he re-created a southern plantation and gave Bostonians a glimpse of the Old South. Haverly began as a blackface minstrel in the 1860s but soon abandoned performance in favor of management. He brought to minstrelsy the mammoth scale that had already infected other forms of entertainment (circus, theater, opera, variety), and engineered numerous "monster shows" in the 1880s by buying up small troupes and combining them.[83] One of his earlier efforts was his white "Mastodon Minstrels" in 1878, but the size of that troupe—forty—paled in comparison to the hundred black performers that he brought to the Oakland Garden in 1880: twenty endmen, three middle men, forty female jubilee singers, twenty musicians, and seventeen vocalists.[84]

Among the performers were banjoists Horace Weston and the Bohee Brothers (who had played in rival Tom shows), Billy Kersands, Tom McIntosh (who joined the Hyers Sisters Combination later that year), James Grace, Pete Devonear, James Bland, Wallace King, and Sam Lucas (the latter two having performed extensively with the Hyers sisters). The show opened in the pavilion, where a hundred-voice jubilee chorus sang Foster's "Way Down upon the Suwanee River" in front of a painted river scene by the renowned German scenic artist William Voegtlin, who had supplied equally impressive vistas for the Howards' Tom shows.[85] The minstrels appeared on several raised tiers, and the specialty songs of the first part consisted largely of commercial spirituals, with only one by a white composer (Will Hays):

"Den I Must Go" (Fred Lyons, 1880)
"Listen to Dem Silver Trumpets" (James Bland, 1880)
"Dar's a Meetin' Here Tonight" (Pete Devonear, 1875)
"Dese Bones Will Rise Again" (George Scott, 1880)
"Keep in de Middle ob de Road" (Will S. Hays, 1878)
"Dem Silver Slippers" and "When We Meet in the Sweet Bye and Bye" (Sam Lucas, both 1879)

The rest of the show was likewise plantation themed, with the farce *Brudder Bones' Baby!*, "the Alabama Slave" Alex Hunter in imitations, a banjo orchestra, Billy Kersands in comic specialties, the Hamtown Sextette followed by the Bogtowns in burlesques of jubilee troupes (see chap. 6), the Bohee Brothers playing banjo while singing and dancing, and the concluding farce, *Six o'Clock in Georgia!* It was only after the pavilion performance ended, however, that the truly novel performance began.

Charles H. Hicks, manager of the Oakland Garden, had constructed a miniature prewar southern plantation south of the lake (where, in a surreal juxtaposition, a replica of the HMS *Pinafore* was moored—a rage for Gilbert and Sullivan was sweeping the country). The audience migrated from stage to field—"nature's stage"—where they could view the big house, slave quarters, slaves at work in the cotton fields, whipping post, and a mounted overseer with his pack of bloodhounds. One hundred costumed "slaves" populated the fields, singing plantation songs (presumably spirituals or commercial spirituals, but also minstrel songs), dancing, and "indulging in all the antics peculiar to the race."[86] There was a loose script that portrayed a runaway slave returning to his home, his reunion with his family, his detection by the overseer, and the overseer's refusal to whip the errant slave. This open-air theatrical spectacle

was a forerunner of the even larger-scale theatrical "ethnographies" of plantation life of the 1890s, like *Black America*, and was basically an expansion of the
plantation scene in *UTC* productions.[87]

Haverly's carnival was a hit; it ran two weeks at Oakland Garden and then
moved to New York and Brooklyn, where it played in theaters without the
miniature plantation, before returning to Boston for another week in late August. When Haverly returned with his minstrel carnival he made sure to secure
crowd favorites Sam Lucas and the Hyers sisters, who had been performing in
Escape from Slavery.[88]

The summer of 1880 at the Oakland Garden illustrated a new level of "verisimilitude" in theatrical representations of slave life and music. These spectacles
were appreciated more for their sensory delights than for any negligible dramatic content, since the extensive scenery tended to impede comprehension of
the dialogue. The shows were hybrids: part dramatic company, part concert, and
part minstrel/variety show. The Forest Garden, for example, staged an outdoor
"colored camp-meeting" with thirty-five specialty artists—in essence, a variety
show.[89] The Oakland Garden's plantation was recycled in summer productions
throughout the 1880s, with Sam Lucas and his various troupes using it as a venue
for summer concerts. In 1888 Lucas even appeared in an open-air production
of *Uncle Tom's Cabin*, leading the jubilee singers himself in a variety of commercial spirituals.[90]

Haverly toured the country for a year, then took his mammoth company to
England in summer 1881. By 1883 he was broke and the rival Callender organization, now managed by Gustave and Charles Frohman (white), surpassed
Haverly's in plantation realism, using actual logs, tree stumps, moss, and a
cypress tree in their opening plantation scene onstage.[91] That same year saw
the birth of another large show in a "realistic" vein, Buffalo Bill's *Wild West and
Congress of Rough Riders of the World*, which premiered in Omaha, Nebraska,
landed on Coney Island in Brooklyn that August, and toured the country until
1913. Meanwhile Callender divided his monster group into three companies,
putting his celebrity troupe in the Northeast, another in the Midwest, and the
third in the South.[92] Such extravaganzas continued through the 1890s.

In 1892 a racially integrated show called *South before the War* opened in
Louisville, Kentucky, and toured the East, Midwest, and West until at least
February 1901. Its producers were white showmen John Whallen, a southerner
who had fought in the Confederate Army, and Harry Martell, a northerner,
but the "creative genius of its first two seasons" was black musician, actor, and
entrepreneur Billy McClain.[93] McClain (ca. 1857–66 to 1950) "devised the show,
hired and staged the acts," but because of his race was not given credit.[94] Like

its Oakland Garden forebears of 1880, *South before the War* combined realistic spectacle (cottonfield, levee scene, camp meeting) with entertainment (singing, dancing, comic skits, specialty acts)—there was "no drama to speak of."[95] Rather, it pictured "the pleasant side of slavery," in the words of the *New York Clipper*.[96] Among the white cast members was Charley Howard—the lyricist for "Carry the News" (chap. 5). Still appearing as the "aged darkey," the blackface was counterfeit but the age was not; he died in 1895. Ironically, Howard's blackface character appeared in the plantation scene with genuine African Americans. The show's music looked forward to the emerging ragtime craze at the same time that it anchored the present in the past with the usual sentimental plantation songs. The camp meeting scene, according to the *New York Clipper*, "with all its comic probabilities, its exhorters, and a congregation of many types, furnished much amusement,"[97] in the same style as the minstrel plantation scenes of Tom shows. The evening concluded with a cakewalk.

Little is known about the specific music of the show, which in any case was probably as fluid as the "storyline." The male quartets of *South before the War*—who took the place of jubilee troupes in earlier, similar entertainments—probably sang few if any real spirituals, but they did sing commercial spirituals, such as Billy McClain's "De Gospel Pass" (1893), which he dedicated to Charley Howard, and "Hand Down de Robe," written for Billy Williams.[98]

In terms of spirituals, *South before the War* made its most significant impact as an employer of quartets—the Standard, Southern, Eclipse, Twilight, and Buckingham Quartettes being among the earliest.[99] For the Standard Quartette, which was with the show from 1893 to 1895, the consequence of this wide exposure was a series of recordings that included folk and commercial spirituals—the earliest aural evidence of performance practice descended from the jubilee tradition.[100]

Other shows followed in this vein, but the black outdoor spectacle had its apotheosis in *Black America*, which opened on 25 May 1895 in South Brooklyn's Ambrose Park fairground. Billy McClain teamed with white producer Nate Salsbury (1846–1902), who had helped launch Buffalo Bill's Wild West show in 1883 and produced it in Ambrose Park just the year before. Billed as a "Grand Picturesque Out-door Spectacle of Plantation Life in the Sunny South," *Black America* was Haverly's Oakland Garden plantation on a much grander scale, with not one hundred but five hundred African Americans impersonating slaves—the largest all-black cast ever assembled. Before the formal show began visitors could wander through a slave village of 150 log cabins (which were built to house the cast) and see a meeting house, mules, wash tubs, real cotton bushes, a cotton gin, and bales of cotton.[101] It was as if the "living pictures" that were so popular on variety and dime museum programs had been transported to their home environment. A stage show ran twice daily, beginning with a band concert, followed by a choral portion by the "freedmen of the South," and concluding with variety acts. Several jubilee choirs and sixty-three vocal quartets were engaged.[102] A Boston program gives the following song selections in the second part:

1. Camp Meeting Refrain: "Dese Bones Shall Rise Again." BLACK AMERICA LEGION
2. The "MYSTIC" and "CONSERVATORY" QUARTETTES of powerful Male Voices.
3. The celebrated "ORIOLE" and "RUSSELL" QUARTETTES from Charleston.
4. The original DOUBLE AMERICAN QUARTETTE.
5. The famous "ORIOLE" QUARTETTE.
6. The "STANDARD" and "KEYSTONE" QUARTETTES.
7. Characteristic Plantation Song: "See How I Laugh." OLD DOMINION CLUB.
8. Cabin Refrain: "Oh, My Baby." By MAMMOTH CHORUS.
9. "Carry Me Back to Old Virginia." WILLIAM BANKS AND ENTIRE COMPANY.
10. "Wake Up, You Lazy Coon." ENTIRE VOCAL CORPS.
11. "Old Black Joe." Rendered by JOE SOMERVILLE AND QUARTETTES.
12. "Kentucky Home." MISS BESSIE LEE, The Celebrated Soprano. Specially engaged.
13. "Roll, Jordan, Roll." HALLIDAY SISTERS WITH CHORUS.
14. "Watermelon Spoiling at Johnson's." COMPANY.
15. Camp Meeting Song: "Stand on the Walls of Zion." BLACK AMERICA CHORUS.[103]

Among the named selections, only "Roll, Jordan, Roll" and "Stand on the Walls of Zion" were actual spirituals; "Dese Bones" was a commercial spiritual, by the black composer George C. Scott (1880).[104]

After seven weeks the show traveled to Boston, where it spent another seven weeks at the Huntingdon Avenue Grounds before going on tour. It closed six months after it opened.

Despite its purported realism, *Black America* was shackled to minstrel stereotypes. Producer Nate Salsbury displayed the same limited recognition of black artists as white impresarios before him: "The white man can imitate the Negro, but no Negro that I've ever seen was a success as an actor. Singing and dancing are the Negro specialties; and they would do well to stick to them as closely as possible."[105]

Black America inspired another ethnographic show, *Darkest America*, which opened in 1896 and ran for four years. It was conceived on a much smaller scale, with a troupe of about fifty artists. Longtime minstrel Al G. Fields (white) was the impresario, and Sam Lucas was among the leading entertainers. *Darkest America* was intended "to provide snapshots of black progress 'from Plantation to Palace,'" according to a program, but not surprisingly it did so "with little concern for historical accuracy," as Errol Hill and James Hatch note.[106] As with *Black America*, there were plantation scenes with camp meeting shouters and chanters, steamboat scenes, a gambling den (which catches fire), and in a scene later added by Billy McClain, a portrayal of Washington DC's black society.

Concluding Thoughts

Postbellum stage productions of *Uncle Tom's Cabin* were opportunistic, remaking themselves to fit the trends of the times. It's only logical, then, that they became extensions of the jubilee and minstrel industries, reinvigorating the popular but well-worn play with jubilee singers and spirituals, both traditional and commercial. Indeed, in the words of one critic, the actors took second place to the jubilee singers.[107] Tom shows gave new force to spirituals by inserting them into a narrative, and spirituals raised the emotional bar of Tom shows while endowing them with purported authenticity. Hearing spirituals sung by blacks in slave attire and situated amid realistic scenery made tangible what audiences could only fantasize during a Fisk Jubilee concert. And the plantation festival, with its camp meeting shouters, frenzied dancing, and chanting gave audiences a glimpse of what they assumed to be black religious worship, in all its barbarism and abandon.

Uncle Tom's Cabin brought traditional and commercial spirituals to greater numbers of people than any previous American entertainment. Thomas Gossett estimates that for every person who read the novel (only the Bible outsold it in the nineteenth century), "perhaps as many as fifty people would eventually see the stage production."[108] And the audience was the most diverse ever brought into American theater. Stowe's work, being a "moral drama," was the first play that ministers actually urged their congregants to see. Managers did their part in attracting new audiences by having special performances for schoolteachers, half-price performances, special church productions (using church choirs), and juvenile troupes (consisting only of child actors). Women and children crowded the matinees. People went to see the play over and over again, often in the same year.

The educational function of *Uncle Tom's Cabin* was the key to its success until the early 1880s, when Tom shows devolved into spectacles. In fact, the very first production of the play in 1852 was at a dime museum. Dime museums, which often cost more than a dime to enter, were private collections of objects that peaked in popularity in the 1880s and 1890s. Designed as wholesome entertainment for the family, curiosity seekers might encounter wax tableaus, animal menageries, a hall of mirrors and other arcade amusements, freaks, artifacts (Daniel Boone's rifle, Egyptian mummies, ship models), and in the auditorium, a stage show featuring variety, plays, minstrels, and other popular entertainment. Although they tended to rely on sensationalism, their arguable educational value was in keeping with the Victorian belief that "leisure time should not be spent in idleness and frivolity but in edifying and constructive activities."[109] They remained an important venue for Tom shows even after the war.

When the Hyers sisters mounted *Out of Bondage*, it was significant that they appeared under the auspices of the Redpath Lyceum Bureau and that Redpath's advertisements labeled it—like *Uncle Tom's Cabin*—a "moral" drama,[110] implying that audiences could improve themselves by attending. This educational thrust remained as Tom-type shows evolved and audiences were transformed from spectators to participant-observers, mingling with the performers at Haverly's Colored Carnival or *Black America*. What began as an attempt to compete in the Tom market by infusing *Uncle Tom's Cabin* with spirituals and jubilee singers ended some twenty years later with audiences becoming interactive participants in ethnographic representations of slave life. The "educational" value of Tom shows implied by dime museum and lyceum bureau patronage, and the moral edification asserted by marketing, were naturally suspect, for in showing "life among the lowly" the shows commodified, distorted, and freely falsified history to please the public, as Andrea Dennett has written of dime museums.[111]

The popularity of Tom shows and environmental spectacles came at a price for black artists. K. Stephen Prince has noted with regard to postbellum minstrelsy that it "functioned not by innovation but by repetition," endlessly reproducing "a standard set of tropes," such as the faithful slave, the kind master, the plantation song and dance, and so on.[112] Tom shows and their offshoots did likewise, even more perniciously, because they were the largest employer of black performers for the last quarter of the century. As a result, long after Emancipation, it was virtually impossible for blacks to find stage roles in a production that didn't explicitly concern race.

As black minstrel troupes found ways to subtly defy white definitions of black bodies onstage, black artists sought to expand black identity in race-based dramas and music. *Out of Bondage* was revolutionary as a music drama performed by and largely created by blacks (who, for example, improvised stage action and musical interpolations), despite having a white playwright and a large dose of minstrel elements. Its spirituals signified the past of slavery, to be educated out of the black characters by play's end. (This paralleled the original desire of the Fisk Jubilee Singers—to leave behind the songs of the painful past and sing the cultivated music of the white tradition.) In *Peculiar Sam*, however, spirituals weren't merely a pretense for performance but rather illuminated characters and action. Significantly, Hopkins didn't leave spirituals "down on the plantation" at the end of the play but rather acknowledged their foundation to the identity of her educated, geographically transplanted, socially reconstructed characters. In both the Hyers and Hopkins plays spirituals had a pride of place that was lacking in *UTC* onstage, where they were confined to the scenic outskirts and were used to intensify two expressive modalities: sorrow (death scenes) and jubilation (camp meeting).

Tom shows employed unprecedented numbers of blacks in onstage roles. Although jubilee troupes were generally part of touring companies, supernumeraries (who were often required to sing and dance) were hired locally. The best of them received good pay: from $50 to $150 per week in large cities.[113] Several Tom shows playing simultaneously in one city could drain local black talent completely, forcing producers to use inferior performers or seek singers and dancers elsewhere.

Tom shows could also be considered an artistic cauldron that brought together black performers who had started out on different career paths. James Waddy from the Hampton singers, the Hyers sisters from the world of art music, the Wilmington Jubilee Singers, Sam Lucas, Billy and Cordelia McClain from minstrel and variety, and many others all brought their creativity and musical experience to Tom shows and their offshoots, extending the musical hybridity of spirituals and popular music that had begun with minstrelsy. Indeed, there were probably few if any popular entertainment performers, white or black, who didn't perform in some version of *UTC*, whether legitimate productions, parodies, anti-Tom plays, or Tom-related sketches, songs, or characters.

The preexisting jubilee troupes that joined Tom shows had already been presenting costumed sketches as part of their concert performances. College troupes and the more serious independent troupes like Donovin's Tennesseans avoided the play altogether. For better or worse, spirituals gave black entertainers entrée into the world of Tom shows and spectacles. Over time the role of spirituals in these entertainments diminished to make room for new musical styles. The labels "jubilee singers" and "jubilee music" persisted, however—a sign of the increasingly blurry boundaries between modes of entertainment.

CHAPTER 8

Blurring Boundaries between Traditional and Commercial

By the late 1870s a jubilee craze was in full swing. Whether you were a working-class male who frequented minstrel and variety halls or a respectable woman who attended matinees, a churchgoer who shunned the theater or a theatergoer who shunned the church, young or old or white or black, rich or middle class or poor, educated or not, urban or rural, northern or southern or western, you were likely to encounter some manner of jubilee song. The blatant commercialization of spirituals had dulled the altruistic sheen of the earliest student jubilee singers. As impresarios and performers competed in this new cultural marketplace, it wasn't always easy to recognize what was "traditional" and what was "commercial."

The term "jubilee singers" as coined by George White in 1871 meant a group of African American students singing arranged spirituals on behalf of an educational institution for freedmen. This definition sufficed through 1874, after which other types of performers began appropriating it. Student jubilee singers had created the "jubilee marketplace," but minstrels and variety performers expanded and helped maintain it, until the term "jubilee singer" became so diluted as to be essentially meaningless. All manner of jubilee singers represented themselves as tradition-bearers, giving rise to frequent skirmishes over legitimacy that were played out in marketing. As traditional spirituals, contrafacta, parodies, answer songs, and parodies of parodies cycled back on each other, the boundaries between them and their performers blurred.

The large majority of jubilee troupes that entered the field from 1875 to 1885 were independent ventures (see table 4.1). Even the Fisk Jubilee Singers were reborn as an independent enterprise after the original troupe dissolved in 1878: first under George White in 1879, and again in 1882 by Fisk singer Frederick Loudin, their first black director.[1] The most successful of the independent troupes flavored their jubilee concerts with minstrel ingredients and performed in a range of settings that included variety theaters, musical plays onstage, and the more usual jubilee venues: legitimate theaters, churches, charity events, orphanages, and the like. Their flexibility contributed to their longevity. Some, like the Wilmington Jubilee Singers, even performed in tandem with white minstrels. Although the Fisk Jubilee Singers were still the gold standard, with an unassailable reputation supported by a Christian missionary cause, by 1880 some U.S. audiences began to comment on a lack of "authenticity" in their sound, which by that time had been honed by almost a decade of training and discipline. One critic wrote that the Fisk singers lacked "the genuine and hearty manner, and peculiar dialect, wont to be given by colored singers, from the plantations and campmeetings of the south, and which charmed and fascinated the people of the north in the years after the war."[2] Similar appraisals dogged the North Carolinians; in 1874 their "untrained" voices were appreciated as an "accurate representation" of their race, but by 1875 they had improved so much that "their voices are getting too fine for the kind of music they are singing."[3] This perception created a space for competitors.

Jubilee Singers and Minstrels: Emerging Alliances

The Wilmington Jubilee Singers organized at the beginning of 1874. Like the Fisks, they won the patronage of Henry Ward Beecher, and like the Tennesseans, their jubilee concerts included "scenes from the South" (chap. 4). In early 1876 the Wilmingtons joined an *Uncle Tom's Cabin* company, after which their entertainments began to take on elements of variety shows, even as they still performed sacred concerts of jubilee songs. Their concerts of spirituals and theatrical tableaus found a home in New York's stately Steinway Hall on one night and in the New York Parisian Varieties or Chateau Mabille Varieties on another—where one could otherwise find female minstrels, the can-can, and lots of "naughty but nice" ladies (see figure 8.1). In these latter venues the Wilmingtons were, as theater historian George Odell put it, "reputable people in questionable surroundings."[4] The company expanded its personnel and became a variety combination for a while in 1876. Their company "combined" races in addition to an array of acts:

THE WILMINGTON COLORED JUBILEE SINGERS AND COMBINATION COMPANY.

The largest, oldest, and best band of slave vocalists in America. Organized 1869. Endorsed by press and public. 8 colored and 6 white performers. Part or entire entertainments furnished. Minstrelsy, variety, sketch, Sunday sacred concerts, clog, song-and-dance, duets, Irish biz, etc. For terms, dates, etc. address HARRY YORK, 228 West 18th St., N.Y. "Uncle Tom's Cabin," 16 characters.[5]

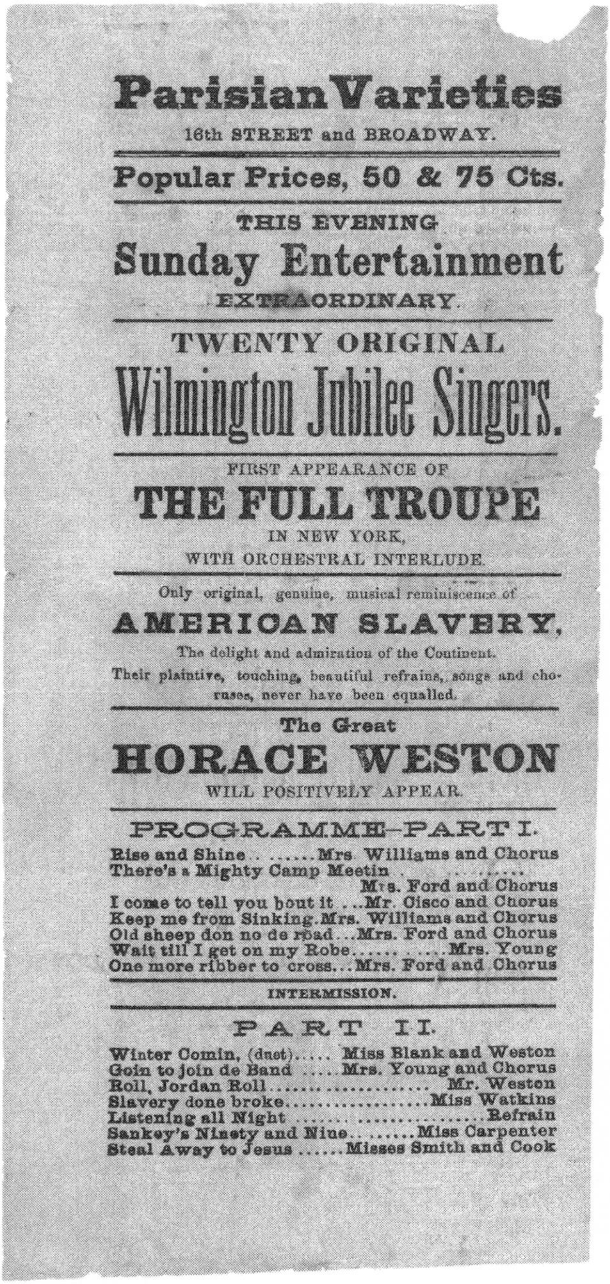

Parisian Varieties

16th STREET and BROADWAY.

Popular Prices, 50 & 75 Cts.

THIS EVENING

Sunday Entertainment

EXTRAORDINARY.

TWENTY ORIGINAL

Wilmington Jubilee Singers.

FIRST APPEARANCE OF

THE FULL TROUPE

IN NEW YORK,
WITH ORCHESTRAL INTERLUDE.

Only original, genuine, musical reminiscence of

AMERICAN SLAVERY,

The delight and admiration of the Continent.

Their plaintive, touching, beautiful refrains, songs and choruses, never have been equalled.

The Great

HORACE WESTON

WILL POSITIVELY APPEAR.

PROGRAMME—PART I.

Rise and Shine . . . . . . .Mrs. Williams and Chorus
There's a Mighty Camp Meetin . . . .
          Mrs. Ford and Chorus
I come to tell you bout it . . .Mr. Cisco and Chorus
Keep me from Sinking. Mrs. Williams and Chorus
Old sheep don no de road . . .Mrs. Ford and Chorus
Wait till I get on my Robe . . . . .Mrs. Young
One more ribber to cross . . .Mrs. Ford and Chorus

INTERMISSION.

PART II.

Winter Comin, (duet). . . . . Miss Blank and Weston
Goin to join de Band . . . . Mrs. Young and Chorus
Roll, Jordan Roll . . . . .Mr. Weston
Slavery done broke. . . . . .Miss Watkins
Listening all Night . . . . .Refrain
Sankey's Ninety and Nine. . . . . . . .Miss Carpenter
Steal Away to Jesus . . . . . .Misses Smith and Cook

FIGURE 8.1. Reputable performers in a questionable
venue: the Wilmington
Jubilee Singers' program of
spirituals, enlivened by banjoist Horace Weston (ca. 1876).
Jubilee singing was an anomaly at the Parisian Varieties
Theatre, which favored shows
with such titles as "Legs on
the Brain," as well as other
variety acts. MS Thr 556,
folder 628, Houghton Library,
Harvard University.

In other words, the Wilmingtons fulfilled anyone's jubilee or minstrel or variety needs. The white performers, actors from an *Uncle Tom's Cabin* production in which the Wilmingtons appeared, were presumably responsible for the "Irish biz" and clog duets. The ad erroneously claims the troupe organized in 1869—an obvious attempt to imply that they, and not the Fisks, were the original jubilee singers.

A playbill from October 1876 listing personnel and their specialties suggests that the variety and minstrel influences were holding sway in their shows at this time:

THE WILMINGTON JUBILEE SINGERS
W. [William] E. Gillespie, Proprietor

Geo. W. Woods, The Acknowledged Bone Soloist of America.
Will H. Vane, The Great Manipulator of the Banjo, and Song and Dance Artiste, conceded to be the best Performer on the Large and Small Banjo in America.
Harry York, The Popular American Ethiopian Comedian and Orator.
Samuel Hill, The Great Plantation Essence Dancer, and Character Artist.
Harry Henderson, The Favourite Tenor Vocalist.
Horace St. Clair, The wonderful Dialect Comedian.
Alexander Davis, The Celebrated Cane Brake Warbler.
Eligah White, The Famous Cotton-field Vocalist and Humorist.
Charles Washington, The Cultured Baritone.
Peter Stokes, Camp Meeting Basso.
Isaac Cisco, The Renowned Tenor.
Miss Ida Washington, The Beautiful Quadroon Prima Donna "The Star of the South"
Miss Rebecca Samuels, The Sweet-voiced Creole Alto Songstress.
Miss Fanny Davis, The Accomplished Mulatto Balladist.
Miss Hannah Mason, The Plantation Oddity.[6]

Bones, dialect ("Ethiopian") comedy, essence dancing, and cane-brake warbling were the stuff of minstrelsy, not of legitimate jubilee concertizing.

In October 1876 the Wilmingtons traveled to England, hoping to share in the fame and fortune that the Fisk Jubilee Singers continued to enjoy there. After one week manager Gillespie deserted them during a performance. Shortly thereafter white minstrel entrepreneur Sam Hague—who had brought a group of Georgia Minstrels to England in the 1860s—assumed proprietorship of the Wilmingtons.[7] Hague's business plan was to shadow the Fisk Jubilee Singers. An irritated America Robinson wrote to her sweetheart back at Fisk: "These

Wilmington Jubilee Singers are imitating us in everything—our posters, programmes &c. The man who is their manager is a very unprincipled man. I am
truly sorry they are here. They are not far from us. They are deceiving the people
too."[8] Not only was Hague content to let the public believe the Wilmingtons
were the Fisk singers, but he also falsely claimed that the troupe was raising
money for the maintenance of a school in Wilmington, North Carolina.

When the Fisks left Britain for Holland in late January 1877, the Wilming-
tons were still on their tail but beginning to falter financially. In the spring Ida
Washington, the troupe's prima donna, and her husband, baritone Charles
Washington, applied to Fisk president E. M. Cravath for positions with the
Fisk troupe, claiming that Hague had treated them badly. (Hague apparently
disagreed; he sued Mr. Washington for breach of promise.) Cravath turned
them down. Jubilee singer America Robinson expressed little sympathy for
Ida Washington, claiming that at a Fisk concert "she sauced Mr Cravath" and
spoke in her letter of application "of her talents in a way that plainly shows
that she thinks Mr C ought to feel honored to have her &c."[9] The next year
the Wilmingtons, still in England, had acquired a new manager, the Reverend
Parsons of Brighton. But they fell out with him as well, claiming their pay was
two weeks in arrears, and Parsons severed his connection with the troupe with
the wish that he had never taken them on. In the end, the Wilmingtons were
forced to solicit donations to pay their way back to the states.[10]

What was left of the troupe apparently dissolved shortly thereafter (a few
stayed in England). A male quartet of Wilmingtons appeared on a December
1880 program by a newly organized band of Christy Minstrels, under the
management of Frederick Kyle, at Horticultural Hall in Boston. This appearance
may have resulted from Hague's intervention, for the interlocutor of the Christy
troupe, James W. Lamont (white), had been a member of Hague's Minstrels in
Liverpool. Although the response to the program overall was mixed, the Wilmington quartet was a hit, being twice recalled for its plantation melodies and
camp meeting refrains.[11] If the Wilmingtons began their career giving "portraits,
not caricatures, of the slave as he was," they ended it giving the reverse—not
necessarily by choice but owing to the pressures of a highly competitive jubilee
marketplace.[12]

Several other jubilee groups walked a tightrope between jubilee concertizing and minstrelsy, among them Sheppard's Jubilee Singers (see chap. 4). They
typically sang spirituals at respectable variety theaters, such as Tony Pastor's in
New York, as well as in concert halls. In January 1876 they were the headline act
at the Howard Atheneum, a variety theater in Boston, followed by twenty-one
artists in the novelty olio. The *Boston Daily Globe* raved about their "real wild

'spirituals,' as sung at camp-meetings and around the hearth-fires," which were "given with a rude energy and a natural pathos never yet successfully imitated by cultured vocalists [such as the Fisk Jubilee Singers], and . . . they received the heartiest applause."[13] Imagine twenty minutes of spirituals, followed by the serio-comic vocalist Jennie Morgan (white), the dancing team of (James) Sanford and (Charles) Wilson (who were former blackface burlesque Jubilee Singers; chap. 5), and blackface comedian Harry Bloodgood (an early performer of "Rock'a My Soul"; chap. 5), among others. The *Globe's* delight in Sheppard's Jubilees was perhaps in part explained by its frustration with the Hyers sisters, whose rendering of jubilee songs at a competing concert on the Sheppards' opening night they deemed ponderous. Despite their obvious sweetness of voice, wrote the reviewer, the Hyers company "in refining the character of their vocalism have fallen into the error of dragging too much, so that last evening it was almost impossible to recognize 'The Old Folks at Home' and other favorites in their altered time."[14]

Not only did Sheppard's troupe appear on a white variety bill in Boston, but they also teamed with a quartet from Haverly's Colored Minstrels, who were mounting a "Colossal Colored Carnival" in Boston that January, at Beethoven Hall. J. H. Haverly (1837–1901, born Christopher Haverly) was one of the most influential minstrel impresarios of all time, beginning as a manager of Cal Wagner's Minstrels in 1870 and gradually buying interests in other white troupes over the years. He bought Callender's Colored Minstrels in 1878 and immediately began hiring additional performers until he had one hundred performers, which supported eight corps of jubilee singers.[15] (Haverly had similarly gigantic white troupes as well.) The pairing of Haverly's minstrel quartet and Sheppard's jubilee troupe solved two problems by avoiding competing concerts while promoting two different troupes.[16]

Whereas Sheppard's jubilee singers would seem to have the greater claim to legitimacy, Haverly wasted no opportunity to promote his "genuine" colored minstrels, all of whom were "natural singers, natural dancers, natural humorists, and natural performers."[17] Sheppard's singers likewise assured the public of their authenticity by explaining that troupe leader Andrew Sheppard had been a slave for thirty years, owned by General Robert E. Lee (see figure 8.2). They too were "natural," making "no pretentions as to musical abilities" and being "unable to read or write." The program begins with the same combination of Lord's Prayer and "Steal Away" that opened almost every Fisk Jubilee concert.

Despite Haverly's perpetuation of black stereotypes, he seemed to have a genuine appreciation for black folk culture. Unlike some white managers, Haverly treated his black employees with respect and even generosity—when Charles

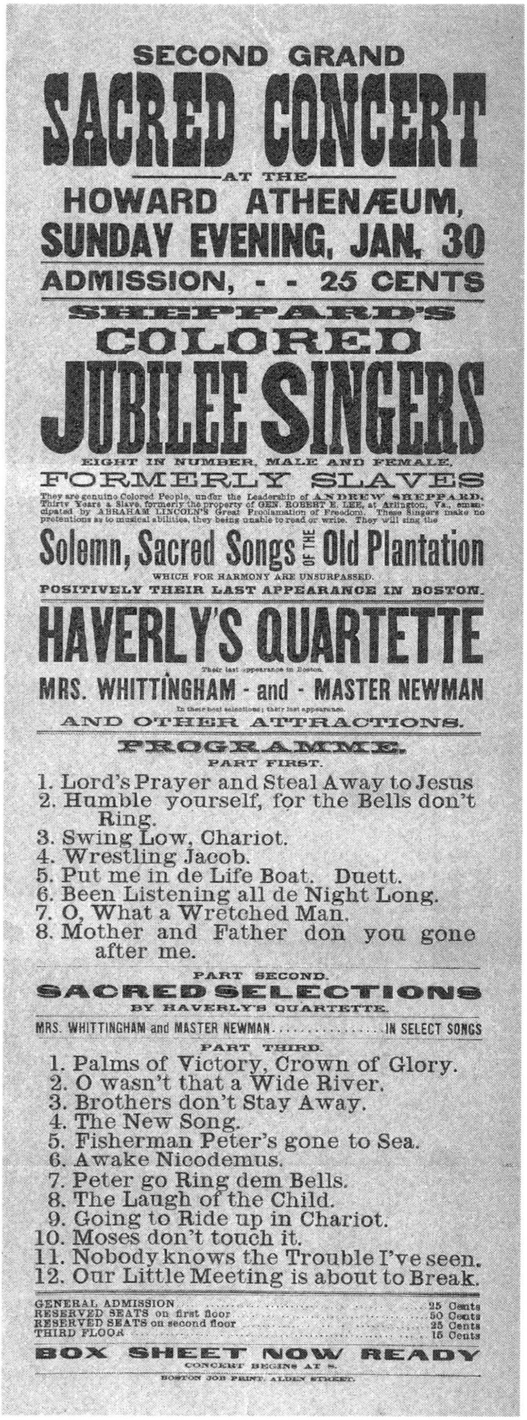

SECOND GRAND

SACRED CONCERT

AT THE

HOWARD ATHENÆUM,

SUNDAY EVENING, JAN. 30

ADMISSION, - - 25 CENTS

SHEPPARD'S

COLORED

JUBILEE SINGERS

EIGHT IN NUMBER, MALE AND FEMALE.

FORMERLY SLAVES

They are genuine Colored People, under the Leadership of ANDREW SHEPPARD, Thirty Years a Slave, formerly the property of GEN. ROBERT E. LEE, at Arlington, Va., emancipated by ABRAHAM LINCOLN'S Great Proclamation of Freedom. These Singers make no pretentions as to musical abilities, they being unable to read or write. They will sing the

Solemn, Sacred Songs OF THE Old Plantation

WHICH FOR HARMONY ARE UNSURPASSED.

POSITIVELY THEIR LAST APPEARANCE IN BOSTON.

HAVERLY'S QUARTETTE

Their last appearance in Boston.

MRS. WHITTINGHAM - and - MASTER NEWMAN

In their best selections; their last appearance.

AND OTHER ATTRACTIONS.

PROGRAMME.

PART FIRST.

1. Lord's Prayer and Steal Away to Jesus
2. Humble yourself, for the Bells don't Ring.
3. Swing Low, Chariot.
4. Wrestling Jacob.
5. Put me in de Life Boat. Duett.
6. Been Listening all de Night Long.
7. O, What a Wretched Man.
8. Mother and Father don you gone after me.

PART SECOND.

SACRED SELECTIONS

BY HAVERLY'S QUARTETTE.

MRS. WHITTINGHAM and MASTER NEWMAN................IN SELECT SONGS

PART THIRD.

1. Palms of Victory, Crown of Glory.
2. O wasn't that a Wide River.
3. Brothers don't Stay Away.
4. The New Song.
5. Fisherman Peter's gone to Sea.
6. Awake Nicodemus.
7. Peter go Ring dem Bells.
8. The Laugh of the Child.
9. Going to Ride up in Chariot.
10. Moses don't touch it.
11. Nobody knows the Trouble I've seen.
12. Our Little Meeting is about to Break.

GENERAL ADMISSION........25 Cents
RESERVED SEATS on first floor........50 Cents
RESERVED SEATS on second floor........25 Cents
THIRD FLOOR........15 Cents

BOX SHEET NOW READY

CONCERT BEGINS AT 8.

BOSTON JOB PRINT, ALDEN STREET.

FIGURE 8.2. Undated (ca. 1881) playbill for a sacred concert in Boston by Sheppard's Colored Jubilee Singers and Haverly's Quartette, from Haverly's Colossal Colored Carnival minstrel troupe. MS Thr 556, folder 573, Houghton Library, Harvard University.

V. Delaney, a member of Haverly's Genuine Colored Minstrels, died from consumption at the age of thirty in New York, Haverly paid to transport the body back to Delaney's hometown of St. Louis.[18] As for the Sheppard Jubilees, their brushes with variety and minstrelsy didn't derail them from jubilee singing; nine years later they were offering concerts of spirituals and asserting their superiority to the Fisk Jubilee Singers (see figure 8.3).[19] Although the program was their usual mix of spirituals and white parlor songs, one "jubilee" song was an interloper: Sam Lucas's commercial spiritual "Children, I'm Gwine to Shine."

Lucas had written the song circa 1881 for the white duo Billy "Williams" Carmody (1854–1910) and William J. "Sully" Sullivan (1858–after 1911). Williams and Sully made their reputations singing "camp meeting melodies" (commercial spirituals) in blackface and played variety halls for eleven years from 1876.[20] Some of the Sheppard patrons probably recognized Lucas's "Children" from performances in variety halls. Others, however, could be forgiven if they thought "Children" was a traditional spiritual. Despite some gentle humor ("Oh, Gabriel done said to de Children all / In de morning he was gwine to call, / If he bust his horn I'll lend him mine, / Oh children I'm a gwine to shine"),[21] the lyrics avoid broad minstrel stereotypes, and the music has folklike elements (see example 8.1). It blended both musically and lyrically with the traditional spirituals and parlor songs on the program.

EXAMPLE 8.1. Excerpt from the chorus to Lucas's "Children, I'm Gwine to Shine." Folk traits include ambiguous pitch (the E natural in measure 2 and E♭ in measure 3); a gapped-scale melody; and an internal refrain in the verse. Transcribed from *Plantation Songs and Jubilee Hymns*, 37.

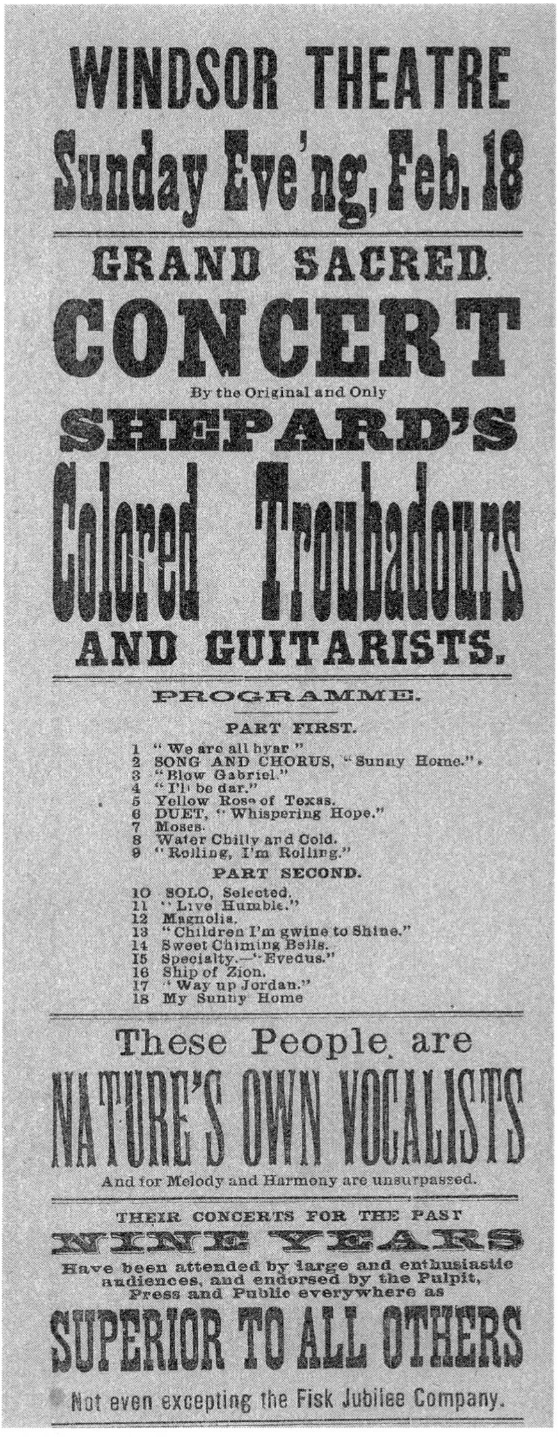

WINDSOR THEATRE
Sunday Eve'ng, Feb. 18

GRAND SACRED
CONCERT
By the Original and Only
SHEPARD'S
Colored Troubadours
AND GUITARISTS.

PROGRAMME.

PART FIRST.

1 "We are all hyar"
2 SONG AND CHORUS, "Sunny Home."
3 "Blow Gabriel."
4 "I'l be dar."
5 Yellow Rose of Texas.
6 DUET, "Whispering Hope."
7 Moses.
8 Water Chilly and Cold.
9 "Rolling, I'm Rolling."

PART SECOND.

10 SOLO, Selected.
11 "Live Humble."
12 Magnolia.
13 "Children I'm gwine to Shine."
14 Sweet Chiming Bells.
15 Specialty.—"Evedus."
16 Ship of Zion.
17 "Way up Jordan."
18 My Sunny Home

These People are
NATURE'S OWN VOCALISTS
And for Melody and Harmony are unsurpassed.

THEIR CONCERTS FOR THE PAST
NINE YEARS
Have been attended by large and enthusiastic audiences, and endorsed by the Pulpit, Press and Public everywhere as
SUPERIOR TO ALL OTHERS
Not even excepting the Fisk Jubilee Company.

FIGURE 8.3. Program circa 1882 for a sacred (Sunday) concert by Sheppard's Colored Troubadours and Guitarists, formerly known as Jubilee Singers. Amid the traditional spirituals is Sam Lucas's commercial spiritual "Children, I'm Gwine to Shine." MS Thr 556, folder 571, Houghton Library, Harvard University.

Sam Lucas's Jubilee Journey:
A Nexus between Folk and Popular

Although certain commercial spirituals were called "jubilee songs" on programs, in reviews, and in printed music, Sam Lucas was unique in branding himself a "jubilee singer" and in forming a jubilee group in 1881 to highlight the popular songs of black composers, as well as his own character songs.[22] His jubilee troupe never performed jubilee songs in the original sense of arranged traditional spirituals. Instead, he mixed commercial spirituals, cultivated songs, instrumental selections, and comedy, forging a new kind of concert that was part variety, part band concert, and part art music.

The blueprint for this concert format emerged in early 1880, when Lucas and the Hyers sisters performed a mix of art songs, sacred music from the white tradition, and commercial spirituals (indicated in bold):

Quartet, "Crusaders," Hyers Sisters Quartet
Jubilee, "I must go," Mr. Fred Lyons, and members of the company.
 [composed by Lyons, published 1880]
Soprano solo, "Miserere." (By request) Miss Anna Hyers, assisted by Miss
 Emma L. Hyers.
Violin solo Mr. James H. Harris
Jubilee, "Dese Bones," By members of the company.
 [composed by George W. Scott, published 1880]
Motto songs Mr. Sam Lucas
Tenor solo. "Castle Walls," Mr. Charles E. Bentley
Quartette. "Turkish Patrol," Hyers Sisters Quartet.
 (This quartet was arranged especially by Mr. Sawyer for the Hyers Sisters
 quartet.)
Jubilee, "Put on my Long White Robe," Mr. Sam Lucas and Hyers Sisters
 Company. [composed by Lucas, published 1879]
Duet, "I will magnify Thee, oh Lord," Miss Anna Hyers and Mr. Charles E.
 Bentley.
Quartet. (Sacred.) Hyers Sisters Quartet
Contralto solo. "O Fond Dove, Oh Fair Dove," Miss May Reynolds.
Jubilee, "I's gwine in de valley," Mr. Scott and company.
 [composed by Lucas, published 1879]
Quartet. "Good Night." Hyers Sisters Quartet.[23]

The commercial spirituals, all by black songwriters, are consistently introduced with the word "jubilee." They represent an interesting departure from the Hyers sisters' earlier sacred concerts, which featured Fisk-style traditional spirituals.

A concert from early 1876, for example, featured art music solos in the first half and, in the second, the entire company singing "Gwine Up," "Keep Me from Sinking Down," "Swing Low," and "The Danville Chariot"—all from the Fisk and Hampton repertories.[24]

Lucas formed his first jubilee troupe in the summer of 1880. He was living in Boston at the time, where jubilee singing often floated on the air of the city's many parks. At Oakland Garden, for example, there was Haverly's Colossal Colored Carnival, offering commercial spirituals on a reconstructed plantation (chap. 7). Those who preferred whiteface entertainment could go to Oakland Garden on another day and hear "jubilee hymns" sung by a quartet from the theatrical troupe of Boston's own Little Corinne. Corinne, who at the age of nine was already an experienced entertainer and audience darling, often interpolated commercial spirituals into her plays. She was especially known for her energetic performance of James Bland's commercial spiritual "Oh! Dem Golden Slippers" (1879), which she sang while portraying Cinderella in *The Magic Slipper*.[25] Finally, those who preferred their jubilee songs via white men in blackface could patronize the Olympia Quartette (Boston-bred William Keough, William J. Sullivan, Hugh Mack, and a man named O'Hara) in Ocean Garden at City Point, who according to the publicity "shouted" camp meeting songs as part of a vaudeville entertainment.[26] All of these entertainers stretched the term "jubilee" to cover not only a traditional or commercial spiritual but also any energetic performance that loosely alluded to slave culture.

In the fall Hathaway and Pond (now manager-owners of the Redpath Bureau) assembled for their lyceum series the Ideal Colored Company—named after the white Boston Ideal Opera Company formed in 1879. Included were Lucas, the Hyers, rising prima donna Marie Selika (ca. 1849–1937), Cuban classical violinist Joseph R. Brindis, and James M. Waddy—former bass of the Hampton Institute Singers (see chap. 4). A prominent feature of the Ideals' entertainment was Sam Lucas and quartet in "jubilee selections." On a December 1880 program at the Park Theatre in Boston, for example, the Ideal Quartet opened the concert with jubilee songs, and "Mr. Sam Lucas and quartet" performed more jubilees in the middle of the program.[27]

Lucas as Jubileer

By summer of 1881 Lucas and his Ideal Jubilee Singers had become an independent star attraction rather than a supporting act, playing venues like Boston's Oakland Garden and Forest Garden, and Dorchester's Webster Garden.[28] Although Lucas's formidable comic talents were always on display, he seems to have sidestepped ridicule in his jubilee melodies, imbuing them with a degree of earnestness. This conclusion remains conjecture without detailed descriptions of performances, but a *Boston Globe* reviewer implies as much in writing about Haverly's jubilee singers, who reprised their act that June without Lucas. The direction of the jubilee chorus by celebrated comic Billy Kersands, noted the reviewer, gave "full scope to his faculty for burlesque" and won many encores; at the same time, the reviewer "could not help thinking that such treatment detracted much from the natural charm of the jubilee melodies."[29] This came at a time when Lucas was trying to break free of the minstrel stranglehold and enter the legitimate theatrical sphere.

In the summer of 1881 Lucas also partnered with other jubilee groups, like the Norfolk Jubilee Singers (with whom he closed the summer season at the Oakland Garden, on 11 September) and the Harper's Ferry Jubilee Singers (on 6 November at the Academy of Music in Chelsea).[30] The Harper's Ferry troupe had been appearing the previous week in C. H. Smith's Double Mammoth *Uncle Tom's Cabin*, starring Lucas as Uncle Tom, but the identity of these particular Norfolk Jubilee Singers—another name that several different troupes claimed—remains a mystery. In summer of 1882 Lucas advertised his act as the Sam Lucas Jubilee Songsters, which consisted of Flora Johnson, Scott Wilson, the DeWolf Sisters, George Roushe, and Jacob Sawyer on piano. In fall of 1882 he reconstituted his Ideal Jubilee Concert Company with at least one new member—his wife, Alice Lucas—and in 1883 the Ideals were represented by the Slayton Lyceum Bureau. Through 1885 Lucas continued to collaborate with the most talented African American artists in the profession (sometimes including the Hyers, sometimes not) as he assembled various jubilee troupes and concert companies and traveled throughout the Northeast and Midwest.[31]

Although many other African Americans wrote commercial spirituals (James Bland being the most well known and prolific), Lucas was the only one to present them consistently within a jubilee concert context, as opposed to a minstrel show. Lucas had been vocal about liberating himself from the minstrel profession and its ossified racist caricatures. Biographical puff pieces focused on his value as a performer, emphasizing not only his talent but his refinement and ability to earn top dollar. A profile published in 1882 noted that "while there are several comedians of the sunny soil now before the public, who may attempt to hold a position as enviable as Mr. Lucas now holds, not one has had the ambition, energy and education to aspire beyond the stereotyped, big mouthed, bone rattling, heel shuffling, mouth contortioned [a dig at Billy Kersands], conventional minstrel performances." To the contrary, "Mr. Lucas" displayed a "gentlemanly demeanor" and "many noble characteristics" as well as "a circle of friends which many artists enviously acknowledge."[32] Perhaps Lucas's programming of commercial spirituals under the guise of "jubilee songs" was a canny move to attract audiences by capitulating to stereotype while offering an entertainment that largely avoided the strictures of minstrelsy. In this way he could try to reeducate audiences about what to expect from black performers.

The songs from Lucas's jubilee group period have a sincere quality about them. Lucas published seventeen of his twenty-one known commercial spirituals in a span of only three years—four in 1879, four in 1880, and nine in 1881—largely to refresh the repertory of his jubilee groups, it seems.[33] Some of them, such as "What Kind of Shoes You Gwine to Wear," were only slightly altered versions of traditional spirituals, as was "De Young Lambs Must Find de Way" (1880), which used the same internal refrain as the Hampton Institute Singers' spiritual, titled "De Ole Sheep Done Know the Road."[34]

Although newspapers announced the appearance of Lucas's jubilee troupe, they didn't describe the performances, so sheet music provides the only clues to performance practice. The chorus of "Talk about Your Moses" (1880), for example, is filled with the sort of "concert effects" for which the Fisk Jubilee Singers were renowned: punctuating silences, fermatas, dynamic contrast, and humming (see example 8.2).[35] The tempo marking at the beginning of the obligatory dance before the verse—"moderato, maestoso"—counters minstrelsy's norm of uninhibited energy. The sheet music has it both ways when it comes to marketing, with the cover announcing "the great end song and chorus" (implying humor) and the title page labeling it a "camp meeting hymn" (which could mean any number of things). The verse lyrics are of the exhorting variety (parenthetical texts are internal refrains):

1. If you was me and I was you (Sing glory, Hallelujah),
   I wonder what dis child would do (Sing glory in my soul.)
   I'd sing dat song in de morning bout eight, (Sing glory, Hallelujah),
   Now join in de chorus and don't be late (Sing glory in my soul).

2. Didn't Moses smote de big red sea (Sing glory, Hallelujah),
   For to make some room for you and me (Sing glory in my soul.)
   Oh, de sea got rough and de host got lost (Sing glory, Hallelujah),
   And we're all left to pay de cost (Sing glory in my soul).

3. Now all my friends dats here tonight (Sing glory, Hallelujah),
   Just learn to shout and try to do right (Sing glory in my soul).
   Dat you may reach dat happy land (Sing glory, Hallelujah),
   And dere you'll be a happy band (Sing glory in my soul).

EXAMPLE 8.2. The chorus of "Talk about Your Moses" by Lucas, illustrating "concert effects" made famous by the Fisk Jubilee Singers: punctuating rests, fermatas, humming, and dynamic contrast. The chorus lyrics are indistinguishable from those of traditional spirituals. Music Division, Library of Congress.

Although most commercial spirituals exploited the student jubilee tradition for comic potential, "Moses," like several others by Lucas, seemed to pay homage to the jubilee tradition. The second verse, for example, presents a common metaphor for the liberation of African slaves: Moses parting the Red Sea and leading the Israelites to freedom, and God causing the pursuing Egyptians to drown. The last line of the verse, however, seems to comment on the situation of blacks after emancipation, whose freedom came with a high cost. Sung for black audiences, that line--set off by a pause or otherwise emphasized-- would be certain to elicit noisy affirmation from listeners.

From Commercial to Folk: "Every Day'll Be Sunday"

Like the Wilmington Jubilee Singers before them, the Original Nashville Students were an independent troupe that offered programs of spirituals and plantation sketches in costume. The members, who were neither students nor from Nashville, seem to have formed in 1882 in Chicago. Initially called the Original Tennessee Jubilee and Plantation Singers, they toured small towns on the western lecture circuit under the proprietorship of H. T. Wilson and Harry B. Thearle (white), of the World Lyceum Bureau (Chicago), performing in YMCAs, libraries, town halls, churches, and opera houses.[36] Thearle (1858–1914) was the son of a prominent clergyman, the Reverend Fred G. Thearle, who was manager of the Baptist Book Publishing Company, a frequent tenor in church choirs, and perhaps most significantly, had been involved with "colored Sunday schools in the South" earlier in his career.[37] The son seems to have inherited the father's religious disposition and appreciation for black folk culture, for one of the earliest acts he acquired as lyceum agent was a band of jubilee singers.

By 1883 the troupe had a new name: the Nashville Students. The west was getting crowded with Tennesseans: Donavin's Original Tennesseans were touring at the time, as were Tennessee Jubilee Singers in productions of *Uncle Tom's Cabin* and minstrel shows. As had other jubilee troupes, they added "Original" to their name in a futile effort to distinguish them from the others. Even so, some newspapers misidentified them as representing a college in Tennessee, and other troupes tried to pose as Nashville students and benefit from the prestige that Thearle's group had earned.[38]

The troupe had eight or nine members, and their shows consisted of a first part presenting traditional spirituals mixed with other songs, a second part featuring solos and the male quartet, and a third with a sketch in full plantation costume. The entertainment concluded with a comical musical sketch, "An Evening with Uncle Rasper." For the 1885–1886 season the Nashville Students appeared under the auspices of the prestigious Redpath Lyceum Bureau, still with Thearle as their proprietor. An excerpt from that season's program follows:

Note.—The "NASHVILLE STUDENTS" claim to possess cultivated voices and to be competent to sing what is commonly termed classical music; but it is not their mission, and they leave that field to the white concert companies. But they DO claim to sing the original Jubilee and Plantation Melodies, as sung by the children of bondage in their own peculiar manner in religious and social meetings and on the plantation.

PART FIRST

1. Opening Chorus.—Company
2. Keep a moving.—Miss Nellie Scott Tipton
3. My Lord is Writing Down Time—Miss Franklin Hawkins
4. Every Day Will Be Sunday, bye and bye—Chas. Moore
5. How I long to go—Aug. L. Wright
6. "Selected"—Miss Helen Sawyer
7. Listen to dem ding dong bells.—W. J. Moon
8. O, I'll Meet You Dar—Walter Tipton
9. Gospel Train—All Aboard.
   Piano Selections—Geo. B. McPherson[39]

Nos. 2, 3, 5, and 9 are traditional spirituals. Interspersed among them are two commercial spirituals, both by Sam Lucas: "Every Day Will Be Sunday, Bye and Bye" (the title wasn't standardized) and "O, I'll Meet You Dar." "Listen to Dem Ding Dong Bells" is a novelty song by Jacob J. Sawyer about going to church, with a chorus featuring "ringing" patterns in the bass—a popular musical trope at the time.[40] Sawyer had been a student at Hampton (but never a jubilee singer) who had later worked as a pianist with the Hyers sisters and with Sam Lucas in his jubilee troupes in 1882, and who in 1884 was pianist and music director for the Nashville Students. The assertion in the program that they sing the "original Jubilee and Plantation Melodies" is complicated by the inclusion of new compositions with a plantation theme. Similarly, the Nashville Students offer contradictory images: dignified comportment and dress while singing spirituals, and minstrelized humor in costume during the concluding sketch. In their programs the traditional and commercial merged.

If audiences expected Lucas's "Every Day Will be Sunday, Bye and Bye" to be a traditional spiritual, the song itself didn't disappoint: its persistent melodic repetition, internal refrain, gapped scale (B♭, C, D, F, A), and hint of melisma on the word "shine" in the chorus are all folk traits (see example 8.3).

The Southern Jubilee Singers also programmed "Every Day'll Be Sunday." Managed by an African American lawyer named R. C. O. Benjamin, the troupe toured the Los Angeles area in 1887 under the auspices of the Woman's Christian Temperance Union. According to manager Benjamin they perpetuated the glees and songs of the jubilee singers' forebears, and audiences received them enthusiastically. Like the Nashville Students they attempted a finale consisting

EXAMPLE 8.3. Chorus to "Every Day'll Be Sunday" by Sam Lucas (1881), displaying folk traits. Music Division, Library of Congress.

of a skit with costumes and props, but unlike the Nashville Students their "flat acting" failed to impress. In their Los Angeles area concerts they sang traditional spirituals ("We Are All Here," "Gwine to Hail," "Rolling and Rocking," "Gwine to Ride Up in de Chariot"), a couple of parlor songs ("Evangeline," "Dream of Me"), and one commercial spiritual: "Every Day'll Be Sunday."[41]

"Every Day'll Be Sunday" was also in the repertory of the Canadian Jubilee singers, who actually *were* from Canada (Ontario). Organized in 1884, they toured for five years in Great Britain and then returned to North America.

Their songster, *Songs Sung by the Famous Canadian Jubilee Singers* (plus their Royal Paragon Male Quartette and Imperial Orchestra), has numerous spirituals copied directly from the Fisk anthologies, as well as a section giving lyrics but no music to fifty-four spirituals.[42] Among them are a handful of commercial spirituals: Lucas's "Talk about Your Moses" (no. 40), "Every Day'll Be Sunday" (no. 50), and "Swing Dose Gates Ajar" (no. 33).[43] "Every Day'll Be Sunday" appears on a spread with three other spirituals, without composer attribution, giving the impression that it's a traditional song.

Through programs and songsters that intermingled the commercial with the traditional, through publicity that asserted folk identity ("camp meeting song," "jubilee song"), and in the absence of songwriting credit, commercial spirituals like "Every Day'll Be Sunday" gradually entered folk tradition. The introduction of recordings in the 1890s abetted and extended this process.

The Standard Quartette recorded Lucas's song around 1894 or 1895.[44] It was one of the many black quartets that proliferated in the 1890s, heirs to the jubilee style of singing. Formed around 1891, the Standard Quartette toured independently as well as with the show *South before the War* (chap. 7). The quartet made numerous recordings of "old-fashioned songs" by 1890s standards, encompassing various styles: comic minstrel (e.g., "Who Broke the Lock on the Henhouse Door?"), plantation ("My Old Kentucky Home"), sentimental ("O Promise Me"), and jubilee ("Swing Low, Sweet Chariot").[45]

The Standards' recording of "Every Day'll Be Sunday" exemplifies the concert style originated by the Fisk Jubilee Singers twenty-five years earlier, featuring trained voices, a stately tempo, a solo call answered by a cappella harmony, precise intonation, and clear enunciation. But folk traits are also present, as they were with the Fisk students. For example, the recording begins with the refrain rather than the verse. The cadences overlap and run on. The verse has a chantlike, gapped melody, following the general contours of Lucas's melody but even less active (see example 8.4), making it more typical of black folk song as described in verbal accounts from before the Civil War. Only the chorus, lyrics, and melody of the internal refrain ("Every day'll be Sunday by and by") identify this as Lucas's song. In addition, the dotted rhythms of Lucas's chorus are smoothed out in the Standards' recording.

A comparison of different versions of Lucas's song illustrates the persistence of certain formulaic phrases and ideas in "Every Day'll Be Sunday." For example, the Fisk Jubilee Singers' spiritual "Oh Yes! Oh, Yes!" includes the line "as I went down in the valley to pray," found in both the Lucas and Standards versions. Both the Fisk and the Standard Quartette versions mention meeting Satan on the way. Lucas's narrator meets a character named Eli instead of Satan, but all

EXAMPLE 8.4. The first verse of "Every Day'll Be Sunday" alternating a solo call with a choral refrain. *Top line*: Transcribed from the Standard Quartette's recording. *Second line*: Lucas's composition as printed in the sheet music. The melodic contour of the Standard Quartette's version is much more static. Although it's difficult to pick out the specific pitches of the choral response on the recording, the four-part response follows Lucas's harmony of I–V7–I.

three versions describe a greeting (e.g., "What do you think he said to me" or "How do you do?").

Sheet music may have supported the success of Lucas's song in the commercial realm, but "Every Day'll Be Sunday" had a healthy life in oral transmission as well. The history of Lucas's commercial spiritual is one of ongoing borrowing and modification within an oral tradition that eventually erased his ownership of this song. Two twentieth-century sources, for example, present the song without credit: a recording by the white Zonophone Quartette circa 1906 and the 1910 songster *Wehman Bros.' Good Old-Time Songs* (lyrics only).[46]

Parodies of Lucas's Commercial Spirituals

Although white performers often sang Lucas's commercial spirituals—as well as those by other black composers—they also parodied them. For example, Lucas wrote two commercial spirituals expressly for Lotta (Charlotte Crabtree, chap. 7) and Edward Marble, which were almost immediately burlesqued by white entertainers. One, Lucas's "De Gospel Cars," was an earnest spiritual in the vein of "Talk about Your Moses," published in 1880. The white entertainer Bobby Kirk created a parody that appeared that same year in *Harrigan and Hart's "Mulligan Guard's Surprise"* songster, as well as three others. Labeled an "end song," Kirk's lyrics replace Lucas's liberation message with formulaic minstrel humor and stereotypes:

Lucas's verse 1	Kirk's verse 1
Dar is a road dat Moses made,	As I was crossin o'er de fields,
De angels bid you come.	Angels bid you come.
From earth to Heab'n dis line extends,	A rattlesnake bit me on de heel,
De angels bid you come.	Angels bid you come.
No fare for you am dar to pay,	I went home and laid on de shed,
De angels bid you come.	Angels bid you come.
For Moses am himself de way,	When all dem niggers dey thought
	I was dead.
De angels bid you come.	Angels bid you come.[47]

Lucas's other song for Lotta, "Oh, I'll Meet You Dar" (programmed by the Nashville Students, as discussed previously), was also parodied, by Ned Goss (1848–1882). Goss and his partner James Fox had long performed as "jubilee singers" in blackface, appearing with Simmons, Slocum, and Sweatnam's Minstrels in Philadelphia in 1878, and Harrigan and Hart's company in New York from 1879. They sang several contrafacta of Lucas's spirituals. Whereas Lucas's first verse refers to "de people" around town, Goss differentiates "the white folks" and "the colored folk." His derogatory second verse describes a "gun boat of nigger men" and a "yaller gal" that the singer can "see home."[48]

Although there was nothing unusual in a minstrel writing a parody of another composer's commercial song, white-on-black parody had more sinister consequences. As shown in these two examples, not only did these white parodists capitalize on black creativity through appropriation, replacing the black composer, but their lyrics and performances also re-placed black minstrel performers—and by extension black society—under white control.

Lucas himself wrote his share of songs that perpetuated minstrel stereotypes—it was the rare black artist who could survive professionally without doing so. "De Coon Dat Had de Razor" (1885), for example, reflected the more violent imagery of the emerging "coon song" genre. Although the music was credited to Lucas, his sobriquet for the lyrics, Professor Wm. F. Quown, pun though it was, may have been an attempt to distance himself from the song's racist imagery.[49]

Concluding Thoughts

In eschewing commercial spirituals the Fisk Jubilee Singers represented one extreme of the jubilee performance spectrum. At the other extreme were minstrel and vaudeville entertainers who exploited jubilee song style to parody plantation life, camp meetings, jubilee singers, or African Americans generally. In between were hundreds of black entertainers trying to earn a living by singing spirituals and commercial spirituals, veering toward one pole or the other as circumstance required. Some, like the Wilmingtons, began as concert artists but ended up as minstrel or variety entertainers. Others, like the Nashville Students, successfully incorporated variety entertainment in their programs while maintaining their reputation as concert artists. As the category of jubilee singer loosened, the boundaries between the altruistic and the purely commercial, between the folk and the popular, and between "high" and "low" began to blur.

Sam Lucas's career illustrates these processes. In basing many of his compositions on folk spirituals, he helped spread their sound. In writing commercial spirituals with noncomic lyrics for his own jubilee troupe, he reoriented in some measure a genre that had relied largely on irreverence—proof being the performance of his songs by legitimate jubilee troupes.

Numerous other African American composer-performers wrote commercial spirituals as well; those with published songs include James Bland, Gussie Davis, Harry Davis, Pete Devonear, James Grace, Henry Hart, John H. Jordan, Dan Lewis, Fred Lyons, James S. Putnam, Albert Saunders, Jacob J. Sawyer, and George W. Scott.[50] The entertainment world was small, and the black entertainment world smaller, so that most of these composers crossed paths (see figure 8.4). The composers of Lucas's generation were generally self-taught musicians, the exceptions being Sawyer (1856–1885) and Gussie Davis (1863–1899), who both studied music in Cincinnati, at the College of Music and the Nelson Musical College, respectively, and who both wrote a large body of songs that were far more ambitious than commercial spirituals. (Davis's career rested on songs written in the late 1880s and 1890s during the rise of Tin Pan Alley.) Sawyer and Bland also went to college, although neither graduated; Sawyer attended Hampton Institute, and Bland briefly was a prelaw student at Howard University before abandoning his studies for the minstrel stage in 1875. Although Sawyer worked in a Boston bank and Bland undoubtedly could have had a job in business or government—his father worked in the U.S. Patent Office—both men chose the uncertain world of entertainment.

If by 1880 a jubilee singer could be anything from a concert artist to a minstrel parodist, and if traditional spirituals could be found on the concert stage

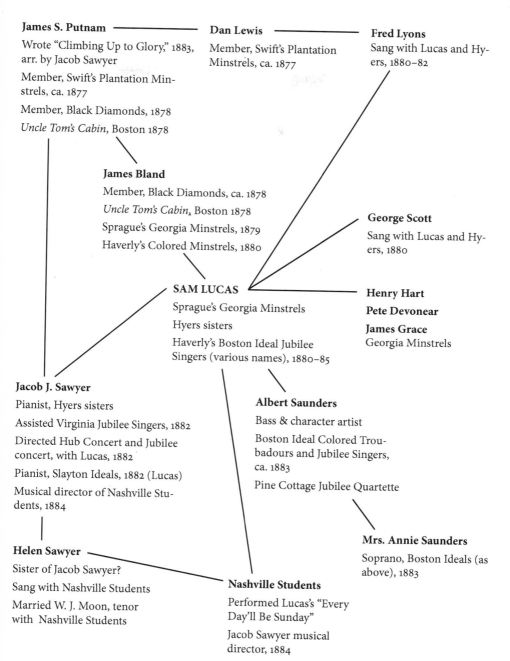

James S. Putnam ——————

Wrote "Climbing Up to Glory," 1883, arr. by Jacob Sawyer

Member, Swift's Plantation Minstrels, ca. 1877

Member, Black Diamonds, 1878

Uncle Tom's Cabin, Boston 1878

Dan Lewis ——————

Member, Swift's Plantation Minstrels, ca. 1877

Fred Lyons

Sang with Lucas and Hyers, 1880–82

James Bland

Member, Black Diamonds, ca. 1878

Uncle Tom's Cabin, Boston 1878

Sprague's Georgia Minstrels, 1879

Haverly's Colored Minstrels, 1880

George Scott

Sang with Lucas and Hyers, 1880

SAM LUCAS

Sprague's Georgia Minstrels

Hyers sisters

Haverly's Boston Ideal Jubilee Singers (various names), 1880–85

Henry Hart

Pete Devonear

James Grace

Georgia Minstrels

Jacob J. Sawyer

Pianist, Hyers sisters

Assisted Virginia Jubilee Singers, 1882

Directed Hub Concert and Jubilee concert, with Lucas, 1882

Pianist, Slayton Ideals, 1882 (Lucas)

Musical director of Nashville Students, 1884

Albert Saunders

Bass & character artist

Boston Ideal Colored Troubadours and Jubilee Singers, ca. 1883

Pine Cottage Jubilee Quartette

Mrs. Annie Saunders

Soprano, Boston Ideals (as above), 1883

Helen Sawyer ——————

Sister of Jacob Sawyer?

Sang with Nashville Students

Married W. J. Moon, tenor with Nashville Students

Nashville Students

Performed Lucas's "Every Day'll Be Sunday"

Jacob Sawyer musical director, 1884

FIGURE 8.4. The world of entertainment was small in the nineteenth century. Using Sam Lucas as a point of reference, this diagram shows the web of relationships between the more active composer-performers of spirituals. All except Lucas and Jacob J. Sawyer spent their careers in minstrelsy.

as well as in Tom shows and commercial entertainments, how was the public to view the black entertainer at this time? For example, was Lucas a minstrel performer? vaudeville performer? concert artist? comedian? legitimate actor? Was he a race activist or an accommodationist? religious or sacrilegious? He was probably all of these things at different times and to different degrees. Multiple and sometimes contradictory images of him circulated simultaneously, as did the various versions of his commercial spirituals. The same could be said of most black performers of the time.

A program circa 1883 illustrates this ambiguity at work. Titled "Boston Ideal / Colored Troubadours / and Jubilee Singers," it aims for comprehensiveness in referencing Slayton's Ideals (concert music), Troubadours (cultivated popular song; the term made its way into Lucas's "Ideal Colored Troubadours" in 1885), and Jubilee Singers (connoting spirituals).[51] Even in 1883, a decade into the jubilee phenomenon, the term "jubilee" was valuable in branding concerts by black composers, whether or not "tradition" was in evidence.

It's easy to perceive jubilee singers like the Fisks, the Hamptons, and the Tennesseans as activists, as Doug Seroff did when he wrote of the later Fisk Jubilee Singers' "civil rights tours" of 1879–1882. It's more challenging to consider African American composers and performers of commercial spirituals in that light. On the face of it, their exploitation of a folk tradition for minstrel, variety, and vaudeville entertainment might connote pollution, vulgarity, and poor taste. Yet the determination of black performers to program black compositions and their clear admiration for certain white minstrel performers—to whom they dedicated songs, with whom they collaborated, and with whom they occasionally performed—complicate such a position, as do expressions of race pride and engagement with social issues in certain of their songs.

For example James Putnam, who wrote his share of coon songs in the 1880s (and a commercial spiritual called "I'll Be Ready When the Great Day Comes," one of the top-selling songs of 1883), wrote a "jubilee song" called "Climbing Up to Glory" that exhorts listeners to keep inching toward heaven, not individually but as a community, hand in hand. The refrain urges brothers to come along, sisters to come along, and *class leaders* to come along—a highly unusual term to find in any commercial spiritual, particularly one by Putnam. Jacob Sawyer arranged the music for the sheet music edition, whereas more typically the publisher would hire a white arranger.

Jacob Sawyer had a varied career, working with the Hyers sisters combination starting in 1877 and later as pianist and/or music director for the Virginia Jubilee Singers, Haverly's Minstrels, Sam Lucas's various jubilee troupes, the Maryland Jubilee Singers, and the Nashville Students.[52] With a body of eighteen instrumental compositions (mazurkas, waltzes, schottisches, polkas, and marches for solo piano), twenty-four vocal songs (eleven of which were commercial spirituals), and six arrangements—published over a mere six years (1879–1885)—he was also one of his generation's most prolific songwriters.[53] His musical output and his formative years with the Hyers troupe reflected his preference for music that promoted social advancement. His first set of published pieces was the "Out of Bondage Waltzes" (op. 2, 1879), written for Joseph Bradford's music drama for the Hyers about the transformative consequences of education. (It was highly unusual for such a composition to be given an opus number.)

Almost all of Sawyer's commercial spirituals date from 1883, when he was pianist for Sam Lucas's jubilee troupe, which that year was called the Slayton Ideals (not to be confused with the later Slayton Jubilee Singers, a different troupe that was popular on the Chautauqua circuit in the late 1890s until the 1920s). Although Sawyer's lyrics on the whole can't be considered "progressive," his songs have their moments of dignity. For example, "Ring Dem Chimin' Bells" celebrates "Massa Linkum" setting the slaves free. Despite the dialect and the paternalistic term of "children" for the former slaves, the chorus's slow-moving chordal harmony creates the possibility of a stirring, hymnlike affirmation of the power of black voices. The topic of emancipation also surfaces in Sawyer's "Yes, I'll Be Dar."[54]

There are also examples of protest in commercial spirituals, as in "Ole' Nicker Demus" by Sam Lucas and "All de Darkies Gittin' Up" by Jim Grace, who performed in both Callender's and Haverly's minstrel troupes in the 1870s and 1880s.[55] Lucas's lyrics convey black superiority: "You Talk about your white folks, O, my Lord! . . . Dey say dat de darkey can't stand in der shoes, / But Old Nicker Demus was der ruler ob de Jews!" The chorus reinforces this message: "If I want a good man, a darkey I will choose, / for old Nicker Demus was de ruler ob de Jews!" Although the third and fourth verses somewhat undercut the chorus in asserting the "darkey's" loyalty and willingness to do white folk a good turn, it's impossible to know whether, or in what manner, black performers sang these verses.

Grace's song, on the other hand, is unusually direct in its criticism of whites. The narrators are a band of sinners who have lost their way because Satan stole their compass to see if they had "pluck" (which they do—hence the phrase "All de darkies gittin' up"). The second verse exclaims: "Ole massa he's a hypocrite, / He prays so loud on Sunday, / And when we're in de cornfield, / He whips us all on Monday." Things deteriorate for massa in the third verse; the slaves, having rejected sin and set off on the path to glory, note that when they see old massa at the golden gate, "he'll find he's come too late."

Lyrics by black songwriters that directly promote race pride are admittedly the exception rather than the rule, for good reason. Black songwriters were in an altogether different position from the Fisk Jubilee Singers, who after eight years of touring could afford to speak out against the race prejudice they encountered. For example, George White's reconstituted, independent troupe of Fisks announced to a Louisville, Kentucky, audience in 1880 that they had been denied access to a first-class railroad car—after having been feted in Europe by kings and emperors and prime ministers. When they sang "Gospel Train" at a concert shortly after this announcement ("The fare is cheap and all can go, / The rich and poor are there, / No second-class on board the train, / No difference in the fare"), the house nearly came down with screams and applause of support.[56] But black minstrel entertainers were patronized by the working and middle class, not by powerful clergy and European aristocracy. Although black performers certainly tailored their songs and messages to local communities based on geography and race, minstrel and variety artists had to please a wider range of people who, after all, attended minstrel and variety shows for entertainment, not edification. In addition, the largest black minstrel troupes were still managed by whites—the minstrel overseers. If certain concert spirituals became protest songs in the hands of the Fisk Jubilees, however, perhaps certain commercial spirituals served a similar, if more veiled, function in the hands of commercial singers, dancers, and comedians. Black entertainers would have to walk this fine line between unfiltered creative expression and fulfilling audience expectations not only for the rest of the nineteenth century but throughout the twentieth.

Conclusion
Lessons and Legacies

The earliest literary recognitions of black music, outlined in the introduction, set up an artificial dichotomy between "white" and "black" traditions, suggesting for each of these two categories an essence and a stability that didn't exist. Concert spirituals, commercial spirituals, and indeed the entire black entertainment industry of the nineteenth century were shaped by a common dynamic. Music, dance, comedy, performance practice, and other expressive strategies that had emerged among black Americans—and that were closely bound up with their social and religious lives—were made to conform to the preferences and expectations of white audiences. The earliest jubilee singers sang spirituals molded by white arrangers. Black minstrels performed caricatures of slave culture that had been imagined by white performers. As black performers discovered, the commercial sphere was ruled by white taste, and success rested on maintaining the fiction that they were offering up an authentic slice of black culture. The earnestness of the student jubilee singers, the seeming willingness of black commercial entertainers to enact slave caricatures, and the occasional collaborations between white and black performers obscured the coercion that drove their performances. Mel Watkins has argued that in order to carve out more autonomy, black performers had to maintain a delicate balance, satirizing white notions about black people without reinforcing negative stereotypes.[1] But as the foregoing chapters have shown, they had other options as well, even though the chance for success was limited: create their own plays and songs and sketches, manage their own performing troupes, even pursue entertainment genres that didn't center on racial identity.

Why did the spiritual become the signature song for this emerging, complicatedly racialized entertainment industry? The answer lies in the spiritual's emotive power, which allowed it to serve as a potent mediator between concert jubilee singers and their white audiences. Nineteenth-century audiences were easily moved to tears, and there was a plethora of sentimental parlor songs to tug at their heartstrings. White men and women who heard the Fisks and other student jubilee groups were therefore predisposed to react emotionally, and to do so openly. Fisk's "services of song" further primed audiences with messages of missionary zeal followed by "strangely" beautiful music, which, thanks to the strategic blending of musical elements, audiences could perceive as at once familiar and exotic. The inclusion on early jubilee programs of popular songs from the white tradition—especially Civil War songs and plantation songs such as "Massa's in the Cold, Cold Ground" by Stephen Foster—"sharpened the image of the Jubilee Singers as former slaves by providing images of locales and a way of life that the spirituals did not provide," as William Austin observed.[2] The slave's sentimental attachment to the plantation in Foster songs, the jubilant abolitionist message of "John Brown's Body" (a favorite of Fisk audiences), and the spirit of the spirituals—defiant, sorrowful, joyful, faith-filled—served up a concoction of mixed messages, each of which was consistent with the romantic racialism of the time period.

Student jubilee concerts served as a forum in which whites with no previous experience of plantation slavery could imagine that they suddenly understood the pain of the freedmen. In so doing they became what Saidiya Hartman calls a "proxy" for the formerly enslaved singers. Such empathy led some whites to a more enlightened understanding of black Americans, but as Hartman elaborates, there was also a danger that this "too-easy intimacy," this "consideration of the self," occurred at the expense of the singers, who might disappear under the sympathetic white gaze.[3] That this indeed happened is evident in reactions that designated the Fisk students as "children of bondage," for example, even though some had been born free and none were children. The singers were seen as a symbol rather than as individuals, and their spirituals represented an imaginary Other that encompassed essentialized notions of blackness, slavery, and ultimately Africa.

Concerts by groups like Donavin's Original Tennesseans, the Wilmington Jubilee Singers, and the Nashville Students heightened audience identification with slavery through costumes and sketches, offering a presumably ethnographic portrayal of slave life. Minstrel shows (already well established, and even tired, cultural institutions by the mid-1870s) and stage productions of *Uncle Tom's Cabin* renewed themselves by appropriating jubilee songs and singers. The minstrels parodied jubilee groups, then competed with them by performing commercial spirituals and Hamtown acts in the parallel sphere of popular entertainment. The incorporation of jubilee singers conferred on Tom shows a new credibility in the mid-1870s; it not only drove a new marketing strategy centered on "authenticity," but it gave audiences a reason to keep attending once the cause of emancipation had been won. Spectacles like *Black America* offered immersive experiences by expanding the illusory ethnographic reach. Spectators became participants as they wandered through elaborate outdoor sets with cotton fields, cabins, animals, and field hands. Sounds, smells, tactility, and weather left little to the patrons' imagination and certainly transformed the experience of listening to jubilee singers.

Over a twenty-year span in the 1870s and 1880s, then, spirituals went from being an innovation—a means by which young blacks could achieve an education while in turn educating others in some degree about black culture—to a commodity that was appropriated and transformed according to context. In the first instance the concert spiritual allowed white audiences to indulge in "the spectacular nature of black suffering." In the second, the commercial spiritual facilitated "the dissimulation of suffering through spectacle"[4]—a kind of "ideological repair" that served to reassure white northerners in particular that slavery, with its camp meeting jubilees and corn husking songs and nimble dances, had not been all suffering all of the time.[5] The spiritual worked in these wildly divergent performance contexts because it was malleable and ubiquitous. The properties of slave spirituals were recognizable even in commercial permutations, such was the success of jubilee troupes in winning over their audiences until spirituals had become a pervasive cultural presence.

Certainly there were other types of music derived from black culture that appeared in mass entertainments at the time, notably instrumental music, which usually accompanied jigs, reels, buck and wing, and other dances onstage. In the rural South during slavery, "musicianers" (folk instrumentalists) had provided the backbone to frolics, "the secular counterpart of the Sunday prayer meeting," in the words of Paul Cimbala. But "musicianers did not respond to the political challenge of Reconstruction."[6] Whereas spirituals underwent stylistic development and prompted public discourse about racial uplift, in the public imagination instrumental music remained rooted in the antebellum past until the early 1890s;[7] when performed onstage it was in the context of minstrelsy, variety, Tom shows, or the circus. (The many black brass bands at the time didn't play folk music, although they played commercial spirituals. The early twentieth century witnessed the first band arrangements of traditional spirituals, by N. Clark Smith for the Tuskegee Institute Band.)[8] Because of its association with an antiquated past, instrumental folk music didn't figure into discussions of race development, regardless of how esteemed a performer might be. Jubilee troupes in the Fisk mold called upon instruments of the middle class when accompaniment was needed—piano, pump organ, and guitar.

Although most jubilee troupes were initially under white management, black directors, composers, and arrangers became increasingly common in the mid-1870s and 1880s. There was Leroy Pickett, who arranged spirituals and sang for Donavin's Original Tennesseans, and who by the early 1880s was their manager. Samuel B. Hyers initially managed his famous daughters. Thomas J. Gatewood managed the early career of the Centennial Jubilee Singers. There was Frank A. Stewart, a tenor with Donavin's Original Tennesseans (1874) for eight years before he organized the Stewart-Wilberforce Concert Company in 1881. That troupe toured for two years as an organ of the nation's oldest historically black university, Wilberforce University (1856, Xenia, Ohio), before becoming a private venture in 1884, with Stewart as proprietor and manager. There was James O. Crosswhite, who assumed management of the Boston Ideal Colored Troubadours and Jubilee Singers in 1883 after being a featured soloist with Al Holden's Louisiana Jubilees, a Tom jubilee troupe. Robert Hamilton, a singer with the 1872 original Hampton students, managed a traveling group of jubilee singers in connection with Norfolk Mission College in 1886 and 1887 before teaching at Tuskegee. P. T. Wright managed a variety troupe known as the Nashville Students starting in 1888 (to be distinguished from Thearle's Nashville Students, a more conventional jubilee troupe on the Fisk model).[9] Mr. and Mrs. William Carter, who sang with Thearle's Nashville Students in 1890, went on to become managers and proprietors of the Canadian Jubilee Singers. And then there was the forerunner of them all: Charles "Barney" Hicks (d. 1902), who organized the first successful black minstrel troupe, Brooker and Clayton's Georgia Minstrels, and went on to associate himself with every significant black minstrel troupe for the rest of the century. His career illustrates the challenges of being a black impresario at the time: not only was it difficult for black managers to get bookings in white-owned theaters, but Hicks's relentless entrepreneurial spirit was effectively throttled by his white competitors. As Ike Simond recalled, "Hicks was a very dangerous man to all outside managers and they all were afraid of him; when he was at the head of a company he was a cross-roader [grifter] for a man's life; the Frohmans kept him in their employ for years, in order to keep him from starting out for himself."[10] (See web table 4.4, Biographical Dictionary of Jubilee Concert Troupes, for more on these individuals and jubilee troupes.)

The most celebrated among black managers and proprietors was former original Jubilee Singer Frederick J. Loudin, who reorganized a troupe of Fisk Jubilee Singers after George White was incapacitated in an accident. Loudin never attended Fisk but was devoted to the university; older than the other original troupe members, he had long played a leadership role among the singers. Like White, Loudin used the Fisk name even though the university didn't sponsor his troupe. Loudin's Fisk Jubilee Singers toured the United States for two years starting in 1882. Confronted with racism and poor financial receipts at home, they embarked on an ambitious six-year world tour, disbanding upon their return. (In Liverpool they sang spirituals in a venue uncharacteristic for Fisk groups—Hengler's Circus. The crowd of some seven thousand was reportedly the largest paid-admission audience for any incarnation of the Fisk singers.)[11] At the tour's conclusion, and after a fifteen-year career in the jubilee business, Loudin returned to his hometown of Ravenna, Ohio, where he became the largest stockholder of what would become the F. J. Loudin Shoe Manufacturing Company. He couldn't ignore the lure of jubilee singing, however, and he mingled touring with shoe manufacturing until 1902, when he collapsed while performing in Scotland; he died in 1904.

The jubilee entertainment industry also opened doors for black women, more often in vocal and instrumental performance than in management. In the jubilee realm the Hyers sisters were the best known, although Pauline Hopkins had local repute in Boston as a playwright and singer. Several former Fisk Jubilee Singers managed and performed in jubilee troupes later in their careers, including Jennie Jackson (Jennie Jackson DeHart's Jubilee Singers) and Maggie Porter Cole, although before long her troupe was taken over by white manager Charles Mumford and became known as Mumford's Fisk Jubilee Singers. Most female performers were recognized for singular achievement as part of a larger group rather than as solo acts. Georgia (Georgie) Allen was one exception. She sang with Slavin's Georgia Jubilee Singers in the Howards' production of *Uncle Tom's Cabin* (see her two solos on the concert program in figure 7.3). In 1877 she was promoted from jubilee singer to cast member in the role of Emmeline—a slave who is sold, along with Tom, to Legree in act 5 of Aiken's play as revised by G. C. Howard—becoming one of the earliest African Americans to have a speaking role in *Uncle Tom's Cabin* onstage. Invoking the memories of Elizabeth Taylor Greenfield and Jenny Lind, the publicity machine proclaimed her "far superior to the Black Swan" and dubbed her the "Southern Nightingale."[12] She tried her hand at leading her own jubilee band, the Georgie Allen Colored Jubilee Singers. In February 1878 they closed the afternoon variety bill at Gilmore's Garden in New York with "good, old-fashioned songs and plantation melodies," probably when the Howard production was on hiatus, but the group seemed to disappear after that.[13]

Such breakout moments for women performers were few in number, however. It was more common for them to meet their future husbands while performing together; notable examples include Sarah Miles of Slavin's *Uncle Tom's Cabin* jubilees (married to Alexander Taylor), Ida Washington of the Wilmington Jubilee Singers (married to Charles Washington), Jennie Robinson of Donavin's

Tennesseans and later Stewart-Wilberforce Concert Company (married to Frank Stewart), and Cordelia McClain (married to Billy McClain). Women also served as pianists for troupes, as did Carrie Alden with Pauline Hopkins's groups circa 1880 (among other jubilee groups). Several women combined accompaniment and directing duties, as did Ella Sheppard with the Fisks. Mrs. William Carter, who had performed with her husband in Thearle's Nashville Students, later shared management and proprietorship duties with her husband for the Canadian Jubilee Singers (ca. 1895–1990). Like Frederick Loudin, three women of the original Fisk Jubilee Singers had afterlives in the profession by organizing and touring with their own troupes: Maggie Porter, who with her husband, Daniel Cole, founded the Original Jubilee Singers in 1882 (also known as the Fisk Jubilee Singers, creating confusion with Loudin's troupe); Mabel Lewis, who settled in Cleveland with her husband, Martin Imes, and organized a local choir there; and Jennie Jackson, who created the Jennie Jackson DeHart Jubilee Club (ca. 1884), also known as the Jennie Jackson Concert Company. Thanks to the pioneers of the first black entertainment industry, the greatest late nineteenth-century black women performers were able to make their reputations primarily outside of the jubilee business. These included vocalists Nellie Brown Mitchell, Marie Selika Williams, and Matilda Sissieretta Jones.[14]

Remuneration of black entertainers varied according to economic vicissitudes, geographical region, the scale of the organization, time of year, and demand. The one constant was that blacks almost always made less than their white counterparts. An exception in the jubilee realm was the original Fisk Jubilee Singers, who received $500 annually in 1873–1874—far more than white teachers at Fisk received—and between $700 and $1,000 annually from 1876—enough to buy a plot of land or a house.[15] The pay of minstrel and variety performers depended not only on market forces but on the performer's role within the organization as well. For example, in 1873 the unknown Sam Lucas was invited to join Callender's Georgia Minstrels for a salary of $4 per week (including travel and lodging); when he was promoted to endman he received a raise to $10 per week, and by 1874 he was making $20 per week—by which time he had reached Callender's limit.[16] Thanks to jubilee fever, black minstrels enjoyed a short period of being in greater demand than whites—the public clamored for genuine rather than corked-up performers. As Robert Toll notes, between 1865 and 1890 over half of the want ads for "colored entertainers" in the *New York Clipper* appeared during four years, between 1880 and 1884. As a result of this demand the salary of comic Billy Kersands jumped from $15 per week in 1879 to $80 per week in 1882.[17] Such surges in pay were temporary, however. (By way of comparison, the white song and dance team of Booker and Canfield joined

J. H. Haverly's minstrels in 1873 at a salary of $300 per week, or $150 each—one of the highest salaries for such an act at the time.)[18]

Even though both whites and blacks sang and wrote commercial spirituals, only blacks formed legitimate jubilee troupes to sing traditional spirituals. Spirituals were black creations, despite any borrowings from white hymns and tunes, and despite initial transcriptions and arrangements by whites. There is nevertheless an irony in calling an entertainment realm dominated by white management and white performers a "black entertainment industry," especially because the violence experienced by black performers in the United States prompted so many of them to tour abroad—from jubilee troupes to minstrel troupes to individual performers like Fisk Singer Thomas Rutling or minstrel James Bland, who spent the height of his career in England (1881–1901). Nevertheless, the phrase points to an important truth at a historical turning point in American entertainment: the emergence of jubilee groups and the developments in black minstrelsy depended on the lived experience of black artists, their recent history as enslaved people, their creativity, their labor, and their talent. Even though both whites and blacks sang and wrote commercial spirituals, only black jubilee troupes sang traditional spirituals.

Although there were no known white jubilee troupes in the United States—the Hutchinson Family's concert spirituals to the contrary—whites did sing spirituals in American Sunday schools and homes, influenced largely by the original Fisk Jubilee Singers and later incarnations. In Scotland, however, the practice of singing spirituals in worship seems to have led to the formation of white jubilee groups in the 1890s. The Reverend McInnes Neilson, pastor of the First Congregational Church in Ravenna, Ohio, heard Frederick Loudin's Fisk troupe sing many times in Britain. He observed that even though "it needs the Negro to do the dialect justice, yet that did not prevent the white people, usually a quartet or a quintet of consecrated men and women, from adopting the name 'The Jubilee Singers,' and establishing themselves in their own towns to sing these weird and fascinating melodies." He noted that there was such a quintet in his hometown, ten miles from Glasgow, and found similar groups in "a great many towns in Scotland" who performed for religious services, without remuneration.[19]

Spirituals in the Popular Sphere: Canon Formation

One musical consequence of the jubilee industry was the establishment of a canon of spirituals. Their popularity was measured not just by frequency of performance by concert jubilee groups but by repeated parody (e.g., "Go Down,

Moses"--Sam Lucas's "Carve Dat Possum"; "Swing Low, Sweet Chariot"--Delehanty and Hengler's "Sing Low"; "There's a Meeting Here Tonight"-- Pete Devonear's commercial spiritual of the same name). The publishing industry further reflected and boosted popularity by issuing different versions of the most beloved spirituals (e.g., solo piano arrangements, often as a medley; guitar or banjo accompaniments), as well as by anthologizing them in collections of American songs and even college songs.[20] Table 9.1 presents a canon of spirituals whose numerous public performances, reinforced by music publication, can be documented from 1872 to the turn of the century. The list could well be extended as programs, playbills, and newspaper reports become readily available.

Given that some long-lived jubilee troupes advertised over a hundred songs in their repertory, the list may seem relatively short. It should be noted that at any one time, however, a troupe's active repertory was likely to be half the size advertised. Lack of rehearsal time due to rigorous touring schedules, illness, and inadequate facilities on the road discouraged the addition of too many new songs in a given season. At the same time, consecutive performances at the same venue required a change of program. The challenge in identifying the most canonical spirituals lies in determining whether a troupe actually performed the songs that their publicity advertised. Newspaper reviews didn't always list song titles—especially once the novelty of jubilee concerts had diminished. In addition, jubilee troupes often economized by printing a generic program that could be used throughout a season, implying a limited repertory that may in fact have been broader. Finally, printed programs often had a slot for "Selections" that could be announced from the stage—an opportunity for managers to retain some flexibility and for audiences to play an active role in programming by making requests. There was no doubt, however, that certain spirituals were universally acclaimed. It was for this reason that the Fisk Jubilee Singers developed a formula that several rival groups adopted, opening every one of their concerts with "Steal Away," followed immediately by the chanting of the Lord's Prayer.

The End of One Era and Beginning of Another

The jubilee industry was largely worn out by 1890. The *Brooklyn Eagle* hinted at its demise when it noted in 1888 that the public was moving on to new fads: "Lady fencers are appearing all around the country. They promise to be as thick as the . . . Jubilee Singers used to be" (1 July). Despite some exceptional forays into plantation nostalgia in the 1890s, such as *Black America* and *South before the War*, popular music had largely moved on to coon songs, the cakewalk, ethnic

Been a Listening
Bright Sparkles in the Church-Yard
Didn't My Lord Deliver Daniel?
Gideon's Band / Band of Gideon
Give Me Jesus
Go, Chain the Lion Down
Go Down, Moses
Good News, de Chariot's Comin'
Gospel Train / Get on Board
Great Camp-Meetin' in de Promised Land
Gwine to Ride up in the Chariot
Gwine Up
Hard Trials
He Arose / He Rose from the Dead / Dust and Ashes
He's the Lily of the Valley
Humble Yourself (The Bell Done Ring)
I'll Hear the Trumpet Sound
I'm a-Rolling
Inching Along
In Dat Great Gittin-up Mornin'
Judgment Day Is Rolling Round / How I Long to Go
Keep Me from Sinking Down
Mary and Martha
My Brethren, Don't Get Weary / Don't Get Weary
My Lord, What a Mourning/Morning
My Lord's Writing All the Time
My Way's Cloudy
Nobody Knows de Trouble I See, Lord
Nobody Knows the Trouble I've Had/Seen
Oh, Wasn't That a Wide River?
Old Ark's a Movering
Old Sheep Done Know de Road
Peter, Go Ring Them Bells
Reign, Master Jesus
Ride on, King Jesus
Rise and Shine / Rise! Shine! And Give God the Glory
Rocks and the Mountains
Roll, Jordan, Roll
Room Enough / O Brothers, Don't Stay Away
Steal Away
Swing Low, Sweet Chariot (Coming for to carry me home)
Swing Low, Sweet Chariot (Don't you leave me behind)
There's a Meeting Here Tonight
This Old Time Religion / Give Me This Old Time Religion
Turn Back Pharaoh's Army
View the Land / Way Over Jordan
We'll Die in the Field / I Will Die in the Field / What Do You Say, Seeker
What Kind of Shoes Are You Going to Wear?
Wrestling Jacob

Note: Given that titles weren't standardized, two commonly used titles sometimes appear in this list, indicated by a slash. Similar titles on separate lines indicate unique words and tune.

novelty songs, and ragtime. There were still concert jubilee groups, but with a few exceptions—including Thearle's Nashville Students, which petered out in the 1890s—they relied on the Chautauqua circuit for their subsistence, or else represented local churches and communities, foregoing a national profile. By the late 1890s the foundation of a new, less homogeneous black entertainment industry was being laid—by black artists singing art songs and opera; black instrumentalists playing art, dance, and marching band music; solo concert artists singing spirituals; and composers/dancers/singers/actors revitalizing musical comedy.

The descendants of the first generation of black minstrels came of age during the 1880s and 1890s, as Jim Crow legislation was being enacted. They included Bob Cole, Will Marion Cook, Paul Laurence Dunbar, Ernest Hogan, James Weldon Johnson, J. Rosamond Johnson, Ada Overton, Will Vodery, George Walker, and Bert Williams. Although still bound in many ways by minstrel convention, this new generation changed the conversation in their musical comedies, moving locales of plays to Africa (e.g., Williams and Walker), writing large-scale songs that loosened the straitjacket of the verse-chorus formula (e.g., Cook), and injecting subversive wit into characters and plots. Nevertheless, as Karen Sotiropoulos notes, although "black performers enacted fictive types onstage to debunk racial mythologies offstage," they underestimated white determination to control and own black culture.[21] As a result, they still were subject to the demands visited by white impresarios and advertisers, the constraints of white audience expectations, and the eager appropriation by white songwriters, performers, and publishers of their songs, dances, and performance practices.

With this second wave of black entertainers cresting around the turn of the century, the South became a lucrative field for black performers. Ernest Hogan and Billy McClain's Smart Set became the first big black musical comedy troupe to tour the South successfully; in addition the South was crowded with large black minstrel companies that played outdoors in tents. Indeed this period marked the first time in which black minstrels outnumbered whites. These shows introduced ragtime, blues, and early blueswomen such as Ma Rainey and Bessie Smith.[22]

If spirituals were no longer the currency of popular entertainment by the 1890s, neither were they central to the black church. The praise houses, camp meetings, and churches that had been important environments for the creation and performance of folk spirituals had moved from the center to the periphery as African American religion and worship diversified after the Civil War.[23] As slavery receded from the personal experience of new generations, and as education erased black folk culture as a rung on the ladder to success, there was a backlash in urban communities against rural religious practice. One leader of the backlash was Daniel Alexander Payne (1811–1893), who as bishop of the African Methodist Episcopal Church (1852–1893) raised funds to purchase Wilberforce University, over which he presided as president from 1865 to 1876. He was one of the most influential African Americans of the nineteenth century. On a trip east in 1878 he attended a bush meeting, where the worshippers performed a ring shout "in a most ridiculous and heathenish way," as he phrased it in his autobiography, before piling on additional pejoratives such as "rude," "extravagant," "stupid," "headstrong," and "disgrace."[24] A similarly negative stance was still evident among upwardly mobile blacks at the turn of the century, as evidenced by an article in a black newspaper warning participants at a camp meeting, especially ladies, to exercise restraint—apparently on account of white guests, who wouldn't approve of demonstrative behavior: "Our modern ladies cannot afford to use the familiarity with white guests in Minnesota, as our old foreparents did in the South 32 years ago. . . . Every Afro-American who attends this camp meeting should be as reserved as when attending a church."[25] Educated urban blacks favored European anthems and hymns in their church services, and they offered church concerts featuring classical music, recitations, and orations.[26] Rather than anticipate the afterlife—the message of so many spirituals—they were ready to embrace the contemporary world, as revealed in this comment from a black newspaper in 1891 regarding the canonical spiritual "Give Me Jesus": "Brothers please quit singing that song, 'Take all the world and give me Jesus.' That talk used to go, but it don't go now."[27]

As a result of these cultural shifts, black folk culture was at risk of being forgotten. Although some jubilee troupes and writers had been sounding the alarm about vanishing folk music for years ("This is one of the last—*the* last and only chance to many," wrote one journalist in 1872 of the Fisk Jubilee Singers, "that will ever be afforded for hearing the quaint and wild strains in which the Southern negroes give vent to their pent up feelings"),[28] preservation efforts were slow to materialize. It wasn't until 1893 that Alice Bacon, a white teacher at the Hampton Normal School, implored students, graduates, and friends of Hampton University to collect and preserve black folklore: "Even now the children are growing up with little knowledge of what their ancestors have thought or felt or suffered." Ironically, she noted, it was institutions like Hampton, "eradicating the old, and planting the seeds of the new," that were pivotal agents in this crisis.[29] Bacon's Hampton Folk-Lore Society was an important early platform for African Americans to speak and write about black folk culture, although its contributions to the study of spirituals were slight, owing to the lack of a trained musician among the researchers and the difficulty of capturing a live performance without a recording device.[30] This wasn't to say that folk spirituals were a dead tradition. They were still vital in rural regions of the South especially. As Zora Neale Hurston noted decades later, "Contrary to popular belief their creation is not confined to the slavery period. Like the folk-tales, the spirituals are being made and forgotten every day."[31]

At the turn of the century a number of whites began publishing folkloric research on spirituals and even performing them in public. William Eleazar Barton (1861–1930), a cousin of Red Cross founder Clara Barton, was a prominent clergyman, seasoned musician, and gifted writer whose deep experience among the black mountain people of Kentucky and Tennessee informed his fascinating articles on *Old Plantation Hymns* (1899).[32] Barton's voice was one of a growing chorus of critics who found the arranged jubilee songs deficient in conveying folk practice, and his transcriptions from live performances contain remarkable detail. In the same year Jeannette Robinson Murphy (1865–1946), a white southerner, published her first article on black folklore. Murphy gained quite a following by singing, teaching, and lecturing on African American folk-tales and folksongs for white northerners, using dialect and even dressing up as a black domestic servant, trafficking in the "mammy" figure that remained a staple of stage and screen in the twentieth century.[33] Catherine Smiley ("Kitty") Cheatham of Nashville (1864–1946), like Murphy, grew up after the war hearing spirituals sung by ex-slaves. Her relationship to spirituals was unique in that Ella Sheppard's mother had been a servant to Cheatham's maternal grandmother, and at Ella Sheppard Moore's invitation Cheatham visited Fisk University in 1914 to tell students about her work and plead the cause of preserving the spirituals. The beneficiary of Harry T. Burleigh's tutelage, Cheatham sang the composer's concert spirituals in many of her concerts in New York, often accompanied by Burleigh himself, as well as in Europe.[34] John Wesley Work, professor of Latin and history at Fisk University, named Cheatham among a handful of people whom he regarded as agents of preservation in his 1915 book *Folk Song of the American Negro*. The others in his exclusive group included George White, Adam Spence, E. M. Cravath, Ella Sheppard Moore, Harry T. Burleigh, W. E. B. Du Bois, Henry Krehbiel, Antonin Dvořák, C. J. Ryder, and Samuel Coleridge-Taylor.[35] Lucy McKim, Thomas Fenner, and many others also deserve to be recognized in that company. Although beyond the scope of this study, the twentieth century brought a large contingent of black researchers in addition to those already named, among them James Weldon Johnson and J. Rosamond Johnson, Zora Neale Hurston, John Wesley Work II, John Wesley Work III, and Nicholas Ballanta-Taylor.[36]

Even after the jubilee entertainment industry had wound down, one corner remained and even thrived: the Chautauqua, an outgrowth of the lyceum movement. Its first incarnation was the New York Chautauqua Institute, founded in 1874 by Methodist minister John Heyl Vincent as an adult education program with a primarily religious focus. By 1880 the summer programs at the institute's scenic retreat on Lake Chautauqua near Lake Erie had become more ecumenical and well known, and as usual, the Fisk Jubilee Singers (the independent troupe led by George White) were first on the scene. Other communities followed suit with their own Chautauquas, leading in 1904 to the circuit Chautauqua: a sophisticated entertainment package comprising lectures, music, dramatic arts, comic entertainment, and children's activities that traveled throughout the country.[37] Most jubilee troupes in the 1890s and after 1900 made their living primarily on the Chautauqua circuit, singing arranged spirituals and popular songs, although by the mid- to late 1890s the arrangements had been modernized to barbershop-style harmonies. Examples of well established groups include Glazier's Jubilee Singers, Slayton's Jubilee Singers (reorganized in 1891), the Brockway Jubilee Singers, and the Camp Nelson Jubilee Singers—who were organized by the Salvation Army (see web table 4.1, Biographical Dictionary of Jubilee Concert Troupes).

The Legacy of the Jubilee Entertainment Industry

Commercial spirituals live on today largely in archives of sheet music and in digital repositories; they are understandably problematic compositions that require careful contextualization in order to understand the cultural work they accomplished. One commercial spiritual that has so far managed aural immortality is James Bland's "Oh, Dem Golden Slippers" (1879). A popular inclusion in American songbook anthologies well into the twentieth century, a staple of family and community sings, and an instrumental standard (allowing circumvention of objectionable lyrics) in brass, string, and jazz band repertories, it has been a continuous presence in the history of popular song. In 1905 it was played for the Philadelphia Mummer's Parade and subsequently gave its name to the Mummer's Strut—or Golden Slipper—becoming the event's unofficial anthem to the present day. In the 1880s Bland's lighthearted commercial spiritual became the basis of a contrafactum hymn written for the Salvation Army, in an ironic reversal of influence; the refrain implored, "Oh! my loving Saviour! oh! my loving Saviour / Sinner won't you come with me? We'll walk those golden streets."[38]

Jubilee choirs, on the other hand, continue to carry on the legacy of the early student groups. After a brief lapse following the demise of the original Jubilee Singers, the university organized a new official troupe, and today the Fisk Jubilee Singers remain firmly embedded in the school's identity. The contemporary singers concertize nationally and internationally, record, and act as ambassadors for the spiritual at the same time that they perform a wide-ranging repertory of art music. In 2008 they received the National Medal of Arts, the country's highest recognition of artistic excellence. The choir's consciousness of the past is ever-present: as of this writing, one of their web pages features an 1872 photograph of the Jubilee Singers with a portrait of original singer Jennie Jackson directly above it; present-day Jubilee Singers are superimposed on her chest so that her head towers above them—a visual symbol that today's singers stand on the shoulders of the pioneers, whose eyes watch over them, in appreciation, benevolence, and protection.[39]

There are other distinguished college choirs devoted to preserving and extending the legacy of arranged spirituals. Choirs with roots in the nineteenth century include the Hampton University Concert Choir, Tuskegee Choir, and Wilberforce University Choir. The Howard University Choir, Florida Agricultural and Mechanical University Concert Choir, Dillard University Concert Choir, and Spelman College Glee Club (for women's voices) joined them in the twentieth century, as did groups from many other historically black colleges and universities. All of them sing a varied repertory of art, popular, and traditional music, not only from African and African diasporic genres but from around the world. Not surprisingly, the concert spirituals sung by today's choirs bear no aural resemblance to the arrangements pioneered by George White, reflecting instead a century and a half of new compositional trends, new vocal and choral techniques, and different politics about the presentation of black music. Rather than replicating the past these choirs pay tribute to concert spirituals in contemporary musical language—which was precisely what White did.

In addition to university choirs, there are also independent groups that present spirituals in concert (in addition to other African and African American musics): the Princely Players (Nashville), the Albert McNeil Jubilee Singers (Los Angeles), the Georgia Sea Islanders, and the Plantation Singers (Charleston, South Carolina) are a mere few among many. There are church choirs devoted to preserving the legacy of spirituals as well. Some of these groups have sought to incorporate historical performance practices rooted in black folk tradition, with its heterogeneity, cross rhythms, improvisation, and communal participation.[40]

. . .

The earliest concert arrangements of spirituals and commercial spirituals existed in a symbiotic relationship. As the jubilee industry took shape, a continuum emerged in which hundreds of African Americans found a place to engage in folk-oriented, concert, and popular entertainments. If most of the commercial songs generated during this confluence of performance genres were ignoble, they nonetheless played an important role in the social life of African American music at the time, and they provided a livelihood for the first generation of black performers. To remember student jubilee singers at the expense of black minstrel performers and their parodies of camp meetings and spirituals, to valorize one and denigrate the other, imposes a hierarchy on the historical past that obscures the manifold contributions of black entertainers and reifies black folk culture as authentic to the black experience at the expense of fully engaging the diversity and complexity of that experience. Indeed, the very complexity that led black minstrels to engage with spirituals is at the crux of understanding the climate and conditions in which all performers of the era operated.

Historical knowledge is always in flux. During the decade this book was written new digital repositories of images, recordings, newspapers, and primary sources flooded the internet, causing me to veer between elation and despair. Books have to end, but this history does not. Our knowledge of the spiritual, its singers, and its chroniclers will continue to expand, transform, and allow for new interpretations in the future, as new voices add to the old.

Notes

INTRODUCTION

1. Thompson, *Ring Shout*, 5.

2. Ibid., 63, 80, 81, 133; the quote is from p. 84.

3. For more detailed surveys of prewar black musicians see Southern, *Music of Black Americans*, 100–121; Toll, *Blacking Up*, 195–200; and Trotter, *Music and Some Highly Musical People*.

4. Southern, *Music of Black Americans*, 107.

5. Trotter gives Greenfield's year of birth as 1809 (p. 68) and Southern gives it as 1824 (p. 102), but records of the now defunct Olive Cemetery in Philadelphia, where Greenfield was buried, give her birth year as 1819.

6. See Trotter, *Music and Some Highly Musical People*, 114–30, for a detailed treatment of Holland's career.

7. Hill and Hatch, *History of African American Theatre*, 26. They provide a detailed overview of the African Grove on pp. 24–36.

8. *New York American*, 27 April 1826, cited in Hill and Hatch, *History of African American Theatre*, 31.

9. Quoted from the Fisk Jubilee Singers' website, http://www.fiskjubileesingers.org (accessed 20 May 2017).

10. Loudin: "A Humiliating Fact," *Cleveland Gazette*, 12 July 1890, cited in Abbott and Seroff, *Out of Sight*, 79; Southern, *Music of Black Americans*, 134; Watkins, *On the Real Side*, 114.

CHAPTER 1. The Folk Spiritual

1. White and White based this correspondence on Karin Barber's description of oriki as "essentially and not accidentally fragmentary and non-narrative"; *Sounds of Slavery*, 67.

2. Southern, *Music of Black Americans*, 199–201. Thomas Wentworth Higginson first noted the preference for Old Testament stories in spirituals, and Lawrence Levine illustrates how the selective approach to Christianity relates to pan-African cosmologies; Higginson, *Army Life*, 205, and Levine, *Black Culture*, 30–38. Floyd, *Power of Black Music*, chap. 1, is also illuminating on this connection. On spiritual texts and form see Southern, *Music of Black Americans*, 180–204; Maultsby, "Black Spirituals"; and Lovell, *Black*

Song, chap. 15. For a more in-depth treatment of folk spirituals and a useful synthesis of existing literature see Darden, *People Get Ready!* chaps. 1–5.

3. White and White, *Sounds of Slavery*, 59.

4. "Untitled Manuscript," in J. W. Work III, Jones, and Adams, *Lost Delta Found*, 53. Although Work was doing fieldwork in the Mississippi delta in the early 1940s, his observations about folk practice are confirmed by numerous nineteenth-century sources.

5. Hurston, "Spirituals and Neo-spirituals," 223.

6. Frederick Douglass discusses "Run to Jesus" as a code song (*Life and Times*, 197); former slave Wash Wilson mentions "Steal Away" as a code song in *Texas Narratives*, vol. 16, pt. 4, p. 198, https://memory.loc.gov/mss/mesn/164/164.pdf, in Works Projects Administration, *Slave Narratives, 1936–1938* (Washington, DC: Library of Congress, 1941). Josephine Wright gives a good overview of spirituals in plantation life based on oral histories in "The Third Culture."

7. Levine, *Black Culture*, 31; see also 30–80.

8. Raboteau, *Slave Religion*, 222.

9. Southern, *Music of Black Americans*, 72–80; see also Braithwaite, "Originality in the Hymnals of Richard Allen." There were autonomous black congregations in the South as well as the North at the time, some with black leaders and others with white; the earliest independent black church was founded between 1773 and 1775 in South Carolina (Raboteau, *Slave Religion*, 139).

10. Southern, *Music of Black Americans*, quotes contemporaneous accounts on 78, 79.

11. Hankins, *Second Great Awakening*, 11, 16, 18, 41.

12. Southern, *Music of Black Americans*, 83.

13. See accounts quoted in Southern, *Music of Black Americans*, 84–85; these date variously from 1819, 1820, and 1850.

14. John F. Watson, *Methodist Error* (Trenton, NJ, 1819), 63–64; quoted in Southern, *Music of Black Americans*, 85. The form and performance practice of folk spirituals bore a close resemblance to that of corn-shucking songs; see Abrahams, *Singing the Master*, especially chap. 4.

15. Levine, *Black Culture*, 22.

16. *Georgia Narratives*, vol. 4, pt. 4, p. 18, https://memory.loc.gov/mss/mesn/044/044 .pdf, in Works Projects Administration, *Slave Narratives, 1936–1938* (Washington, DC: Library of Congress, 1941). Titles alone don't prove that any of these songs are spirituals, of course. Cordelia Thomas was eighty at the time of her interview, so she was likely born circa 1858; she admits that she relied on the stories of her parents in her narrative and was probably describing life immediately before the war.

17. See Allen et al., *Slave Songs*, xiii–xv; Floyd, *Power of Black Music*, 43–45. Lorenzo Dow Turner found an Arabic equivalent to the word "shout" that was present in West African languages, which he spelled phonetically as ʃaut and defined as "to move around the Kaaba (the small stone building at Mecca which is the chief object of the pilgrimage of Mohammedans) until exhausted"; *Africanisms in the Gullah Dialect*, 202.

18. Epstein, *Sinful Tunes*, 192.

19. Towns, *Alabama Narratives*, vol. 1, http://www.gutenberg.org/files/36020/36020

-h/36020-h.html; Grant, *South Carolina Narratives*, vol. 14, pt. 2, p. 185, https://memory
.loc.gov/mss/mesn/142/142.pdf; in Works Projects Administration, *Slave Narratives,
1936–1938* (Washington, DC: Library of Congress, 1941).

20. They are quoted in Raboteau, *Slave Religion*, 213–14.

21. *Georgia Narratives*, vol. 4, pt. 2, p. 120, https://memory.loc.gov/mss/mesn/042/042
.pdf, in Works Projects Administration, *Slave Narratives, 1936–1938* (Washington, DC:
Library of Congress, 1941).

22. Jackson, *White and Negro Spirituals*, 267. Southern gives several examples of this
process in *Music of Black Americans*, 185–89.

23. F. J. Work, *Folk Songs*, 82–84.

24. Southern, *Music of Black Americans*, 185.

25. Hurston, "Spirituals and Neo-spirituals," 224.

26. See Locke, *New Negro*, and Hurston, "Spirituals and Neo-spirituals," 224. Raboteau has a good overview on the Herskovits-Frazier debate (*Slave Religion*, 48–92). For
helpful interpretive overviews of black music historiography see Radano, *Lying Up a
Nation*, chap.1; and Ramsey, "Cosmopolitan or Provincial?"

27. The debate can be followed by reading, in order, Epstein, "A White Origin?";
Tallmadge, "The Black in Jackson's White Spirituals"; and Garst, "Mutual Reinforcement."

28. Jackson, *White and Negro Spirituals*, 267.

29. Quoted in Epstein, *Sinful Tunes*, 280.

30. Levine, *Black Culture*, 24.

31. This summary is based on Epstein, *Sinful Tunes*, 243–50. The words to "Go Down,
Moses" were also published in *Continental Monthly* 2, no. 1 (1862): 113. Epstein identifies
Baker as a violinist who played with conductor Louis Jullien; she surmises he was an
Englishman, though little else is known about him.

32. McPherson, *Battle Cry of Freedom*, 371.

33. For numbers and origins of slave importations to the Sea Islands see the following in Holloway, *Africanisms*: Holloway, "Origins of African American Culture," esp.
21–28, 35; Holloway, "Sacred World of the Gullahs"; and Margaret Washington, "Gullah
Attitudes toward Life and Death," esp. 152–54.

34. James Miller McKim was a Quaker and an active abolitionist. The family home of
his wife, Sara Allibone Speakman, was a regular stop on the Underground Railroad in
Chester County, PA. For more on the McKim family and Lucy in particular see Epstein,
Sinful Tunes, 260–61 and 314–20, and Charters, *Lucy McKim Garrison*.

35. She described these songs in "Songs of the Port Royal 'Contrabands,'" *Dwight's
Journal of Music*, 8 Nov. 1862.

36. Allen and his wife arrived in November 1863 to teach and discovered that Allen's
cousin, Ware, had been there since 1862. Since Lucy McKim's first visit in 1862, she had
married Wendell Phillips Garrison, son of abolitionist William Lloyd Garrison and
founder of *The Nation* (1865, headquartered in New York City).

37. Higginson's numerous publications on slave song remain valuable today for their
ethnographic detail: *Army Life*; "Negro Spirituals"; and Mary Thacher Higginson, *Letters and Journals*.

38. See Epstein, *Sinful Tunes*, 303–42, for a thorough primary source–based history; Radano, *Lying Up a Nation*, esp. 206–29, for an incisive cultural interpretation; and Charters, *Lucy McKim Garrison*, her first full-length biography.

39. Charters, *Lucy McKim Garrison*, 11.

40. Cruz, *Culture on the Margins*, 3.

41. Ibid., 119.

42. Ibid., 22. See 128–29 for his discussion of spirituals as artifacts.

43. Ibid., 127. His detailed argument is well worth reading in full.

44. Radano, *Lying Up a Nation*, 211, 213.

CHAPTER 2. The Jubilee Singers of Fisk University

1. Foreword, *Fisk University News* 2, no. 5 (1911): 2.

2. DeBoer, *His Truth Is Marching On*, 4–5. By contrast, William Lloyd Garrison's American Anti-Slavery Society (founded 1833) employed African Americans only in clerical positions, and Quaker organizations likewise lacked black leadership.

3. "Constitution of the American Missionary Association," 185-, AMA Archives. The emphasis on evangelicalism was meant to exclude Unitarians, who had separated from the Congregationalists at the beginning of the century.

4. "Census Report of Colored Population in Nashville" (10 Aug. 1865), W. T. Clarke, Asst. A-G to General [Clinton B.] Fisk, cited in McDaniel, *John Ogden*, 31. There were two or three mission schools, including the McKee School, run by the Presbyterian Joseph Gillespie McKee; see Ward, *Dark Midnight*, 34–44, 51–57.

5. McDaniel, *John Ogden*, 32.

6. Richardson, *History of Fisk University*, 3.

7. "Tennessee," *American Missionary* [March] 1866, a digest of reports extracted and reprinted from Nashville's several newspapers, quoted in McDaniel, *John Ogden*, 38.

8. Richardson, *History of Fisk University*, 7, 10–12, 18. The reference to "white niggers" comes from A. K. Spence to E. M. Cravath, 8 May 1871, Nashville, AMA Archives.

9. Richardson, *History of Fisk University*, 17.

10. Ibid., 15.

11. Information about George White's life has been compiled from Pike, *Jubilee Singers*, 42–48; Marsh, *Story of the Jubilee Singers* (1886), 12–13; Spence, "Character Sketch of George L. White," 2–5; Taylor, "Reminiscences of Jubilee Singers," 29; and *Dictionary of American Biography*, s.v. "White, George Leonard," 100–101. Ward has written the most complete biography to date in *Dark Midnight*, 13–15, 73–74, and passim.

12. *Report of Special Committee to Investigate the Indian Problem of the State of New York, Appointed by the Assembly of 1888* (Albany: Troy Press Co., Printers, 1889), 59; see also 23, 61.

13. Ward, *Dark Midnight*, 15.

14. Spence, "Character Sketch of George L. White," 5. Mary grew up on the Fisk campus. Original Jubilee Singer Ella Sheppard Moore supplied Mary with much of the information in her article.

15. Playbill, Fisk School Grand Musical and Literary Entertainment, Thur., 11 June 1868, at Masonic Hall, George L. White Scrapbook 1867–72, FULSC.

16. In February 1871, for example, his student Benjamin Holmes (a future Jubilee Singer) invited White and his choir to sing for the Sunday school Union meeting at the Second Christian Church; Holmes to White, 22 Jan. 1871, AMA Archives.

17. White to Edward P. Smith, 7 Nov. 1868, AMA Archives. At this time Fisk cofounder Smith was working for the AMA as a general field agent in New York.

18. White to Smith, 21 Nov. 1868, AMA Archives.

19. Ibid. Italicized words were underlined in the original.

20. Will S. Hays, "Little Sam" (n.p.: J. L. Peters, 1867), sheet music cover, Brown University Library, https://repository.library.brown.edu/studio/item/bdr:22751/.

21. See Mahar, *Behind the Burnt Cork Mask*, chap. 1, for a detailed overview of developments in minstrel shows from the 1840s to 1860.

22. Katherine K. Preston notes that the presence of lower- and middle-class operagoers was occasionally acknowledged but largely ignored in antebellum journalism on opera performances; *Opera on the Road*, 18. On opera in blackface minstrelsy see Mahar, *Behind the Burnt Cork Mask*, esp. chap. 3.

23. G. F. Root, *Story of a Musical Life*, 83, 98, 97.

24. Her maternal grandmother was Cherokee, her maternal grandfather an enslaved African, and her paternal grandfather a white planter; Ward, *Dark Midnight*, 4–5.

25. Pike, *Jubilee Singers*, 52–53. Although Pike presents the Jubilee Singers' biographies in the first person, as if they were their own words, he admits in the preface that "the personal histories were gathered chiefly by a former teacher of Fisk University." This could have been Mary F. Wells, who accompanied the Jubilee Singers on their first tour but then returned to work at her former AMA school in Alabama. Although the general outlines of the stories can be relied on, there are conflicting details in the various sources on Ella Sheppard's early life, which include Ella Sheppard Moore's pamphlet "Before Emancipation" (located in FULSC); and Moore, "Historical Sketch," 41–58. Ward's biography of Sheppard is excellent; see *Dark Midnight*, 1–12, 71–73.

26. Moore, "Before Emancipation," 2. Andrew Ward presents the Sheppard family tree in *Dark Midnight*: Ella's paternal grandfather, James Glover Sheppard, was a white planter who sired Ella's father Simon by one of his slaves. When James Glover Sheppard's white son, Benjamin Harper Sheppard, married Phereby, Benjamin's half-brother Simon became his slave (4).

27. Ibid., 1–2.

28. Fox, "'The Jubilees!'" 36.

29. Moore, "Before Emancipation," 2–3. In Pike, *Jubilee Singers*, 49–50, Sheppard states that this early part of her life was recounted to her by her father, as she was only three.

30. Ward, *Dark Midnight*, 72.

31. Sheppard's recollection comes from Pike, *Jubilee Singers*, 52. Ward identified Rivi as a teacher at Glendale; *Dark Midnight*, 72.

32. Pike, *Jubilee Singers*, 52.

33. H. H. Wright, "Jubilee Songs at Chapel Exercises," 24.

34. Wells, "Character Sketch," 17.

35. Ward, *Dark Midnight*, 85.

36. Taylor, "Reminiscences of Jubilee Singers," 28.

37. Anonymous clergyman visiting Fisk, in Alrutheus Ambush Taylor, *The Negro in Tennessee, 1865–1880* (Washington, DC: Associated Publishers, 1941), 221–22; cited in Ward, *Dark Midnight*, 103.

38. A. K. Spence, "The Origin of the Jubilee Singers," *Fisk Herald* 8, no. 3 (1890): 1. The date of summer 1871 comes from Spence, undated lecture, Mary Elizabeth Spence Collection, Notebooks, FULSC; quoted by Ward, *Dark Midnight*, 110.

39. Moore, "Historical Sketch," 43.

40. Allen et al., *Slave Songs*, 10.

41. Moore, "Historical Sketch," 43.

42. H. H. Wright, "Jubilee Songs at Chapel Exercises," 24.

43. Taylor, "Reminiscences of Jubilee Singers," 28.

44. F. J. Work, *Folk Songs*, 114.

45. Ibid. *Elijah*: oratorio by Felix Mendelssohn (1846); *Messiah*: oratorio by George Frideric Handel (1742); and *The Creation*: oratorio by Joseph Haydn (1798).

46. For a concise summary of the Hutchinsons' career see Hamm, *Yesterdays*, 141–61; for a more in-depth account see Gac, *Singing for Freedom*. On the Luca family see Southern, *Music of Black Americans*, 106–7; Trotter, *Music and Some Highly Musical People*, 88–113.

47. Hutchinson, *Story of the Hutchinsons*, 2: 4.

48. Ibid., 5.

49. Playbill for concert in the Star Lecture Course, Tues., 13 Dec. 1870, Farwell Hall, Ludlow Patton's Hutchinson Family Scrapbook, item 80r, Wadleigh Memorial Library, Milford, New Hampshire. I'm grateful to Alan Lewis for directing me to the playbill.

50. Hutchinson, *Story of the Hutchinsons*, 2: 13.

51. Ibid.

52. "Popular Music," *Brooklyn Daily Eagle*, 2 Dec. 1864.

53. Gac, *Singing for Freedom*, 245.

54. The two troupes may not have sung the same version of "Great Is the Lord"; the words, from Psalm 48, were set by many composers. For more on specific performances of these songs see Graham, "Fisk Jubilee Singers," appendix B. Cockrell, *Excelsior*, lists the repertory sung by the Hutchinsons in the 1840s.

55. The Fisk Jubilee Singers sang these songs in 1872; the first two were published in Seward, *Jubilee Songs* (1872a), and "Wait a Little While" was published in Marsh, *Story of the Jubilee Singers* (1875).

56. Spence to Cravath, 6 Apr. 1871, Nashville, AMA Archives. The relationships among Cravath, Spence, and White were complicated and fascinating; Ward depicts them compellingly in *Dark Midnight*, chaps. 9–10.

57. John Lawrence to E. M. Cravath, 31 Mar. 1871, Nashville, AMA Archives.

58. To some extent these fears regarding ego were borne out; see Graham, "On the Road to Freedom."

59. Spence to Cravath, 6 Apr. 1871, Nashville, AMA Archives.

60. White to Cravath, 26 Apr. 1871, Nashville, AMA Archives.

61. White to Cravath, 12 Sept. 1871, Nashville, AMA Archives.

62. Richardson, *History of Fisk University*, 26; Moore, "Historical Sketch," 46.

63. Spence to Cravath, 9 Oct. 1871, Nashville, AMA Archives.

64. Pike, *Jubilee Singers*, 95, quoting an unidentified Cincinnati newspaper in October 1871; Moore, "Historical Sketch," 47.

65. Marsh, *Story of the Jubilee Singers* (1886), 19–20. Marsh seems to have assisted with the later campaigns of the Jubilee Singers; in 1875 he was treasurer of Oberlin (OH) College, and from 1878 to 1881 he served as the town's mayor; Wilbur H. Phillips, *Oberlin Colony: The Story of a Century* (Oberlin, 1933).

66. White to Cravath, 12 Sept. 1871, Nashville, AMA Archives.

67. Moore, "Historical Sketch," 46. The advance agent was G. Stanley Pope.

68. Ibid., 47.

69. Ward, *Dark Midnight*, 141. Ward (435n55) found the first mention of a building fund in an Akron broadside in the Jubilee Singers Scrapbook, FULSC.

70. Moore, "Historical Sketch," 47.

71. Ibid., 48.

72. Another reason for the gradual change may have been singer resistance, which figures in Arna Bontemps's novel *Chariot in the Sky*, based on primary research in the Fisk Library archives. In the novel, when White announces that the students will be singing spirituals on tour, Greene Evans chooses to leave the troupe (Edmund Watkins replaced him). Other singers succumb but are unhappy about the decision (see pp. 178–86).

73. Program, 19 March 1872, New England, town unidentified, George L. White Scrapbook 1867–72, FULSC.

74. The *Brooklyn Daily Eagle* conferred this nickname (10 March 1869). Beecher, a New Englander, was the son of Lyman Beecher, a pivotal figure in the Second Great Awakening. Educated at Amherst College and Lane Seminary (Cincinnati, Ohio), he entered the ministry in 1837, serving in Indiana before becoming the first pastor of the new Plymouth Church in 1847.

75. Among Protestants, Congregationalist ministers were the highest paid; the next tier below Beecher earned in the neighborhood of $10,000. "The Men Who Preach to Brooklyn," *Brooklyn Eagle*, 4 Feb. 1877; see also Joseph Howard Jr., *Life of Henry Ward Beecher* (Philadelphia: Hubbard Bros., 1887), 626–27.

76. "World Wide Tribute," *Brooklyn Daily Eagle*, 26 June 1887, a literary memorial to Beecher published after his death in March of that year.

77. "Why Beecher Played Truant," *Washington Post*, reprinted in *Brooklyn Daily Eagle*, 12 March 1887; "World Wide Tribute," *Brooklyn Daily Eagle*, 26 June 1887.

78. Beecher, *Plymouth Collection of Hymns and Tunes; for the Use of Christian Congregations* (New York: A. S. Barnes, 1873), iii.

79. The singers were Asa, John, Judson, and Abby—temporarily reunited. Beecher was so impressed with them that he tried to hire the Hutchinsons to direct the church choir, but they declined; Hutchinson, *Story of the Hutchinsons*, 2: 94, 260. Although John Hutchinson implies that the concert occurred around 1843–1844, Beecher wasn't in Brooklyn yet. A more likely date is March 1850 (see p. 260).

80. "The Negro," *Brooklyn Daily Eagle*, 11 March 1877.

81. Ibid. Beecher's congregation was middle class, white, and according to James Parton, "the sort of people who take the 'Tribune,' and get up courses of lectures in the country towns." For a more detailed social profile of the church see Parton, "Henry Ward Beecher's Church," *Atlantic Monthly* 19 (1867): 42.

82. Pike, *Jubilee Singers*, 112.

83. "Beecher: His Reception in the South," *Brooklyn Eagle*, 17 May 1879.

84. Pike, *Jubilee Singers*, 107, 108.

85. Sizer, *Gospel Hymns*, 6–7; Benson, *English Hymn*, 483–85.

86. Sizer, *Gospel Hymns*, 9; Benson, *English Hymn*, 484.

87. It was on Phillips's model that Dwight Moody and Ira D. Sankey (both of whom had worked for the YMCA) would base their famous partnership of preaching and singing the gospel at extended mass meetings.

88. Pike, *Jubilee Singers*, 126.

89. The first narrative was written by Pike; later revisions were made by J. B. T. Marsh. See Epstein, "The Story of the Jubilee Singers," for a thorough documentation of the Jubilee narratives.

90. "The World Moves," *Burlington (VT) Weekly Free Press*, 14 Mar. 1873.

91. Typescript, n.d., Mary C. Terrell Papers f. 87, Negro Spirituals, 1–2, Howard University, Moorland-Spingarn Research Center, Manuscript Division. Terrell is describing the September 1927 funeral of Charlotte Little, wife of Colonel Arthur West Little, one of the few white officers of the famous African American 369th Infantry in World War I. Noble Sissle and a quartet from the Kentucky Choir sang spirituals at the service.

CHAPTER 3. The Fisk Concert Spiritual

1. The following primary sources inform this vignette. Financial appeal: "The Jubilee Singers in Stockport" (England), *Stockport and Cheshire News*, George L. White Scrapbook, FULSC. Performing in Newark: Ward, *Dark Midnight*, 166–68. "Steal Away": *Tonic Sol-fa Reporter*, quoted in Pike, *Singing Campaign for Ten Thousand Pounds*, 33–34. "In or out of body": Pike, *Jubilee Singers*, 109. "Turn Back Pharaoh's Army": *Tonic Sol-fa Reporter*, quoted in American Missionary Association, *Twenty-Seventh Annual Report*, 51; *Liverpool Daily Albion*, 16 Jan. 1874, George L. White Scrapbook, FULSC. Jackson, "I'll Hear the Trumpet Sound": Theodore Cuyler, *New York Tribune*, 19 Jan. 1872; *North British Daily Mail* (Glasgow, Scotland), 27 Oct. 1873; all from George L. White Scrapbook, FULSC.

2. See Epstein, "Story of the Jubilee Singers," 153.

3. Epstein, "Theodore F. Seward," 39.

4. A partial list of Seward's publications through 1872 includes, as editor with assistance from Lowell Mason and William Bradbury, *The Temple Choir* (1867)—which George White had requested that the AMA purchase for use in worship at Fisk (see chap. 2); and as author with Lowell Mason, *The Pestalozzian Music Teacher* (New York: C. H. Ditson, 1871) and *The Coronation* (New York: Biglow and Main, 1872).

5. Pike writes: "Mr. T. F. Seward, editor of the New York Musical Gazette, had them at Rev. Dr. Mix's Church, Orange, N.J., for a concert" (*Jubilee Singers*, 112, 115). The concert probably took place in January 1872. I have been unable to verify whether Seward was employed in Mix's church.

6. Epstein, "Theodore F. Seward," 36, 39.

7. "I'se a Travlin' to de Grave" is for solo voice and piano, and "Keep Me from Sinking Down" for four voices and piano. Stoeckel was the first European-trained music teacher in New Haven; he was appointed Instructor of Vocal Art, Organist, and Chapelmaster at Yale in 1855 and became the first director the Yale Glee Club in 1861. See Judith Ann Schiff, "Old Yale: The Battell Connection," *Yale Alumni Magazine* (October 2002); David Stanley Smith, *Gustave J. Stoeckel: Yale Pioneer in Music* (New Haven: Yale University Press, 1939); "Robbins Battell's Good Works," *New York Times*, 7 Feb. 1895; *National Cyclopaedia of American Biography*, suppl. 1, s.v. "Battell, Robbins" (New York: James T. White, 1910), 254.

8. Battell's name appears regularly in AMA receipts as a donor to black schools; e.g., *American Missionary* 32, no. 11 (1878): 347.

9. Cuyler, "Our Native Music—The Jubilee Singers," *New York Tribune*, 19 Jan. 1872; Davidson to Cravath, 11 Mar. 1872, AMA Archives; cited in Ward, *Dark Midnight*, 184. Although Davidson doesn't mention it, the Fisk song "Room Enough" had a tune cognate in "I Can't Stay Behind" (with different words) from *Slave Songs*.

10. The program is in the George L. White Scrapbook 1877–78, FULSC; see also Allen et al., *Slave Songs*, 93.

11. Epstein, "Theodore F. Seward," is particularly critical of Seward.

12. Curwen's system was developed from a method devised by Sarah Glover of Norwich, England. For more background, see Theodore F. Seward and H. E. Krehbiel, "The Tonic Sol-fa System," *The Century* 35, no. 2 (Dec. 1887): 314–19.

13. Ella Sheppard notes in her diary that Seward used Tonic Sol-fa to jot down spirituals sung by Frederick Douglass in Feb. 1875; cited in Ward, *Dark Midnight*, 281. At least one of these spirituals, "Run to Jesus," appeared in *Jubilee Songs* (see e.g., Pike, *Singing Campaign for Ten Thousand Pounds*).

14. The entries are dated, respectively, 17, 22, 27, 30 July; 3–4 Aug.; 5, 7, 9 Aug. (Jubilee Singers Archive, FULSC).

15. Apparently it was published in two editions, one by Thos. J. Dyer, Printer, and one by Wm. Byles and Sons. Both are very rare, and neither is dated.

16. Rutling, *Tom*, 20.

17. One of these, "Move Along," was actually transcribed by Ella Sheppard.

18. These six are "Go Chain the Lion Down" (which Seward notates in G major and Rutling in G minor, among other discrepancies); "The General Roll" (which Rutling ornaments differently); "Been a Listening" (Rutling provides tempos and modifies Seward's rhythms); "Keep Your Lamps Trimmed" (Rutling modifies Seward's melody and form); "Go Down, Moses" (Rutling modifies Seward's melody in several places, notates it in G minor rather than F minor, and includes seven verses that cohere narratively, as opposed to Seward's twenty-five mostly disjunct verses); and "Don't You Get Weary" (known as "A

Great Camp-Meeting in the Promised Land" in Seward, the most significant difference in Rutling's score being the anticipation of the beat on the phrase "don't you get weary," which makes the tune more syncopated). Both "Inching Along" and "I'm a Rolling" diverge slightly from Seward.

19. Rutling, *Tom*, 20.

20. Spence, "Character Sketch," 4.

21. See, e.g., "A Little More Faith in Jesus" (parallel octaves in the bass and soprano/alto parts), "Old Ship of Zion" and "Judgment Day Is Rolling Round" (open fifths). These were "mistakes" in art music but common in the part writing of American hymnody and popular song.

22. In Seward's first (1872a) publication of *Jubilee Songs*: "I'll Hear the Trumpet Sound," "I've Just Come from the Fountain," "I'm a Trav'ling to the Grave," "I'm a Rolling." First published in Seward's second (1872b) edition: "Oh! Holy Lord," "He Arose," "These Are My Father's Children," "Reign, Oh! Reign," "I Ain't Going to Die No More," "The General Roll," "Oh! Let Me Get Up," and "Oh! Sinner Man."

23. Murphy, *Southern Thoughts for Northern Thinkers*, 24.

24. Spence, "Character Sketch," 4.

25. "The Jubilee Singers," *Lancaster Guardian* (England), 11 Dec. 1875, Jubilee Singers Archives, FULSC.

26. *Tonic Sol-fa Reporter*, reporting on a performance in London on 6 May 1873; quoted in Pike, *Singing Campaign for Ten Thousand Pounds*, 33–34.

27. Spence, "Character Sketch," 4.

28. Maggie Porter Cole to Mr. Allison (Fisk Alumni Secretary), Detroit, 28 Sept. 1934, Jubilee Singers Archives, FULSC.

29. Taylor, "Reminiscences," 30.

30. Review in the *Tonic Sol-fa Reporter*, quoted in American Missionary Association, *Twenty-Seventh Annual Report*, 51.

31. Unknown to Fred, 18 Dec. 1874, Spence Family Collection, FULSC, quoted in Anderson, *"Tell Them We're Singing for Jesus,"* 174; see 172–85 for a helpful biography.

32. *Blairgowrie News* (Scotland), 6 Oct. 1876, George L. White Scrapbook, FULSC.

33. *There Breathes a Hope*; John Wesley Work II (first tenor), James Andrew Myers (second tenor), Alfred Garfield King (first bass), and Noah Walker Ryder (second bass). An excellent source on early recordings by the Fisk Jubilee Singers is Tim Brooks, *Lost Sounds*, chap. 14.

34. J. W. Work II, "The Jubilee Songs Today," 22–23.

35. P. Turner, *Dictionary of Afro-American Performers*, 173. The meeting was in Concord, NH.

36. *Earliest Negro Vocal Groups*, vol. 2; *Church Choirs, Vocal Groups and Preachers*, vol. 3. Nathaniel Dett notes that the melody sung by Europe's singers, "while possibly less striking, is by far the more popular" (*Religious Folk-Songs of the Negro*, 52n).

37. Murphy, *Southern Thoughts for Northern Thinkers*, 24.

38. *Dwight's Journal of Music*, 5 April 1873: 412.

39. *Tonic Sol-fa Reporter*, quoted in American Missionary Association, *Twenty-Seventh Annual Report*.

40. Murphy, *Southern Thoughts for Northern Thinkers*, 24. Italics in the original.

41. *Brooklyn Union*, 2 Jan. 1872, George L. White Scrapbook, FULSC.

42. Griffin, "The Slave Music of the South," *American Missionary* 36, no. 3 (1882): 70.

43. Hurston, "Characteristics of Negro Expression," 26.

44. Undated clipping, *Evening Courier* (Newark, NJ), quoted in Ward, *Dark Midnight*, 167.

45. Article by "C.B." [Colon Brown, lecturer in music], Andersonian University, *North British Daily Mail* (Glasgow, Scotland), 27 Oct. 1873; reprinted in *Dwight's Journal of Music*, 29 Nov. 1873: 131.

46. Mason, "Elementary Department. Theoretical," in Seward et al., *Temple Choir*, 17.

47. Ibid.

48. Spence, "Character Sketch," 4.

49. Cole, "Maggie Porter-Cole," *Fisk News*, Dec. 1939, quoted in Ward, *Dark Midnight*, 116; letter to the editor, [*Boston Daily Advertiser*?], ca. 30 March 1872, George L. White Scrapbook 1867–72, FULSC.

50. Wilson, "Heterogeneous Sound Ideal."

51. Spence, "Character Sketch," 4.

52. Article by "C.B." [Colon Brown, lecturer in music], Andersonian University, *North British Daily Mail* (Glasgow, Scotland), 27 Oct. 1873; reprinted in *Dwight's Journal of Music*, 29 Nov. 1873: 131.

53. Quoted in "Songs of the South," *Memphis Daily Appeal*, 3 March 1872. The review concerned the Jubilees' concert at Steinway Hall, New York.

54. Pike, *Jubilee Singers*, 116.

55. See Anderson, *"Tell Them We're Singing for Jesus,"* and Ward, *Dark Midnight*, for singer biographies.

56. Cuyler presided as minister from 1860 to 1890; in 1874 his church's membership numbered about 1,600 and he was widely published in the U.S. and British religious and popular press. See Theodore Ledyard Cuyler, *Recollections of a Long Life* (1902; reprint Teddington, Middlesex: Echo Library, 2008); "Theodore L. Cuyler, D.D.," *New York Times*, 26 Oct. 1874. As largely as Cuyler figured in the fortunes of the Jubilee Singers, he strangely doesn't mention the troupe in his autobiography.

57. Kyla Wazana Tompkins, *Racial Indigestion: Eating Bodies in the Nineteenth Century* (New York: New York University Press, 2012), 8.

58. "The Jubilees," *Daily National Republican*, 29 Feb. 1872; "The Songs of the South," *Memphis Daily Appeal* (quoting the *New York Evening Post*), 3 March 1872.

59. These events took place in March 1872. Ward, *Dark Midnight*, describes the visit in detail, 170–77.

60. "The Concert of the Colored Jubilee Singers," *New York Sun*, 11 Mar. 1872.

61. "The Jubilee Singers Coming," *St. Johnsbury (VT) Caledonian*, 12 April 1872, quoting a review in the *Newark Courier*.

62. "The Fisk Jubilee Singers," *Brooklyn Eagle*, 24 Jan. 1872; Richardson, *History of Fisk University*, 16.

63. The source is not attributed, but this may come from the *Boston Daily Advertiser*, ca. 30 March 1872 (George L. White Scrapbook 1867–72, FULSC). The writer is signed "L."

64. Pike, *Jubilee Singers*, 147–48.

65. "The Concert of the Colored Jubilee Singers," *New York Sun*, 11 Mar. 1872.

66. Pike, *Jubilee Singers*, 111–12; a clipping of the woodcut illustration is in the George L. White Scrapbook, FULSC. *Day's Doings* was an illustrated weekly published by James Watts until 1873, when Frank Leslie purchased it.

67. Cole, "An Ex-Slave's Impressions of Henry Ward Beecher," *Henry Ward Beecher as His Friends Saw Him* (New York: Pilgrim Press, 1904), 121.

68. Review in the *New York Evening Post*, quoted in "The Songs of the South," *Memphis Daily Appeal*, 3 Mar. 1872.

69. Quotation from *Cincinnati Gazette*, reprinted in "The Tennesseans," *Chicago Daily Tribune*, 3 Feb. 1874. For further considerations of spirituals as literature, see Lovell, *Black Song*, and Peters, "The Poetics of the Afro-American Spiritual."

70. F.B.A., "Freaks of Hymnology," *The Galaxy* 24, no. 5 (1877): 670. Despite its title the article is a tribute to the gospel hymns that emerged during the religious revivals of the 1870s.

71. Colon Brown, lecturer on music, Andersonian University, Glasgow, testimonial on advertisement for a service of song by the Jubilee Singers at Free Trade Hall, Manchester, Tues., 13 Jan. 1874, George L. White Scrapbook 1873–74, FULSC. This was excerpted from Brown's article for the *North British Daily Mail*, Glasgow, 27 Oct. 1873. Brown wrote his article to explain the artistic merit of the jubilee songs to those who found them puzzling; Marsh, *Story of the Jubilee Singers* (1886), 66.

72. *Herald of Freedom* (June 1844), reprinted in Hutchinson, *Story of the Hutchinsons*, 1: 117–18.

CHAPTER 4. Innovators, Imitators, and a Jubilee Industry

1. Moore, "Historical Sketch," 49, 50; Marsh, *Story of the Jubilee Singers* (1886), 40–42; "World's Peace Jubilee. Saturday's Concert," *Boston Globe*, 24 June 1872.

2. "World's Peace Jubilee. The Music Yesterday," *Boston Globe*, 24 June 1872. The Jubilees' last appearance at the festival was on June 25.

3. White to G. D. Pike, 21 Oct. 1872, AMA Archives.

4. Talbot, *Samuel Chapman Armstrong*, 63.

5. This history of Hampton is based on Engs, *Freedom's First Generation*, 5–16; and Foner, *Reconstruction*, 5.

6. Talbot, *Samuel Chapman Armstrong*, 138.

7. Engs, *Freedom's First Generation*, 118. See also Talbot, *Samuel Chapman Armstrong*, 160. The school was funded with $9,000 from the AMA and $10,000 from the Honorable Josiah King of Pittsburgh, executor of the Avery estate, which included a legacy of $250,000 for "Negro" education.

8. Catalogue of the Hampton Normal and Agricultural Institute 1874–1875, in Harlan, ed., *Booker T. Washington Papers*, 2: 34.

9. Arthur P. Davis, "William Roscoe Davis and His Descendants," *Negro History Bulletin* 13 (1950): 80–81, cited in Engs, *Freedom's First Generation*, 118.

10. Engs, *Freedom's First Generation*, 114–15.

11. Armstrong and Ludlow, *Hampton and Its Students*, 127, 128.

12. Pike, *Jubilee Singers*, 145.

13. Ludlow, "The Hampton Student Singers," *Southern Workman*, May 1894, 73. Although Armstrong and Ludlow say that Fenner came to Hampton in June 1872 (*Hampton and Its Students*, 128), this would have been an introductory visit only. Tourjée recommended Fenner to Armstrong for the job of choir director. For biographical details on Fenner see the Fenner Family Tree, Thomas P. Fenner and Sabra Dyer, http://www.fennertree.com/thomas-fenner-1829-1912/.

14. Article by Sallie Davis Thoroughgood in *Southern Workman* (March 1928); cited in Smith, "Hampton Institute Choir," 33.

15. "Concerts of the Hampton Students," *New York Times*, 7 March 1873.

16. *Twenty-Two Years' Work*, 55–56.

17. Ibid., 89.

18. Ibid., 40, 56.

19. "The Ideal Colored Company, Tonight," *Boston Daily Globe*, 28 Nov. 1880; *Boston Daily Globe*, 4 Jan. 1885; Simond, *Old Slack's Reminiscence*, 22. Sam Lucas was the first African American to play Uncle Tom; other blacks who played him were Harry Singleton and Dick Hunter.

20. *Boston Daily Globe*, 14 Oct. 1876; untitled paragraph, *American Missionary* 20, no. 11 (Nov. 1876): 246.

21. A detailed itinerary is given in Armstrong and Ludlow, *Hampton and Its Students*, 132–50.

22. Ludlow, "The Hampton Student Singers," 74.

23. Salaries varied by experience, but $500 per year was typical for the 1873–1874 season (see Graham, "On the Road to Freedom").

24. *Vermont Phoenix* (Brattleboro), 16 Oct. 1874.

25. Ads for "The Jubilee Singers," *Brooklyn Eagle*, 13 Jan. 1873 and 6 Feb. 1873; *Brooklyn Eagle*, 18 Jan. 1873.

26. Armstrong and Ludlow, *Hampton and Its Students*, 137.

27. Pike to AMA secretary George Whipple, 16 Jan. 1874, AMA Archives, cited in Ward, *Dark Midnight*, 250–51.

28. "The Hampton Colored Students," *New York Times*, 24 March 1873.

29. "Concert This Evening," *Boston Daily Globe*, 23 May 1873.

30. "Negro Folk Songs. Slave Melodies of the South.—The Jubilee and Hampton Singers," *Dwight's Journal of Music* 32, no. 26 (5 April 1873): 411–12.

31. "The Jubilee Singers," *Brooklyn Eagle*, 23 Feb. 1875.

32. "Our Letter from New York," *Song Journal*, 23 April 1873: 488.

33. In Armstrong and Ludlow, *Hampton and Its Students*, 172. Although there is no evidence that Fenner knew of Allen et al.'s *Slave Songs*, there are five concordances between *Slave Songs* and the 1874 edition of the Hampton songs: no. 34 "Stars Begin to Fall" / "My Lord, What a Mornin'"; no. 35 "King Emanuel" / "King Emanuel"; no. 74 "Nobody Knows the Trouble I've Had" / "Nobody Knows de Trouble I've Seen"; no. 79 "In the Mansions Above" / "In Bright Mansions Above"; and no. 100 "The Golden Altar" / "John Saw."

34. *Fisk Jubilee Singers*, vol. 2; *Earliest Negro Vocal Groups*, vol. 4.

35. Hampton teacher Isabel B. Eustis described an 1875 performance of this song in "Reminiscences," *Southern Workman* (May 1894): 77.

36. "The Hampton Singers," *New York Times*, 21 Nov. 1873.

37. The succession of choir directors in Fenner's wake included most notably singer Robert Hamilton (1880–1888) and Frederic G. Rathbun (1888–1892). For more on the Hampton Music Department's later history see Miyakawa, *"Sometimes I Feel Like a Motherless Child."*

38. Hampton repertory was published in the following: *Cabin and Plantation Songs* (Fenner 1874, 1877, 1889; Fenner and Rathbun 1891, 1893; Fenner, Rathbun, and Cleaveland); and Dett, *Religious Folk-Songs of the Negro*.

39. Although the group formed in 1873, they began their first tour in January 1874; "Tennesseans! Slave Cabin Concerts," ad, *Decatur (IL) Daily Republican*, 4 May 1874.

40. Haley, *Afro-American Encyclopaedia*, 296, 298. The history of CTC is convoluted, but in brief: In 1900 Central Tennessee College was renamed Walden University; in 1915 its Meharry Medical College became an independent institution. Walden University became Walden College in 1922 and operated until 1925, when it closed.

41. Latimer, "J. W. Donavin's Tennesseans," 42. Latimer's article has excellent further background on Donavin, Central Tennessee College, and the Tennesseans.

42. Advertisement for a series of five concerts at Kingsbury Music Hall in Chicago. "Amusements: The Tennesseans," *Chicago Daily Tribune*, 4 Feb. 1874.

43. "Amusements: The Tennesseans," *Chicago Daily Tribune*, 5 Feb. 1874. "Old-fashioned music" had been a prewar trend most famously exemplified by "Old Folks" concerts, first professionalized in 1856 by "Father" Robert Kemp (1820–1879). Performers in Revolutionary-period costumes singing old-fashioned music became a national enthusiasm, representing an era of lusty, communal singing. After Kemp's retirement in 1868 various "old folks" troupes continued to perform, updating their repertory to the more recent past. On the history of old folks concerts see Judith T. Steinberg, "Old Folks Concerts and the Revival of New England Psalmody," *Musical Quarterly* 59, no. 4 (1973): 602–19.

44. *Selections of Plantation Songs*, introduction by J. W. Donavin, back inside cover.

45. Ad, "The Tennesseans," *Chicago Daily Tribune*, 4 Feb. 1874; *Selections of Plantation Songs* (eleventh annual tour); "Amusements: The Tennesseans," *Chicago Daily Tribune*, 10 Feb. 1874.

46. *Songs of the Tennesseans*; *Selections of Plantation Songs*.

47. See multiple untitled notices in *Columbus (NE) Journal*, 14 April 1886.

48. "Amusements: The Tennesseans," *Chicago Daily Tribune*, 7 Feb. 1874.

49. "Amusements: The Tennesseans," *Chicago Daily Tribune*, 10 Feb. 1874.

50. George L. White to E. M. Cravath, 13 Oct. 1874, Nashville, AMA Archives. Both the Fisks and the Tennesseans performed at the Nashville Exposition in October 1874, which was attended by seven thousand to eight thousand people.

51. Frederick A. Chase (Fisk teacher and Spence's brother-in-law) to E. M. Cravath, 7 Oct. 1874, Nashville, AMA Archives.

52. Gilbert to Cravath, 9 Jan. 1878, Nashville, AMA Archives.

53. J. Braden, "Central Tennessee College," in A. W. Cummings, *The Early Schools of Methodism* (New York: Phillips and Hunt, 1886), 3: 400. Rust Hall was dedicated on 7 October 1875.

54. *Selections of Plantation Songs.* The two troupes were Donavin's Original Tennesseans, J. W. Donavin (proprietor), L. K. Donavin (manager), and George B. Donavin (business manager); and Donavin's Famous Tennesseans, J. W. Donavin (proprietor and manager) and S. K. Donavin (business manager).

55. *Selections of Plantation Songs.*

56. Latimer, "J. W. Donavin's Tennesseans," 46.

57. Advertisement, *Wichita (KS) Daily Eagle*, 10 Sept. 1895; "The Tennesseans," *People's Voice* (Wellington, KS), 30 Jan. 1896; "Tonight Is the Time," *Wichita Daily Eagle*, 5 Feb. 1896.

58. "Bellaire Letter, Bellaire, O., April 26, 1875," *Belmont Chronicle* (St. Clairsville, OH), 29 April 1875.

59. Multiple sources give varying birth and death dates. According to an 1867 advertisement, Emma Louise was eight years old and Anna ten, making their birth dates ca. 1857 and 1855, respectively (*Sacramento Daily Union*, 20 April 1867); this conclusion is reinforced by an 1874 article that gives the sisters' ages as seventeen and nineteen ("The Hyers Sisters at Castleton," *Rutland [VT] Daily Globe*, 16 June 1874). It's certain that by 1900 Anna Madah was performing alone; Emma Louise seems to have died between 1898 and 1900. The dates given by Buckner, "Spectacular Opacities," seem accurate.

60. Advertisement, *Sacramento Daily Union*, 20 April 1867.

61. *Reading (PA) Times*, 6 June 1873: 1; *New Journal* (Wilmington, DE), 3 June 1873: 3; "The Colored Race as Vocalists," *New York Sun*, 6 March 1873; "The Hyers Sisters," *Brooklyn Daily Eagle*, 20 Mar. 1873, regarding a performance at Plymouth Church on 19 March.

62. Advertisement, *Brooklyn Daily Eagle*, 30 Sept. 1873.

63. "Jubilee Concert—The Hyer Sisters," *Brooklyn Daily Eagle*, 2 Oct. 1873.

64. Advertisement, *Brooklyn Eagle*, 29 Oct. 1873.

65. "The Hyers' Sisters at Castleton," *Rutland (VT) Daily Globe*, 16 June 1874.

66. "Amusements," *Boston Daily Globe*, 25 Dec. 1874; Trotter, *Music and Some Highly Musical People*, 170.

67. Ostendorf, *Black Literature in White America*, 77.

68. "Freedmen's Concert," *Boston Daily Globe*, 17 June 1873; see also advertisement in *Boston Daily Globe*, 21 June 1873.

69. *Shaw University Bulletin: Diamond Jubilee Souvenir Program* 10, no. 2 (Dec. 1940).

70. "Jubilee Concert," *Rutland (VT) Daily Globe*, 9 Aug. 1873: 1; "Rutland County," *Rutland (VT) Daily Globe*, 15 Aug., 1873; untitled notice, *Green-Mountain Freeman* (Montpelier, VT), 20 Aug. 1873; "Southern Items," *Weekly Caucasian* (Lexington, MO), 20 Dec. 1873.

71. *Kingston (NY) Daily Freeman*, 24 Mar. 1874: 3.

72. *Pittston (PA) Gazette*, 21 May 1874: 3.

73. They sang at Beecher's Plymouth Church on 4 May 1875 (Odell, *Annals*, 10: 83).

74. Abbott, "'Do Thyself,'" 3.

75. "Jubilee Singers," *Brooklyn Eagle*, 16 Dec. 1874, which describes their performance at the Reverend Dr. Duryea's Classon Avenue Presbyterian Church.

76. Poster/program dated Tues., 17 Nov. [1874], AMA Archives.

77. See Keck, "Promoting Black Music."

78. Pike, *Jubilee Singers*, 116.

79. "Plymouth Church Service," *New York Times*, 1 Feb. 1875.

80. Programme of the Tennesseans Slave Cabin Concerts, n.d., W. S. Hoole Special Collections, University of Alabama Libraries.

81. A brochure describing the twentieth-century Jacksons can be found in the Iowa Digital Libraries collection, Traveling Culture: Circuit Chautauqua in the Twentieth Century: http://digital.lib.uiowa.edu/cdm/ref/collection/tc/id/51134.

82. "Red Wing and Vicinity," *Grange Advance* (Red Wing, MN), 19 Aug. 1874.

83. Untitled notice, *St. Cloud (MN) Journal*, 27 Aug. 1874.

84. "North Carolinians," *Ottawa (IL) Free Trader*, 4 Sept. 1875.

85. He is listed as "proprietor" of the "Madison City Directory" (State of Wisconsin, n.d.) during Governor Washburn's tenure, which was from 1872 to 1874. Census data come from the 1870 and 1880 federal censuses. For examples of Brand's compositions see "Sounds from the Old Camp Ground" (Chicago: Root and Cady, 1868), LC, https://www.loc.gov/item/ihas.200001228/, and "They've Burned My Little Bed" (Boston: White, Smith, 1880), LC, https://www.loc.gov/resource/sm1880.06146.0/?sp=4.

86. The *Carroll County (Lanark, IL) Gazette* reported in 1875 that "a group of Negro performers named the 'North Carolinians' organized by the Prof. in his travels were appearing locally" ("Calendar and History 1980: Happy 150th Anniversary Tom Crain," Lanark Museum, Lanark, IL: http://genealogytrails.com/ill/carroll/carrollcalendar1980.html).

87. The earliest located written record of their performances dates from 24 Dec. 1875, when they sang a sacred (Sunday) concert at Tony Pastor's New Theatre in New York.

88. Playbill, Howard Athenaeum [1876], HTC, minstrel playbills.

89. "Introductory," *New York Clipper*, 21 July 1877: 134.

90. Lampert, "Bringing Music to Lyceumites," 68, 69.

91. The Hyers sisters' concert took place on 2 Oct. (ad, *Boston Daily Globe*, 28 Sept. 1875). Although they were the first black entertainers to appear in a lyceum course, they weren't the first African Americans, as Frederick Douglass was already a popular lecturer on the circuit. In Nov. 1875 Redpath sold his bureau to George Hathaway and Major J. B. Pond. In 1880 Hathaway bought out Pond and became sole owner. The agency retained Redpath's name (Tapia, *Circuit Chautauqua*, 15).

92. "The Nashville Students," *Wood River Times* (Hailey, ID), 17 June 1884: 3.

93. Ad for Jubilee Singers, *Boston Globe*, 5 Oct. 1879.

94. Lampert, "Bringing Music to Lyceumites," 81.

95. "The Chautauqua Assembly," *New York Times*, 8 Aug. 1880: 2.

96. Cruz, *Culture on the Margins*, 115, 116.

CHAPTER 5. The Minstrel Show Gets Religion

1. Blackface performance includes not only the formal minstrel show but individual blackface acts in variety shows and theatrical productions. Although postbellum minstrelsy remains under-studied, sources with valuable selective information include Southern, *Music of Black Americans* and "Georgia Minstrels"; Toll, *Blacking Up*; and the following memoirs of late nineteenth-century minstrelsy: Fletcher, *One Hundred Years*; Handy, *Father of the Blues*; Rice, *Monarchs of Minstrelsy*; and Simond, *Old Slack's Reminiscence*. Taylor and Austen's *Darkest America* explores the legacy of blackface minstrelsy, but unfortunately the section on postbellum minstrelsy is the weakest in an otherwise excellent book. For overviews of antebellum minstrelsy, see Cockrell, *Demons of Disorder*; Lhamon, *Jump Jim Crow* and *Raising Cain*; Lott, *Love and Theft*; Mahar, *Behind the Burnt Cork Mask*; and Nathan, *Dan Emmett and the Rise of Early Minstrelsy*.

2. The Shaking Quakers act was based on a song by Even "Eph" Horn called "Fi-Hi-Hi" (New York: Firth, Pond, 1851). The Shakers were a Protestant denomination with settlements north of New York City and in New England and had nothing to do with the Quakers; rather "Shaking Quakers" was a derogatory description of their ritual singing, which incorporated dancing, shaking, and gesturing. See Mahar, *Behind the Burnt Cork Mask*, 29–30, 48, 50.

3. This is verse 3 of Emmett, "Jordan Is a Hard Road to Trabel" (Boston: Oliver Ditson, 1853); searchable at Brown Digital Repository, https://repository.library.brown.edu/.

4. Rieser, *Chautauqua Movement*, 25–32; "Introductory," *New York Clipper*, 11 Aug 1877: 158; see also Aron, *Working at Play*, chap. 4.

5. Sam Lucas used the same comic setup in verse 3 of his commercial spiritual "Down By de Sunrise" (Boston: White, Smith, 1884): Jackariah climbs a tree to get a better view of the Lord, but the limb breaks and he falls. Like folk songs, minstrel songs often relied on variations of stock verses.

6. Rice, *Monarchs of Minstrelsy*, 51. An image of Howard in character appears on the cover of "The Old Home Ain't What It Used to Be," Duke University Libraries Digital Collections, http://library.duke.edu/digitalcollections/media/jpg/hasm/lrg/b0949-1.jpg.

7. "Negro Minstrelsy," *New York Clipper*, 10 Sept. 1870: 183. For biographies of Simmons and Slocum, see Rice, *Monarchs of Minstrelsy*.

8. Wittig's publication was announced in the *New York Clipper*, 3 Dec. 1870: 279, under "Musical." The other versions were easy solo piano arrangements by E. Mack for the "Sunbeams" series (Philadelphia: Lee and Walker, 1871), LC, and by J. J. Haman for "Ballads without Words" (Philadelphia: Lee and Walker, 1871), LC; and a quadrille arranged by Ross for an instrumental medley (Philadelphia: Lee and Walker / W. H. Boner, 1871), CPM.

9. Their appearance at Bryant's Opera House, New York, is cited in Brown, "Early History of Negro Minstrelsy."

10. "Variety Halls," *New York Clipper*, 1 Oct. 1870: 207. For more on McAndrews see Toll, *Blacking Up*, 45, 51; Rice, *Monarchs of Minstrelsy*, 79.

11. "Amusements," *Brooklyn Eagle*, 17, 19, and 20 Dec. 1870.

12. "Negro Minstrelsy," *New York Clipper*, 24 Dec. 1870: 303.

13. "Negro Minstrelsy," *New York Clipper*, 7 Jan. 1871: 319.

14. "Amusements, etc.," *Daily Alta California* (San Francisco), 24 Feb. 1871: 1.

15. All citations are from "Negro Minstrelsy," *New York Clipper*. Emerson: 25 Feb. 1871: 375. Welch: 11 Feb. 1871: 359; 22 April 1871: 23.

16. "The Globe," program for Emerson's California Minstrels, 29 Aug. 1872, HTC, minstrel playbills, https://iiif.lib.harvard.edu/manifests/view/drs:46588334$8i.

17. "Variety Halls," *New York Clipper*, 1 July 1871: 102; "Negro Minstrelsy," *New York Clipper*, 9 Sept. 1871: 183; "City Summary," *New York Clipper*, 23 Sept. 1871: 198; "Negro Minstrelsy," *New York Clipper*, 25 Nov. 1871: 271; ad, Alhambra Theatre, *Daily Alta California* (San Francisco), 4 Sept. 1871. The information on Welch performing with Simmons and Slocum comes from Rice, *Monarchs of Minstrelsy*, 123.

18. For more on these see Toll, *Blacking Up*, 198–99 and 275–76; Peterson, *African American Theatre Directory*, 217; and Southern, "Georgia Minstrels."

19. See Toll, *Blacking Up*, 204, and his chronological list of black minstrel troupes, 275–80.

20. Ad, *Tiffin (OH) Tribune*, 9 Nov. 1871: 2, and *Petroleum Centre (PA) Daily Record*, 29 Nov. 1871: 2.

21. "Georgia Minstrel Troupe," *Western Reserve Chronicle* (Warren, OH), 15 Nov. 1871: 3. Grace's song remains unidentified.

22. All citations from *New York Clipper*: "Negro Minstrelsy," 3 Feb. 1872: 351; 29 June 1872: 103; 18 Jan. 1873: 335; 14 Sept. 1872: 191. "Variety Halls," 26 Oct. 1872: 239; 18 Jan. 1873: 335.

23. McAndrews sang it the week of 24–29 March 1879 on a variety bill at the London Theatre, Bowery, New York (Odell, *Annals*, 10: 669). Lyrics to the song can be found in the following songsters: *Cool Burgess' "In the Morning by the Bright Light" Songster* (New York: New York Popular Publishing, n.d. [1880 or later]), 18, HTC, songsters; and *Olympia Quartette Songster* (New York: New York Popular Publishing, n.d. [ca. 1881]), 28, LC, Music Division, Dumont Collection.

24. Cartee, "Rock'a My Soul" (Boston: G. D. Russell, 1871), LC, https://www.loc.gov/item/sm1871.00387/. The second printing of *Slave Songs* was advertised in *The Nation*, 4 May 1871: 311.

25. The tune name in John Playford's *Dancing Master* is "The Dargason" (London: Thomas Harper, 1651), fol. 71; http://imslp.org/wiki/The_Dancing_Master_(Playford,_John); in the Irish fiddle tradition it's a jig known as "The Irish Washerwoman"; various settings can be found at *The Session*, https://thesession.org/tunes/92. Jackson asserts a corollary between the fiddle tune and the spiritual in *White and Negro Spirituals*, 226–27.

26. Programme of the Tennesseans Slave Cabin Concerts, n.d., W. S. Hoole Special Collections, University of Alabama Libraries; Graham, "Fisk Jubilee Singers and the Concert Spiritual," 529. Perkins, writing in 1922, didn't think the Fisk version was accurate, noting the difficulty in comprehending the melody and notating it exactly. He pointed out that different sections of the South had different renditions and claimed the spiritual was "provincial to Mississippi, Louisiana, and western Alabama" ("Negro Spirituals," 239).

27. The ring shout reference is posited by "The Spirituals Project—Sankofa—Rock a mah Soul," University of Denver, 2014, http://videocast.du.edu/video/the-spirituals-project-sankofa-rock-a-mah-soul.

28. "The Younger Generation in Minstrelsy and Reminiscences of the Past," *New York Clipper*, 27 March 1915: 5–7.

29. The two took a fifteen-month hiatus beginning in 1875, when they dissolved their partnership and Delehanty teamed with James H. Cummings. Delehanty reunited with Hengler in 1876; "To the Public," in *Delehanty and Cummings' "Sunset in the South" Songster* (New York: A. J. Fisher, 1875), 3, HTC, songsters. From that point on they were constant friends and colleagues, performing together until consumption overtook Delehanty in 1880. Hengler also died young, in 1888. See also Rice, *Monarchs of Minstrelsy*, 184; "Current Events," *Brooklyn Eagle*, 14 May 1880.

30. *Thatcher, Primrose and West Songster* (New York: New York Popular Publishing, n.d.), HTC, songsters. Although this songster dates from 1883 or later judging from its contents, this particular song probably dates from ca. 1875.

31. *Delehanty and Hengler's Song and Dance Book* (New York: Robert M. De Witt, Publisher, 1874), 162, HTC, songsters.

32. "To the Public," *Delehanty and Cummings' "Sunset in the South" Songster* (New York: A. J. Fisher, 1875), 3, HTC, songsters. Italics in the original.

33. "City Summary," *New York Clipper*, 22 June 1872: 94.

34. Program for "The Original Georgia Minstrels," Charles Callender, proprietor, and Chas. B. Hicks, business manager, for Wed. evening, 29 Jan. 1873 at Horticultural Hall, no city, HTC, minstrel playbills.

CHAPTER 6. Commercial Spirituals

1. Dennison, *Scandalize My Name*, 297–98.

2. Ibid., 298; Hamm, *Yesterdays*, 271; Toll, *Blacking Up*, 235–44; Southern, "Georgia Minstrels," 173 (Southern is talking specifically about black minstrel composers).

3. See Graham, annotated index, for a complete list of these songs, including analyses and links to online sheet music.

4. Dennison, *Scandalize My Name*, 299.

5. Southern, "Georgia Minstrels," 173; Jackson, *Down-East Spirituals*, 2.

6. See sheet music in the Lester S. Levy Sheet Music Collection: http://levysheetmusic.mse.jhu.edu/catalog/levy:054.053. Whereas the verse uses a five-tone gapped scale, the chorus is diatonic and uses passing chromatic tones in the melody and a V of ii harmony in one measure, which provides a sharp musical contrast to the verse.

7. "City Summary," *New York Clipper*, 13 Dec. 1873: 294. Other white troupes performed the song as well: Little Mac's California Minstrels in 1876, sung by Charles Reed (Little Mac's California Minstrels program, printed in *Beethoven Programme* [Beethoven Hall, Boston], 15 Sept 1876); and Campbell's Minstrels in late 1877 and probably into 1878, sung by George Milbank (Campbell Minstrels playbill, Associate Hall, Somerville [MA], 17 Dec. 1877); HTC, minstrel playbills.

8. Browne, *Early Minstrel Songs*. Browne (1878–1954?) was a highly regarded actor and singer from 1900 to 1925, appearing in musical and dramatic theater, as well as in silent films. He served as director and announcer for the Columbia Broadcasting System from 1926 to 1931, after which he turned to full-time work in the Christian Science Church, becoming president of the Mother Church in Boston in 1948. "Scientists Elect First Church Head," *New York Times*, 8 June 1948; Brian Golbey, liner notes to Browne, *Early Minstrel Songs*.

9. On Browne's recording, "Gospel Train" is paired in a medley with the hit song "Children, Don't Get Weary," a commercial parody of a traditional spiritual that was published as sheet music by Oliver Ditson (Boston) in 1879 (LC, https://www.loc.gov/item/sm1877.10128/) and had been transcribed by Allen et al. in *Slave Songs*.

10. John Reginald Blake, "The Decadence of Minstrelsy," *The Theatre* 4, no. 6 (5 Mar. 1888): 107; the reminiscence refers to Bryant and endman Nelse Seymour together. Bryant was born Daniel Webster O'Brien (1833–1875), and Nelse Seymour was born Thomas Nelson Sanderson (1835–1875).

11. In 1880 a reorganized and independent troupe of Fisk Jubilee Singers sang "Gospel Train" in protest of the segregation and exclusion they repeatedly endured on trains and in hotels and restaurants; see Seroff, "'Voice in the Wilderness,'" 147–49.

12. To give a few examples: the Hutchinsons were parodied by Christy's Minstrels in 1857 (see program in HTC, https://iiif.lib.harvard.edu/manifests/view/drs:46006405$2i) and by Carncross and Dixey's Minstrels, 31 Dec. 1862 and 31 Dec. 1863, at Eleventh St. Opera House, Philadelphia, NYPL, Lincoln Center, minstrels U.S., scrapbook. Kelly and Leon's minstrels presented the "Kneelson Concert" at Hooley's Opera House in Brooklyn ("Negro Minstrelsy," *New York Clipper*, 7 Jan. 1871: 319); the female impersonator known as Eugene (Eugene d'Ameli, 1836–1907) appeared as Nilsson at Hooley's the following week ("Negro Minstrelsy," *New York Clipper*, 14 Jan. 1871: 327); and the next week Martha Wren and James Collins starred in a musical sketch called "The Arrival of Kneelson" at Tony Pastor's theater in New York ("City Summary," *New York Clipper*, 21 Jan. 1871: 334). Thatcher and Ryman's Minstrels burlesqued "Sarah Heart-Burn" at Tony Pastor's Theatre, 9 May 1881 (Odell, *Annals*, 11: 317). For minstrel critiques of Lincoln and other politicians, see Saxton, "Blackface Minstrelsy," 21–22.

13. "Negro Minstrelsy," *New York Clipper*, 1 Mar. 1873: 383; "Musical," *New York Clipper*, 1 Feb. 1873: 351.

14. The *New York Clipper* noted, "The burlesque of 'The Carolina Singers' will be presented for the first time" at their Opera House, 17 Feb. 1873; "Negro Minstrelsy," *New York Clipper*, 22 Feb. 1873: 375; "Musical," *New York Clipper*, 1 Feb. 1873: 351.

15. Amusements ad, *Chicago Daily Tribune*, 4 Feb. 1874; amusements ad and "Review of Amusements," *Chicago Daily Tribune*, 15 Feb. 1874.

16. Pike, *Jubilee Singers*; "Variety Halls," *New York Clipper*, 18 May 1873: 55.

17. From biographies of James H. Budworth and Bob Hart in Brown, "Early History of Negro Minstrelsy."

18. This imagined speech is slightly altered and redacted from a stump speech in H. H. Wheeler (comp.), *Up-to-Date Minstrel Jokes* (Boston: Up-to-Date Publishing, 1902), 64–65.

19. Seroff, "Fisk Jubilee Singers in Britain," 48. It's hard to know whether Imes personally witnessed the performance, for the Jubilee Singers' extracurricular activities were closely monitored by the Fisk managers, and were more likely to include opera, the symphony, band concerts, and religious events.

20. *Blairgowrie News* (Scotland), 6 Oct. 1876; *Craven Herald* (England), 6 Jan. 1877; both in George L. White Scrapbooks, FULSC.

21. New York: J. L. Peters, 1873, LC, https://www.loc.gov/item/sm1873.11978/.

22. Birdoff, *World's Greatest Hit*, 135.

23. From the introduction by E. D. Gooding, *Ham-Town Students Songster*. Gooding's birth and death dates aren't known, but Allston Brown's earliest mention of him is with Birch, Bowers, and Fox's Minstrels in 1858 ("Early History"); Gooding was working as a stage manager in New York in the 1880s.

24. The Olympic was at 624 Broadway and was managed by John R. Poole; "Amusements," *New York Times*, 8 Feb. 1875. On Sanford's initial burlesque of the Fisks see "Amusements," Hooley's Opera House, *Brooklyn Eagle*, 3–8 March 1873.

25. "City Summary," *New York Clipper*, 4 Sept 1875: 182, and 26 Feb. 1876: 382; "A Few Words," *Ham-Town Students Songster*.

26. Winans, "Early Minstrel Show Music," 141–62. For more on the quartet tradition, especially among African Americans, see Gage Averill, *Four Parts, No Waiting: A Social History of American Barbershop Harmony* (New York: Oxford University Press, 2003), and Lynn Abbott, "'Play That Barber Shop Chord': A Case for the African-American Origin of Barbershop Harmony," *American Music* 10, no. 3 (1992): 289–325.

27. The Tennesseans' repertory is listed in their ad under "Amusements," *Brooklyn Eagle*, 18 Jan 1874.

28. See, e.g., Alan Lomax, *Georgia Sea Island Songs* (New World Records, 1977).

29. *Ham-Town Students Songster*, 9. The Hamptons' score is in Armstrong and Ludlow, *Hampton and Its Students*, 188.

30. "The Park Theatre," *Brooklyn Eagle*, 7 Sept. 1875.

31. The Ham Town impersonators belonged to the Orpheus Quartette, consisting of H. C. Depew, H. S. Dale, Parr, and J. A. Sturgess, who performed standard repertory in whiteface in the same show. Playbill, Harry Bloodgood's Minstrels [McDonough Hall, Middletown, CT], 22 Nov. [1877], HTC, minstrel playbills.

32. "Amusements—St. Charles Theatre," *New Orleans Daily Democrat*, 26 Oct. 1877: 5.

33. "City Summary," *New York Clipper*, 19 July 1879: 134.

34. Haverly's Colossal Colored Carnival [1883], Oakland Garden Programme, Boston; the Blackville Jubilees: Haverly's Colossal Colored Carnival and Genuine Colored Minstrels [1880], Haverly's Niblo Garden, New York, HTC, minstrel playbills.

35. "To-night the Original Black Diamonds," program, HTC, American minstrel show collection. Although undated, the year 1875 handwritten on the program has been reproduced in various sources as factual. But the program's first part features Bland's "new" song "Carry Me Back to Ole Virginny" (published 1878) as well as "Whisper Softly Baby's Dying" (presumably by L. C. Wegefarth, published 1881 by Oliver Ditson). Even though songs typically circulated in performance before being published, the six-year gap between 1875 and 1881 would have been unusual. The year 1878 seems more likely

because of the repertory, and is supported by a notice in the *New York Clipper* ("Amusements in Boston, Mass.," 25 May 1878: 70), which lists members of the Black Diamonds as participating in a stage production of *Uncle Tom's Cabin*. The Black Diamonds' program was printed in Boston.

36. Southern, "Georgia Minstrels," 172–73.

37. "Amusements," *Philadelphia Inquirer*, 23 Nov. 1875.

38. "The Georgia Minstrels," *Boston Daily Globe*, 30 Mar. 1875. On audiences see "Musical Notes," *Boston Daily Globe*, 1 April 1875.

39. "Musical Notes," *Boston Daily Globe*, 1 April 1875. The invitation was issued in "Musical Notes," *Boston Daily Globe*, 10 April 1875.

40. "Hamlin's," *Chicago Daily Tribune*, 1 July 1879.

41. "Callender's Georgia Minstrels," *Boston Daily Globe*, 11 and 20 April 1877; "Callender's Georgia Minstrels," *Wheeling (WV) Daily Intelligencer*, 21 Jan. 1878: 4.

42. Callender's Original Georgia Minstrels, Hooley's Opera House, *Brooklyn Daily Programme*, 21 Aug. 1874, NYPL, Lincoln Center, minstrels U.S., programme. Sheet music published by John F. Perry, Boston, 1875.

43. "The Georgia Minstrels," *Boston Daily Globe*, 30 Mar. 1875; and "Dramatic and Musical Notes," *Boston Daily Globe*, 21 Apr. 1875.

44. For more on Devonear's songs see Graham, annotated index.

45. Robinson, *From Log Cabin to the Pulpit, or, Fifteen Years in Slavery*, 3rd ed. (1913, published by the author), 79, electronic edition: University of North Carolina Library, Documenting the American South, http://docsouth.unc.edu/fpn/robinson/robinson.html. Josephine Wright identifies four sources of "There's a Meeting" in "Songs of Remembrance," *Journal of African American History* 91, no. 4 (2006): 418.

46. Ad for the Tennesseans, *Chicago Daily Tribune*, 4 Feb. 1874 (they used the title "Just Fix Your Feet for Travelin'"); program for Jackson Jubilee Singers, 17 Nov. 1874, AMA Archives, and reprinted in chap. 4; Pike, *Singing Campaign for Ten Thousand Pounds*. The Fisks used different lyrics for the verses than the Tennesseans.

47. See Graham, Songs of Sam Lucas, and "Composing in Black and White." Lucas didn't write all the songs published under his name.

48. For more on Lucas's biography see Graham, "Composing in Black and White." The following sources supply biographical data: Fletcher, *One Hundred Years*; Hill and Hatch, *History of African American Theatre*; Holly, "Sam Lucas"; Johnson, *Black Manhattan*; *Sam Lucas' Plantation Songster*, unsigned biographical sketch; Simond, *Old Slack's Reminiscence*; Southern, *Biographical Dictionary*.

49. I gratefully acknowledge the excellent archival research of high school student Ben Nichols, whose paper "Samuel Lucas—Actor, Composer, Member of Fifth Regiment United States Volunteer Colored Infantry" was published in the 2003 anthology *Ohio's African American Civil War Heritage*, by the Research History Class of Washington High School (Washington Court House, OH) and sponsored by the Ohio Bicentennial Underground Railroad Committee. Lucas's military and pension documents, and those of his half-brother, Clarence Powell, can be accessed at the National Archives and Records Administration.

50. "Long Sam Lucas: Artist of Negro Minstrelsy," *New York Sun*, 22 Oct. 1911.

51. *Ham-Town Students Songster*, 28; Browne, *Early Minstrel Songs*; *Uncle Dave Macon Classic Sides*.

52. Music for the Nation, "Greatest Hits, 1870–85: *Variety Music Cavalcade*," LC, http://www.loc.gov/collections/american-sheet-music-1870-to-1885/articles-and-essays/greatest-hits-1870-85-variety-music-cavalcade/.

53. Biographical information on Hays is from Spaeth, *History of Popular Music*, 158, and Charles Eugene Claghorn, *Biographical Dictionary of American Music* (West Nyack, NY: Parker Publishing, 1973), 204.

54. *Callender's Georgia Minstrels Songster* (San Francisco: Francis and Valentine, 1878). *Katie Cooper's "Cindy Jane" Songster* gives Charles Anderson as the song's performer (New York: New York Popular Publishing, n.d. [1882 or later]), 35, HTC, songsters.

55. *The A. H. Sheldon Songster* (New York: A. J. Fisher, 1881), 41, HTC, songsters. I've corrected the obvious typo in the first two words, which were printed "Make hasts." For more details on this song and its parodies, see Graham, annotated index.

56. "Angel Gabriel" (New York: J. L. Peters, 1875), LC, https://www.loc.gov/item/sm1875.03069/.

57. A sampling of recordings that give the song a country or old-time treatment include Norman and Nancy Blake on *The Hobo's Last Ride* (1996); Chloe and Jan Davidson on a compilation CD titled *Nightshoots and Morningsongs* produced by the John C. Campbell Folk School in Brasstown (2007); Flying Jenny on the album *Flying Jenny* (2003). In addition, over the years Stewart's song has been reinterpreted as gospel: e.g., the Black Swan Classic Jazz Band gave it a stylistic makeover (*A Joyful Noise*, 2000), excerpted on their website: http://www.bscjb.com/recording_samples/.

58. "Stewart's Last Song," from 26 June *Cincinnati Gazette*, reprinted in *New York Times*, 28 June 1884.

59. According to Davis: "I fell in with a man who is dead now, but to whom I owe all my points and knowledge about song writing. . . . that was James E. Stewart, the author of 'Only to see her face again,' 'Cricket on the Hearth,' and 'Jenny, the flower of Kildare,' who died in the workhouse in Cincinnati" ("Irene, Good Night," *Cleveland Gazette*, 4 Feb. 1888, reprinted in Josephine Wright, comp., *Black Perspective in Music* 6, no. 2 [1978]: 189–230).

60. Dennison, *Scandalize My Name*, xi.

61. Sam Lucas recounts this in "Long Sam Lucas: Artist of Negro Minstrelsy," *The Sun* (New York), 22 Oct. 1911.

62. Dennison, *Scandalize My Name*, 298.

63. Gottschild, *Digging the Africanist Presence*, 112.

64. Dennison, *Scandalize My Name*, 298.

65. Dunson, "Black Misrepresentation," 55.

66. See Graham, "Composing in Black and White."

67. Moton, *Finding a Way Out*, 59–60. Moton retells this story with the date of 1878 in "Negro Folk Music," *Southern Workman* (June 1915): 329. It's not clear what song he was referencing.

CHAPTER 7. Spirituals in Uncle Tom Shows, Melodramas, and Spectacles

1. This composite description is based on several primary sources and imagined from the viewpoint of a young white female; some phrases have been quoted directly from the following: "Dramatic," *New York Clipper*, 16 Jan. 1875: 334; "'Uncle Tom's Cabin' at the Boston," *Boston Daily Globe*, 4 April 1876; "Hooley's," *Brooklyn Eagle*, 7 Nov. 1876; script of *Uncle Tom's Cabin* "perfected by G[eorge] C. Howard," 1875, based on original script by George L. Aiken, act 4, scene 4 (Uncle Tom's Cabin and American Culture, scripts, http://www.iath.virginia.edu/utc/onstage/scripts/schp.html); Birdoff, *World's Greatest Hit*, 190–91.

2. Serial publication ran occasionally from 5 June 1851 to 1 Apr. 1852; the first stage adaptation was at the Baltimore Museum, Baltimore, MD, on 5 Jan. 1852.

3. "Sweet Singers Wanted," *New York Times*, 10 Feb. 1878.

4. Riis surveys the use of music in his article "Music and Musicians in . . . *Uncle Tom's Cabin*." Root, "Music of Uncle Tom's Cabin," examines Stowe's use of music as a literary device in her novel.

5. Birdoff, *World's Greatest Hit*, 5; for other overviews of the genesis of Tom shows see Gossett, *Uncle Tom's Cabin and American Culture*, and John Frick, "Uncle Tom's Cabin on the Antebellum Stage," Uncle Tom's Cabin and the Making of American Culture (Web), http://utc.iath.virginia.edu/interpret/exhibits/frick/frick.html. The following website contains an overview of scripts, and portions of them: http://www.iath.virginia.edu/utc/index2f.html.

6. This was reported in national newspapers, e.g.: "Anniversary of This Institution," *Chicago Daily Tribune*, 2 Jan. 1876; "The Fisk University," *New York Times*, 2 Jan. 1876.

7. There were 10 million recorded admissions. By way of context, the population of the United States at that time was 46 million, and the population of Philadelphia under 1 million; Stephanie Grauman Wolf, "Centennial Exhibition," *Encyclopedia of Greater Philadelphia* (Mid-Atlantic Regional Center for the Humanities, Rutgers University, 2013), http://philadelphiaencyclopedia.org/archive/centennial/.

8. "Hampton at the Centennial," *Southern Workman* (May 1876): 35; also "Centennial Views," *Southern Workman* (Jan. 1877): 6.

9. "Grand Opera House," *New York Tribune*, 21 Oct. 1876.

10. "The Drama, Park Theater," *New York Tribune*, 24 May 1876. Philadelphia theaters actually suffered a decline in attendance when the Centennial Exhibition commenced that continued through the hot summer months, although business recovered in the fall; "Green-Room Notes," *Chicago Daily Tribune*, 21 May 1876, and "The Outer World," 4 June 1876.

11. Untitled item, *New York Clipper*, 4 Nov. 1876: 250.

12. "City Summary," *New York Clipper*, 29 Jan. 1876: 350.

13. "Plymouth Church—The Jubilee Concert," *Brooklyn Eagle*, 1 May 1875; ads for the Wilmington Singers, *Brooklyn Eagle*, 30 Apr. 1875 and 12 May 1875.

14. "The Concert at Plymouth Church," *Brooklyn Eagle*, 17 May 1875.

15. Birdoff, *World's Greatest Hit*, 30–43; "Obituary Notes" [Mr. George C. Howard], *New York Times*, 20 Jan. 1887; George C. Howard Biographical Sketch, Harry Ransom Humanities Research Center, University of Texas at Austin, http://norman.hrc.utexas .edu/fasearch/findingAid.cfm?eadid=00058.

16. Riis, "Music and Musicians," 274; "City Summary," *New York Clipper*, 29 Jan. 1876: 350.

17. The website Uncle Tom's Cabin and American Culture contains maps with troupe itineraries: http://www.iath.virginia.edu/utc/onstage/performin/tourshp.html. Although Stowe makes abundant references to music in her novel, religious music manifests predominantly as hymns, with allusions to camp-meeting hymns and spirituals; see Root, "Music of *Uncle Tom's Cabin*"; Boots, *Singing for Equality*, chap. 10.

18. Ad, *Clipper*, 11 Mar. 1876: 395. The Wilmingtons appeared in *UTC* on 14 Feb. 1876, at the Theatre Comique in Williamsburgh, NY (Odell, *Annals*, 10: 83).

19. E.g., the Tennessee Jubilee Singers, a concert troupe, appeared in *UTC* in San Francisco in early October ("Amusements. Grand Opera House," *Daily Alta California* [San Francisco], 11 Oct. 1876).

20. Their itinerary is reconstructed from notices in the *New York Clipper* and various newspaper ads, Uncle Tom's Cabin and American Culture (website), http://www.iath .virginia.edu/utc/onstage/revus/clipperhp.html and http://www.iath.virginia.edu/utc/ onstage/ads/tsadshp2.html, supplemented with notices from the *Brooklyn Daily Eagle*, *New York Times*, *Boston Post*, and *Boston Daily Globe*. Regarding Slavin's Georgias touring as a concert troupe, see "Dramatic," *New York Clipper*, 14 July 1877: 126.

21. Ad for the Wilkinsons' *UTC*, *New York Clipper*, 2 Mar. 1878: 387.

22. Howard promptbook, George C. Howard and Family Collection, Harry Ransom Humanities Research Center, University of Texas at Austin, available at Uncle Tom's Cabin and American Culture (website), http://www.iath.virginia.edu/utc/onstage/scripts/ aikentshp.html. Handwritten annotations indicate where songs should be inserted.

23. "Dramatic. Brooklyn Theatre," *Brooklyn Eagle*, 26 Sept. 1876.

24. This plot summary follows George Howard's modification of Aiken's original script, in which handwritten annotations describe where to insert the music. Song titles come from a synopsis in the *New York Herald*, 30 Oct. 1876 (advertisement), and various descriptive reviews, quoted and cited as relevant.

25. In the book this hymn is Charles Wesley's "And Let This Feeble Body Fail" (Boots, *Singing for Equality*, 207).

26. "City Summary," *New York Clipper*, 2 Mar. 1878: 390.

27. Extract from the *Baltimore American*, 11 Jan., reprinted in ad for Gilmore's Holliday Street Theatre, *Baltimore Sun*, 14 Jan. 1878.

28. Review of J. Pemberton Smith and G. C. Howard's production at the Fifth-avenue Theatre, New York; *New York Clipper*, 13 April 1878: 6.

29. Ad, "Grand Opera House," *New York Herald*, 11 Oct. 1876; Brooklyn Academy of Music, *Brooklyn Eagle*, 17 Feb. 1877. The jawbone had been a common folk instrument in earlier minstrel music but was no longer used.

30. Correspondent from New York to the *Boston Journal*, reprinted in ad for the Howards' *UTC* at Gilmore's Holliday Street Theatre, *Baltimore Sun*, 7 Jan. 1878.

31. Extract from the *Baltimore American*, 11 Jan., reprinted in ad for Gilmore's Holliday Street Theatre, *Baltimore Sun*, 14 Jan. 1878.

32. Correspondent from New York to the *Boston Journal*, reprinted in ad for the Howards' *UTC* at Gilmore's Holliday Street Theatre, *Baltimore Sun*, 7 Jan. 1878.

33. "Grand Opera House," *New York Herald*, 4 Oct. 1876.

34. These phrases are taken from various reviews quoted in the advertisement for the Grand Opera House, *New York Herald*, 8 Oct. 1876.

35. The script was printed privately; a copy is housed at the New York Historical Society and can be viewed online at Uncle Tom's Cabin and American Culture, http://www.iath.virginia.edu/utc/onstage/scripts/rowehp.html.

36. "A Famous Manager Gone" (Palmer obituary), *New York Times*, 21 July 1878; "A Theatrical Showman Gone," *Brooklyn Eagle*, 21 July 1879; Birdoff, *World's Greatest Hit*, 240–46.

37. Cf. Howards at Gilmore's Holliday Street Theater (ad), *Baltimore Sun*, 7 Jan. 1878, and "City Summary" regarding Jarrett and Palmer's production, *New York Clipper*, 23 Feb. 1878: 382; on Jarrett and Palmer see also "City Summary," *New York Clipper*, 2 Mar. 1878: 390.

38. "'Uncle Tom's Cabin' at Booth's," *New York Times*, 19 Feb. 1878.

39. Birdoff, *World's Greatest Hit*, 257.

40. Ibid., 295–97; "Amusements," *Washington Post*, 5 Mar. 1882.

41. Birdoff, *World's Greatest Hit*, 307–10.

42. Krehbiel, *Afro-American Folksongs*, 17.

43. E.g., "Jubilee Singers," *Brooklyn Eagle*, 19 Apr. 1876.

44. *New York Clipper*, 4 Nov. 1876: 251.

45. Ad, Sacred Concert at Bowery Theatre, *New York Herald*, 30 Jan. 1876.

46. They donated the proceeds from an April concert at the Marcy Avenue Baptist Church in Brooklyn to the Sunday school, and appeared as part of a variety benefit at the Academy of Music for the Catholic Orphan Asylums in October; "Georgia Jubilee Singers," *Brooklyn Eagle*, 21 Apr. 1876; ad, *New York Times*, 24 Oct. 1876.

47. Ad for "Slavin's Uncle Tom Combination," *New York Clipper*, 8 Sept. 1877: 192.

48. Early activities include church concerts at the Fleet Street Methodist Episcopal Church in Brooklyn on 4 May 1876, in which they sang slave songs of the South, and another on 15 May at the New England Church in Williamsburgh; Odell, *Annals*, 10: 162.

49. Ad, "Gilmore's Holliday Street Theatre," *Baltimore Sun*, 9 Jan. 1878. See also Birdoff, *World's Greatest Hit*, 234.

50. "Brooklyn Music Hall," *Brooklyn Eagle*, 11 April 1880.

51. "Dramatic," *New York Clipper*, 9 Feb. 1878: 367; "Notice to Managers," *New York Clipper*, 16 Mar. 1878: 403. Taylor is listed as pianist for the Hyers Sisters' Combination in the Redpath Lyceum Circular of 1876–1877, reproduced in Southern, *African American Theater*, xli.

52. "Notice to Managers," by James H. Slavin, *New York Clipper*, 16 Mar. 1878. Luca: *Folio*, July 1878: 253. Taylor: Trotter, *Music and Some Highly Musical People*, 170.

53. Post-Slavin performances: Georgias in Anderson's *UTC*, cited in Odell, *Annals*,

11: 647; "Pavilion Sunday Concert," *Brooklyn Eagle*, 11 Jul. 1886; "Amusements," *Brooklyn Eagle*, 15 Feb. 1889; "At Prohibition Park," *New York Times*, 4 Jul. 1892; "Young Men's Christian Association," 14 Dec. 1901.

54. Playbill, Eagle Theatre, [16 Feb. 1876], University of California, Davis, special collections, U.S. playbills.

55. The 1876 performance took place on 9 October at the Opera-house in Washington, DC; "Dramatic," *New York Clipper*, 21 Oct. 1876: 238. See also "Home Notes" [Criterion Theatre], *Chicago Daily Tribune*, 20 Nov. 1881; "Lee Avenue Academy," *Brooklyn Eagle*, 17 Dec. 1893.

56. "General Mention," *New York Times*, 25 Sept. 1879; ad for Hooley's Theatre, *Chicago Tribune*, 22 Apr. 1883. An 1896 revival in Washington, DC, had forty jubilee singers, and a 1912 production had jubilee singers, buck and wing dancers, and pickaninnies; ad, *Washington Post*, 1 Nov. 1896 and 20 Feb. 1912. See also Bordman, *Oxford Companion*, 122, 712.

57. For biographical data see "Stevens, John A.," in Albert Ellery Berg, *The Drama, Painting, Poetry, and Song: Embracing a Complete History of the Stage* (New York: Collier, 1884), 322.

58. "The Passing Show," *Weekly Music and Drama* (New York), 27 Jan. 1883: 5.

59. "Plays and Actors," *New York Times*, 25 Mar. 1883; "Grand Opera House," *Brooklyn Eagle*, 8 Apr. and 10 Apr. 1883; "'Passion's Slave' at the Howard," *Boston Daily Globe*, 28 Dec. 1884.

60. "Standard Museum," *Brooklyn Eagle*, 2 Oct. 1888.

61. She had a wildly successful twenty-year career, leaving an estate worth $4 million upon her death. Biographical data are compiled from "Gossip about Lotta," *Boston Daily Globe*, 13 June 1880; Rice, *Monarchs of Minstrelsy*, 170; Francis Wilson, *Francis Wilson's Life of Himself* (Boston: Houghton Mifflin, 1924); Odell, *Annals* (see esp. index for vols. 9, 10); "Lotta Crabtree Is Dead," *Los Angeles Times*, 26 Sept. 1924.

62. Ad, Lotta, Park Theatre, *New York Times*, 26 Dec. 1876.

63. Southern, *African American Theater*, xiv–xv. See chap. 4 for more on the Hyers sisters as well as the lyceum movement.

64. Southern, *African American Theater*, xvi. The quote comes from the *Muscatine (IA) Journal*, 22 May 1877, quoted in the Redpath Lyceum Circular for the 1877–1878 season, reproduced in Southern (xlii).

65. "Out of Bondage," *Boston Daily Globe*, 21 Aug. 1877. Z. A. Coleman later sang bass with the Stewart-Wilberforce Concert Company in 1881, a jubilee group representing Wilberforce University, Xenia, Ohio (see web table 4.4, Biographical Dictionary of Jubilee Concert Troupes).

66. Bradford's script is in the Library of Congress; a facsimile appears in Southern, *African American Theater*.

67. *Muscatine (IA) Journal*, 22 May 1877, quoted in the Redpath Lyceum Circular for the 1877–1878 season, in Southern, *African American Theater*, xlii.

68. D. Brooks, *Bodies in Dissent*, 285. Hopkins was born in Portland, Maine, but moved as an infant to Boston. For her later biography see Southern, *African American Theater*, xxiii, which corrects factual errors in earlier sources, and Ira Dworkin, "Biography of

Pauline E. Hopkins," Pauline Elizabeth Hopkins Society, http://www.paulinehopkins society.org/biography/.

69. The only copy known to exist is the original in four acts, which is housed in Hopkins's papers at FULSC; a facsimile is reproduced in Southern, *African American Theater*. Page numbers refer to the facsimile edition. The play was also reprinted in Hamalian and Hatch, *Roots of African American Drama*, without the interpolations in the second hand.

70. The score is in Seward, *Jubilee Songs*, 1872a.

71. *New York Clipper*, 19 June 1880: 99.

72. "Dramatic," *New York Clipper*, 3 July 1880: 118.

73. "Dramatic," *New York Clipper*, 17 July 1880: 134.

74. D. Brooks, *Bodies in Dissent*, 288–89; *New York Clipper*, 17 July 1880: 134.

75. "Sam Lucas' Theatrical Career Written by Himself in 1909," *New York Age*, 13 June 1916: 6.

76. Patterson, "Remaking the Minstrel," 13, 14. Hopkins wasn't the first to do this; black minstrels had already established a similarly subversive performance strategy.

77. "Local Intelligence," *Vermont Phoenix* (Brattleboro, VT), 2 April 1880: 2.

78. "They Stand at the Head," ad, *New York Clipper*, 10 Jan. 1880: 335.

79. "The Hyer Sisters at the Gaiety," *Boston Daily Globe*, 7 Mar. 1880.

80. "Sacred Concert by the Hyers Sisters," *Boston Daily Globe*, 14 Mar. 1880.

81. "Local Intelligence," *Vermont Phoenix* (Brattleboro, VT), 9 Apr. 1880: 2.

82. "Oakland Garden and Its Attractions," *Boston Daily Globe*, 13 July 1879.

83. On Haverly see Rice, *Monarchs of Minstrelsy*, 120; Toll, *Blacking Up*, 145–51. The "double Uncle Tom" shows were part of this trend in the realm of theater.

84. "Theatrical Notes," *New York Times*, 20 Jun. 1880; ad, *Boston Daily Globe*, 21 June 1880.

85. "A Strong Attraction at the Oakland," *Boston Daily Globe*, 20 June 1880; playbill, Haverly's Gigantic Colored Minstrel Carnival, 5 July [1880], Niblo's Garden Theatre, New York; and program, Haverly's Genuine Colored Minstrels [22 Aug. 1880], Oakland Garden, HTC, minstrel playbills. Haverly took his carnival directly to New York after Boston and gave the same show there.

86. "A Strong Attraction at the Oakland," *Boston Daily Globe*, 20 June 1880.

87. "Dramatic," *New York Clipper*, 3 July 1880: 118.

88. Southern, *African American Theater*, xxv; "Musical Pabulum," *Boston Daily Globe*, 22 Aug. 1880.

89. Ad, Forest Garden, *Boston Daily Globe*, 22 Aug. 1880.

90. "Oakland Garden," *Boston Post*, 31 July 1888.

91. Toll, *Blacking Up*, 206.

92. Ibid.

93. Abbott and Seroff, *Out of Sight*, 362. The most accurate and detailed accounts of these shows are Abbott and Seroff, *Out of Sight*, 360–68 (and elsewhere); and T. Brooks, *Lost Sounds*, 92–102 (in relation to the Standard Quartette). For more on McClain see Cullen, Hackman, and McNeilly, *Vaudeville*, 738; and Bill Reed, *Hot from Harlem: Twelve African American Entertainers, 1890–1960* (Jefferson, NC: McFarland, 2009), 43–51.

94. "Billy McClain," in Cullen et al., *Vaudeville*, 738.

95. "Colored Folks at the Bijou," *New York Times*, 20 Nov. 1894.

96. "World Players," *New York Clipper*, 14 May 1892: 148.

97. 21 Jan. 1893, quoted in Abbott and Seroff, *Out of Sight*, 363.

98. "Variety and Minstrelsy," *New York Clipper*, 4 Mar. 1893: 835; Peterson, *Century of Musicals*, 327.

99. T. Brooks, *Lost Sounds*, 96.

100. See ibid., 92–102; and *Earliest Negro Vocal Quartets 1894–1928*.

101. Hill and Hatch, *A History of African American Theatre*, 143.

102. For descriptions see ibid.; Riis, *Just before Jazz*; Peterson, *Century of Musicals*, 34; Abbott and Seroff, *Out of Sight*, 391–95.

103. Advance program, *Black America*, Huntingdon Avenue Grounds, 1895, HTC, minstrel playbills; boldface in the original.

104. "Stand on the Walls of Zion" doesn't appear in contemporaneous print sources, but the lyrics to "Goin' to Stan' on the Walls of Zion" appear in a collection of spirituals from the Deep South by A. E. Perkins, who was a black school principal in New Orleans and collected folklore from his students; Perkins, "Negro Spirituals," 239. The first stanza is: "Goin' stand on the walls of Zion / An' view that ship come sailin', / Goin' stand on the walls of Zion, / To see it give erway."

105. *Washington Post*, 27 Oct. 1895: 19, quoted in Hill and Hatch, *A History of African American Theatre*, 144.

106. Hill and Hatch, *A History of African American Theatre*, 145. The program they cite was dated February 1897.

107. "Dramatic," *New York Clipper*, 25 May 1878: 70.

108. Gossett, *Uncle Tom's Cabin and American Culture*, 260.

109. Dennett, *Weird and Wonderful*, 6.

110. "New Advertisements," *Ottawa (IL) Free Trader*, 12 May 1877: 5.

111. Dennett, *Weird and Wonderful*, 6.

112. Prince, *Stories of the South*, 181.

113. "Sweet Singers Wanted," *New York Times*, 10 Feb. 1878.

CHAPTER 8. Blurring Boundaries between Traditional and Commercial

1. White got permission to use the Fisk University name for the independent singers, even though the university (and the American Missionary Association) no longer officially sponsored them.

2. *Daily American* (Lawrence, MA), 22 Oct. 1879, George L. White Scrapbook, 1879–81, FULSC, cited by Prince, *Stories of the South*, 272n37.

3. "Red Wing and Vicinity," *Grange Advance* (Red Wing, MN), 19 Aug. 1874; "North Carolinians," *Ottawa (IL) Free Trader*, 4 Sept. 1875.

4. Odell, *Annals*, 10: 96.

5. *New York Clipper*, 29 April 1876: 40.

6. The dates for Friday and Saturday, 20 and 21 Oct., identify the year as 1876, which

also accords with W. E. Gillespie's proprietorship. The performance is for the Music Hall in Chester (no state given) and is reprinted without attribution in Langston Hughes and Milton Meltzer, *Black Magic: A Pictorial History of the Negro in American Entertainment* (Englewood Cliffs, NJ: Prentice-Hall, 1967), 128.

7. "Foreign Show News: Musical," *New York Clipper*, 2 Dec. 1876: 287.

8. Robinson to James D. Burrus, 22 Dec. 1876, Carlisle, England, America Robinson Letters, FULSC.

9. Robinson to Burrus, 3 June 1877, Northampton, England, America Robinson Letters, FULSC; *Guardian*, London, 25 July 1877: 6.

10. George L. White, unidentified clipping, May 1877, Jubilee Singers Scrapbooks, FULSC, cited in Ward, *Dark Midnight*, 335; *Wilmington (NC) Morning Star*, 18 Aug. 1878: 1.

11. "Negro Minstrelsy," *New York Clipper*, 1 Jan. 1881: 323; playbill for Christy Minstrels at Horticultural Hall, Boston, HTC, minstrel playbills.

12. "Plymouth Church—The Jubilee Concert," *Brooklyn Eagle*, 1 May 1875.

13. "At the Other Theatres," *Boston Daily Globe*, 25 Jan. 1876.

14. "The Lyric Stage," *Boston Daily Globe*, 24 Jan. 1876. Spirituals in the Hyers repertory at this time included "Inching Along," "Swing Low," "Danville Chariot," "Gwine Up," and "Keep Me from Sinking Down"; "Sunday Evening Concerts," *Boston Daily Globe*, 15 and 17 Jan. 1876.

15. "Haverly's Colored Minstrels at the Howard," *Boston Daily Globe*, 30 Jan. 1881.

16. "Haverly's Minstrels," *Boston Daily Globe*, 29 Jan. 1876; playbill, Haverly's Minstrels at Beethoven Hall [28 Jan. 1876], HTC, minstrel playbills; playbill, Second Grand Concert at the Howard Atheneum, 30 Jan. [1876], HTC, minstrel playbills.

17. Ad for Haverly's Genuine Colored Minstrels at the Howard Athenaeum, *Boston Daily Globe*, 30 Jan. 1881.

18. "Negro Minstrelsy," *New York Clipper*, 25 Dec. 1880: 315. The members of the company paid for the funeral.

19. Playbill, Windsor Theatre, Sunday evening, 18 Feb. [1883], Shepard's Colored Troubadours and Guitarists, HTC, minstrel playbills.

20. Rice, *Monarchs of Minstrelsy*, 283.

21. *Plantation Songs and Jubilee Hymns*, 35–37. This comes from verse 3.

22. Lucas's troupe may have occasionally performed commercial spirituals by white composers as well: for example, the prolific George Russell Jackson dedicated his commercial spiritual "Oh! When I War Dem Gospel Garments" (1880, music by Herbert Leslie) to Lucas. The two had collaborated on Lucas's song "Grandfather's Old Arm Chair" (1877), for which Russell had written the lyrics.

23. "Musical Pabulum," *Boston Daily Globe*, 14 Mar. 1880.

24. "Sunday Evening Concerts," *Boston Daily Globe*, 15 Jan. 1876.

25. "Little Corinne at Oakland," *Boston Globe*, 27 June 1880; "Stage and Concert Hall" and ad for *Magic Slipper*, *Boston Globe*, 1 April 1880, 5 April, respectively. According to a newspaper article Corinne was born 25 Dec. 1871; upon her parents' deaths she was given to the custody of Mrs. Jennie Flaherty, a comic opera singer who had performed

under the name Jennie Kimball but who now managed Corinne and appeared in her troupe; "Little Corinne in Trouble," *New York Times*, 30 Nov. 1881. Corinne made her debut in her hometown of Boston at the age of five, playing Buttercup in Gilbert and Sullivan's *H.M.S. Pinafore*; "Little Corinne," *Boston Globe*, 14 Dec. 1879.

26. Program for July 1880, HTC, American vaudeville. The Olympia act was originated by Boston native Keogh around 1876. See also ad in *Boston Globe*, 12 Aug. 1883. O'Hara was replaced by William J. Sullivan by 1883. Three years later the Olympia Quartette sang their jubilee hymns with Little Corinne's troupe at the Oakland Garden, on the same day that Sam Lucas performed with his jubilee troupe at the Park Square Garden.

27. Notices and ads for the 5 Dec. concert appear in the *Boston Globe* on 21 and 28 Nov., and 5 Dec. 1880. Programs didn't reveal titles or quartet members.

28. Ads, *Boston Globe*, 28 June, 10 July, 28 Aug. 1881; notices on 10, 17 July 1881.

29. "The Oakland Garden Concerts," *Boston Globe*, 6 June 1881.

30. Ads, *Boston Globe*, 11 Sept. and 6 Nov. 1881; "Musical Matters," 11 Sept. 1881.

31. *The New York Mirror* is a good source for tracking Lucas's Ideals and the Hyers.

32. "Sam Lucas: A Chapter from the Life of the Celebrated Comedian and Vocalist," *Omaha (NE) Daily Bee*, 16 Feb. 1882.

33. See Graham, annotated index, for more on these songs.

34. Traditional lyrics are taken from Armstrong and Ludlow, *Hampton and Its Students*, 198. Graham, Songs of Sam Lucas, has a modern recording of Lucas's song.

35. "Talk about Your Moses" (Boston: White, Smith, 1880), LC, https://www.loc.gov/item/sm1880.14946/. Graham, Songs of Sam Lucas, has a modern recording.

36. Abbott and Seroff say they organized in 1878 but offer no proof (*Out of Sight*, 170). Furthermore, the Nashville Students' songster was published in 1884—if they had been around for six years it seems likely they would have published a songster much earlier than this (Sawyer, *Jubilee Songs and Plantation Melodies*). The back cover states that during the past season (1883–1884) the troupe traveled the country from Maine to California—there are no claims to having been in existence for several years.

37. "Baptist State Convention," *Detroit Free Press*, 23 Oct. 1878.

38. For example, "The Jubilee Singers," *Montana Standard* (Butte, MT), 29 July 1882, claims that the Original Tennessee Jubilee and Plantation Singers "founded the Knoxville College in Tennessee twelve years ago."

39. Program, Original Nashville Students, Season 1885–1886, NYPL, Lincoln Center, minstrels U.S., scrapbook.

40. All three compositions are in the Library of Congress: Lucas, "Every Day'l Be Sunday By and By" (Boston: White, Smith, 1881), https://www.loc.gov/item/sm1881.14723/, and "O, I'll Meet You Dar" (Boston: White, Smith, 1880), https://www.loc.gov/item/sm1880.17549/; Sawyer, "Listen to Dem Ding, Dong Bells" (Cleveland: Brainard's Sons, 1885), https://www.loc.gov/item/sm1885.04773/. See Graham, Songs of Sam Lucas, for a recording of "Every Day'll Be Sunday By and By."

41. "Jubilee Singers: Old Plantation Songs at the First Congregational Church," *Los Angeles Times*, 15 Dec. 1887. Their skit concerned a southern barbershop ("Alhambra," signed by Yusuf, *Los Angeles Times*, 14 Jan. 1888).

42. Although the songster, which was printed in Hamilton, Ontario, isn't dated, it probably was published ca. 1892, since the title page refers to "five years' tour of Great Britain" and "three years' tour of United States."

43. Although "Swing Dose Gates Ajar" was labeled a "spiritual" when it was collected by the Federal Writers' Project, the lyrics reveal it to be a commercial spiritual. Verse 2 reads: "White folks dey brags, but in days way back / Old Eve and Adam both were black, / But they disobeyed the law and they felt its might, / And it scared 'em so bad that they both turned white" (WPA Federal Writers' Project Papers, 1936, University of South Carolina Library, Columbia, SC, http://digital.tcl.sc.edu/cdm/fullbrowser/collection/wpafwp/id/2901/rv/compoundobject/cpd/2903). A minstrel version of "Swing Dose Gates Ajar" with varied lyrics appeared in the travel periodical *The Gripsack* (St. John, New Brunswick), March 1889: 31.

44. *Earliest Negro Vocal Groups*, vol. 2, originally recorded on an unnumbered cylinder for Columbia.

45. Brooks, *Lost Sounds*, 92–102, has an excellent profile of the Standards and their recordings; see also Abbott and Seroff, *Out of Sight*, 368–69.

46. Brooks mentions the Zonophone Quartette in *Lost Sounds*, 99, 540n16; he claims it was a "coon song" but gives no reason for this conclusion. "Sunday" appears on pp. 21–22 of the Wehman songster, HTC, songsters, also available at https://archive.org/details/goodoldtimesongoopublgoog.

47. Sam Lucas, "De Gospel Cars" (Boston: G. D. Russell, 1880), LC, https://www.loc.gov/item/sm1880.13847/; *Harrigan and Hart's "Mullgian Guard's Surprise"* (New York: Popular Publishing Co., n.d. [ca. 1880]), 18, HTC, songsters. The parody also appears in *Cool Burgess' "In the Morning by the Bright Light"* (New York: Popular Publishing, n.d. [1880 or later]), 12, HTC, songsters; *Olympia Quartette Songster* (New York: Popular Publishing, n.d. [ca. 1881]), 14, LC, Music Division, Dumont Collection; and *J. H. Haverly's New Mastodon Minstrel Songster* (New York: Popular Publishing, n.d. [1883]), 13, HTC, songsters.

48. *Goss and Fox's "Huckleberry Picnic" Songster* (New York: Popular Publishing, n.d. [ca. 1879]), 12, HTC, songsters. In addition to "Oh, I'll Meet You Dar" Goss and Fox incorporated a parody of another Lucas spiritual, "Down by the Sunrise," in their "Medley of Hymns," found in *Harrigan and Hart's "Mulligan Guard Chowder" Songster* (New York: New York Popular Publishing, 1879, 30, HTC, songsters. Graham, annotated index, has more on these songs.

49. Lucas, "De Coon Dat Had de Razor" (Boston: White, Smith, 1885), LC, https://www.loc.gov/item/sm1885.19033/.

50. This list is compiled from sheet music, songsters, and programs. For more on these composers and their compositions, see Graham, annotated index. Many other minstrel performers likely wrote songs, which were either never published or didn't survive.

51. NYPL, Lincoln Center, minstrels U.S., scrapbook. The troupe was managed by James O. Crosswhite of Boston, and consisted of J. H. Jordan (musical director), Mrs. Annie Saunders (soprano), Mrs. F.V.E. Jones and Miss May E. Smith (altos), Albert S. Johnson (tenor), and Albert Saunders (bass and character artist).

52. *Twenty-Two Years' Work*, 78. Ike Simond recalls first seeing the Hyers, with Sawyer on piano, in 1877, in Pittsburgh (*Old Slack's Reminiscence*, 6). His work with the Virginia, Lucas, and Maryland jubilee singers can be traced in the *Boston Globe* throughout 1882: e.g., 30 Jan., 23 July, 8 Oct. He was musical director of Haverly's Colored Minstrels in 1881 (see cover of "The Coonville Guards"), pianist for Lucas's Slayton Ideal company in 1883 (see cover to "My Lord Is Writin' Down Time"), and musical director of the Nashville Students in 1884 (see cover to "Hear Dem Ebening Bells"). See also Nico Schüler, "Sawyer, Jacob J.," Oxford Music Online (Oxford University Press), http://www .oxfordmusiconline.com/subscriber/article/grove/music/A2267610.

53. For a works list of his commercial spirituals see Graham, annotated index.

54. "Ring Dem Chimin' Bells" (Chicago: National Music, 1883), LC, https://www.loc .gov/item/sm1883.10664/; "Yes, I'll Be Dar" (Chicago: National Music, 1883), LC, https:// www.loc.gov/item/sm1883.10665/.

55. "Ole' Nicker Demus" (Boston: J. M. Russell, 1881), LC, http://hdl.loc.gov/loc .music/sm1881.13935; "All de Darkies Gittin' Up" (Boston: White, Smith, 1877), LC, http:// hdl.loc.gov/loc.award/rpbaasm.0547.

56. For a full account of this see Ward, *Dark Midnight*, 381–82.

CONCLUSION. Lessons and Legacies

1. Watkins, *On the Real Side*, 114.

2. Austin, "*Susanna*," 282.

3. Hartman, *Scenes of Subjection*, 19. Hartman's analysis revolves around a white man named John Rankin, who in a letter to his brother attempted to express the horrors of slavery by putting himself in the place of a slave being whipped and imagining it in excruciating detail.

4. Ibid., 22. Although Hartman is discussing the beaten black slave body and the auction block as entertainment, her observation also applies to how the spiritual functioned in postwar entertainment.

5. Rydell uses the term "ideological repair" to describe the "ethnological" exhibits of Africans at the 1893 Chicago World's Columbian Exposition ("'Darkest Africa,'" 135).

6. "Black Musicians from Slavery to Freedom," 15. Although the frolic can be seen as a sacred counterpart to religious worship, Cimbala argues that the two were complementary rather than oppositional, equally important in creating community.

7. Ashby discusses how the banjo assumed new social meanings beyond minstrelsy at that time (*With Amusement for All*, 90–92).

8. Graham, "Reframing Negro Spirituals," 625–26.

9. Abbott and Seroff, *Out of Sight*, 172, reprints a notice about Wright from the *Indianapolis Freeman* of 22 Aug. 1891.

10. Simond, *Old Slack's Reminiscence*, 13. Charles, Gustave, and Daniel Frohman were among the foremost theatrical managers of the time, with connections to Callender's Colored Minstrels, Haverly's Mastodon Minstrels (white), and Callender's Consolidated Spectacular Colored Minstrels.

11. Loudin's supplement in Marsh, *Story of the Jubilee Singers* (1892), 131–32.

12. "New Broadway Theatre," *New York Times*, 16 Jan. 1877; "Academy of Music," *Brooklyn Eagle*, 18 Feb. 1877; ad, *Brooklyn Eagle*, 17 Feb. 1877.

13. Ad, "Amusements," *New York Times*, 10 Feb. 1878; the group performed the week of 11 Feb.

14. See Sonya R. Gable-Wilson, "Let Freedom Sing! Four African-American Concert Singers in Nineteenth-Century America" (PhD diss., University of Florida, 2005); and J. Wright, "Black Women in Classical Music in Boston."

15. See Graham, "On the Road to Freedom."

16. Unsigned biographical sketch, *Sam Lucas' Plantation Songster*; "Long Sam Lucas: Artist of Negro Minstrelsy," *New York Sun*, 22 Oct. 1911.

17. Toll, *Blacking Up*, 223.

18. Rice, *Monarchs of Minstrelsy*, 222.

19. "Loudin's Singers," *Cleveland Gazette*, 19 Nov. 1904: 1–2.

20. See Graham, "Reframing Negro Spirituals."

21. Sotiropoulos, *Staging Race*, 258. Her book can function as a sequel to this one.

22. Abbott and Seroff, *Ragged but Right*, gives an excellent overview of these developments.

23. For more background on these trends, see Cornel West and Eddie S. Glaude Jr., eds., *African American Religious Thought: An Anthology* (Louisville, KY: Westminster John Knox Press, 2003), especially Elsa Barkley Brown, "Negotiating and Transforming the Public Sphere: African American Political Life in the Transition from Slavery to Freedom," 435–74.

24. Payne, *Recollections of Seventy Years* (Nashville: AME Sunday School Union, 1888), 253–54, http://docsouth.unc.edu/church/payne70/payne.html#p149.

25. "Afro-American Camp Meeting," *Afro-American Advance* (Minneapolis), 8 July 1899.

26. "Points of View," *Brooklyn Eagle*, 15 April 1900, is a helpful retrospective of changes in the preceding twenty-five years; black newspapers are full of articles and advertisements that reflect these changes in African American churches. In his preface to Coleridge-Taylor's *Twenty-Four Negro Melodies*, Booker T. Washington notes that spirituals in large city churches "are being used but little" (ix).

27. *Topeka (KS) Weekly Call*, 1 Nov. 1891; cited in Abbott and Seroff, *Out of Sight*, 196.

28. *New Haven Palladium*, quoted in Seward, *Jubilee Songs* (1872a). The irony was that, at this time, African Americans never gave "vent to their pent up feelings" by singing an arranged concert spiritual.

29. Bacon's letter was originally printed as an undated pamphlet; the text was also published in *Southern Workman* (Dec. 1893): 180–81. A slightly edited version appeared as "Dear Friends," *Journal of American Folklore* 6, no. 23 (1893): 305–9.

30. The formal study of folklore was just beginning in the United States. The American Folk-Lore Society was organized in Cambridge, MA, in 1888. Closely intertwined with the development of American anthropology, the discipline was slow to turn its attention to African American culture—not for lack of interest, but because the violent social climate of Jim Crow made federal funding politically sensitive.

31. Hurston, "Spirituals and Neo-spirituals," 223.

32. "Old Plantation Hymns," "Hymns of the Slave and the Freedman," and "Recent Negro Melodies" were published in the Sept.–Nov. 1899 issues of *New England Magazine* and later that year in book form (Barton, *Old Plantation Hymns*).

33. See chap. 4 and Murphy, *Southern Thoughts for Northern Thinkers*.

34. Jean Snyder, "Harry T. Burleigh and the Creative Expression of Bi-Musicality: A Study of an African-American Composer and the American Art Song" (PhD diss., University of Pittsburgh, 1992), 293–97; Brian Moon, "The Inimitable Miss Cheatham," Society for American Music, *Bulletin* 32, no. 2 (2006): 25–27; A. W. Kramer, "Kitty Cheatham Urges Fisk University Students to Preserve Old Spiritual," *Musical America*, 30 May 1914: 9.

35. J. W. Work, *Folk Song*, 97–98.

36. Abromeit's *Spirituals: A Multidisciplinary Bibliography for Research and Performance* is a comprehensive guide to researchers.

37. In offering standardized programs to rural towns and large cities alike, "chautauqua gradually broke down the barrier between agrarian and urban attitudes, beliefs, and values, thereby fostering a melting pot ideology for the country," according to historian John Tapia, *Circuit Chautauqua*, 47.

38. *Salvation Soldier's Song Book* (New York: Army Headquarters, 1880), HTC. Bland's original song was published by John F. Perry, Boston, LC, https://www.loc.gov/item/sm1879.01966/.

39. See Fisk Jubilee Singers, "Our History," http://www.fiskjubileesingers.org/about.html, accessed 7 July 2017.

40. Listen, for example, to the Plantation Singers' rendition of "Wade in the Water," which streams on their website: http://www.plantationsingers.com. Reagon, *Wade in the Water*, has excellent recordings featuring both concert and folk styles.

Bibliography

Archives and Abbreviations

AMA	American Missionary Association Archives, Amistad Research Center, Tulane (microfilm at Schomburg Center for Research in Black Culture, New York City)
CPM	Center for Popular Music, Middle Tennessee State University, Murfreesboro, TN
[no abbreviation]	City Museum of New York, New York City
FULSC	Fisk University Library, Special Collections, Nashville, TN
[no abbreviation]	Hampton University Archives, Hampton, VA
HTC	Harvard Theatre Collection, Boston, MA
LC	Library of Congress, Washington, DC
NYPL	New York Public Library for the Arts

Secondary Sources

Abbott, Lynn. "'Do Thyself a' No Harm': The Jubilee Singing Phenomenon and the 'Only Original New Orleans University Singers.'" *American Music Research Center Journal* 6 (1996): 5–47.

Abbott, Lynn, and Doug Seroff. *Out of Sight: The Rise of African American Popular Music 1889–1895*. Jackson: University Press of Mississippi, 2002.

———. *Ragged but Right: Black Traveling Shows, "Coon Songs," and the Dark Pathway to Blues and Jazz*. Jackson: University Press of Mississippi, 2007.

Abrahams, Roger D. *Singing the Master: The Emergence of African-American Culture in the Plantation South*. New York: Penguin Books, 1992.

Abromeit, Kathleen A. *Spirituals: A Multidisciplinary Bibliography for Research and Performance*. Middleton, WI: A-R Editions, 2015.

Allen, William Francis, Charles Pickard Ware, and Lucy McKim Garrison, eds. *Slave Songs of the United States*. 1867. Reprint, New York: Dover, 1995.

American Missionary Association. *The Twenty-Seventh Annual Report of the American Missionary Association and the Proceedings of the Annual Meeting Held at Newark, N.J., Nov. 5th and 6th, 1873*. New York: AMA, 1873.

American Tract Society. *Happy Voices: New Hymns and Tunes.* New York, 1865.

Anderson, Toni Passmore. *"Tell Them We're Singing for Jesus": The Original Fisk Jubilee Singers and Christian Reconstruction, 1871–1878.* Macon, GA: Mercer Press, 2010.

Armstrong, Mary Francis, and Helen L. Ludlow. *Hampton and Its Students.* With fifty cabin and plantation songs, arranged by Thomas P. Fenner. New York: G. P. Putnam's Sons, 1874.

Aron, Cindy Sondik. *Working at Play: A History of Vacations in the United States.* New York: Oxford University Press, 1999.

Ashby, LeRoy. *With Amusement for All: A History of American Popular Culture since 1830.* Lexington: University Press of Kentucky, 2006.

Austin, William. *"Susanna," "Jeanie," and "The Old Folks at Home": The Songs of Stephen C. Foster from His Time to Ours.* 2nd ed. Urbana: University of Illinois Press, 1987.

Bacon, Alice Mabel. "Dear Friends." *Journal of American Folk-Lore* 6, no. 23 (1893): 305–9.

———. "Work and Methods of the Hampton Folk-Lore Society." *Journal of American Folk-Lore* 11, no. 40 (1897): 17–21.

Barber, Karin. "Interpreting Oriki as History and Literature." In *Discourse and Its Disguises: The Interpretation of African Oral Texts,* edited by Karin Barber and P. F. de Moraes Farias, 16–18. Birmingham, UK: University of Birmingham, Center of West African Studies, 1989.

Barton, William E. *Old Plantation Hymns.* With historical and descriptive notes. Boston: Lamson, Wolffe, 1899.

Benson, Louis F. *The English Hymn: Its Development and Use in Worship.* New York: Hodder and Stoughton, 1915.

Birdoff, Harry. *The World's Greatest Hit.* New York: S. F. Vanni, 1947.

Bontemps, Arna. *Chariot in the Sky.* New York: Holt, Rinehart, and Winston, 1951.

Boots, Cheryl C. *Singing for Equality: Hymns in the American Antislavery and Indian Rights Movements, 1640–1855.* Jefferson, NC: McFarland, 2013.

Bordman, Gerald. *Oxford Companion to American Theatre.* New York: Oxford University Press, 1984.

Bradbury, William, comp. *Bradbury's Anthem Book.* New York: Mason Bros., 1860.

———. *Fresh Laurels for the Sabbath School.* New York: Biglow and Main, 1867.

Braithwaite, J. Roland. "Originality in the Hymnals of Richard Allen." In *New Perspectives on Music: Essays in Honor of Eileen Southern,* edited by Josephine Wright and Samuel A. Floyd, 71–99. Warren, MI: Harmonie Park Press, 1992.

Brink, Carol. *Harps in the Wind: The Story of the Singing Hutchinsons.* 1947. Reprint, New York: Da Capo, 1980.

Brooks, Daphne A. *Bodies in Dissent: Spectacular Performances of Race and Freedom, 1850–1910.* Durham, NC: Duke University Press, 2006.

Brooks, Tim. *Lost Sounds: Blacks and the Birth of the Recording Industry, 1890–1919.* Urbana: University of Illinois Press, 2004.

Brown, Col. T. Allston. "Early History of Negro Minstrelsy." In multiple installments: *New York Clipper,* 17 Feb.–13 Dec. 1912 (almost weekly); 11 Jan.–20 Dec. 1913 (occasionally); 14 Feb.–28 Mar. 1914. Reprinted in *Burnt Cork and Tambourines,* edited by William L. Slout. Circus Historical Society, 2005. http://www.circushistory.org/Cork/BurntCork1.htm.

Browne, Harry C. *Early Minstrel Songs Recorded 1916–1923*. British Archive of Country Music CD D 076.

Buckner, Jocelyn L. "'Spectacular Opacities': The Hyers Sisters' Performances of Respectability and Resistance." *African American Review* 45, no. 3 (2012): 309–23.

Charters, Samuel. *Lucy McKim Garrison and "Slave Songs of the United States."* Jackson: University Press of Mississippi, 2015.

Church Choirs, Vocal Groups and Preachers. Vol. 3: 1923–1931. Vienna: Document Records DOCD-5605.

Cimbala, Paul A. "Black Musicians from Slavery to Freedom: An Exploration of an African-American Folk Elite and Cultural Continuity in the Nineteenth-Century Rural South." *Journal of Negro History* 80, no. 1 (1995): 15–29.

Cockrell, Dale. *Demons of Disorder: Early Blackface Minstrels and Their World.* New York: Cambridge University Press, 1997.

———, ed. *Excelsior: Journals of the Hutchinson Family Singers, 1842–1846.* Sociology of Music Series 5. Stuyvesant, NY: Pendragon Press, 1989.

Cole, Maggie Porter. "The Jubilee Singers on the Ocean and in Europe." *Fisk University News* 2, no. 5 (1911): 33–35.

Coleridge-Taylor, Samuel. *Twenty-Four Negro Melodies.* New York: Ditson, 1905.

Cruz, Jon. *Culture on the Margins: The Black Spiritual and the Rise of American Cultural Interpretation.* Princeton: Princeton University Press, 1999.

Cullen, Frank, with Florence Hackman and Donald McNeilly. *Vaudeville Old and New: An Encyclopedia of Variety Performers in America.* Vol. 1. New York: Routledge, 2006.

Darden, Robert. *People Get Ready! A New History of Black Gospel Music.* New York: Continuum, 2004.

DeBoer, Clara Merritt. *His Truth Is Marching On: African Americans Who Taught the Freedmen for the American Missionary Association, 1861–1877.* New York: Garland, 1995.

Dennett, Andrea Stulman. *Weird and Wonderful: The Dime Museum in America.* New York: New York University Press, 1997.

Dennison, Sam. *Scandalize My Name: Black Imagery in American Popular Music.* New York: Garland, 1982.

Dett, Nathaniel, ed. *Religious Folk-Songs of the Negro, as Sung at Hampton Institute.* Hampton: Hampton Institute Press, 1927.

Douglass, Frederick. *Life and Times of Frederick Douglass, Written by Himself.* His early life as a slave, his escape from bondage, and his complete history to the present time, including his connection with the anti-slavery movement. Hartford, CT: Park Publishing, 1882.

Du Bois, W. E. B. *The Souls of Black Folk.* 1903. Reprint, New York: Penguin, 1989.

Dunson, Stephanie. "Black Misrepresentation in Nineteenth-Century Sheet Music Illustration." In *Beyond Blackface: African Americans and the Creation of American Popular Culture, 1890–1930,* edited by W. Fitzhugh Brundage, 45–65. Chapel Hill: University of North Carolina Press, 2011.

Earliest Negro Vocal Groups. Vol. 2: 1893–1922. Vienna: Document Records DOCD-5288.

Earliest Negro Vocal Groups. Vol. 4: 1921–1924. Vienna: Document Records DOCD-5531.

Earliest Negro Vocal Quartets 1894–1928. Vienna: Document Records DOCD-5288.

Engs, Robert Francis. *Freedom's First Generation: Black Hampton, Virginia, 1861–1890.* New ed. New York: Fordham University Press, 2004.

Epstein, Dena J. "Black Spirituals: Their Emergence into Public Knowledge." *Black Music Research Journal* 10 (Spring 1990): 58–64.

———. *Sinful Tunes and Spirituals: Black Folk Music to the Civil War.* 1977. Reprint, with new preface, Urbana: University of Illinois Press, 2003.

———. "The Story of the Jubilee Singers: An Introduction to Its Bibliographic History." In *New Perspectives on Music: Essays in Honor of Eileen Southern*, edited by Josephine Wright and Samuel A. Floyd, 151–62. Warren, MI: Harmonie Park Press, 1992.

———. "Theodore F. Seward and the Fisk Jubilee Singers." In *A Celebration of American Music: Words and Music in Honor of H. Wiley Hitchcock*, edited by Richard Crawford, R. Allen Lott, and Carol J. Oja, 36–50. Ann Arbor: University of Michigan Press, 1990.

———. "A White Origin for the Black Spiritual? An Invalid Theory and How It Grew." *American Music* 1, no. 2 (1983): 53–59.

Fenner, Thomas P., arr. "Cabin and Plantation Songs as Sung by the Hampton Students." In Mary Francis Armstrong and Helen L. Ludlow, *Hampton and Its Students*, 171–256. New York: G. P. Putnam's Sons, 1874.

———, arr. *Cabin and Plantation Songs as Sung by the Hampton Students.* New York: G. P. Putnam's Sons, 1877.

———, arr. *Cabin and Plantation Songs as Sung by the Hampton Students.* New York: G. P. Putnam's Sons / Knickerbocker Press, 1889.

Fenner, Thomas P., and Frederic G. Rathbun, arr. *Cabin and Plantation Songs as Sung by the Hampton Students.* New York: G. P. Putnam's Sons, 1891.

———, arr. *Cabin and Plantation Songs as Sung by the Hampton Students.* Enlarged ed. New York: G. P. Putnam's Sons, 1893.

Fenner, Thomas P., Frederic G. Rathbun, and Bessie Cleaveland, arr. *Cabin and Plantation Songs as Sung by the Hampton Students.* 3rd ed. New York: G. P. Putnam's Sons, 1901.

Fisk Jubilee Singers, in Chronological Order. Vol. 1: 1909–1911. Vienna: Document Records DOCD-5533.

Fisk Jubilee Singers, in Chronological Order. Vol. 2: 1915–1920. Vienna: Document Records DOCD-5534.

Fletcher, Tom. *One Hundred Years of the Negro in Show Business.* New York: Burdge, 1954.

Floyd, Samuel A., Jr. *The Power of Black Music: Interpreting Its History from Africa to the United States.* New York: Oxford University Press, 1995.

Foner, Eric. *Reconstruction: America's Unfinished Revolution, 1863–1877.* New York: Harper and Row, 1988.

Fox, Herbert Jr. "The Jubilees! The Jubilees Forever!" *Nashville!* Jan. 1980, 35–36, 90.

Gac, Scott. *Singing for Freedom: The Hutchinson Family Singers and the Nineteenth-Century Culture of Reform.* New Haven: Yale University Press, 2007.

Garst, John F. "Mutual Reinforcement and the Origins of Spirituals." *American Music* 4, no. 4 (1986): 390–406.

Gossett, Thomas F. *Uncle Tom's Cabin and American Culture*. Dallas: Southern Methodist University Press, 1985.

Gottschild, Brenda Dixon. *Digging the Africanist Presence in American Performance*. Westport, CT: Greenwood Press, 1996.

Graham, Sandra Jean. Annotated Index of Commercial Spirituals. 2015. https://sites.google.com/site/grahamsandraj/home/commercial-spirituals.

———. "Composing in Black and White: Code-Switching in the Songs of Sam Lucas." In *The Oxford Handbook of Music Censorship*, edited by Patricia Hall, 559–92. New York: Oxford University Press, 2017.

———. "The Fisk Jubilee Singers and the Concert Spiritual: The Beginnings of an American Tradition." PhD diss., New York University, 2001.

———. "On the Road to Freedom: The Contracts of the Fisk Jubilee Singers." *American Music* 24, no. 1 (2006): 1–29.

———. "Reframing Negro Spirituals in the Late Nineteenth Century." In *Music, American Made: Essays in Honor of John Graziano*, edited by John Koegel, 603–27. Detroit Monographs in Musicology / Studies in Music, no. 58. Sterling Heights, MI: Harmonie Park Press, 2011.

———. Songs of Sam Lucas. Website with 12 modern recordings. Murfreesboro, TN: Center for Popular Music, 2013. http://popmusic.mtsu.edu/lucas/lucas.html.

Haley, James T. *Afro-American Encyclopaedia; or the Thoughts, Doings, and Sayings of the Race*. Nashville, TN: Haley and Florida, 1895. University of North Carolina Library, Documenting the American South, http://docsouth.unc.edu/church/haley/haley.html.

Hamalian, Leo, and James V. Hatch, eds. *The Roots of African American Drama: An Anthology of Early Plays, 1858–1938*. Detroit: Wayne State University Press, 1991.

Hamm, Charles. *Yesterdays: Popular Song in America*. New York: W. W. Norton, 1979.

Ham-Town Students Songster. Introduction by E. D. Gooding. De Witt's Song & Joke Book Series no. 212. New York, 1875. University of Pittsburgh Digital Library, http://digital.library.pitt.edu/cgi-bin/t/text/text-idx?idno=31735061820282;view=toc;c=ulstext.

Handy, W. C. *Father of the Blues: An Autobiography*. 1941. Reprint, New York: Da Capo Press, 1991.

Hankins, Barry. *The Second Great Awakening and the Transcendentalists*. Westport, CT: Greenwood Press, 2004.

Harlan, Louis R., ed. *Booker T. Washington Papers, 1860–89*. Vol. 2. Urbana: University of Illinois Press, 1972.

Hartman, Saidiya V. *Scenes of Subjection: Terror, Slavery, and Self-Making in Nineteenth-Century America*. New York: Oxford University Press, 1997.

Higginson, Mary Thacher, ed. *Letters and Journals of Thomas Wentworth Higginson, 1846–1906*. Boston: Houghton Mifflin, 1921. https://archive.org/details/lettersandjourno1higggoog.

Higginson, Thomas Wentworth. *Army Life in a Black Regiment*. Boston: Fields, Osgood, 1870. https://archive.org/details/armylifeinblackro0higg_0.

———. "Negro Spirituals." *Atlantic Monthly* (June 1867): 685–94. http://www.theatlantic.com/past/docs/issues/1867jun/spirit.htm.

Hill, Errol G., and James V. Hatch. *A History of African American Theatre*. New York: Cambridge University Press, 2003.

Holloway, Joseph E., ed. *Africanisms in American Culture*. 2nd ed. Bloomington: Indiana University Press, 2005.

Holly, Ellistine Perkins. "Sam Lucas, 1840–1916: A Bibliographic Study." In *Feel the Spirit: Studies in Nineteenth-Century Afro-American Music*, edited by George R. Keck and Sherrill V. Martin, 83–103. New York: Greenwood Press, 1988.

Hurston, Zora Neale. "Characteristics of Negro Expression." In *Negro: An Anthology*, edited by Nancy Cunard, 24–31. 1934. Edited and abridged. New York: Frederick Ungar, 1970.

———. "Spirituals and Neo-spirituals." In *Negro: An Anthology*, edited by Nancy Cunard, 223–25. 1934. Edited and abridged. New York: Frederick Ungar, 1970.

Hutchinson, John Wallace. *Story of the Hutchinsons (Tribe of Jesse)*. 2 vols. Compiled and edited by Charles E. Mann. Introduction by Frederick Douglass. Boston: Lee and Shepard, 1896.

Jackson, George Pullen. *Down-East Spirituals and Others*. New York: J. J. Augustin, 1940.

———. *White and Negro Spirituals*. New York: J. J. Augustin, 1943.

Johnson, James Weldon. *Black Manhattan*. 1930. Reprint, New York: Da Capo Press, 1991.

Jubilee and Plantation Songs. Characteristic Favorites, as Sung by the Hampton Students, Jubilee Singers, Fisk University Students, and Other Concert Companies. Boston: Oliver Ditson, 1887.

Jubilee Songs as Sung by Slayton's Jubilee Singers. Chicago: Thayer and Jackson Stationery for Slayton Lyceum Bureau, n.d.

Keck, George R. "Promoting Black Music in Nineteenth-Century America: Some Aspects of Concert Management in New York and Boston." In *Feel the Spirit: Studies in Nineteenth-Century Afro-American Music*, edited by George R. Keck and Sherrill V. Martin, 157–71. New York: Greenwood Press, 1988.

Krehbiel, Henry Edward. *Afro-American Folksongs: A Study in Racial and National Music*. 1914. Reprint, New York: Frederick Ungar, 1962.

Lampert, Sara. "Bringing Music to Lyceumites: The Bureaus and the Transformation of Lyceum Entertainment." In *The Cosmopolitan Lyceum: Lecture Culture and the Globe in Nineteenth-Century America*, edited by Tom F. Wright, 67–90. Amherst: University of Massachusetts Press, 2013.

Latimer, Marvin E., Jr. "J. W. Donavin's Tennesseans (1873–1895): A Chronicle of an Influential African-American Jubilee Troup, Their Entrepreneurial Director, and Their Music." *Choral Journal* 54, no. 3 (2013): 36–48.

Levine, Lawrence. *Black Culture and Black Consciousness: Afro-American Folk Thought from Slavery to Freedom*. Oxford: Oxford University Press, 1977.

Lhamon, W. T., Jr. *Jump Jim Crow: Lost Plays, Lyrics, and Street Prose of the First Atlantic Popular Culture*. Cambridge: Harvard University Press, 2003.

———. *Raising Cain: Blackface Performance from Jim Crow to Hip Hop*. Cambridge: Harvard University Press, 1998.

Lindfors, Bernth, ed. *Africans on Stage: Studies in Ethnological Show Business*. Bloomington: Indiana University Press, 1999.

Locke, Alain, ed. *The New Negro*. New York: Boni, 1925.

Lost Sounds: Blacks and the Birth of the Recording Industry 1891–1922. Liner notes by Tim Brooks. Archeophone Records 1005.

Lott, Eric. *Love and Theft: Blackface Minstrelsy and the American Working Class*. New York: Oxford University Press, 1993.

Lovell, John, Jr. *Black Song: The Forge and the Flame; The Story of How the Afro-American Spiritual Was Hammered Out*. New York: Macmillan, 1972.

Ludlow, Helen W. "The Hampton Student Singers." *Southern Workman* (May 1894): 72–76.

Mahar, William J. *Behind the Burnt Cork Mask: Early Blackface Minstrelsy and Antebellum American Popular Culture*. Urbana: University of Illinois Press, 1999.

Marsh, J. B. T. *The Story of the Jubilee Singers; With Their Songs*. 2nd ed. London: Hodder and Stoughton, 1875.

———. *The Story of the Jubilee Singers; With Their Songs*. Rev. ed. Boston: Houghton, Mifflin, [1880].

———. *The Story of the Jubilee Singers; With Their Songs*. New ed. London: Hodder and Stoughton, 1886.

———. *The Story of the Jubilee Singers by J. B. T. Marsh, with Supplement Containing an Account of the Six Year's Tour around the World, and Many New Songs, by F. J. Loudin*. Cleveland: Cleveland Printing, 1892.

———. *The Story of the Jubilee Singers by J. B. T. Marsh, with Supplement Containing an Account of the Six Year's Tour around the World, and Many New Songs, by F. J. Loudin*. London: Hodder and Stoughton, 1897.

———. *The Story of the Jubilee Singers by J. B. T. Marsh, with Supplement Containing an Account of the Six Year's Tour around the World, and Many New Songs, by F. J. Loudin*. London, Hodder and Stoughton, 1903.

Mason, Lowell. *The Song-Garden: A Series of School Music Books, Progressively Arranged, Each Book Complete in Itself*. Book 2. New York: Mason Bros., 1864.

Maultsby, Portia. "Black Spirituals: An Analysis of Textual Forms and Structures." *Black Perspective in Music* 4, no. 1 (1976): 54–67.

McDaniel, Dennis K. *John Ogden, Abolitionist Leader in Southern Education*. Philadelphia: American Philosophical Society, 1997.

McKim, Lucy, comp., arr. "Poor Rosy, Poor Gal." Songs of the Freedmen of Port Royal. Philadelphia: n.p., 1862. Lester S. Levy Sheet Music Collection, Johns Hopkins University, http://jhir.library.jhu.edu/handle/1774.2/6860.

———. "Roll, Jordan, Roll." Songs of the Freedmen of Port Royal. Philadelphia: n.p., 1862.

McPherson, James M. *Battle Cry of Freedom: The Civil War Era*. New York: Oxford University Press, 1988.

Miyakawa, Felicia. *"Sometimes I Feel Like a Motherless Child": The Transformative Journey of an American Song*. New York: Oxford University Press, forthcoming.

Moore, Ella Sheppard. "Before Emancipation." Booklet. New York: American Missionary Association, n.d.

———. "Historical Sketch of the Jubilee Singers." *Fisk University News* 2, no. 5 (1911): 41–58.

Moton, Robert Russa. *Finding a Way Out: An Autobiography*. New York: Doubleday, Page, 1920. University of North Carolina Library, Documenting the American South, http://docsouth.unc.edu/fpn/moton/menu.html.

Murphy, Jeannette Robinson. *Southern Thoughts for Northern Thinkers*. New York: Bandanna, 1904. https://archive.org/details/SouthernThoughtsForNorthernThinkers.

Nathan, Hans. *Dan Emmett and the Rise of Early Minstrelsy*. Norman: University of Oklahoma Press, 1962.

Odell, George C. D. *Annals of the New York Stage, 1870–1875*. Vol. 9. New York: Columbia University Press, 1937.

———. *Annals of the New York Stage, 1875–1879*. Vol. 10. New York: Columbia University Press, 1938.

———. *Annals of the New York Stage, 1879–1882*. Vol. 11. New York: Columbia University Press, 1939.

O'Loughlin, Jim. "*Uncle Tom's Cabin* as Dominant Culture." *Journal of Adaptation in Film and Performance* 1, no. 1 (2007): 45–56.

Ostendorf, Berndt. *Black Literature in White America*. Totowa, NJ: Barnes and Noble Books, 1982.

Parkhurst, Mrs. [Susan McFarland Parkhurst], and George Lansing Taylor. "No Slave beneath That Starry Flag." New York: Horace Waters, 1864. LC, https://www.loc.gov/item/ihas.200001756/.

Patterson, Martha. "Remaking the Minstrel: Pauline Hopkins's *Peculiar Sam* and the Post-Reconstruction Black Subject." In *Black Women Playwrights: Visions on the American Stage*, edited by Carol P. Marsh-Lockett, 13–24. New York: Garland, 1999.

Perkins, A. E. "Negro Spirituals from the Far South." *Journal of American Folklore* 35, no. 137 (1922): 223–49.

Peters, Erskine. "The Poetics of the Afro-American Spiritual." *Black American Literature Forum* 23, no. 3 (1989): 559–78.

Peterson, Bernard L., Jr. *African American Theatre Directory, 1816–1960: A Comprehensive Guide to Early Black Theatre Organizations, Companies, Theatres, and Performing Groups*. Westport, CT: Greenwood Press, 1997.

———. *A Century of Musicals in Black and White: An Encyclopedia of Musical Stage Works by, about, or Involving African Americans*. Westport, CT: Greenwood Press, 1993.

Pike, Gustavus D. *The Jubilee Singers and Their Campaign for Twenty Thousand Dollars*. Boston: Lee and Shepard, 1873.

———. *The Singing Campaign for Ten Thousand Pounds; or, The Jubilee Singers in Great Britain. With an Appendix Containing Slave Songs*. New York: American Missionary Association, 1875. http://commons.ptsem.edu/id/singingcaoopike.

Plantation Songs and Jubilee Hymns: A Collection of the Most Popular Ethiopian Old Time Melodies. Boston: White, Smith, 1881. https://play.google.com/store/books/details/Plantation_Songs_and_Jubilee_Hymns?id=FMk2AQAAMAAJ&hl=en.

Preston, Katherine K. *Opera on the Road: Traveling Opera Troupes in the United States, 1825–60*. Urbana: University of Illinois Press, 2001.

Prince, K. Stephen. *Stories of the South: Race and Reconstruction of Southern Identity, 1865–1915*. Chapel Hill: University of North Carolina Press, 2014.

Raboteau, Albert J. *Slave Religion: The "Invisible Institution" in the Antebellum South.* Updated ed. New York: Oxford University Press, 2004.

Radano, Ronald. *Lying Up a Nation: Race and Black Music.* Chicago: University of Chicago Press, 2003.

Ramsey, Guthrie P., Jr. "Cosmopolitan or Provincial? Ideology in Early Black Music Historiography, 1867–1940." *Black Music Research Journal* 16, no. 1 (1996): 11–42.

Reagon, Bernice Johnson. *Wade in the Water: African American Sacred Traditions.* National Public Radio and Smithsonian Institution, 1994. 4-CD set, Smithsonian Folkways, 1996.

Religious Folk Songs of the Negro as Sung on the Plantations. Hampton: Hampton Normal and Agricultural Institute Press, 1918.

Rice, Edward Le Roy. *Monarchs of Minstrelsy, from "Daddy" Rice to Date.* New York: Kenny, 1911.

Richardson, Joe M. *A History of Fisk University, 1865–1946.* University, AL: University of Alabama Press, 1980.

Rieser, Andrew C. *The Chautauqua Movement: Protestants, Progressives, and the Culture of Modern Liberalism.* New York: Columbia University Press, 2003.

Riis, Thomas L. *Just before Jazz: Black Musical Theater in New York, 1890–1915.* Washington, DC: Smithsonian Institution Press, 1989.

———. "The Music and Musicians in Nineteenth-Century Productions of Uncle Tom's Cabin." *American Music* 4, no. 3 (1986): 268–86.

Root, Deane L. "The Music of Uncle Tom's Cabin." *Uncle Tom's Cabin* and American Culture: A Multi-media Archive, website. University of Virginia, 2009. http://jefferson.village.virginia.edu/utc/interpret/exhibits/root/root.html.

Root, George Frederick. *The Story of a Musical Life.* 1891. Reprint, New York: Da Capo Press, 1970.

Rutling, Thomas. *Tom: An Autobiography; with Revised Negro Melodies.* Torrington, N. Devon, England: Thos. J. Dyer, [ca. 1907]. University of Rochester, http://hdl.handle.net/1802/19731.

Rydell, Robert W. "'Darkest Africa': African Shows at America's World's Fairs, 1893–1940." In *Africans on Stage: Studies in Ethnological Show Business,* edited by Bernth Lindfors, 135–55. Bloomington: Indiana University Press, 1999.

Sam Lucas' Plantation Songster. Boston: White, Smith, n.d. HTC, songsters.

Sawyer, Prof. J. J., arr. *Jubilee Songs and Plantation Melodies.* Words and music specially arranged by Prof. J. J. Sawyer and sung by the Original Nashville Students, H. B. Thearle, Proprietor. Chicago: n.p., [1884].

Saxton, Alexander. "Blackface Minstrelsy and Jacksonian Ideology." *American Quarterly* 27, no. 1 (1975): 3–28.

Selections of Plantation Songs as Sung by Donavin's Famous Tennesseans. Delaware, OH: J. W. Donavin, 1883. CPM.

Seroff, Doug. "The Fisk Jubilee Singers in Britain." In *Under the Imperial Carpet: Essays in Black History 1780–1950,* edited by Rainer Lotz and Ian Pegg, 42–54. Crawley: Rabbit, 1986.

———. "'A Voice in the Wilderness': The Fisk Jubilee Singers' Civil Rights Tours of 1879–1882." *Popular Music and Society* 25, nos. 1–2 (2001): 131–78.

[Seward, Theodore F.] *Jubilee Songs: As Sung by the Jubilee Singers of Fisk University.* Preface by Theodore F. Seward. New York: Biglow and Main, 1872a. https://archive.org/details/jubileesongsassuoojubi.

———. *Jubilee Songs: Complete, as Sung by the Jubilee Singers of Fisk University.* Preface by Theo. F. Seward. New York: Biglow and Main, 1872b. Mills Music Library Digital Collections, http://digital.library.wisc.edu/1711.dl/MillsSpColl.JubileeSongs.

Seward, Theodore F., Lowell Mason, and William B. Bradbury. *The Temple Choir: A Collection of Sacred and Secular Music.* Boston: Mason and Hamlin, 1867.

Simond, Ike. *Old Slack's Reminiscence and Pocket History of the Colored Profession from 1865 to 1891.* Chicago: Published by the author, 1891.

Sizer, Sandra S. *Gospel Hymns and Social Religion: The Rhetoric of Nineteenth-Century Revivalism.* Philadelphia: Temple University Press, 1978.

Smith, Llewellyn, and Andrew Ward. *Jubilee Singers: Sacrifice and Glory.* DVD. A production of WGBH Boston for *The American Experience*, 2000.

Smith, Vernon Leon. "The Hampton Institute Choir, 1873–1973." PhD diss., Florida State University School of Music, 1985.

Snyder, Jean E. *Harry T. Burleigh: From the Spiritual to the Harlem Renaissance.* Urbana: University of Illinois Press, 2016.

Songs of the Tennesseans. Arranged by L. N. Pickett. Broadside, n.p., n.d. CPM.

Songs Sung by the Famous Canadian Jubilee Singers, the Royal Paragon Male Quartette, and Imperial Orchestra. Hamilton, Ontario: Duncan Lith., [1892 or later]. https://archive.org/details/cihm_92572.

Sotiropoulos, Karen. *Staging Race: Black Performers in Turn of the Century America.* Cambridge: Harvard University Press, 2006.

Southern, Eileen, ed. *African American Theater.* Vol. 9 of *Nineteenth-Century American Musical Theater.* New York: Garland, 1994.

———. *Biographical Dictionary of Afro-American and African Musicians.* Westport, CT: Greenwood Press, 1982.

———. "An Early Black Concert Company: The Hyers Sisters Combination." In *A Celebration of American Music: Words and Music in Honor of H. Wiley Hitchcock*, edited by Richard Crawford, R. Allen Lott, and Carol J. Oja, 17–35. Ann Arbor: University of Michigan Press, 1990.

———. "The Georgia Minstrels: The Early Years." 1989. Reprinted in *Inside the Minstrel Mask: Readings in Nineteenth-Century Blackface Minstrelsy*, edited by Annemarie Bean, James V. Hatch, and Brooks McNamara, 163–75. Hanover, NH: Wesleyan University Press, 1996.

———. *The Music of Black Americans: A History.* 3rd ed. New York: Norton, 1997.

Spaeth, Sigmund. *A History of Popular Music in America.* New York: Random House, 1948.

Spaulding, H. G. "'Times Hab Badly Change' Old Massa Now; Song of the Freedmen." Boston: Oliver Ditson, 1866. Duke University, Historic American Sheet Music, http://library.duke.edu/digitalcollections/hasm.b0237/.

Spence, Mary E. "A Character Sketch of George L. White." *Fisk University News* 2, no. 5 (1911): 2–5.

Stuckey, Sterling. *Slave Culture: Nationalist Theory and the Foundations of Black America.* New York: Oxford University Press, 1987.

Talbot, Edith Armstrong. *Samuel Chapman Armstrong: A Biographical Study.* 1904. Reprint, New York: Negro Universities Press, 1969.

Tallmadge, William H. "The Black in Jackson's White Spirituals." *The Black Perspective in Music* 9, no. 2 (1981): 139–60.

Tapia, John Edward. *Circuit Chautauqua.* Jefferson, NC: McFarland, 1997.

Tawa, Nicholas. *Sweet Songs for Gentle Americans: The Parlor Song in America, 1790–1860.* Bowling Green, OH: Bowling Green University Popular Press, 1980.

Taylor, Georgia Gordon. "Reminiscences of Jubilee Singers." *Fisk University News* 2, no. 5 (1911): 28–30.

Taylor, Yuval, and Jake Austen. *Darkest America: Black Minstrelsy from Slavery to Hip-Hop.* New York: W. W. Norton, 2012.

There Breathes a Hope: The Legacy of John Work II and His Fisk Jubilee Quartet, 1909–1916. CD with essays by Doug Seroff and Tim Brooks, 2010. Archeophone Records 5020.

Thompson, Katrina D. *Ring Shout, Wheel About: The Racial Politics of Music and Dance in North American Slavery.* Champaign: University of Illinois Press, 2014.

Toll, Robert C. *Blacking Up: The Minstrel Show in Nineteenth-Century America.* New York: Oxford University Press, 1974.

Trotter, James M. *Music and Some Highly Musical People.* Boston: Lee and Shepard, 1878. http://imslp.org/wiki/Music_and_Some_Highly_Musical_People_(Trotter,_James_Monroe).

Turner, Lorenzo Dow. *Africanisms in the Gullah Dialect.* 1949. Reprint, University of South Carolina Press, 2002.

Turner, Patricia. *Dictionary of Afro-American Performers: 78 RPM and Cylinder Recordings of Opera, Choral Music, and Song, c. 1900–1949.* New York: Garland, 1990.

Twenty-Two Years' Work of the Hampton Normal and Agricultural Institute at Hampton, Virginia. Hampton: Normal School Press, 1893. https://archive.org/details/twentytwoyearswoooohamp.

Uncle Dave Macon Classic Sides, 1924–1938. London: JSP Records, JSP7729.

Ward, Andrew. *Dark Midnight When I Rise: The Story of the Jubilee Singers, Who Introduced the World to the Music of Black America.* New York: Farrar, Straus and Giroux, 2000.

Watkins, Mel. *On the Real Side: Laughing, Lying, and Signifying—The Underground Tradition of African-American Humor That Transformed American Culture, from Slavery to Richard Pryor.* New York: Touchstone, 1995.

Wells, Sarah M. "Character Sketch of Professor Adam Knight Spence." *Fisk University News* 2, no. 5 (1911): 17–19.

White, C. A., arr. *Stewart-Wilberforce Concert Co.* [Xenia, OH] 1883.

White, Shane, and Graham White. *The Sounds of Slavery: Discovering African American History through Songs, Sermons, and Speech.* Boston: Beacon Press, 2005.

Wilson, Olly. "The Heterogeneous Sound Ideal in African-American Music." In *New Perspectives on Music: Essays in Honor of Eileen Southern*, edited by Josephine Wright and Samuel A. Floyd, 327–38. Warren, MI: Harmonie Park Press, 1992.

Winans, Robert B. "Early Minstrel Show Music, 1843–1852." In *Inside the Minstrel Mask: Readings in Nineteenth-Century Blackface Minstrelsy*, edited by Annemarie Bean, James V. Hatch, and Brooks McNamara, 141–62. Hanover, NH: Wesleyan University Press, 1996.

Work, Frederick J. *Folk Songs of the American Negro*. Nashville: Work Bros., 1907.

———, ed. *New Jubilee Songs: As Sung by the Fisk Jubilee Singers of Fisk University*. Nashville: Fisk University, 1902.

Work, John W. [III], Lewis Wade Jones, and Samuel C. Adams, Jr. *Lost Delta Found: Rediscovering the Fisk University–Library of Congress Coahoma Country Study, 1941–1942*. Edited by Robert Gordon and Bruce Nemerov. Nashville: Vanderbilt University Press, 2005.

Work, John Wesley [II]. *Folk Song of the American Negro*. Nashville: Press of Fisk University, 1915.

———. "The Jubilee Songs Today: Their Collection and Rendition." *Fisk University News* 2, no. 5 (1911): 21–23.

Wright, H. H. "Jubilee Songs at Chapel Exercises." *Fisk University News* 2, no. 5 (1911): 24–26.

Wright, Josephine R. B. "Black Women in Classical Music in Boston during the Late Nineteenth Century: Profiles in Leadership." In *New Perspectives on Music: Essays in Honor of Eileen Southern*, edited by Josephine Wright and Samuel A. Floyd, 373–407. Warren, MI: Harmonie Park Press, 1992.

———. "The Third Culture—A Conversation about Truth and Reconciliation: An African Americanist's Reflection on the 'Two Cultures' Debate in Post-modern Society." *Forum on Public Policy: A Journal of the Oxford Round Table* (Winter 2007). http://files.eric.ed.gov/fulltext/EJ1098504.pdf.

Index

Examples, figures, and tables are indicated by "*e*," "*f*," and "*t*" after the page number. All titles in quotes are spirituals unless otherwise identified.

scriptions by, 54–55, 58, 58e, 59, 65; favorite spiritual of, 59; and Fisk Jubilee Singers, touring with, 38; at Fisk University, 22; performances by, 25, 27, 56, 176, 255; photograph of, 46f; and Seward, criticism of, 53

Ryder, C. J., 260

sacred concerts, 188, 201, 215, 216
sacred vs. secular song and dance, 3
salaries of black entertainers, 90, 254–55
Salsbury, Nate, 219, 220
Salvation Army, 261
salvation songs, 147
Sam Lucas Jubilee Songsters, 235
Sanford, James, 157–58, 229
Sankey, Ira D., 272n87
Saunders, Albert, 244, 245f, 296n51
Saunders, Annie, 245f, 296n51
Sawyer, Helen, 245f
Sawyer, Jacob J., 166f, 181, 239, 244, 245f, 246–47
Sayler, Bella, 105e
Scandalize My Name (Dennison), 144
Schoolcraft, Luke, 163
schottische rhythm, 177
Scotland, white jubilee groups in, 255
Scott, Delia, 105e
Scott, George C., 215, 220, 245f
Scott, George W., 233, 244
Sea Islands, slave songs from, 10
Second Great Awakening (evangelical movement), 4
secular vs. sacred song and dance, 3
Selika, Marie (later Marie Selika Williams), 234, 254
Seroff, Doug, 156, 246
services of song, 43–44, 45, 48–50, 116, 250
Seward, Theodore Frelinghuysen: criticisms of, 78; and Fisk Jubilee Singers' repertoire, transcription of, 25, 51–55; on form asymmetries, 69–70; on gapped scales, 70–71; on irregularities in spirituals, 79; on rhythm in spirituals, 66; Sheppard and, 28; The Temple Choir compiled by, 25; transcription methods, 273n13. See also "Steal Away"
Seward, Theodore Frelinghuysen, transcriptions of: "Didn't My Lord Deliver Daniel," 66, 67–68e, 69; "The General Roll," 56, 58, 58e; "The Gospel Train," 154e; "He Is the Lily of the Valley," 197t; "Jus Come from

de Fountain," 197t; "Rise and Shine," 102; "Roll, Jordan, Roll," 63e, 65; "Steal Away," 60e

Shaking Quakers (Shakers), 125, 281n2
Shaw Collegiate Institute (later Shaw University), 110
Shaw Jubilee Singers (North Carolina Colored Vocalists), 110–11
sheet music, for commercial spirituals, 147, 180–81
Sheppard, Andrew, 116, 119, 229
Sheppard, Benjamin Harper, 28–29, 269n26
Sheppard, Ella (later Ella Sheppard Moore): as agent of preservation, 260; Cheatham and, 260; duties of, 254; as Jubilee Singers director, 27–28, 39; on Jubilee Singers' name, 40; life and career of, 26–30; in performance, description of, 50; pictures of, 27f, 46f; Pike's biography of, 269n25; published transcriptions of spirituals by, 54; on Seward's transcription methods, 273n13; Spence and, 268n14; on spirituals, 31; on spirituals, learning of, 40; and touring troupe, participation in, 38; Work and, 65
Sheppard, James Glover, 269n26
Sheppard, Phereby, 28–29
Sheppard, Sarah Hannah, 28–29
Sheppard, Simon, 28–29, 269n26
Sheppard's (Colored) Jubilee Singers (later Troubadours and Guitarists), 116, 199, 228–32, 230f, 232f
Sheridan and Mack's Specialty Combination, 163, 164f
Sherman, William T., 42
Shiloh (Covier), 205t
"shouts" and shouting, 5, 199
Simmons, Lew, 128–29, 130, 141, 142
Simmons and Slocum's Minstrels, 128, 133, 153
Simmons, Slocum, and Sweatnam's Minstrels, 243
Simond, Ike, 106, 252, 297n52
singing family phenomenon, 32
"Sing Low, Sweet Children" (Delehanty), 141, 256
Sissle, Noble, 272n91
Six o'Clock in Georgia! (farce), 217
slave-cabin concerts (Tennesseans), 100–101
slaves and slavery: antebellum slave culture in Hampton, VA, 85; as entertainment, ix–x; Fisk concert spirituals and, 81; freed

"Swing Dose Gates Ajar" (commercial spiritual), 241, 296n43

"Swing Low, Sweet Chariot" (Coming for to carry me home): contrafactum of, 156; Fisk Jubilee Singers' performance of, 83; gapped-scale melodies in, 2; internal refrain in, 2; Jackson on, 8; Lucas and Hyers sisters' performance of, 234; as part of canon of spirituals, 256; Ella Sheppard and, 28; in songsters, 102; in *Uncle Tom's Cabin* productions, 195, 196, 198t

"Swing Low, Sweet Chariot" (I don't want to leave me behind), 92, 93e

tableaus, jubilee groups' use of, 163

"Talk about Your Moses" (Lucas), 236–38, 237e, 241

Talley, Thomas W., 27

Tallmadge, William, 8

Tappan, Lewis, 18

Tate, Minnie, 38, 46f

Taylor, Alexander C., 109, 202, 209, 253

Taylor, George Lansing, 24

Taylor, Georgia Gordon (née Georgia Gordon), 22, 30, 31

The Temple Choir (Seward), 24–25

tempo, in Fisk concert spirituals, 59, 60e, 61

Tennesseans. *See* Donavin's (Original) Tennesseans

Tennessee Jubilee Singers, 119, 197–98t, 200, 204t, 207, 238

Terrell, Mary Church, 47, 272n91

testimonies, slave songs as, 13

texture: in Fisk concert spirituals, 56–59, 57e, 58e; in folk spirituals, 2; in Hampton concert spirituals, 94

Thearle, Fred G., 238

Thearle, Harry B., 238

themes, of spirituals, 1

"There's a Meetin' Here To-night" / "Dar's a Meeting Here Tonight" (Devonear): discussion of, 168–71; in *Ham-Town Students Songster*, 158–60; in Haverly's spectacle, 217; as part of canon of spirituals, 256; popularity of, 147; sheet music for, 170–72e; in songsters, 102, 147; Tennesseans' version of, transcription of, 169e

Thomas, Carrie L., 115

Thomas, Cordelia, 5, 266n16

Thompson, Isaac, 202

Thompson, Katrina, ix

Thompson, W. E., 105e

"Times Hab Badly Change' Old Massa Now," 11

tocsins, 147

Toll, Robert, 145, 254

Tom: An Autobiography (Rutling), 54–55

"Tommers" (*Uncle Tom's Cabin* performers), 187

Tompkins, Kyla Wazana, 76

Tom shows. *See* Uncle Tom shows, melodramas, and spectacles

tonality, 70–71, 71e

Tonic Sol-fa system, 53–54

Tourjée, Eben, 44, 87

Towe, Joseph B., 88, 92, 98, 185

Towns, William Henry, 6

traditional spirituals. *See* folk spirituals

"Tramp, Tramping On!" (Mason), 24

Transcendentalism, 121

transmission, of folk, concert, and commercial spirituals, 146t

Tupper, Henry Martin, 110, 111

"Turkey in the Straw" / "Zip Coon," 176

"Turn Back Pharaoh's Army," 33–34, 40, 49–50, 52, 61–62, 69, 158

Turner, Lorenzo Dow, 266n17

Tuskegee Choir, 262

Tuskegee Institute (later Tuskegee University), 17, 86, 88, 251

Uncle Anthony! (Stout), 203, 203t

Uncle Tom's Cabin (Stowe): Brady's production of, 192f; Hyers sisters' production of, 215–16; impact of, on Fisk Jubilee Singers, 75; and jubilee songs and singers, appropriation of, 250–51; as moral drama, 221; plantation scene from, image of, 193f; Smith's Double Mammoth performance of, 235; stage adaptations of, 184

Uncle Tom shows, melodramas, and spectacles, 183–223; black plays and environmental spectacles, 208–21; conclusions on, 221–23; introduction to, 183–86; jubilee singers, other plays with, 202–8; jubilee troupes and, 199–202; origin of jubilee singers in, 186–88; role of black singers in, 188–96; spirituals in, 196–99

Underground Railroad, 172, 214, 267n34

"Under the Palmetto" (Spaulding), 11

Unsworth, James, 153

UTC. See *Uncle Tom's Cabin* (Stowe)

Van Dyke, Charlie, 6

Vernon, Harwood, 9

Vincent, John Heyl, 261

Virginia Choristers, 89

SANDRA JEAN GRAHAM is an associate professor of music at Babson College.

Only a Miner: Studies in Recorded Coal-Mining Songs   *Archie Green*
Great Day Coming: Folk Music and the American Left   *R. Serge Denisoff*
John Philip Sousa: A Descriptive Catalog of His Works   *Paul E. Bierley*
The Hell-Bound Train: A Cowboy Songbook   *Glenn Ohrlin*
Oh, Didn't He Ramble: The Life Story of Lee Collins, as Told to Mary Collins
    Edited by Frank J. Gillis and John W. Miner
American Labor Songs of the Nineteenth Century   *Philip S. Foner*
Stars of Country Music: Uncle Dave Macon to Johnny Rodriguez   *Edited by*
    Bill C. Malone and Judith McCulloh
Git Along, Little Dogies: Songs and Songmakers of the American West
    John I. White
A Texas-Mexican *Cancionero*: Folksongs of the Lower Border   *Américo Paredes*
San Antonio Rose: The Life and Music of Bob Wills   *Charles R. Townsend*
Early Downhome Blues: A Musical and Cultural Analysis   *Jeff Todd Titon*
An Ives Celebration: Papers and Panels of the Charles Ives Centennial
    Festival-Conference   *Edited by H. Wiley Hitchcock and Vivian Perlis*
Sinful Tunes and Spirituals: Black Folk Music to the Civil War   *Dena J. Epstein*
Joe Scott, the Woodsman-Songmaker   *Edward D. Ives*
Jimmie Rodgers: The Life and Times of America's Blue Yodeler   *Nolan Porterfield*
Early American Music Engraving and Printing: A History of Music Publishing in
    America from 1787 to 1825, with Commentary on Earlier and Later Practices
    Richard J. Wolfe
Sing a Sad Song: The Life of Hank Williams   *Roger M. Williams*
Long Steel Rail: The Railroad in American Folksong   *Norm Cohen*
Resources of American Music History: A Directory of Source Materials from
    Colonial Times to World War II   *D. W. Krummel, Jean Geil, Doris J. Dyen,*
    and Deane L. Root
Tenement Songs: The Popular Music of the Jewish Immigrants   *Mark Slobin*
Ozark Folksongs   *Vance Randolph; edited and abridged by Norm Cohen*
Oscar Sonneck and American Music   *Edited by William Lichtenwanger*
Bluegrass Breakdown: The Making of the Old Southern Sound   *Robert Cantwell*
Bluegrass: A History   *Neil V. Rosenberg*
Music at the White House: A History of the American Spirit   *Elise K. Kirk*
Red River Blues: The Blues Tradition in the Southeast   *Bruce Bastin*
Good Friends and Bad Enemies: Robert Winslow Gordon and the Study of
    American Folksong   *Debora Kodish*
Fiddlin' Georgia Crazy: Fiddlin' John Carson, His Real World, and the World of
    His Songs   *Gene Wiggins*
America's Music: From the Pilgrims to the Present (rev. 3d ed.)   *Gilbert Chase*
Secular Music in Colonial Annapolis: The Tuesday Club, 1745–56   *John Barry Talley*
Bibliographical Handbook of American Music   *D. W. Krummel*

Aaron Copland: The Life and Work of an Uncommon Man   *Howard Pollack*
Louis Moreau Gottschalk   *S. Frederick Starr*
Race, Rock, and Elvis   *Michael T. Bertrand*
Theremin: Ether Music and Espionage   *Albert Glinsky*
Poetry and Violence: The Ballad Tradition of Mexico's Costa Chica
    John H. McDowell
The Bill Monroe Reader   *Edited by Tom Ewing*
Music in Lubavitcher Life   *Ellen Koskoff*
Zarzuela: Spanish Operetta, American Stage   *Janet L. Sturman*
Bluegrass Odyssey: A Documentary in Pictures and Words, 1966–86
    Carl Fleischhauer and Neil V. Rosenberg
That Old-Time Rock & Roll: A Chronicle of an Era, 1954–63   *Richard Aquila*
Labor's Troubadour   *Joe Glazer*
American Opera   *Elise K. Kirk*
Don't Get above Your Raisin': Country Music and the Southern Working Class
    Bill C. Malone
John Alden Carpenter: A Chicago Composer   *Howard Pollack*
Heartbeat of the People: Music and Dance of the Northern Pow-wow   *Tara Browner*
My Lord, What a Morning: An Autobiography   *Marian Anderson*
Marian Anderson: A Singer's Journey   *Allan Keiler*
Charles Ives Remembered: An Oral History   *Vivian Perlis*
Henry Cowell, Bohemian   *Michael Hicks*
Rap Music and Street Consciousness   *Cheryl L. Keyes*
Louis Prima   *Garry Boulard*
Marian McPartland's Jazz World: All in Good Time   *Marian McPartland*
Robert Johnson: Lost and Found   *Barry Lee Pearson and Bill McCulloch*
Bound for America: Three British Composers   *Nicholas Temperley*
Lost Sounds: Blacks and the Birth of the Recording Industry, 1890–1919   *Tim Brooks*
Burn, Baby! BURN! The Autobiography of Magnificent Montague
    Magnificent Montague with Bob Baker
Way Up North in Dixie: A Black Family's Claim to the Confederate
    Anthem   *Howard L. Sacks and Judith Rose Sacks*
The Bluegrass Reader   *Edited by Thomas Goldsmith*
Colin McPhee: Composer in Two Worlds   *Carol J. Oja*
Robert Johnson, Mythmaking, and Contemporary American Culture
    Patricia R. Schroeder
Composing a World: Lou Harrison, Musical Wayfarer   *Leta E. Miller and
    Fredric Lieberman*
Fritz Reiner, Maestro and Martinet   *Kenneth Morgan*
That Toddlin' Town: Chicago's White Dance Bands and Orchestras, 1900–1950
    Charles A. Sengstock Jr.
Dewey and Elvis: The Life and Times of a Rock 'n' Roll Deejay   *Louis Cantor*
Come Hither to Go Yonder: Playing Bluegrass with Bill Monroe   *Bob Black*
Chicago Blues: Portraits and Stories   *David Whiteis*

Gone to the Country: The New Lost City Ramblers and the Folk Music Revival
  Ray Allen
The Makers of the Sacred Harp   *David Warren Steel with Richard H. Hulan*
Woody Guthrie, American Radical   *Will Kaufman*
George Szell: A Life of Music   *Michael Charry*
Bean Blossom: The Brown County Jamboree and Bill Monroe's Bluegrass Festivals
  Thomas A. Adler
Crowe on the Banjo: The Music Life of J. D. Crowe   *Marty Godbey*
Twentieth Century Drifter: The Life of Marty Robbins   *Diane Diekman*
Henry Mancini: Reinventing Film Music   *John Caps*
The Beautiful Music All Around Us: Field Recordings and the American Experience
  Stephen Wade
Then Sings My Soul: The Culture of Southern Gospel Music   *Douglas Harrison*
The Accordion in the Americas: Klezmer, Polka, Tango, Zydeco, and More!
  Edited by Helena Simonett
Bluegrass Bluesman: A Memoir   *Josh Graves, edited by Fred Bartenstein*
One Woman in a Hundred: Edna Phillips and the Philadelphia Orchestra
  Mary Sue Welsh
The Great Orchestrator: Arthur Judson and American Arts Management
  James M. Doering
Charles Ives in the Mirror: American Histories of an Iconic Composer
  David C. Paul
Southern Soul-Blues   *David Whiteis*
Sweet Air: Modernism, Regionalism, and American Popular Song
  Edward P. Comentale
Pretty Good for a Girl: Women in Bluegrass   *Murphy Hicks Henry*
Sweet Dreams: The World of Patsy Cline   *Warren R. Hofstra*
William Sidney Mount and the Creolization of American Culture
  Christopher J. Smith
Bird: The Life and Music of Charlie Parker   *Chuck Haddix*
Making the March King: John Philip Sousa's Washington Years, 1854–1893
  Patrick Warfield
In It for the Long Run   *Jim Rooney*
Pioneers of the Blues Revival   *Steve Cushing*
Roots of the Revival: American and British Folk Music in the 1950s
  Ronald D. Cohen and Rachel Clare Donaldson
Blues All Day Long: The Jimmy Rogers Story   *Wayne Everett Goins*
Yankee Twang: Country and Western Music in New England   *Clifford R. Murphy*
The Music of the Stanley Brothers   *Gary B. Reid*
Hawaiian Music in Motion: Mariners, Missionaries, and Minstrels
  James Revell Carr
Sounds of the New Deal: The Federal Music Project in the West   *Peter Gough*
The Mormon Tabernacle Choir: A Biography   *Michael Hicks*
The Man That Got Away: The Life and Songs of Harold Arlen   *Walter Rimler*

The University of Illinois Press
is a founding member of the
Association of American University Presses.

University of Illinois Press
1325 South Oak Street
Champaign, IL 61820-6903
www.press.uillinois.edu